Shojo Beat

Godchild

Earl Cain Series 5

Vol. 3

Story & Art by **Kaori Yuki**

Contents

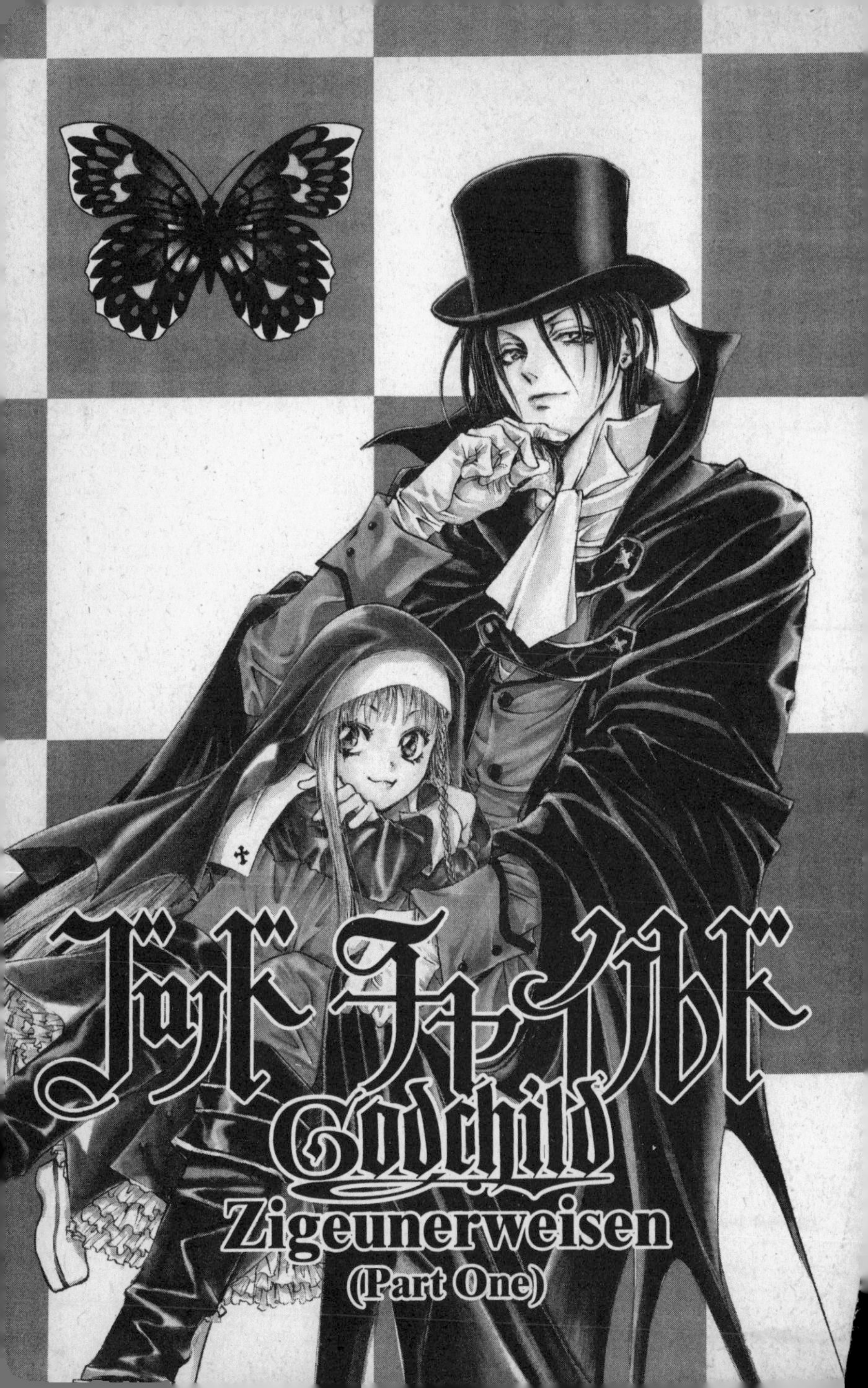
Godchild
Zigeunerweisen
(Part One)

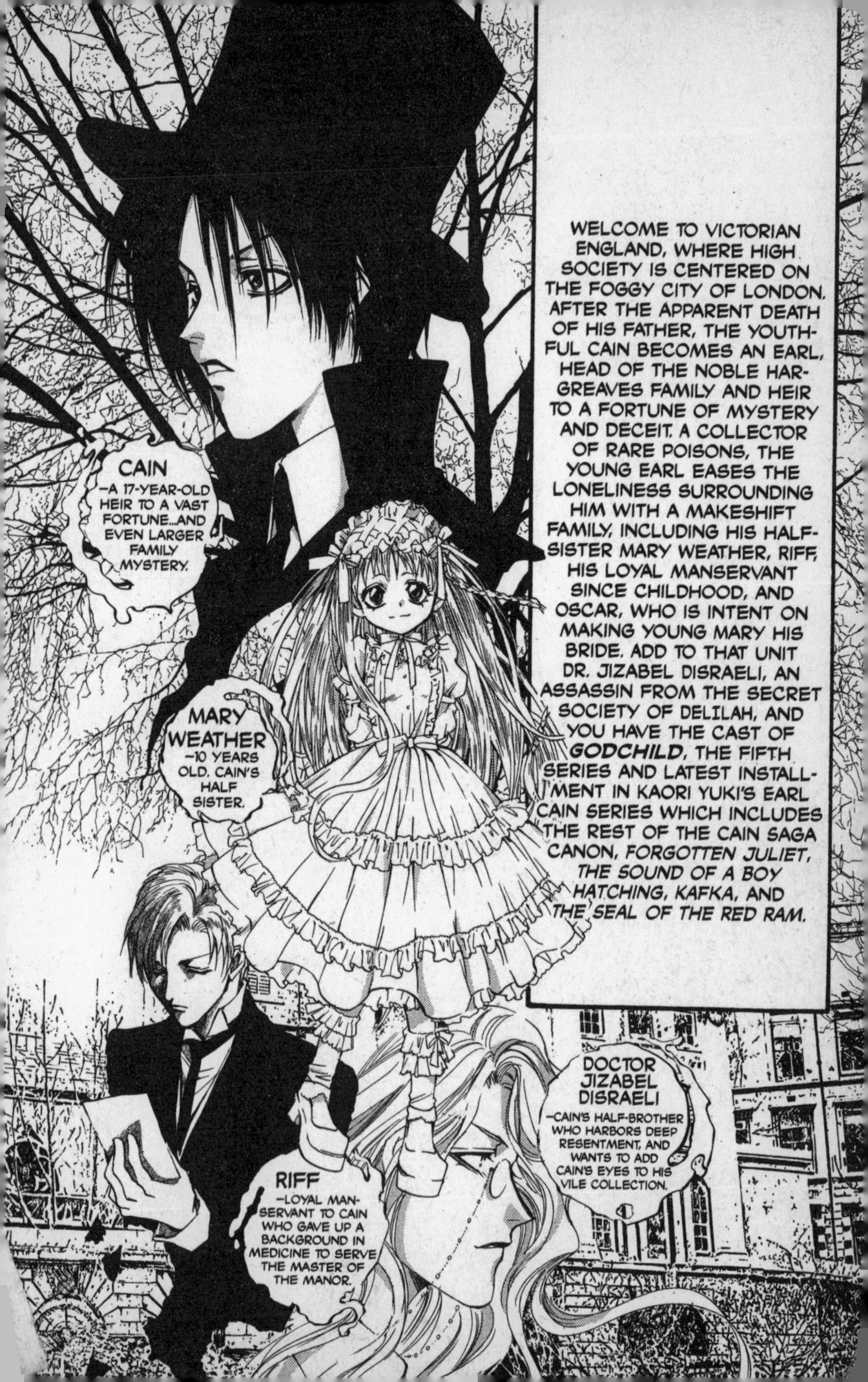
WELCOME TO VICTORIAN ENGLAND, WHERE HIGH SOCIETY IS CENTERED ON THE FOGGY CITY OF LONDON. AFTER THE APPARENT DEATH OF HIS FATHER, THE YOUTHFUL CAIN BECOMES AN EARL, HEAD OF THE NOBLE HARGREAVES FAMILY AND HEIR TO A FORTUNE OF MYSTERY AND DECEIT. A COLLECTOR OF RARE POISONS, THE YOUNG EARL EASES THE LONELINESS SURROUNDING HIM WITH A MAKESHIFT FAMILY, INCLUDING HIS HALF-SISTER MARY WEATHER, RIFF, HIS LOYAL MANSERVANT SINCE CHILDHOOD, AND OSCAR, WHO IS INTENT ON MAKING YOUNG MARY HIS BRIDE. ADD TO THAT UNIT DR. JIZABEL DISRAELI, AN ASSASSIN FROM THE SECRET SOCIETY OF DELILAH, AND YOU HAVE THE CAST OF *GODCHILD*, THE FIFTH SERIES AND LATEST INSTALLMENT IN KAORI YUKI'S EARL CAIN SERIES WHICH INCLUDES THE REST OF THE CAIN SAGA CANON, *FORGOTTEN JULIET*, *THE SOUND OF A BOY HATCHING*, *KAFKA*, AND *THE SEAL OF THE RED RAM*.
CAIN —A 17-YEAR-OLD HEIR TO A VAST FORTUNE...AND EVEN LARGER FAMILY MYSTERY.
MARY WEATHER —10 YEARS OLD. CAIN'S HALF SISTER.
DOCTOR JIZABEL DISRAELI —CAIN'S HALF-BROTHER WHO HARBORS DEEP RESENTMENT, AND WANTS TO ADD CAIN'S EYES TO HIS VILE COLLECTION.
RIFF —LOYAL MANSERVANT TO CAIN WHO GAVE UP A BACKGROUND IN MEDICINE TO SERVE THE MASTER OF THE MANOR.

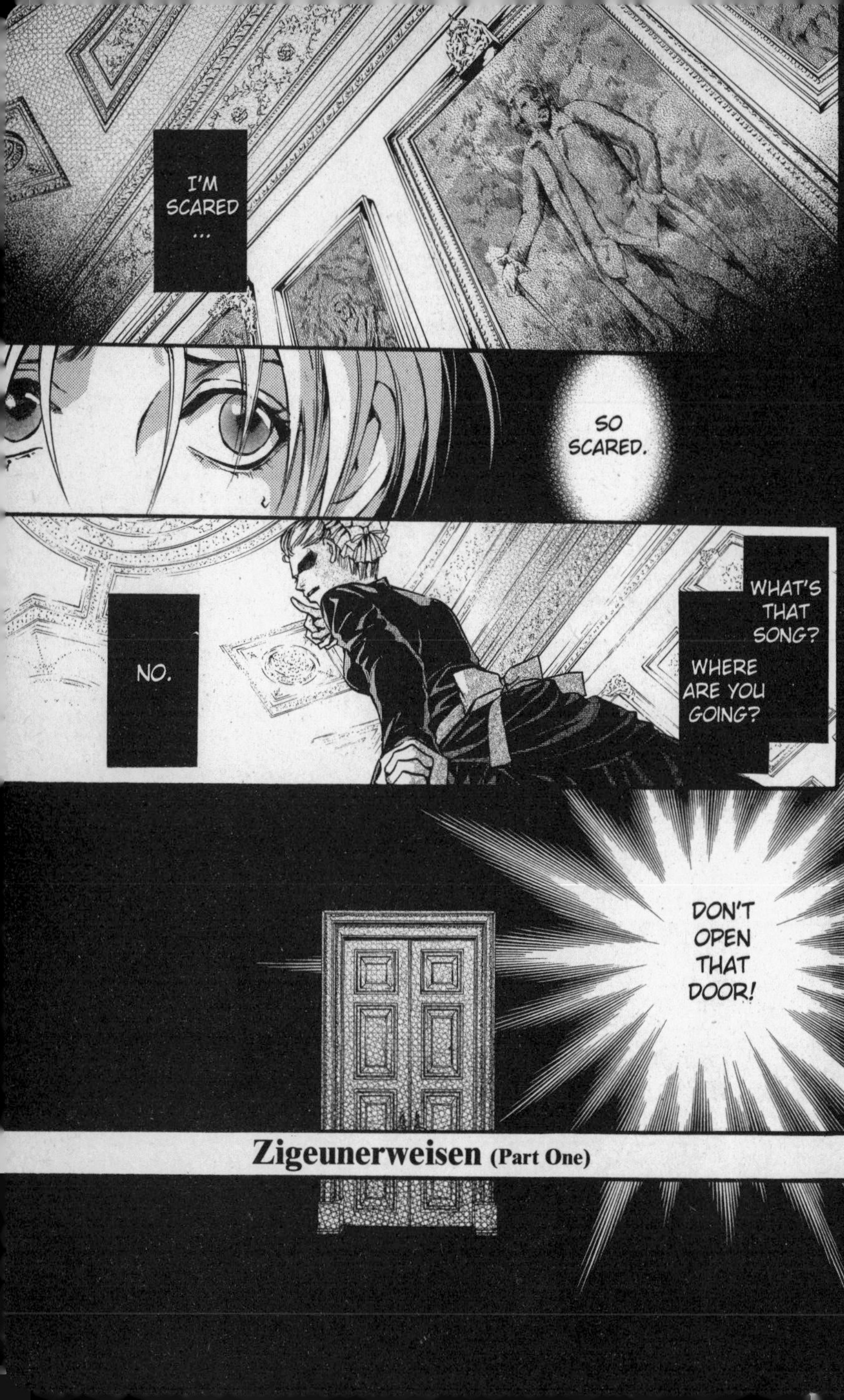

I'M SCARED...
SO SCARED.
WHAT'S THAT SONG?
WHERE ARE YOU GOING?
NO.
DON'T OPEN THAT DOOR!
Zigeunerweisen (Part One)

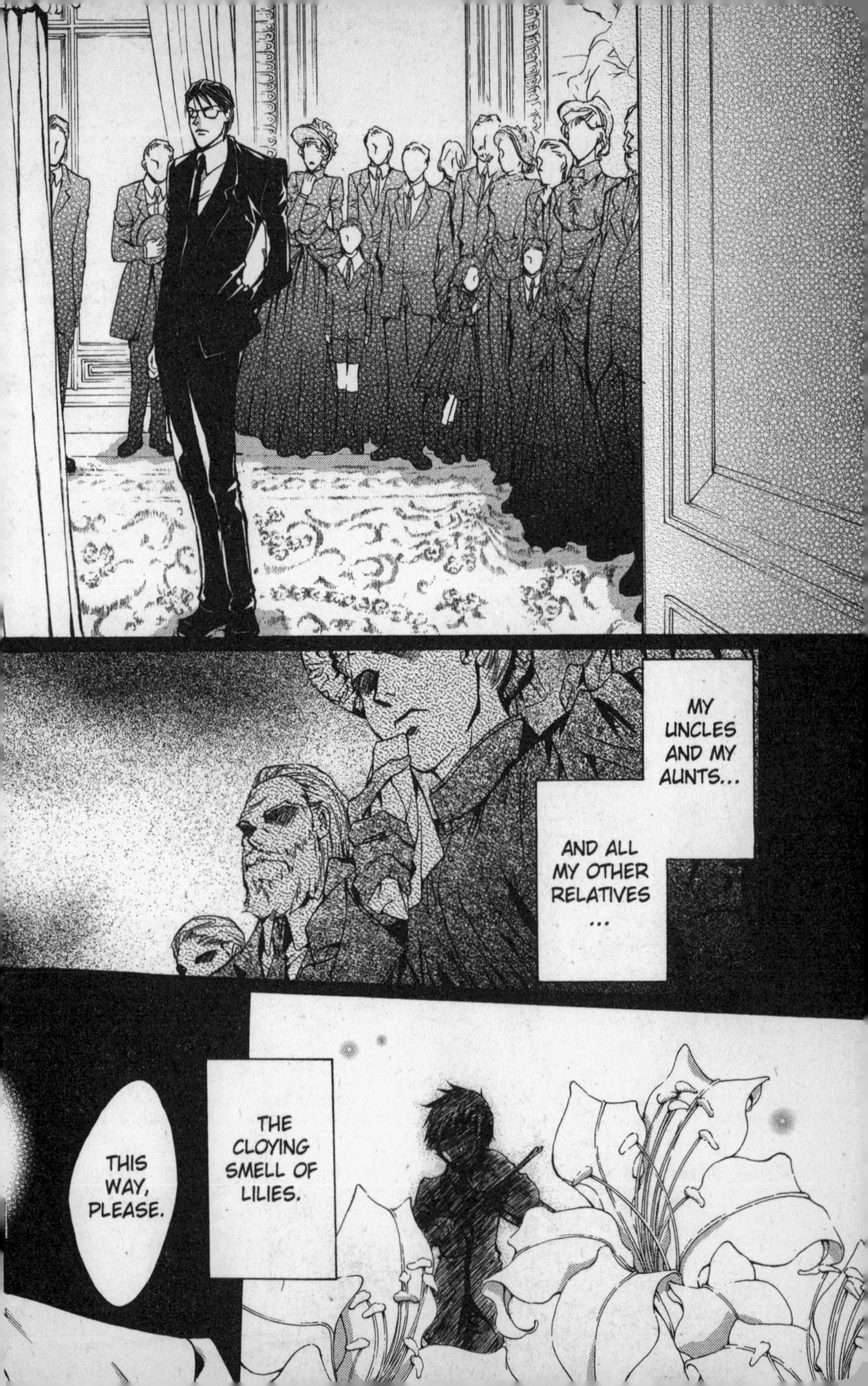
MY UNCLES AND MY AUNTS...
AND ALL MY OTHER RELATIVES ...
THE CLOYING SMELL OF LILIES.
THIS WAY, PLEASE.

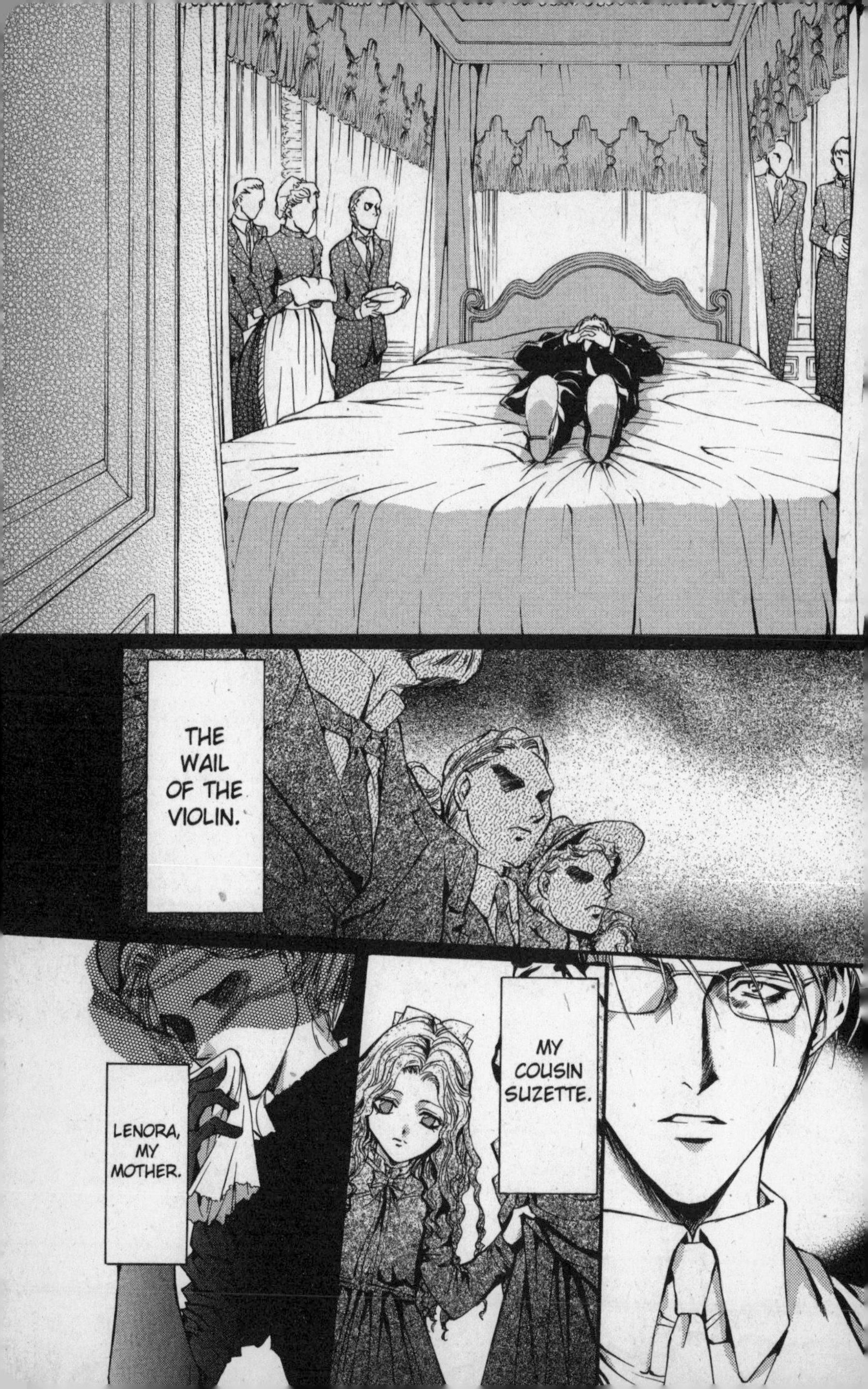
THE WAIL OF THE VIOLIN.
MY COUSIN SUZETTE.
LENORA, MY MOTHER.

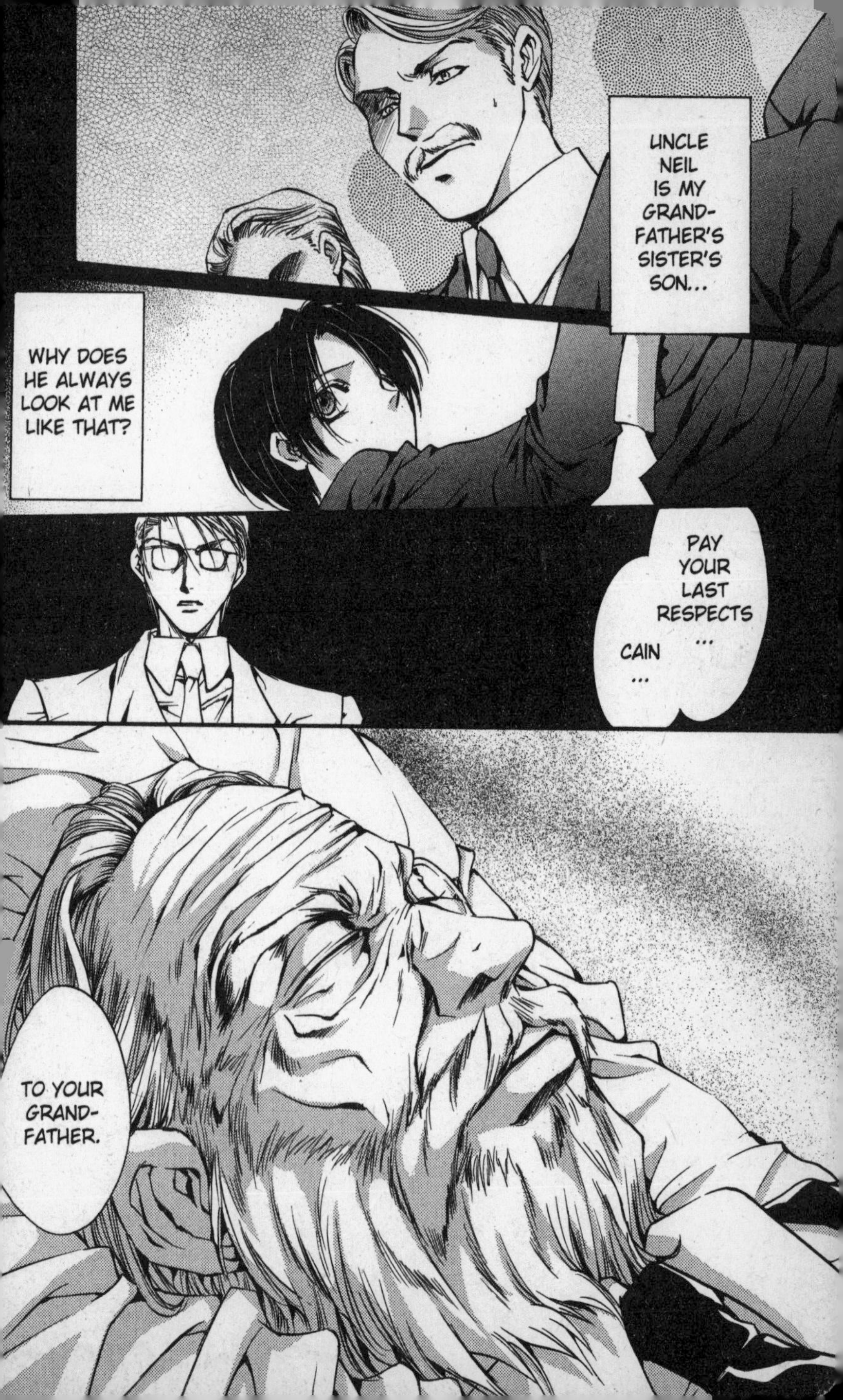
UNCLE NEIL IS MY GRAND-FATHER'S SISTER'S SON...
WHY DOES HE ALWAYS LOOK AT ME LIKE THAT?
PAY YOUR LAST RESPECTS... CAIN...
TO YOUR GRAND-FATHER.

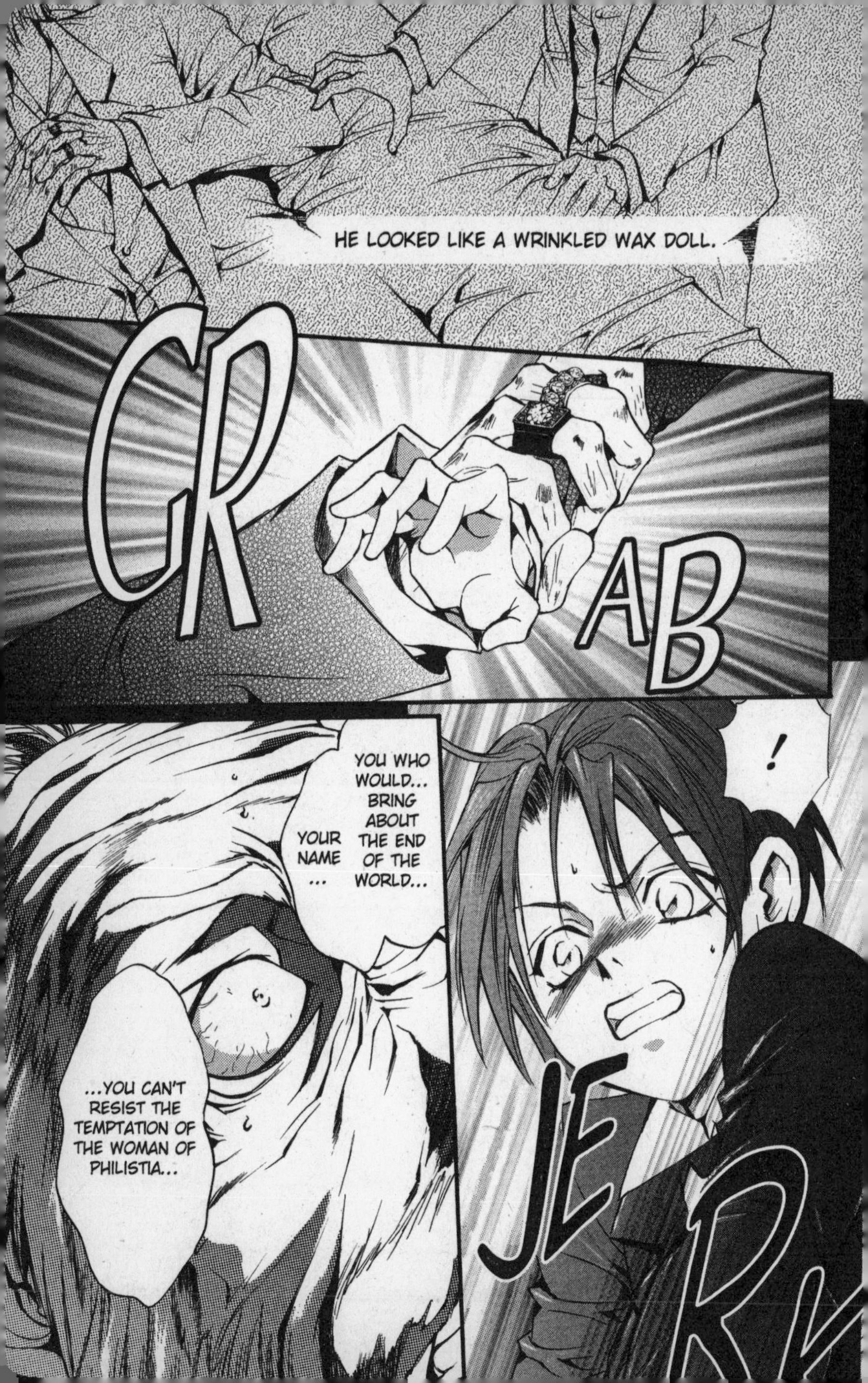
HE LOOKED LIKE A WRINKLED WAX DOLL.
GRAB
!
JERK
YOU WHO WOULD... BRING ABOUT THE END OF THE WORLD...
YOUR NAME ...
...YOU CAN'T RESIST THE TEMPTATION OF THE WOMAN OF PHILISTIA...

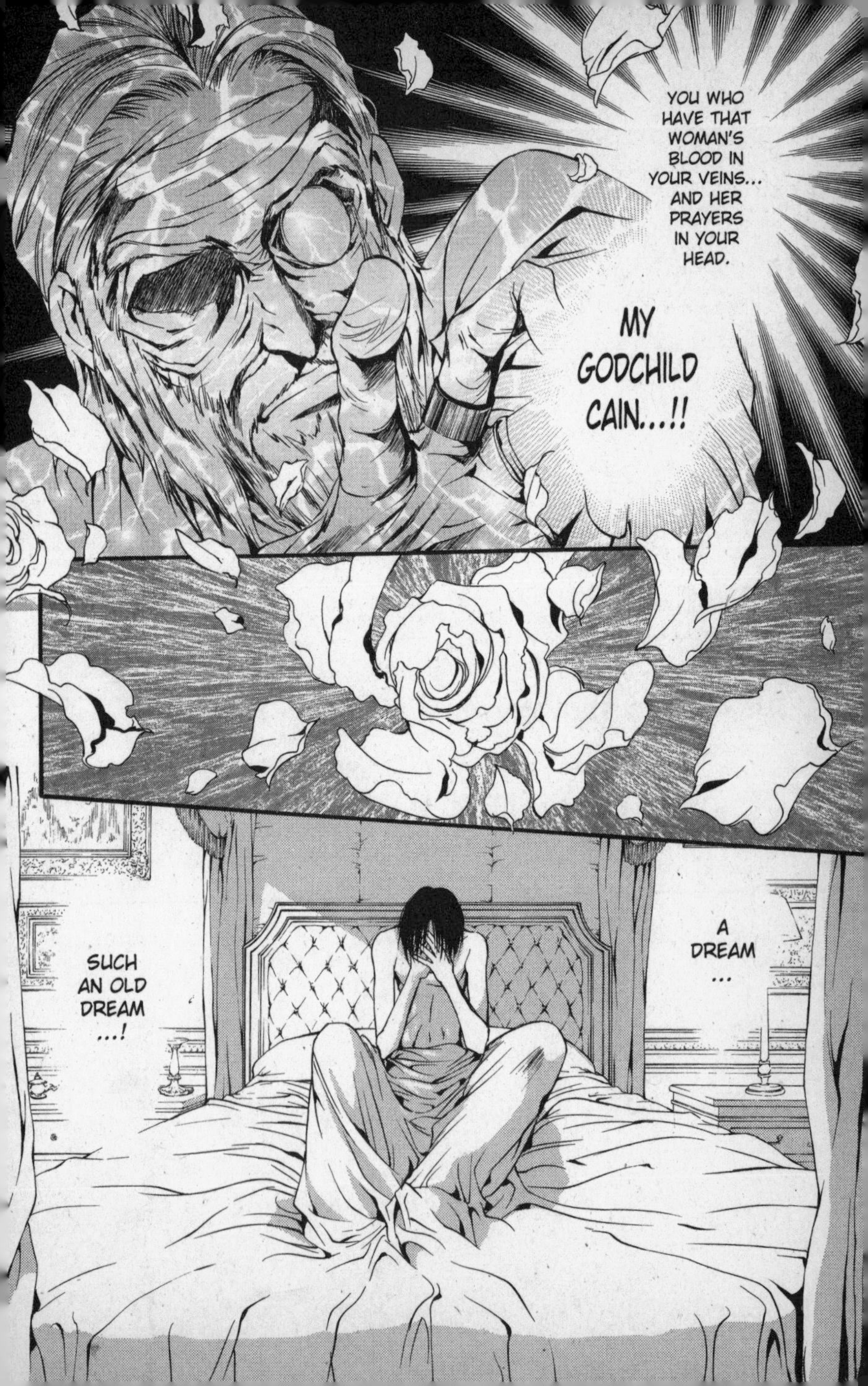
YOU WHO HAVE THAT WOMAN'S BLOOD IN YOUR VEINS... AND HER PRAYERS IN YOUR HEAD.
MY GODCHILD CAIN...!!
A DREAM ...
SUCH AN OLD DREAM ...!

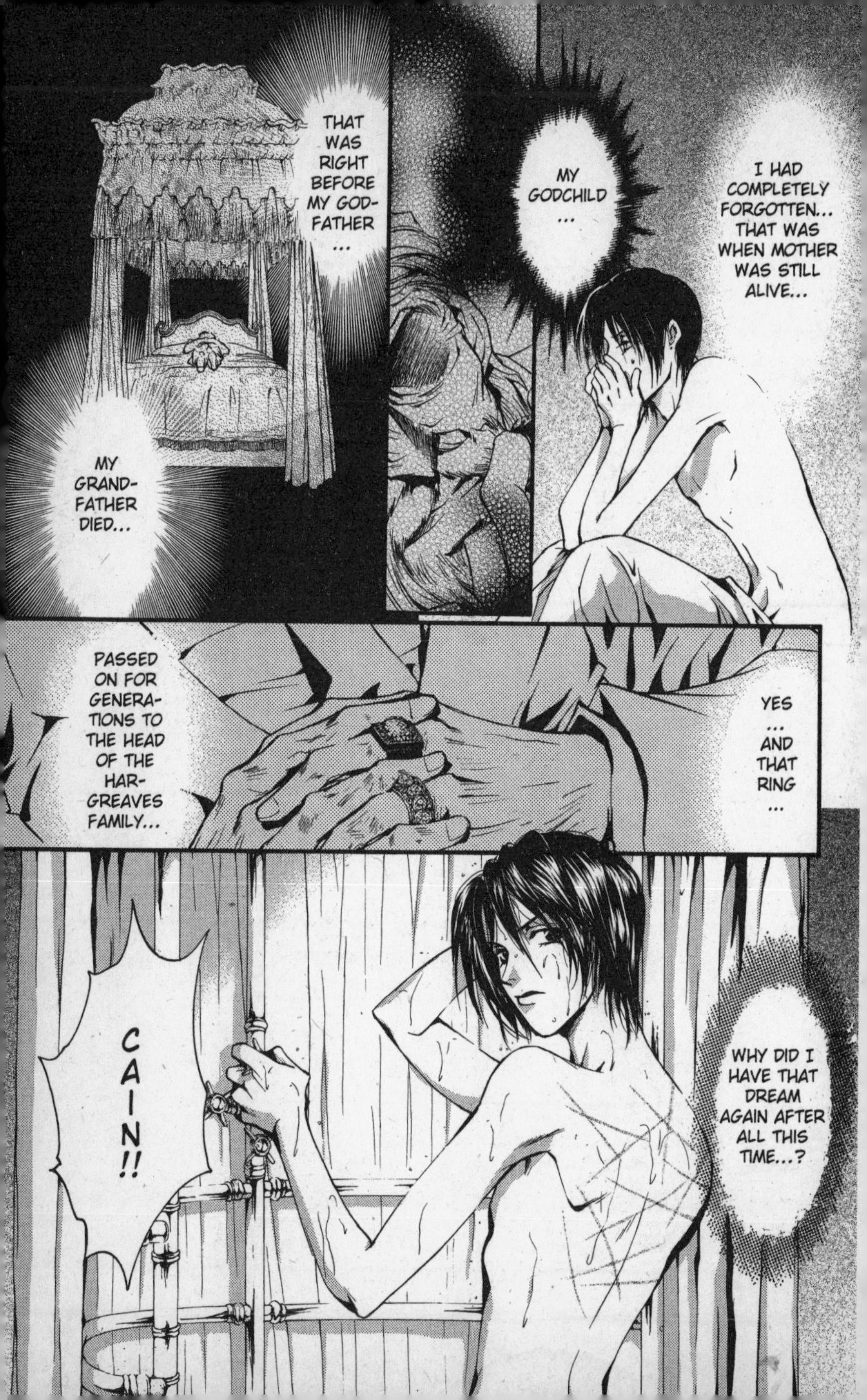
I HAD COMPLETELY FORGOTTEN... THAT WAS WHEN MOTHER WAS STILL ALIVE...
MY GODCHILD ...
THAT WAS RIGHT BEFORE MY GODFATHER ...
MY GRANDFATHER DIED...
YES ... AND THAT RING ...
PASSED ON FOR GENERATIONS TO THE HEAD OF THE HARGREAVES FAMILY...
WHY DID I HAVE THAT DREAM AGAIN AFTER ALL THIS TIME...?
CAIN!!

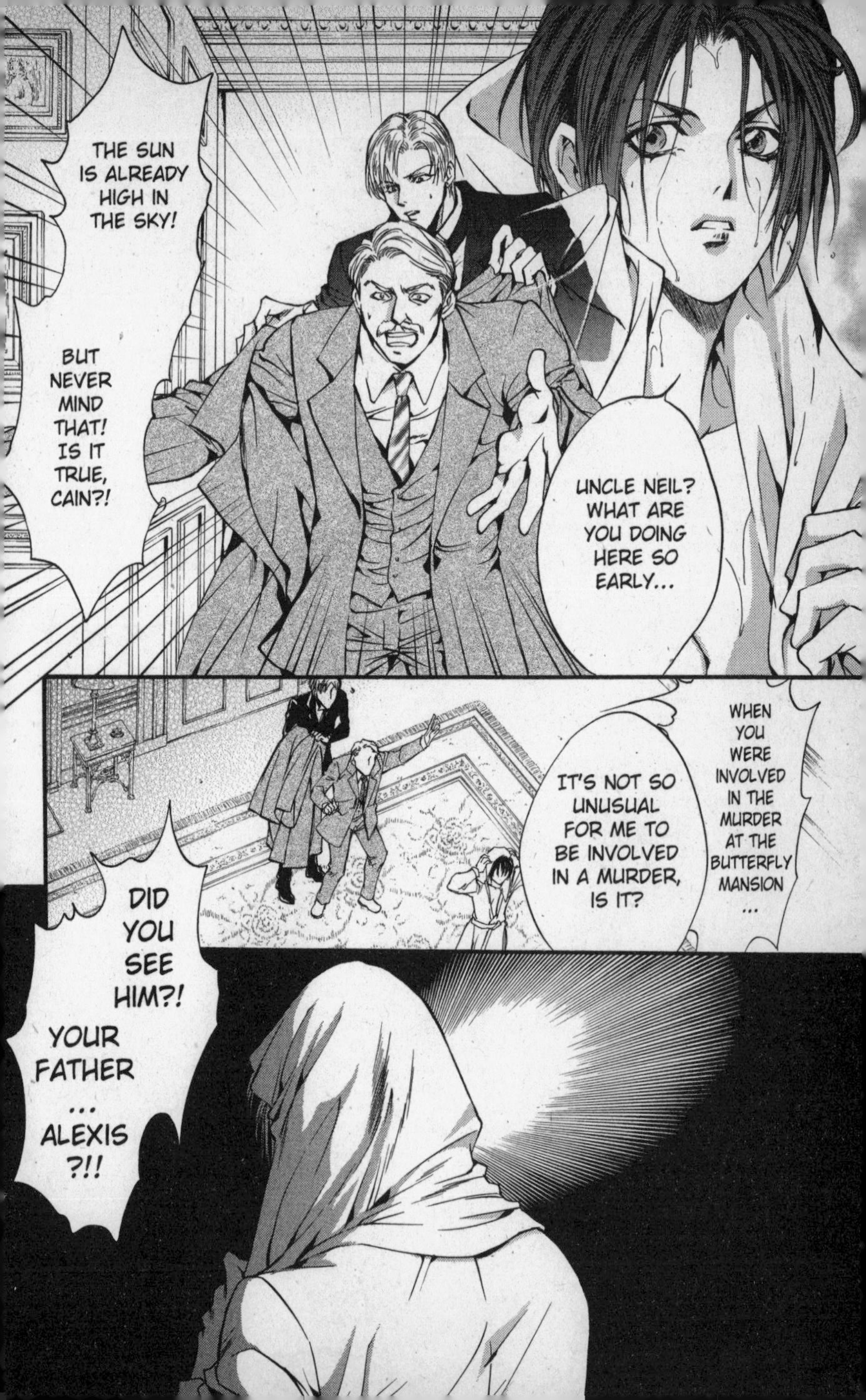
UNCLE NEIL? WHAT ARE YOU DOING HERE SO EARLY...
THE SUN IS ALREADY HIGH IN THE SKY!
BUT NEVER MIND THAT! IS IT TRUE, CAIN?!
WHEN YOU WERE INVOLVED IN THE MURDER AT THE BUTTERFLY MANSION ...
IT'S NOT SO UNUSUAL FOR ME TO BE INVOLVED IN A MURDER, IS IT?
DID YOU SEE HIM?!
YOUR FATHER ... ALEXIS ?!!

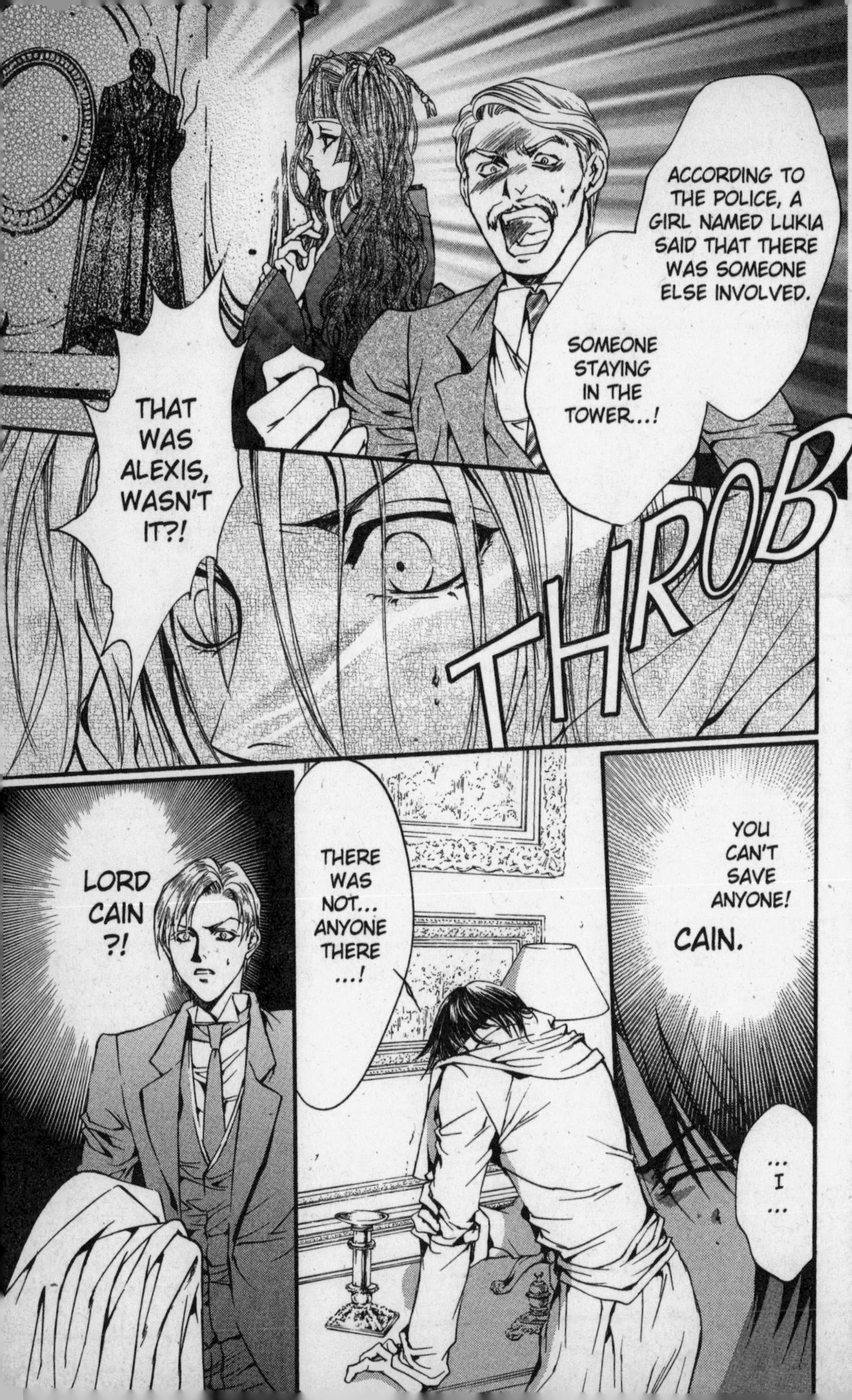
ACCORDING TO THE POLICE, A GIRL NAMED LUKIA SAID THAT THERE WAS SOMEONE ELSE INVOLVED.
SOMEONE STAYING IN THE TOWER...!
THAT WAS ALEXIS, WASN'T IT?!
THROB
YOU CAN'T SAVE ANYONE!
CAIN.
...I...
THERE WAS NOT... ANYONE THERE ...!
LORD CAIN ?!

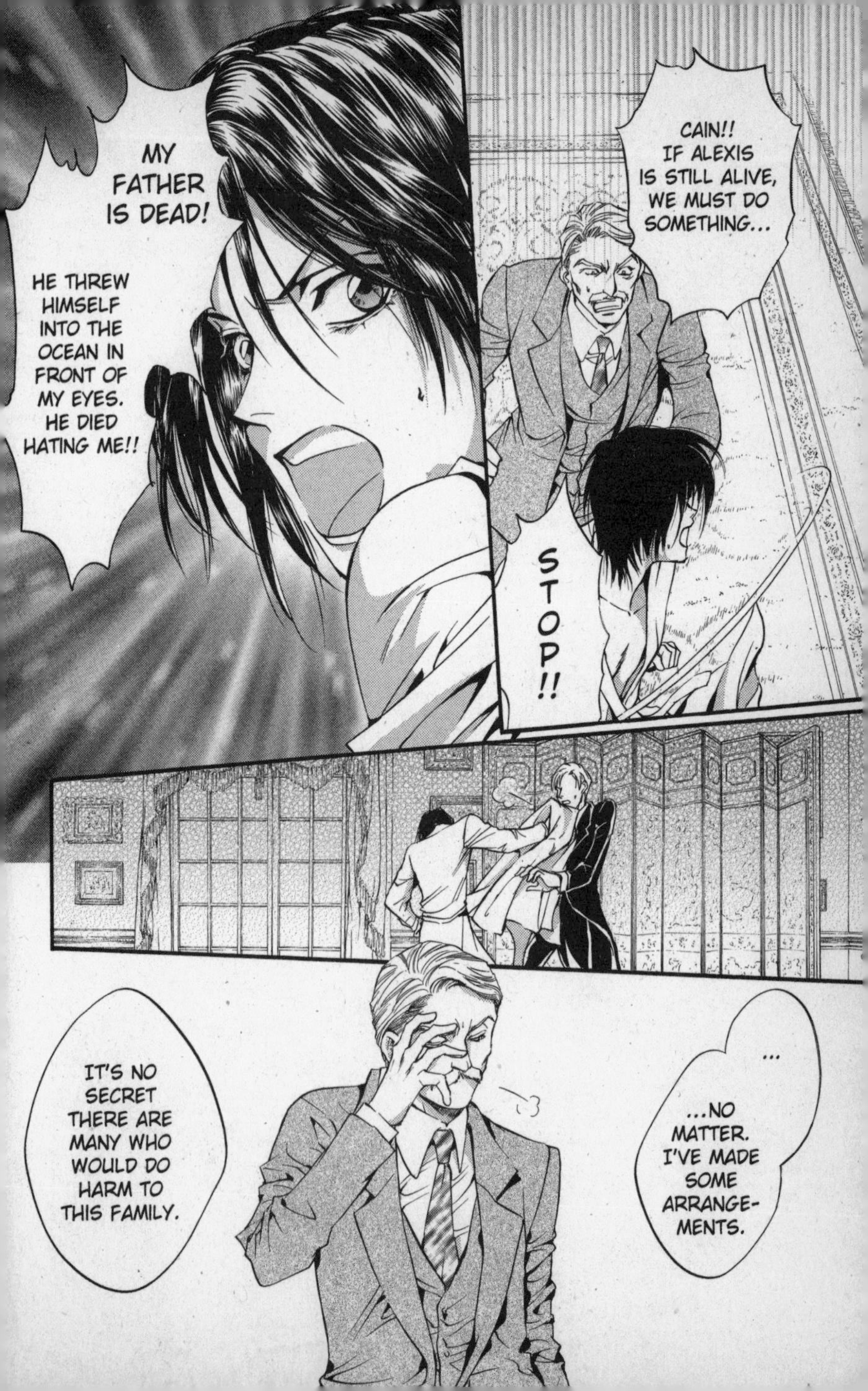
CAIN!! IF ALEXIS IS STILL ALIVE, WE MUST DO SOMETHING...
STOP!!
MY FATHER IS DEAD!
HE THREW HIMSELF INTO THE OCEAN IN FRONT OF MY EYES. HE DIED HATING ME!!
...
...NO MATTER. I'VE MADE SOME ARRANGE-MENTS.
IT'S NO SECRET THERE ARE MANY WHO WOULD DO HARM TO THIS FAMILY.

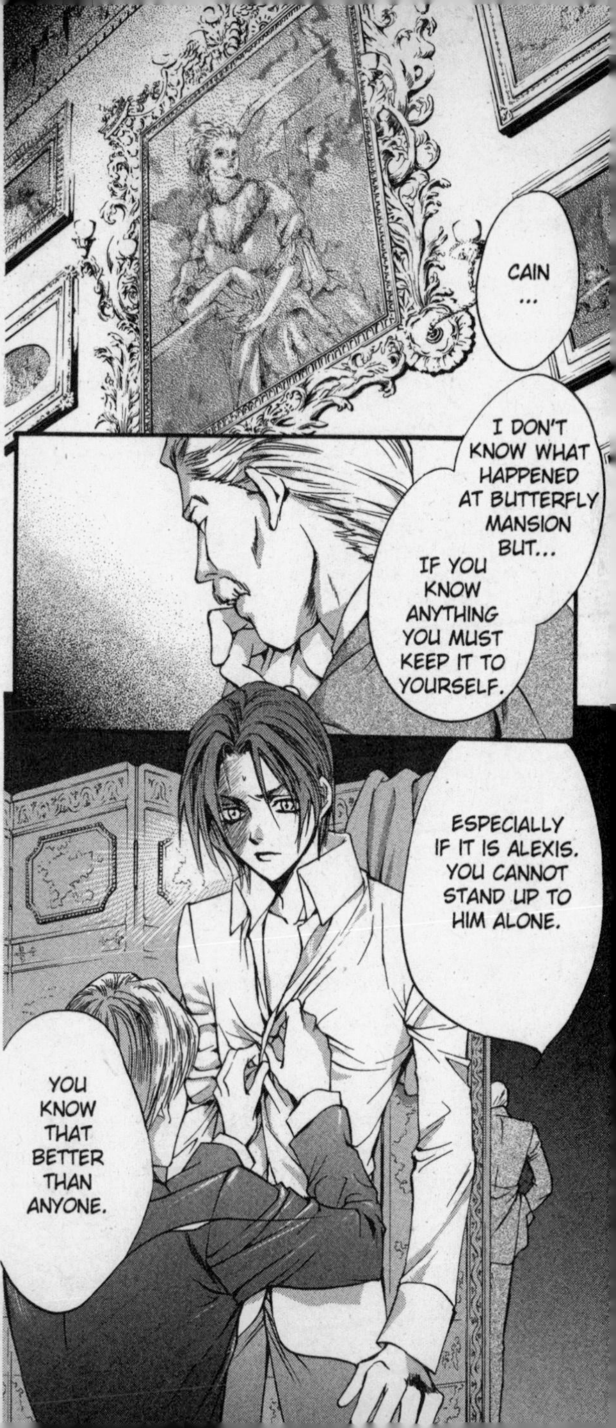
CAIN ...
I DON'T KNOW WHAT HAPPENED AT BUTTERFLY MANSION BUT...
IF YOU KNOW ANYTHING YOU MUST KEEP IT TO YOURSELF.
ESPECIALLY IF IT IS ALEXIS. YOU CANNOT STAND UP TO HIM ALONE.
YOU KNOW THAT BETTER THAN ANYONE.

This is Cain's third volume. It came out really quick. In this volume, readers will finally find out the meaning of the title "Godchild." The scene with Cain's grandpa has been in my head for a long time and I finally got to draw it. Uncle Neil is the grandfather's sister's son or Alexis's cousin. Do you ever speak harshly or rebel against parents and family who love you? That's Cain's problem. He thinks that because there's a bond between he and his uncle that he can get away with saying things that are a little unreasonable. He can't maintain his usual detached demeanor. After all, Cain is still a child. I bought the Zigeunerweisen CD and did a lot of other stuff. I don't know much about Classical music but I do like the sound of the violin.

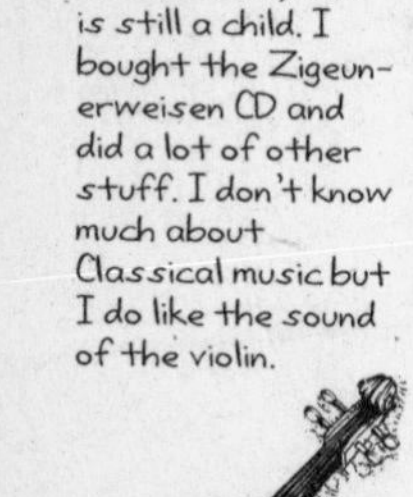

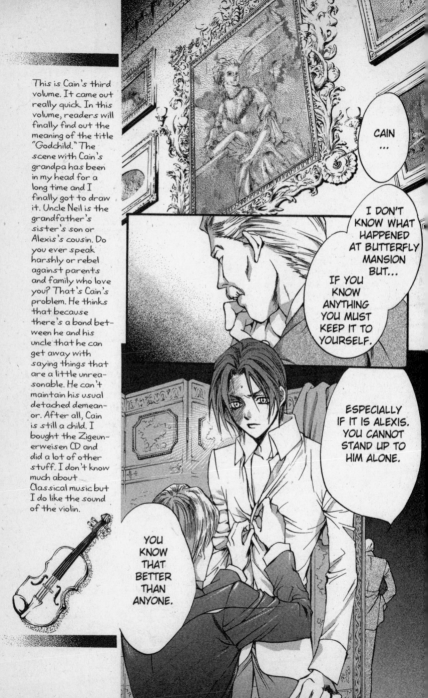

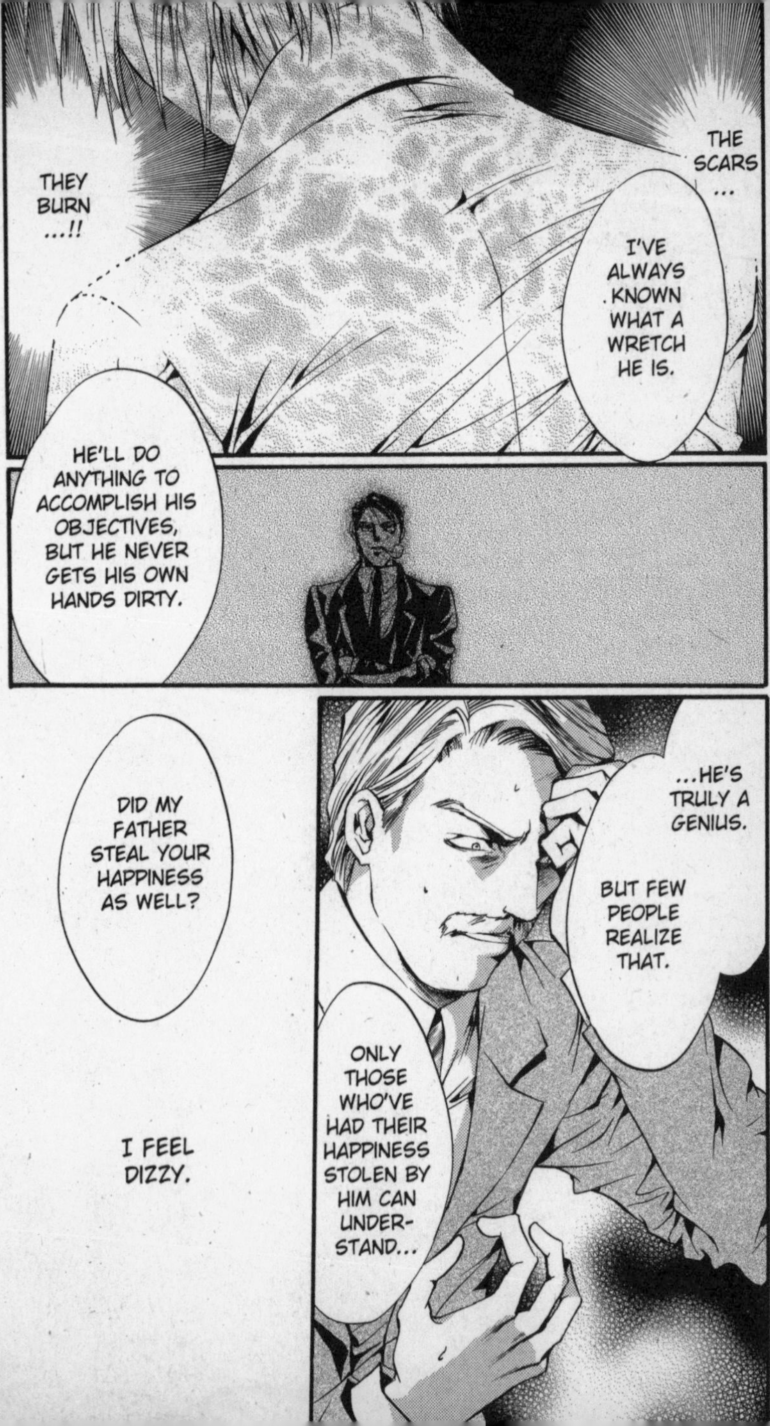
THE SCARS...
I'VE ALWAYS KNOWN WHAT A WRETCH HE IS.
THEY BURN...!!
HE'LL DO ANYTHING TO ACCOMPLISH HIS OBJECTIVES, BUT HE NEVER GETS HIS OWN HANDS DIRTY.
...HE'S TRULY A GENIUS.
BUT FEW PEOPLE REALIZE THAT.
ONLY THOSE WHO'VE HAD THEIR HAPPINESS STOLEN BY HIM CAN UNDER-STAND...
DID MY FATHER STEAL YOUR HAPPINESS AS WELL?
I FEEL DIZZY.

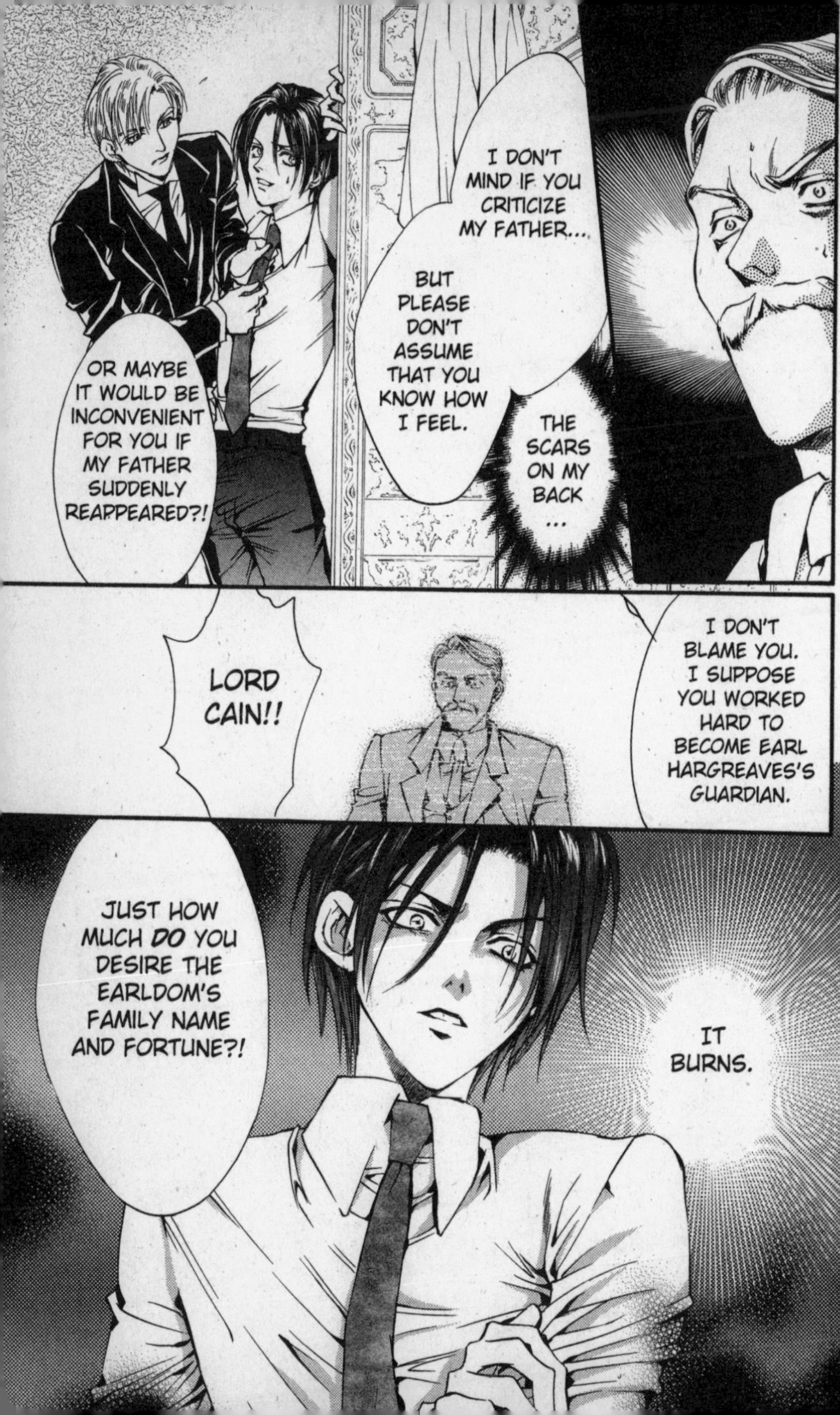
I DON'T MIND IF YOU CRITICIZE MY FATHER...
BUT PLEASE DON'T ASSUME THAT YOU KNOW HOW I FEEL.
THE SCARS ON MY BACK ...
OR MAYBE IT WOULD BE INCONVENIENT FOR YOU IF MY FATHER SUDDENLY REAPPEARED?!
I DON'T BLAME YOU. I SUPPOSE YOU WORKED HARD TO BECOME EARL HARGREAVES'S GUARDIAN.
LORD CAIN!!
JUST HOW MUCH *DO* YOU DESIRE THE EARLDOM'S FAMILY NAME AND FORTUNE?!
IT BURNS.

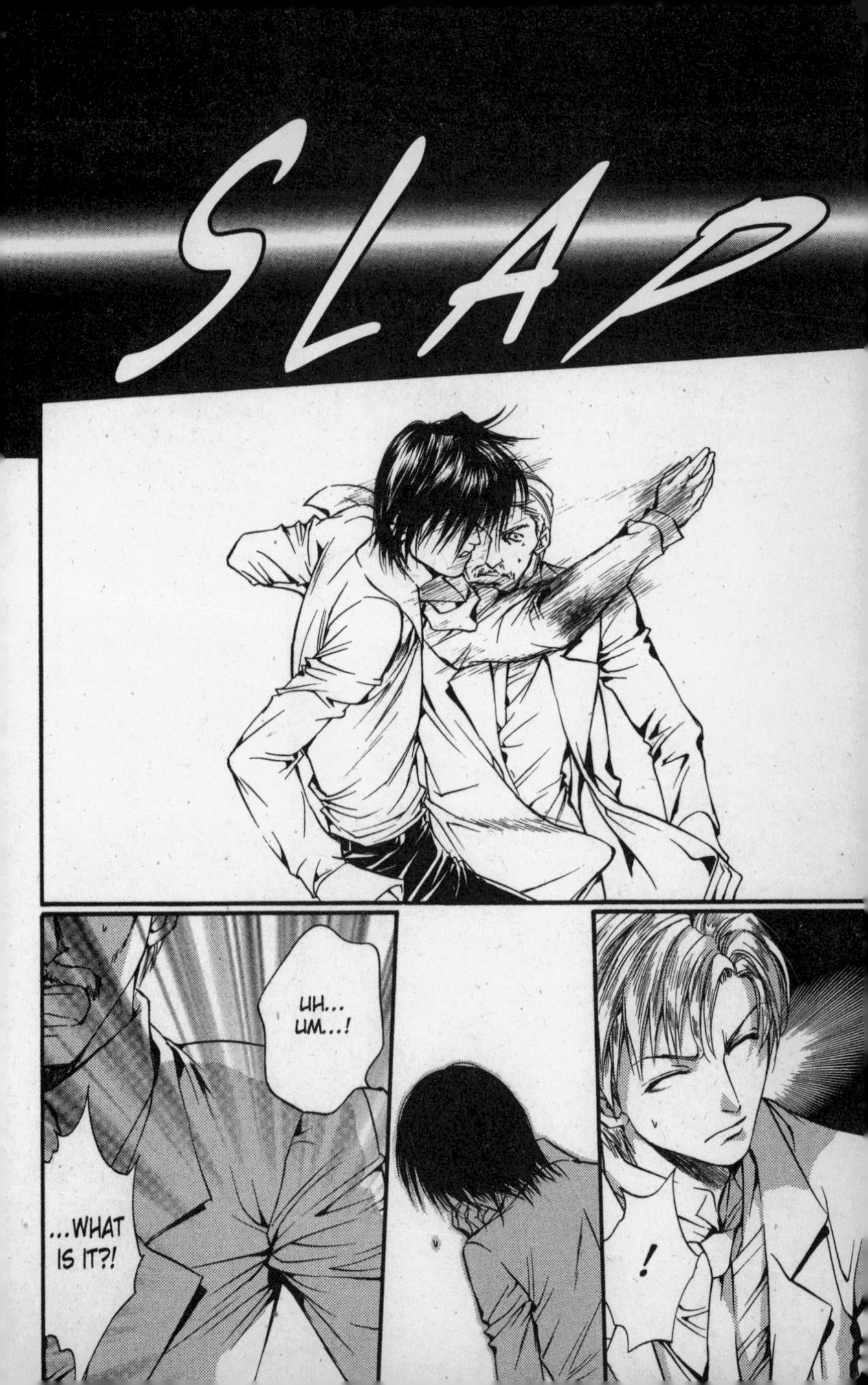
SLAP
!
UH... UM...!
...WHAT IS IT?!

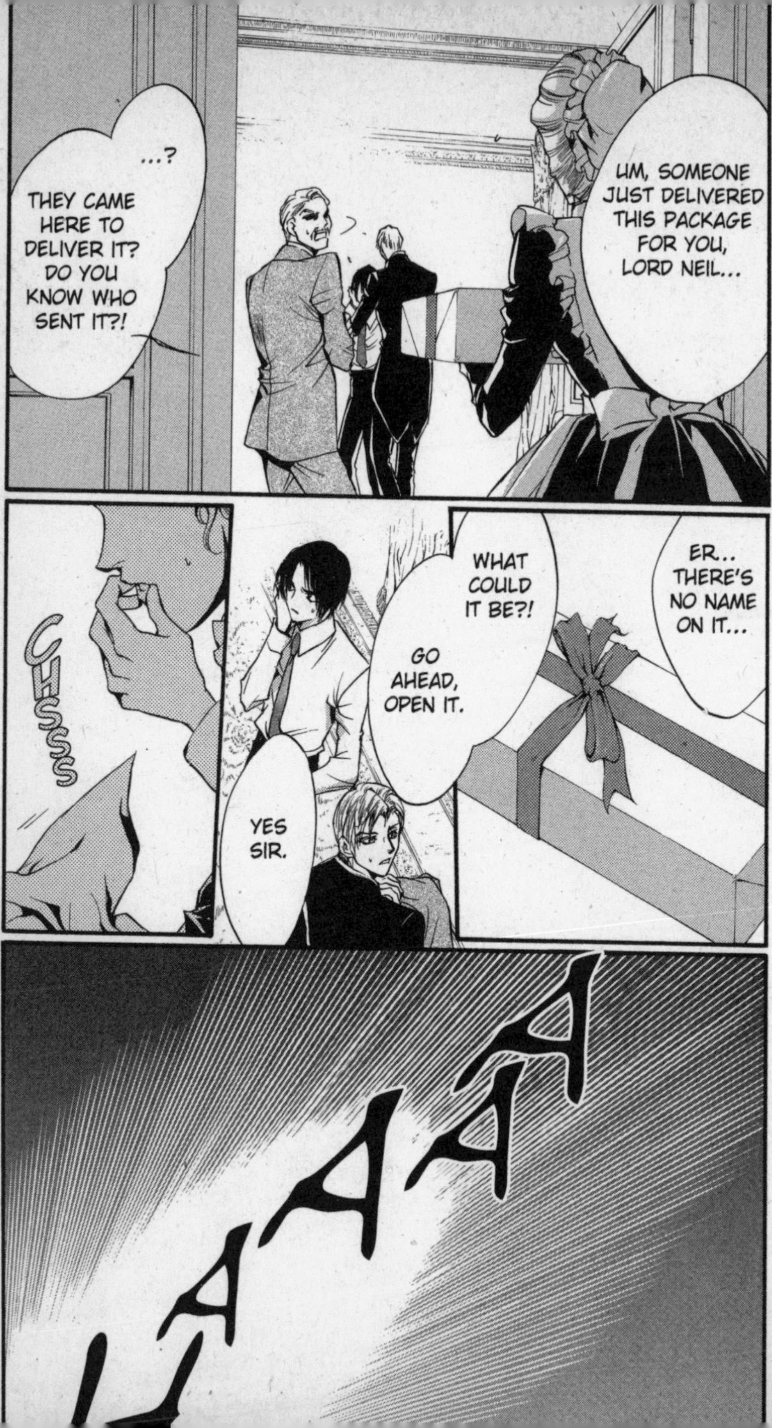
UM, SOMEONE JUST DELIVERED THIS PACKAGE FOR YOU, LORD NEIL...
...?
THEY CAME HERE TO DELIVER IT? DO YOU KNOW WHO SENT IT?!
ER... THERE'S NO NAME ON IT...
WHAT COULD IT BE?!
GO AHEAD, OPEN IT.
YES SIR.
CHSSS
IAAAAA

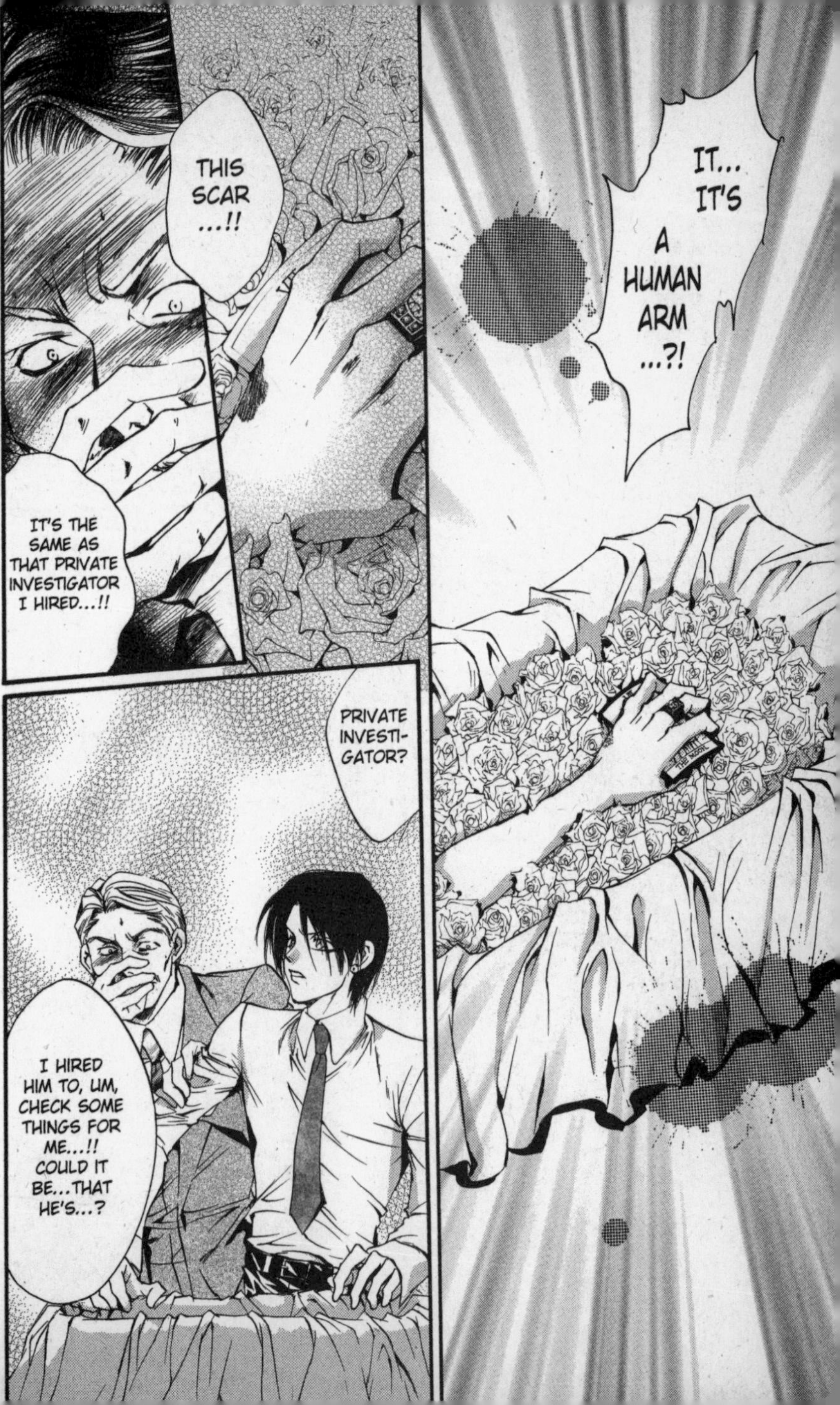
IT... IT'S A HUMAN ARM ...?!
THIS SCAR ...!!
IT'S THE SAME AS THAT PRIVATE INVESTIGATOR I HIRED...!!
PRIVATE INVESTI-GATOR?
I HIRED HIM TO, UM, CHECK SOME THINGS FOR ME...!! COULD IT BE...THAT HE'S...?

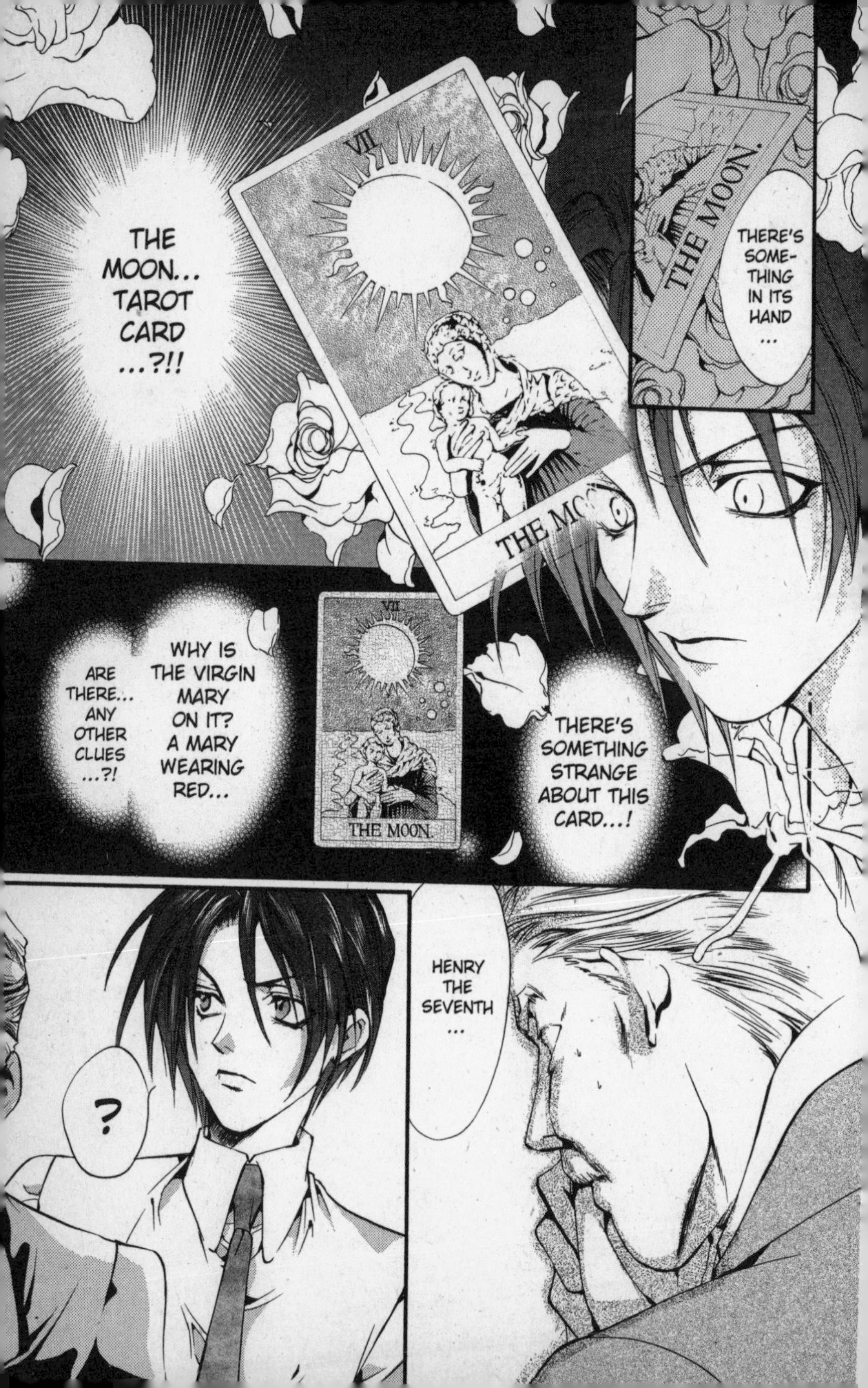
THE MOON.
THERE'S SOMETHING IN ITS HAND...
VII
THE MOON
THE MOON... TAROT CARD...?!!
THERE'S SOMETHING STRANGE ABOUT THIS CARD...!
VII
THE MOON.
WHY IS THE VIRGIN MARY ON IT? A MARY WEARING RED...
ARE THERE... ANY OTHER CLUES...?!
HENRY THE SEVENTH...
?

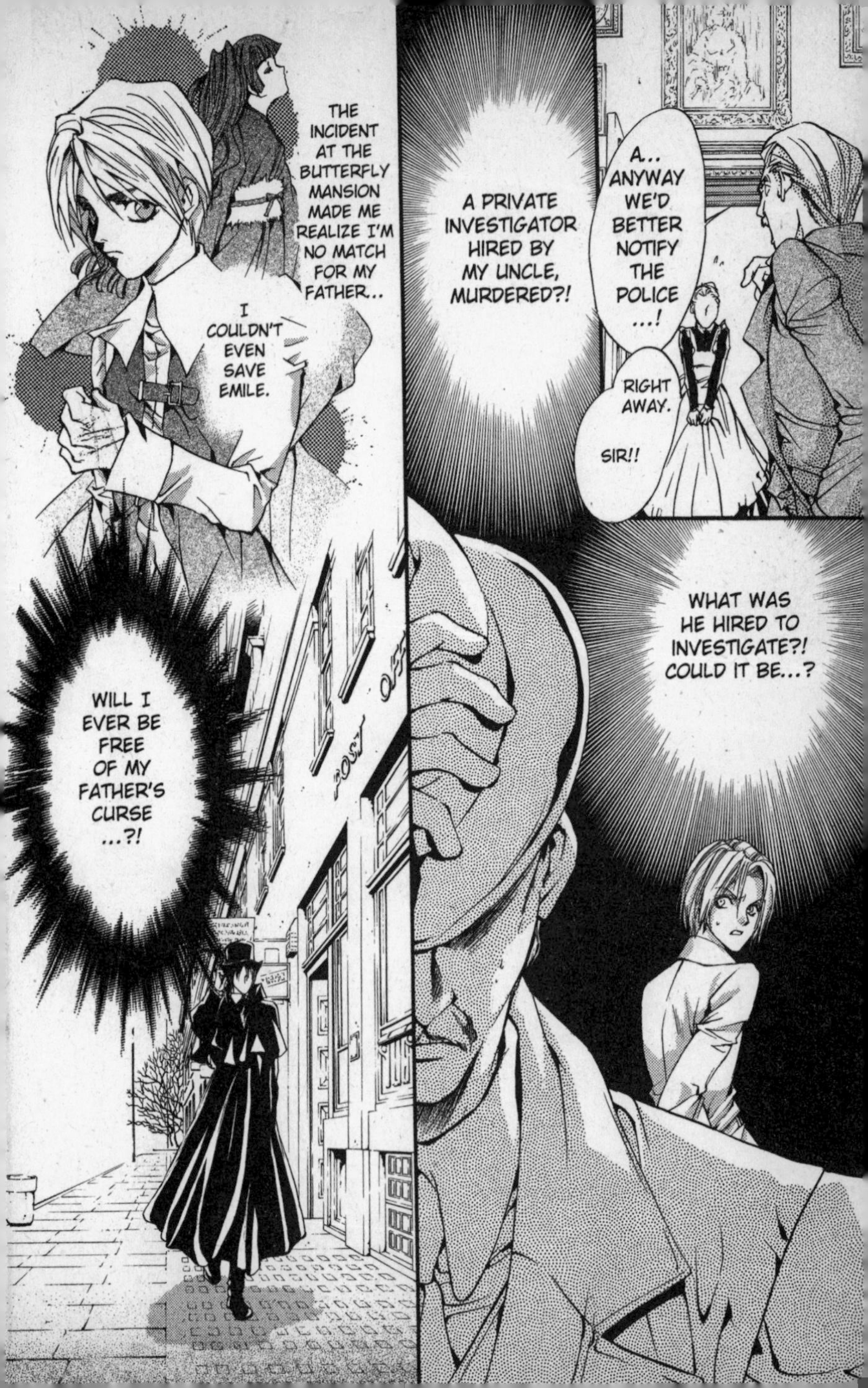
A... ANYWAY WE'D BETTER NOTIFY THE POLICE ...!
RIGHT AWAY.
SIR!!
A PRIVATE INVESTIGATOR HIRED BY MY UNCLE, MURDERED?!
WHAT WAS HE HIRED TO INVESTIGATE?! COULD IT BE...?
THE INCIDENT AT THE BUTTERFLY MANSION MADE ME REALIZE I'M NO MATCH FOR MY FATHER...
I COULDN'T EVEN SAVE EMILE.
WILL I EVER BE FREE OF MY FATHER'S CURSE ...?!

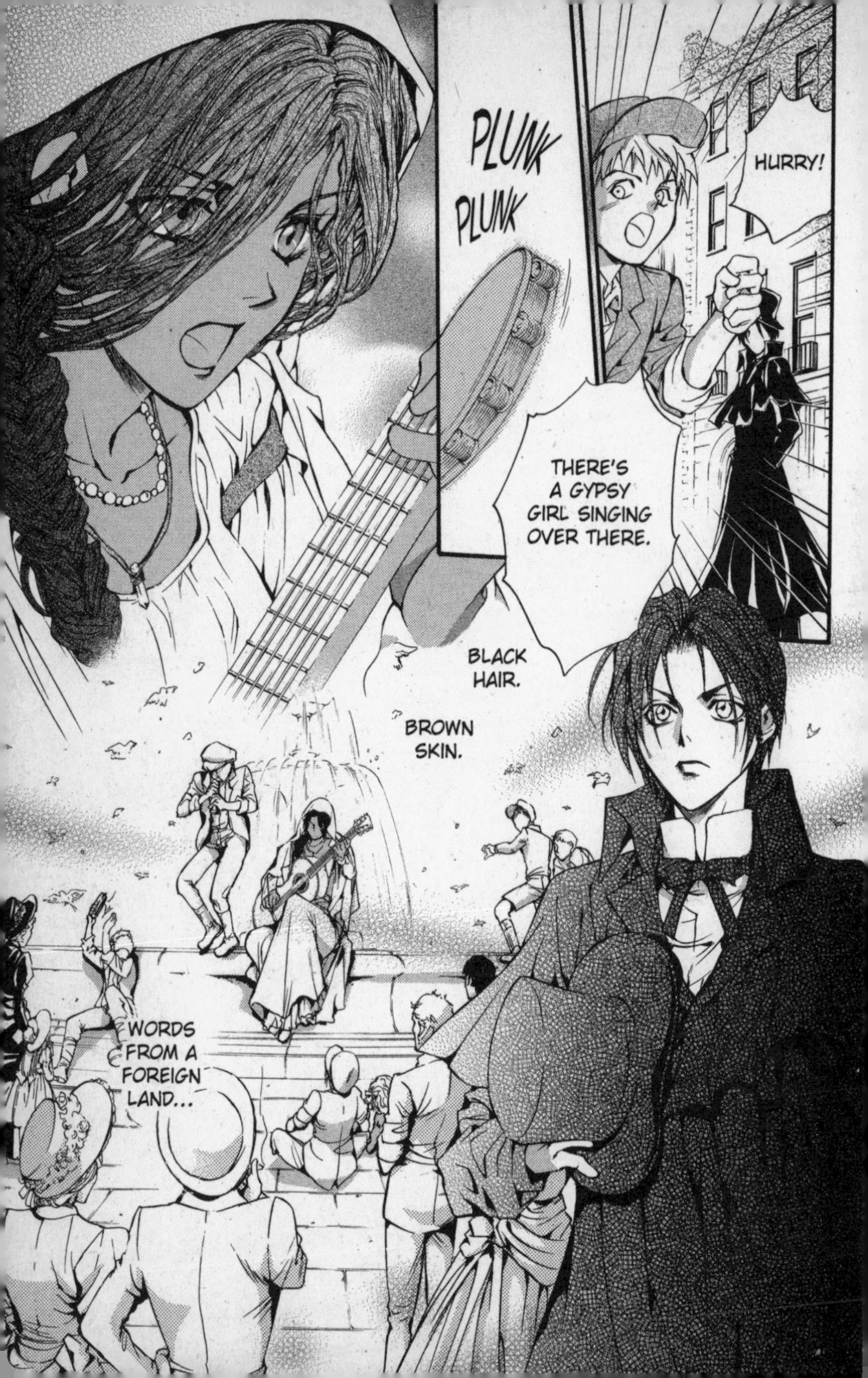
HURRY!
THERE'S A GYPSY GIRL SINGING OVER THERE.
PLUNK PLUNK
BLACK HAIR.
BROWN SKIN.
WORDS FROM A FOREIGN LAND...

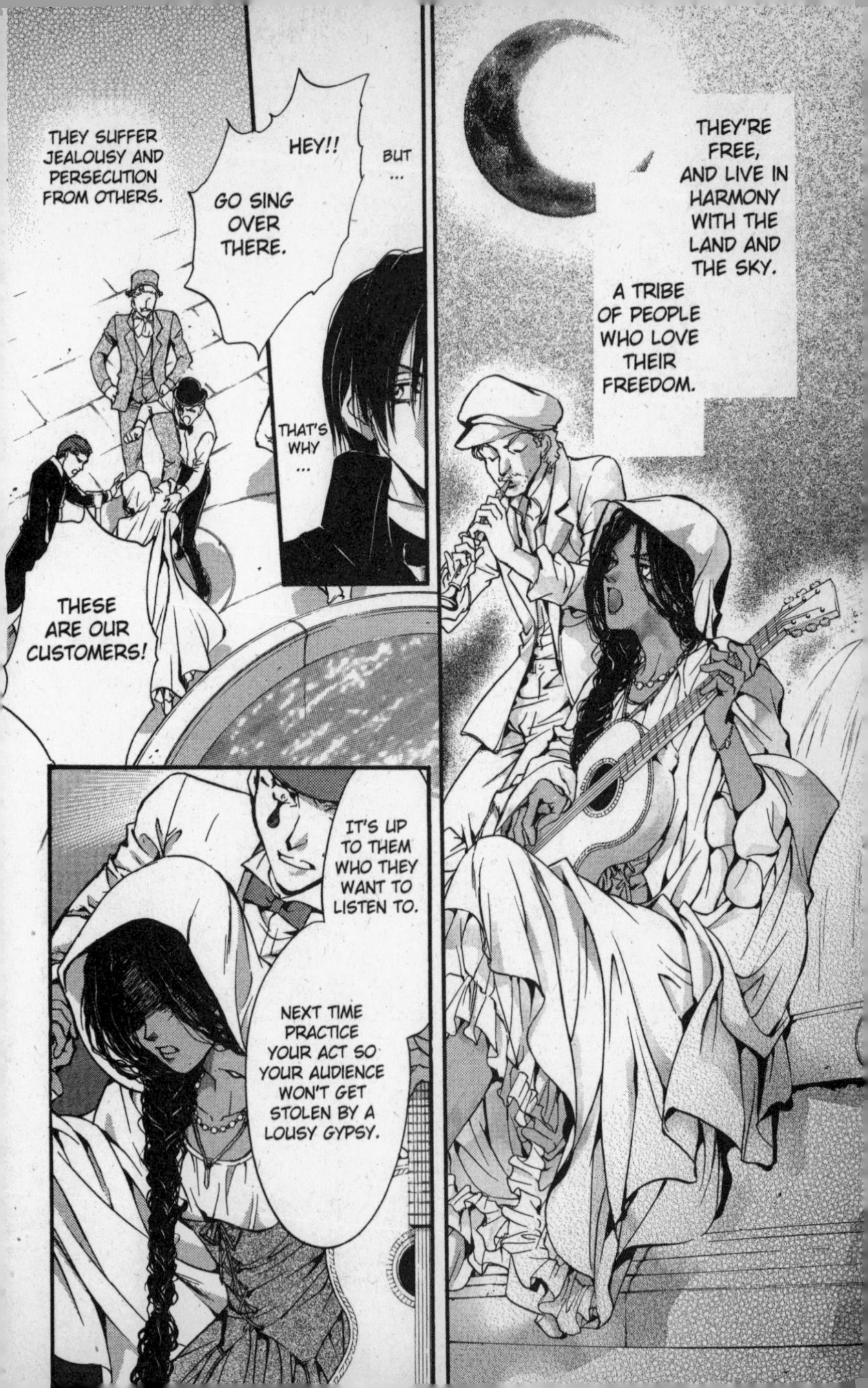

THEY'RE FREE, AND LIVE IN HARMONY WITH THE LAND AND THE SKY.
A TRIBE OF PEOPLE WHO LOVE THEIR FREEDOM.
BUT ...
THAT'S WHY ...
THEY SUFFER JEALOUSY AND PERSECUTION FROM OTHERS.
HEY!!
GO SING OVER THERE.
THESE ARE OUR CUSTOMERS!
IT'S UP TO THEM WHO THEY WANT TO LISTEN TO.
NEXT TIME PRACTICE YOUR ACT SO YOUR AUDIENCE WON'T GET STOLEN BY A LOUSY GYPSY.

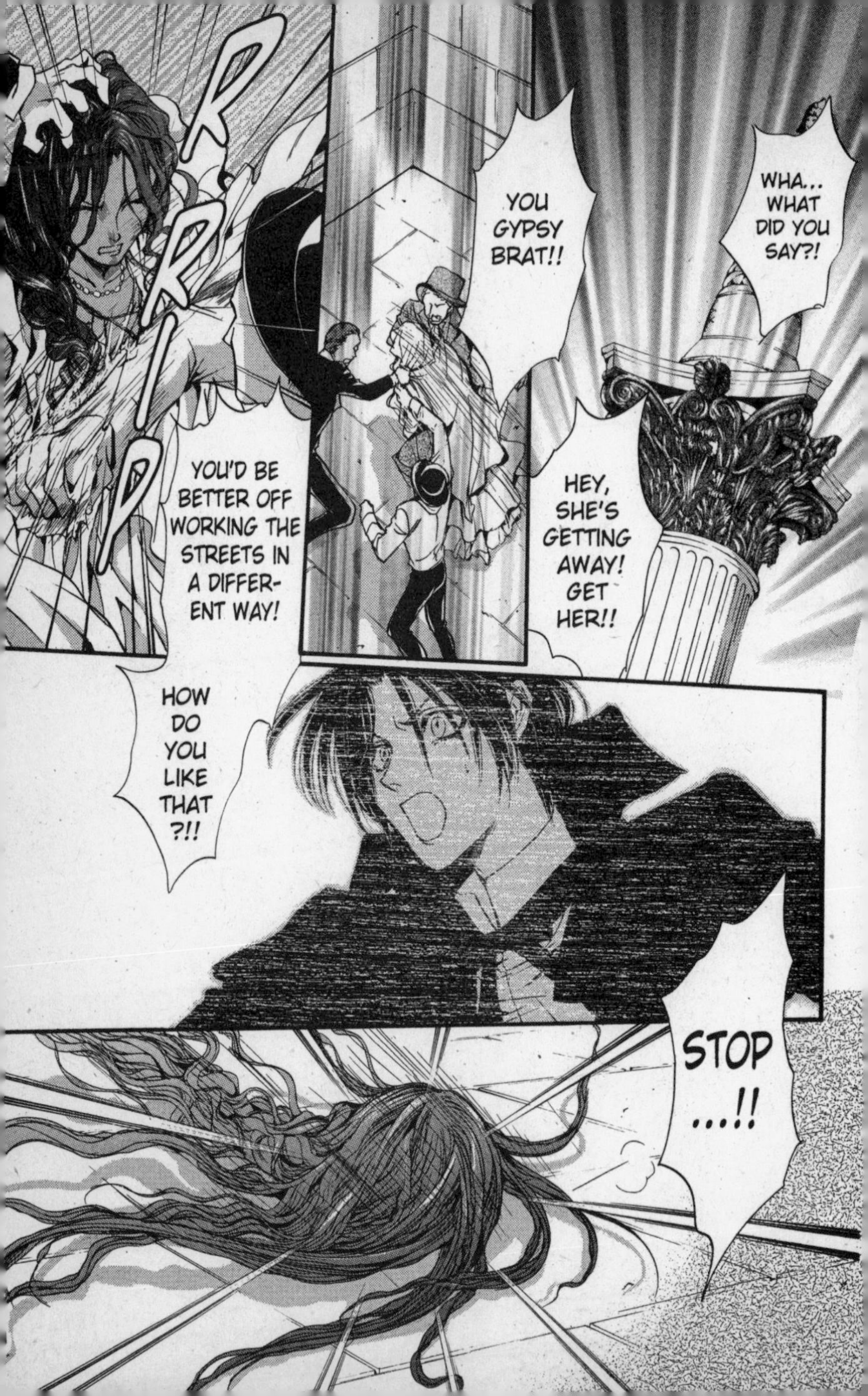
WHA... WHAT DID YOU SAY?!
YOU GYPSY BRAT!!
HEY, SHE'S GETTING AWAY! GET HER!!
RRRIP
YOU'D BE BETTER OFF WORKING THE STREETS IN A DIFFER-ENT WAY!
HOW DO YOU LIKE THAT?!!
STOP...!!

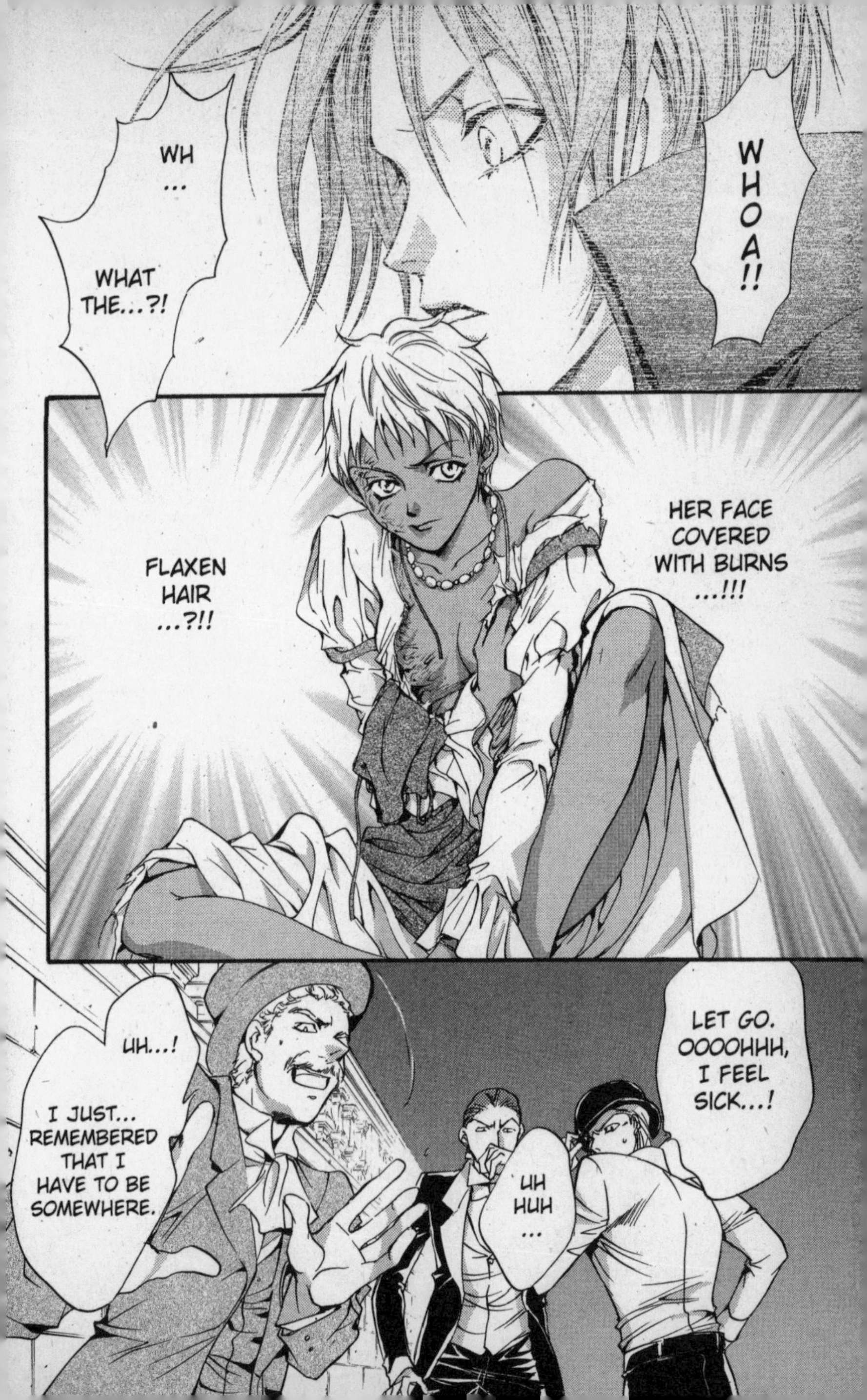
WHOA!!
WH... WHAT THE...?!
HER FACE COVERED WITH BURNS ...!!!
FLAXEN HAIR ...?!!
LET GO. OOOOHHH, I FEEL SICK...!
UH HUH ...
UH...!
I JUST... REMEMBERED THAT I HAVE TO BE SOMEWHERE.

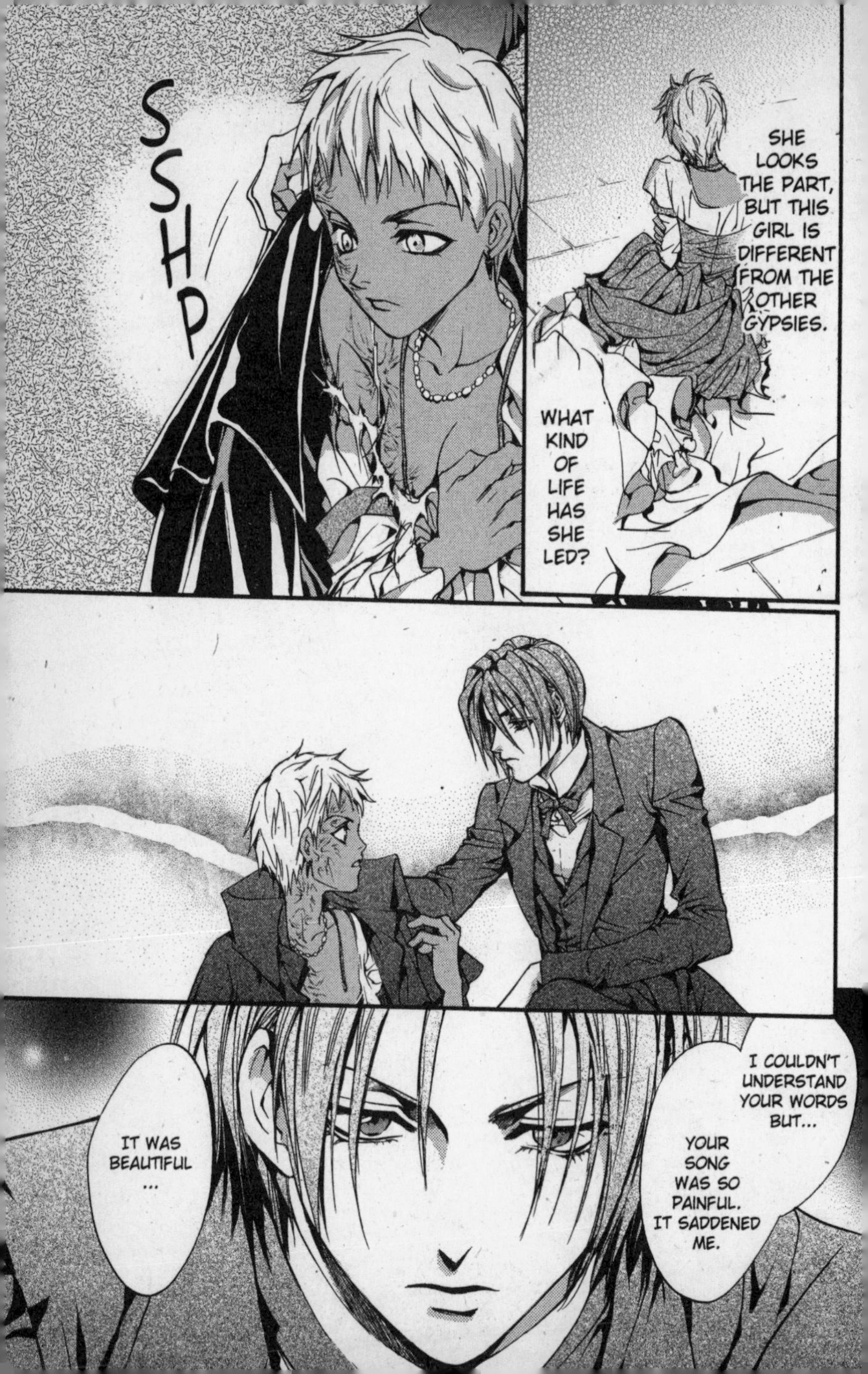
SHE LOOKS THE PART, BUT THIS GIRL IS DIFFERENT FROM THE OTHER GYPSIES.
WHAT KIND OF LIFE HAS SHE LED?
SSHP
I COULDN'T UNDERSTAND YOUR WORDS BUT...
YOUR SONG WAS SO PAINFUL. IT SADDENED ME.
IT WAS BEAUTIFUL ...

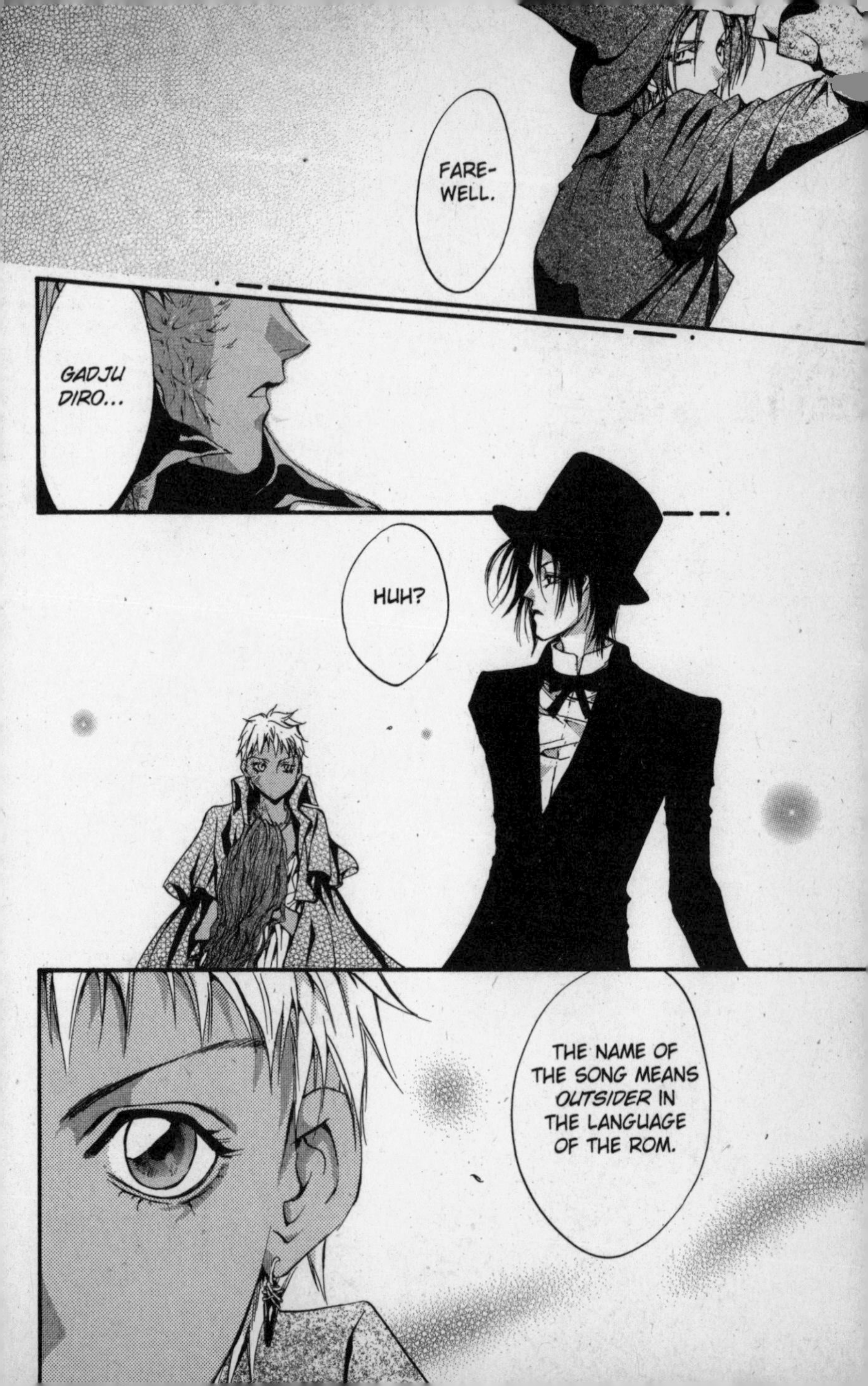
FARE-WELL.
GADJU DIRO...
HUH?
THE NAME OF THE SONG MEANS OUTSIDER IN THE LANGUAGE OF THE ROM.

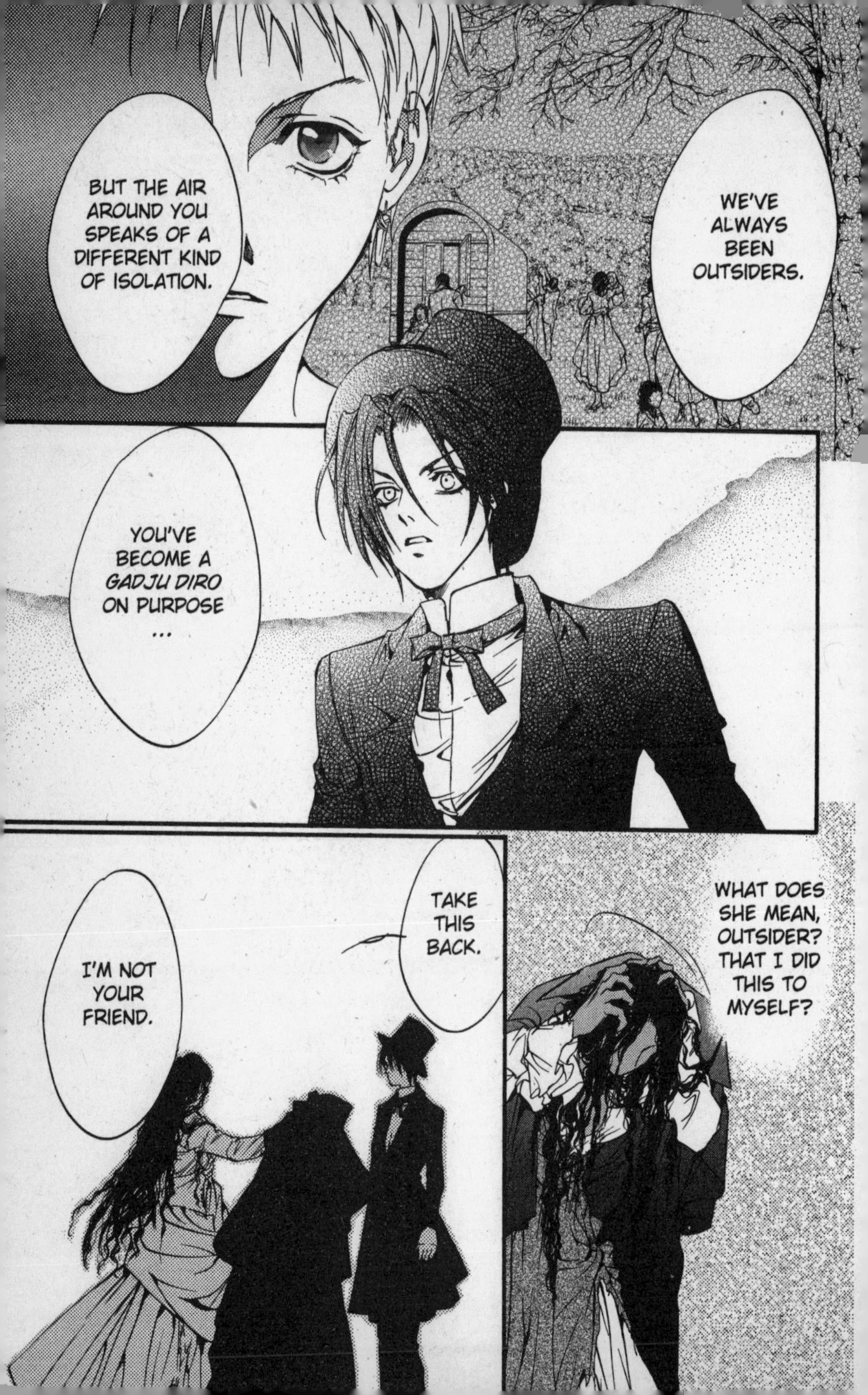
WE'VE ALWAYS BEEN OUTSIDERS.
BUT THE AIR AROUND YOU SPEAKS OF A DIFFERENT KIND OF ISOLATION.
YOU'VE BECOME A *GADJU DIRO* ON PURPOSE ...
WHAT DOES SHE MEAN, OUTSIDER? THAT I DID THIS TO MYSELF?
TAKE THIS BACK.
I'M NOT YOUR FRIEND.

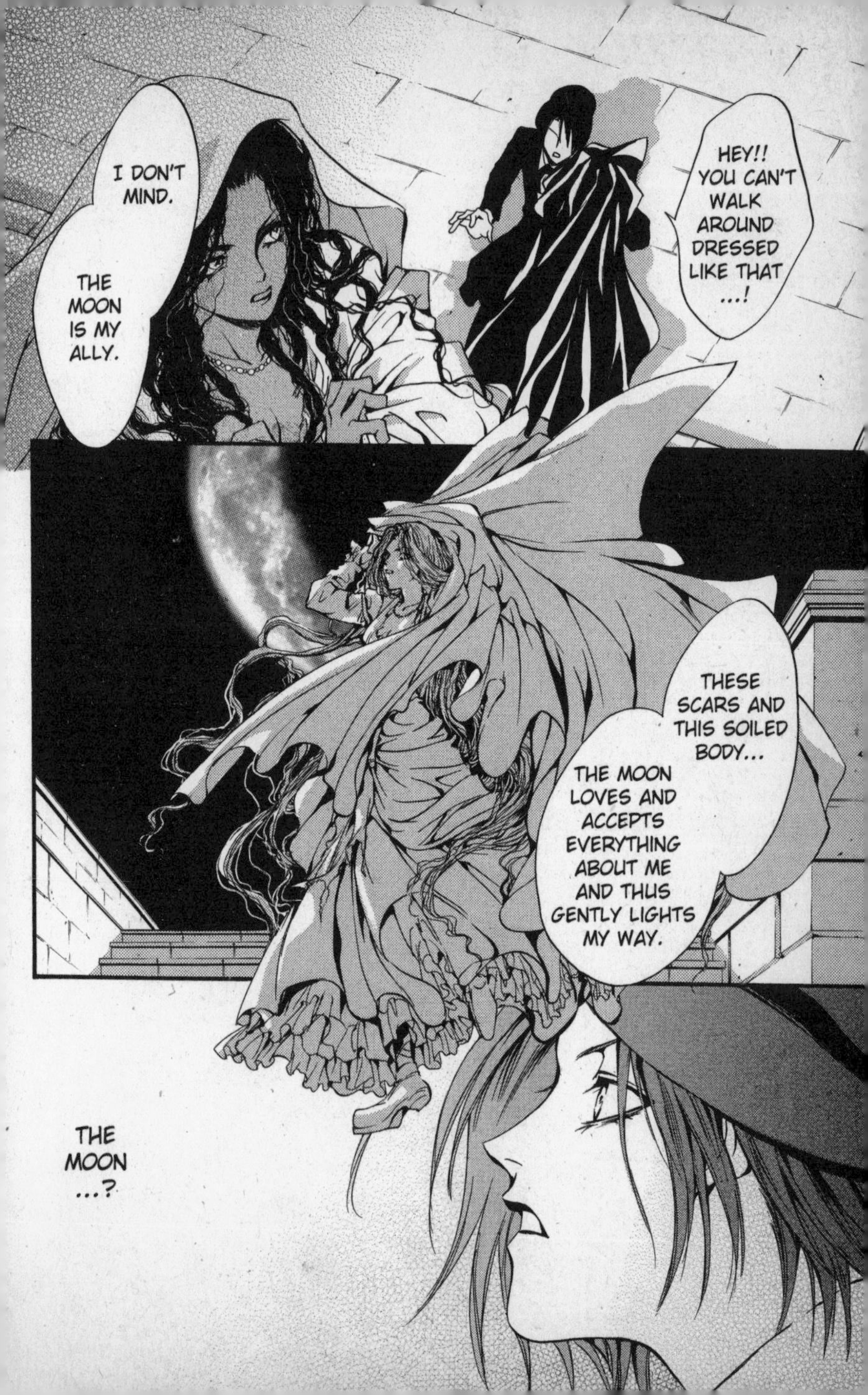
HEY!! YOU CAN'T WALK AROUND DRESSED LIKE THAT ...!
I DON'T MIND.
THE MOON IS MY ALLY.
THESE SCARS AND THIS SOILED BODY...
THE MOON LOVES AND ACCEPTS EVERYTHING ABOUT ME AND THUS GENTLY LIGHTS MY WAY.
THE MOON ...?

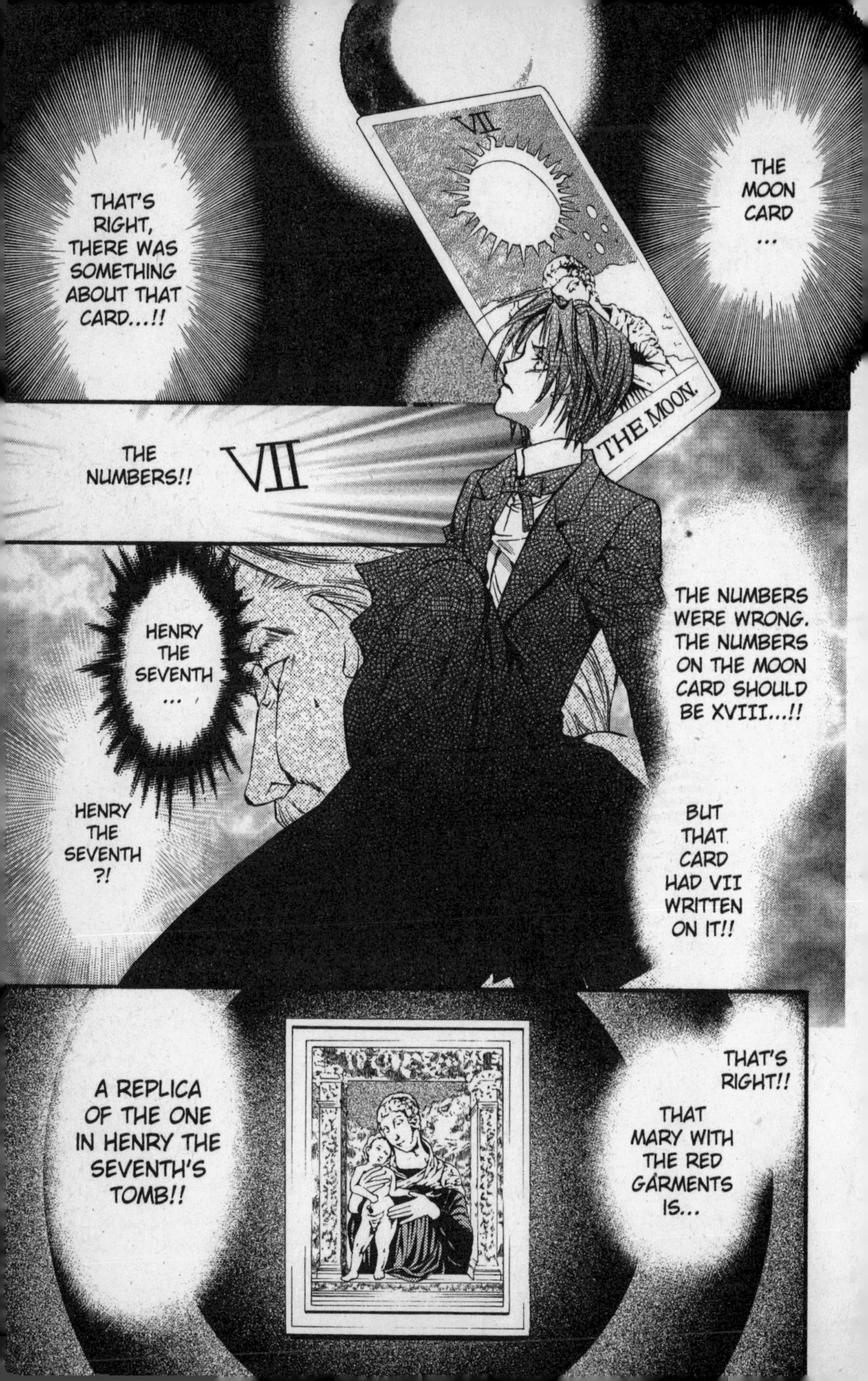
THE MOON CARD ...
VII
THE MOON.
THAT'S RIGHT, THERE WAS SOMETHING ABOUT THAT CARD...!!
VII
THE NUMBERS!!
THE NUMBERS WERE WRONG. THE NUMBERS ON THE MOON CARD SHOULD BE XVIII...!!
BUT THAT CARD HAD VII WRITTEN ON IT!!
HENRY THE SEVENTH ...
HENRY THE SEVENTH ?!
THAT'S RIGHT!!
THAT MARY WITH THE RED GARMENTS IS...
A REPLICA OF THE ONE IN HENRY THE SEVENTH'S TOMB!!

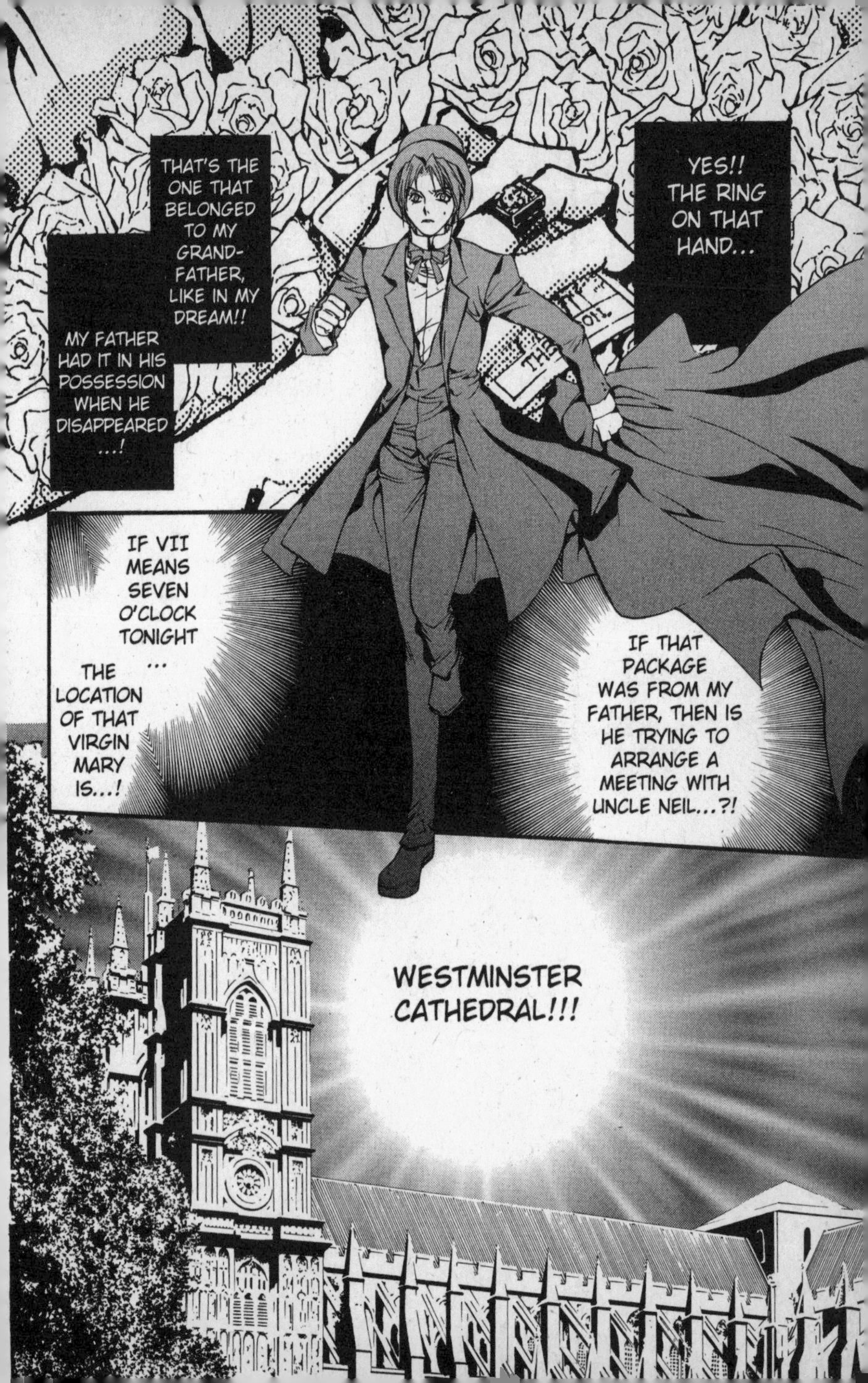
YES!! THE RING ON THAT HAND...
THAT'S THE ONE THAT BELONGED TO MY GRAND-FATHER, LIKE IN MY DREAM!!
MY FATHER HAD IT IN HIS POSSESSION WHEN HE DISAPPEARED ...!
IF THAT PACKAGE WAS FROM MY FATHER, THEN IS HE TRYING TO ARRANGE A MEETING WITH UNCLE NEIL...?!
IF VII MEANS SEVEN O'CLOCK TONIGHT ...
THE LOCATION OF THAT VIRGIN MARY IS...!
WESTMINSTER CATHEDRAL!!!

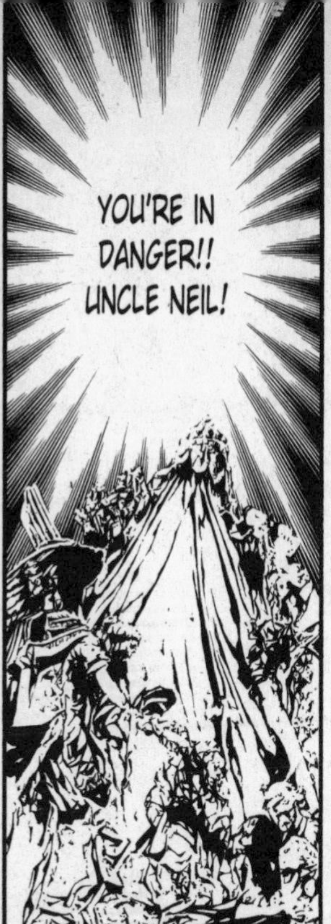
YOU'RE IN DANGER!! UNCLE NEIL!

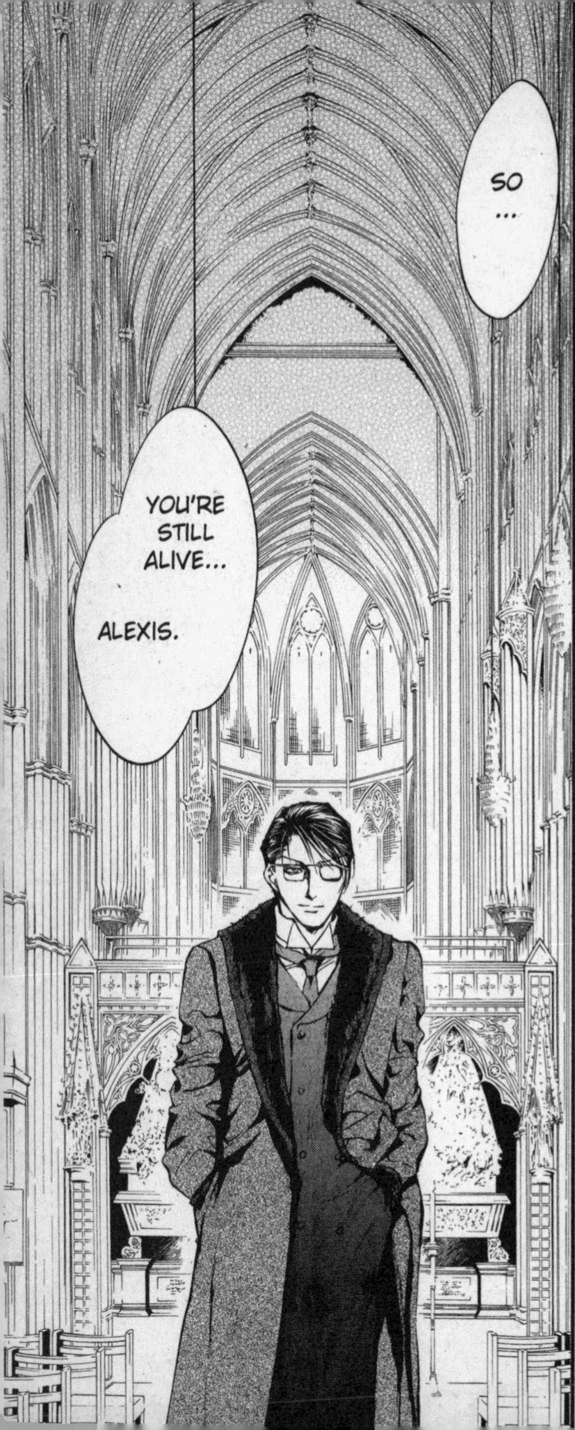
SO ...
YOU'RE STILL ALIVE... ALEXIS.

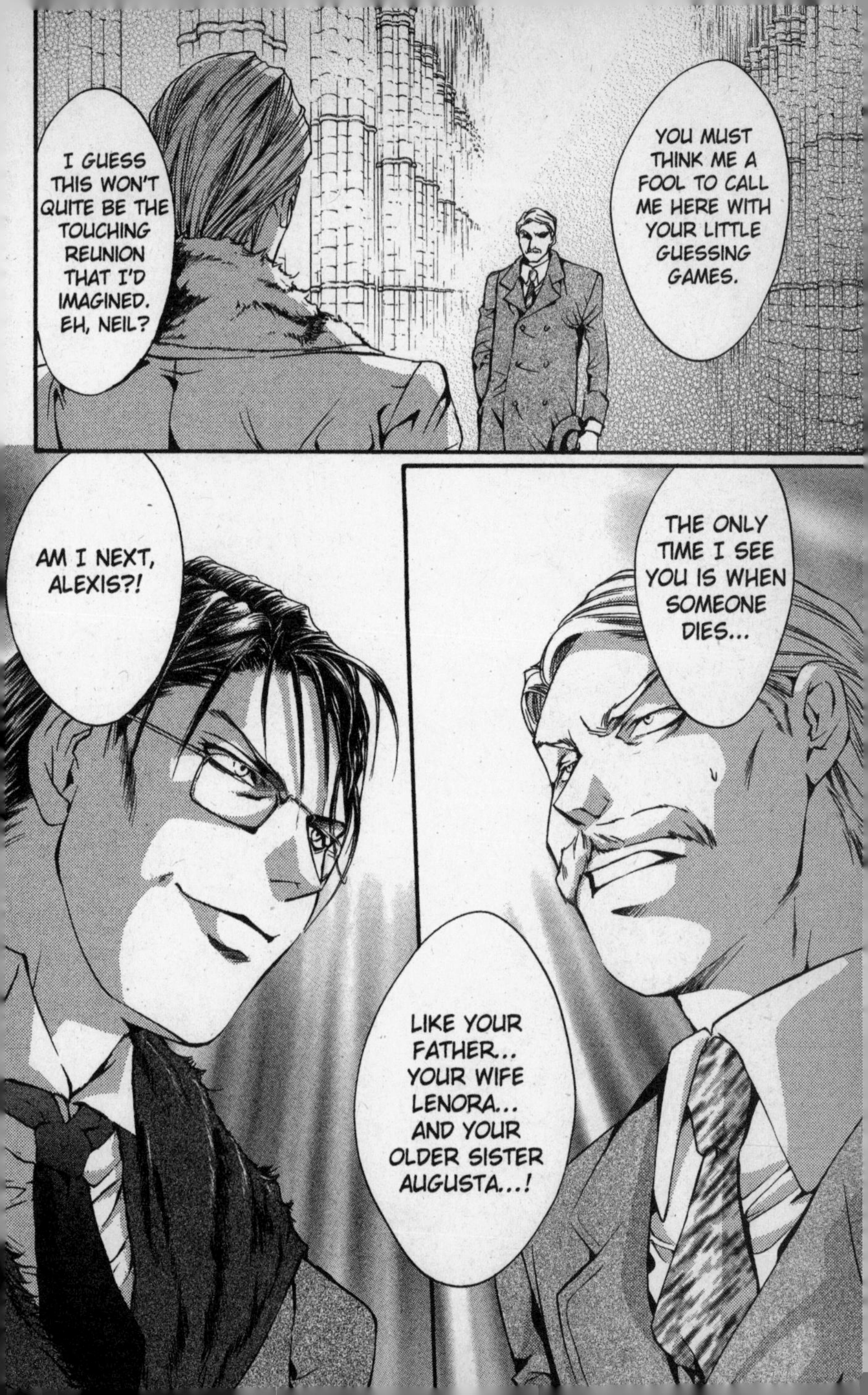
YOU MUST THINK ME A FOOL TO CALL ME HERE WITH YOUR LITTLE GUESSING GAMES.
I GUESS THIS WON'T QUITE BE THE TOUCHING REUNION THAT I'D IMAGINED. EH, NEIL?
THE ONLY TIME I SEE YOU IS WHEN SOMEONE DIES...
LIKE YOUR FATHER... YOUR WIFE LENORA... AND YOUR OLDER SISTER AUGUSTA...!
AM I NEXT, ALEXIS?!

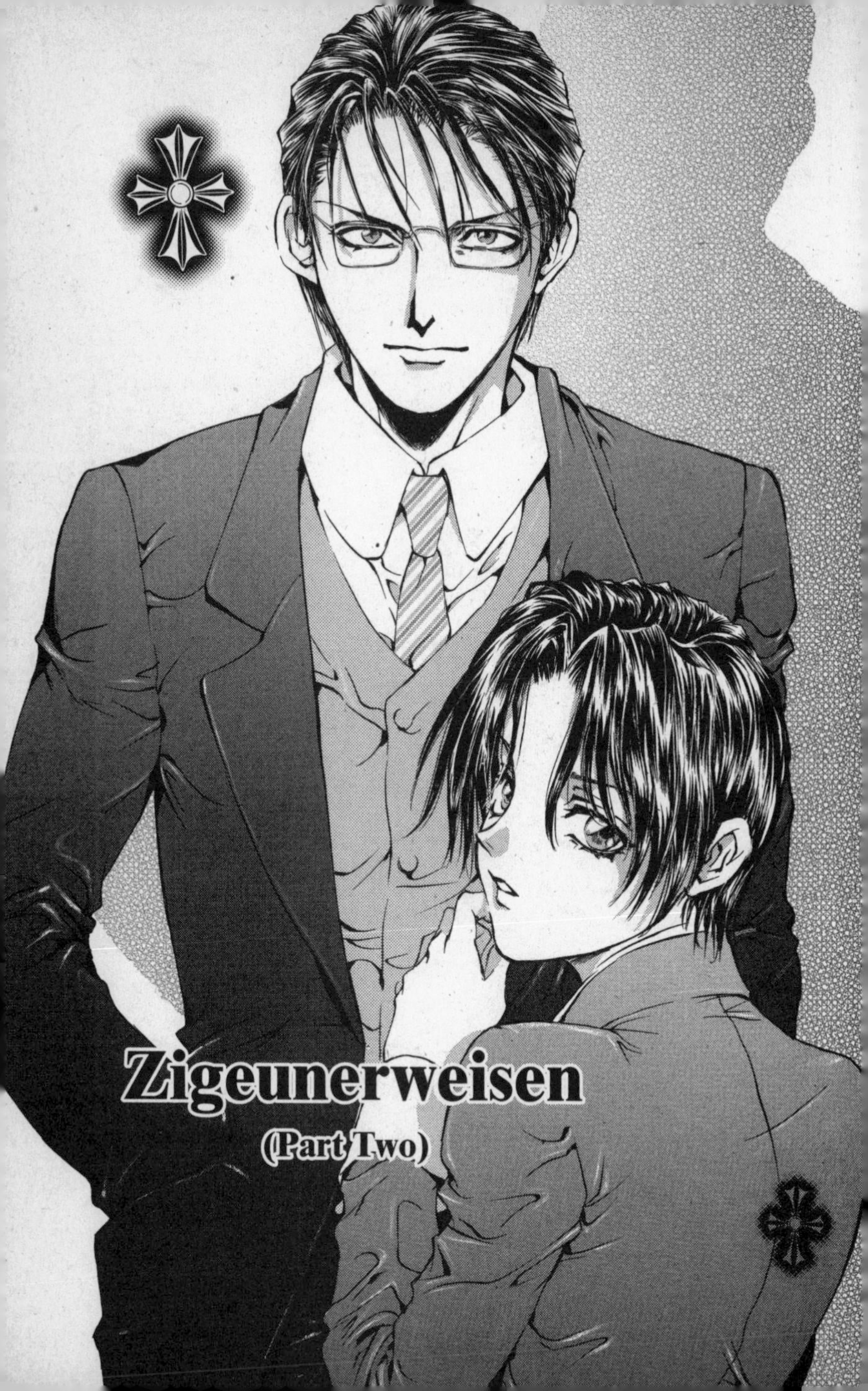
Zigeunerweisen
(Part Two)

Zigeunerweisen (Part Two)

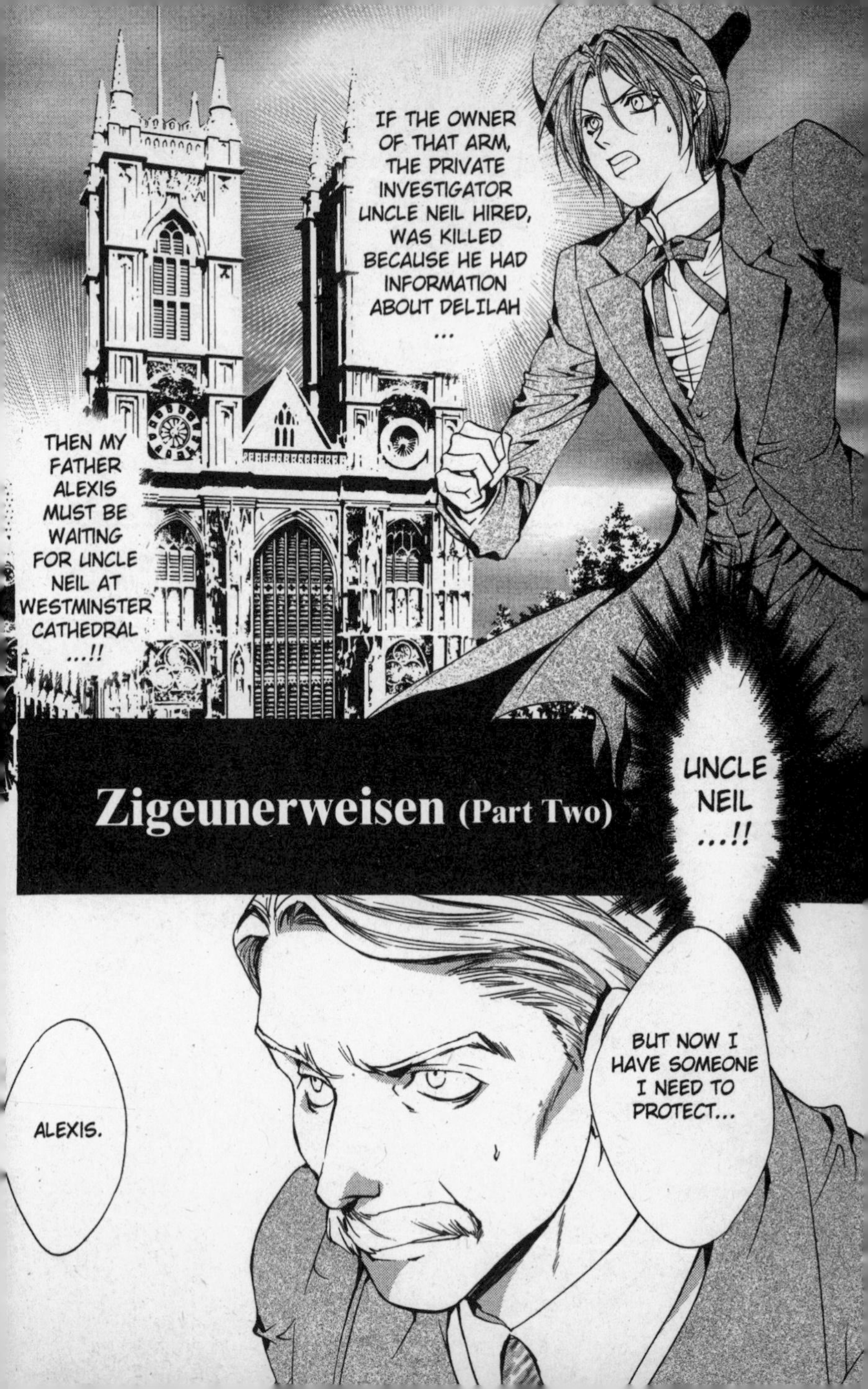
IF THE OWNER OF THAT ARM, THE PRIVATE INVESTIGATOR UNCLE NEIL HIRED, WAS KILLED BECAUSE HE HAD INFORMATION ABOUT DELILAH ...
THEN MY FATHER ALEXIS MUST BE WAITING FOR UNCLE NEIL AT WESTMINSTER CATHEDRAL ...!!
UNCLE NEIL ...!!
BUT NOW I HAVE SOMEONE I NEED TO PROTECT...
ALEXIS.

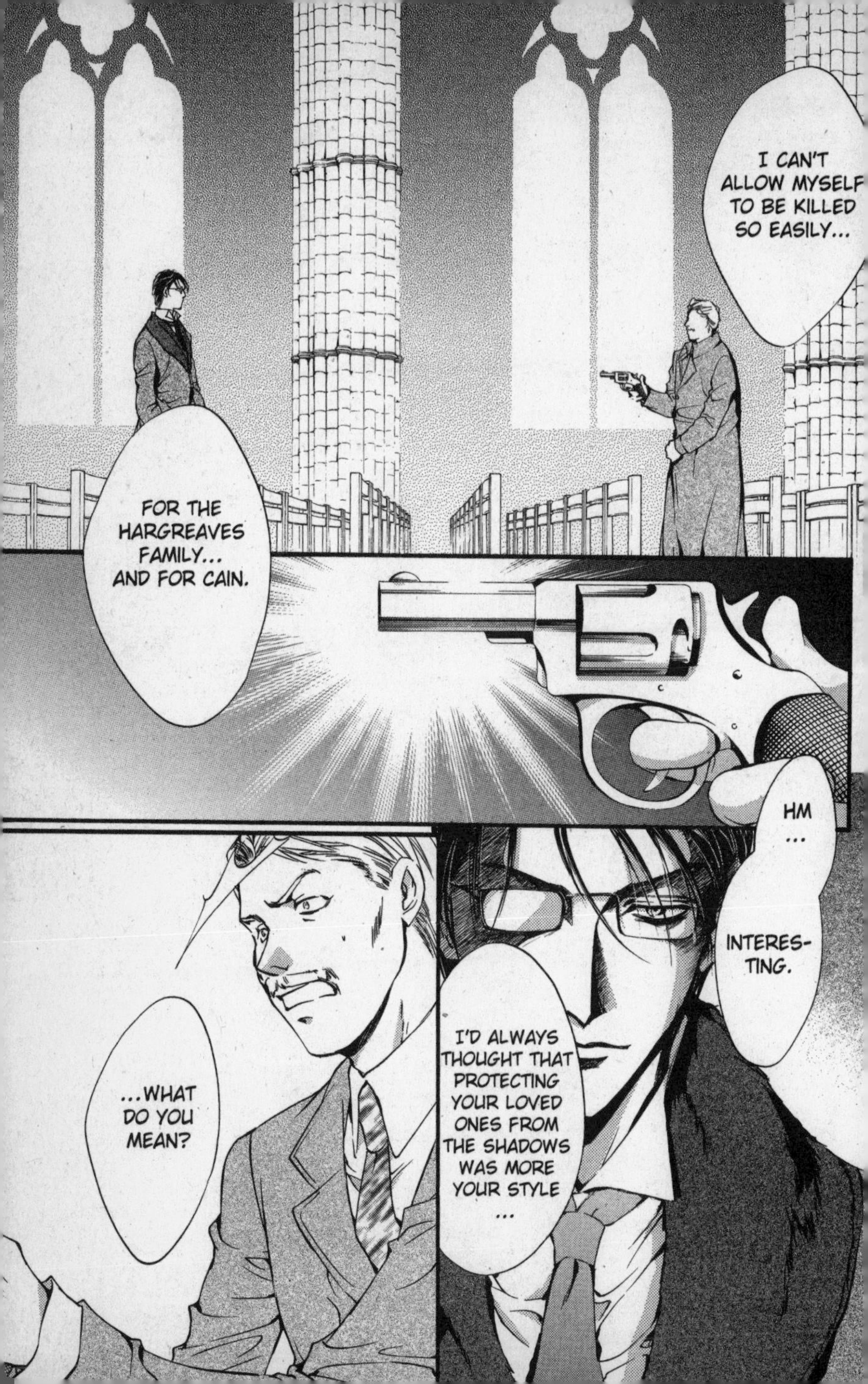
I CAN'T ALLOW MYSELF TO BE KILLED SO EASILY...
FOR THE HARGREAVES FAMILY... AND FOR CAIN.
HM ...
INTERES-TING.
I'D ALWAYS THOUGHT THAT PROTECTING YOUR LOVED ONES FROM THE SHADOWS WAS MORE YOUR STYLE ...
...WHAT DO YOU MEAN?

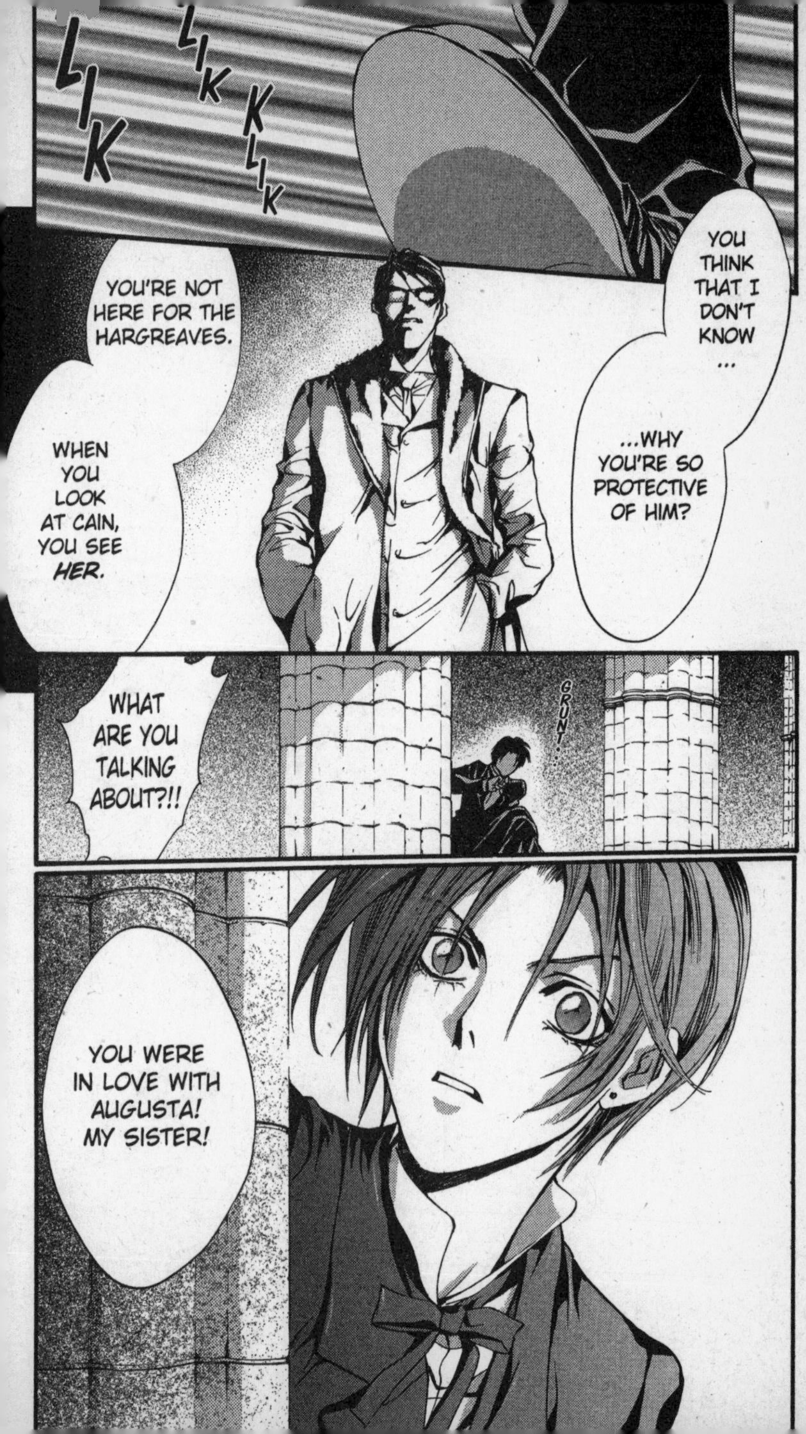

LIK KLIK
LIK
YOU THINK THAT I DON'T KNOW ...
...WHY YOU'RE SO PROTECTIVE OF HIM?
YOU'RE NOT HERE FOR THE HARGREAVES.
WHEN YOU LOOK AT CAIN, YOU SEE *HER*.
GRUNT...
WHAT ARE YOU TALKING ABOUT?!!
YOU WERE IN LOVE WITH AUGUSTA! MY SISTER!

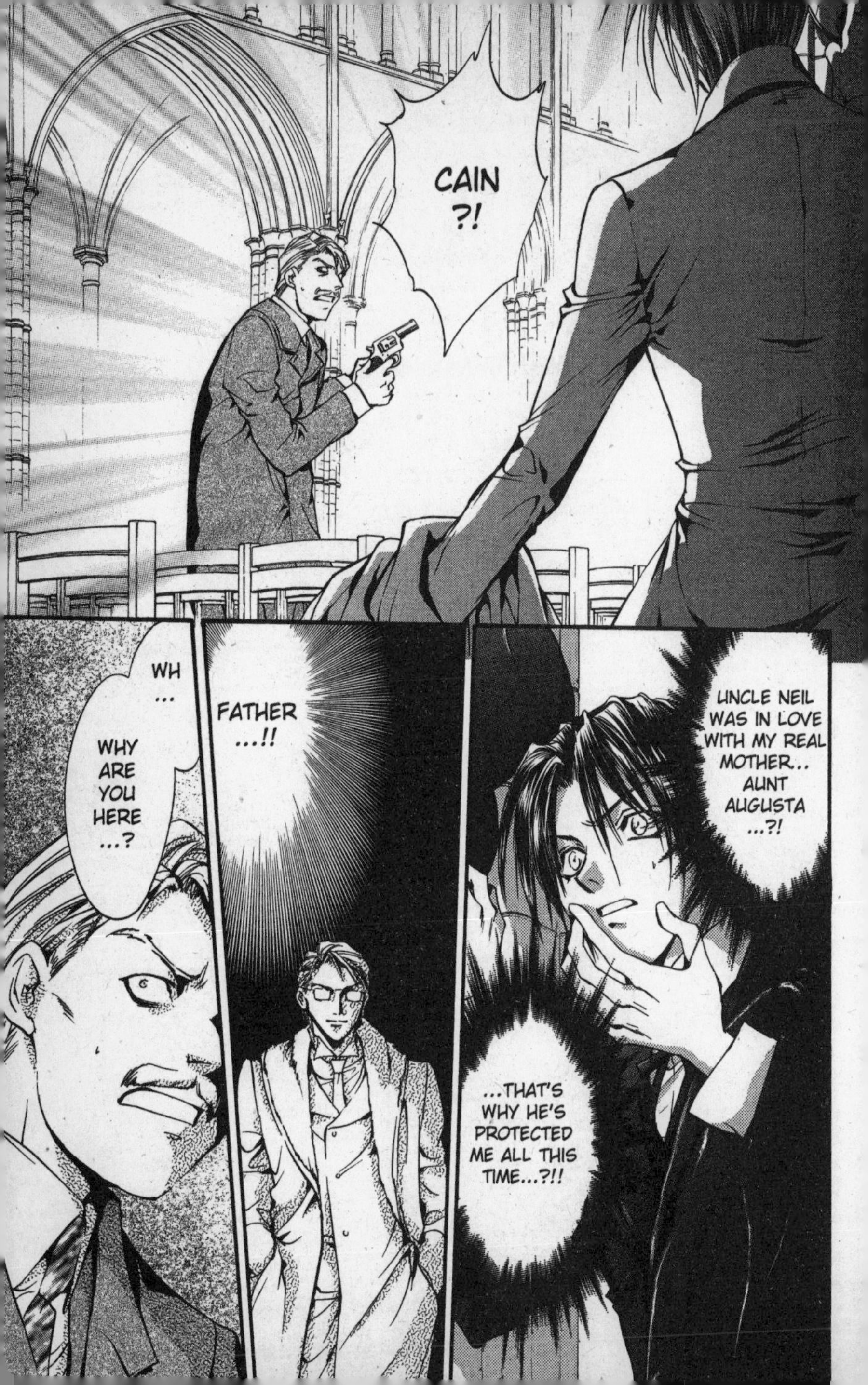
CAIN ?!
UNCLE NEIL WAS IN LOVE WITH MY REAL MOTHER... AUNT AUGUSTA ...?!
...THAT'S WHY HE'S PROTECTED ME ALL THIS TIME...?!!
FATHER ...!!
WH ...
WHY ARE YOU HERE ...?

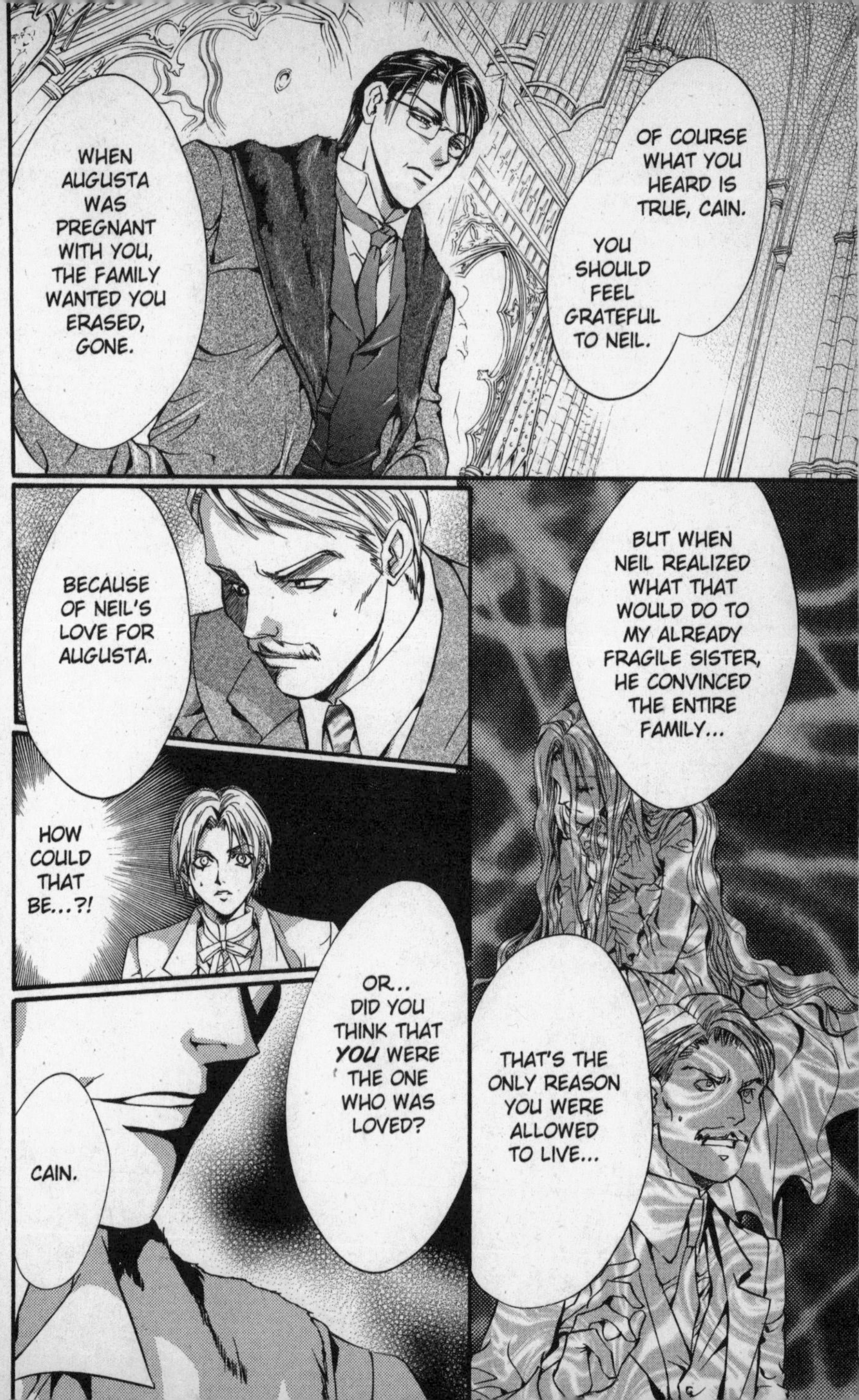
OF COURSE WHAT YOU HEARD IS TRUE, CAIN.
YOU SHOULD FEEL GRATEFUL TO NEIL.
WHEN AUGUSTA WAS PREGNANT WITH YOU, THE FAMILY WANTED YOU ERASED, GONE.
BUT WHEN NEIL REALIZED WHAT THAT WOULD DO TO MY ALREADY FRAGILE SISTER, HE CONVINCED THE ENTIRE FAMILY...
THAT'S THE ONLY REASON YOU WERE ALLOWED TO LIVE...
BECAUSE OF NEIL'S LOVE FOR AUGUSTA.
HOW COULD THAT BE...?!
OR... DID YOU THINK THAT *YOU* WERE THE ONE WHO WAS LOVED?
CAIN.

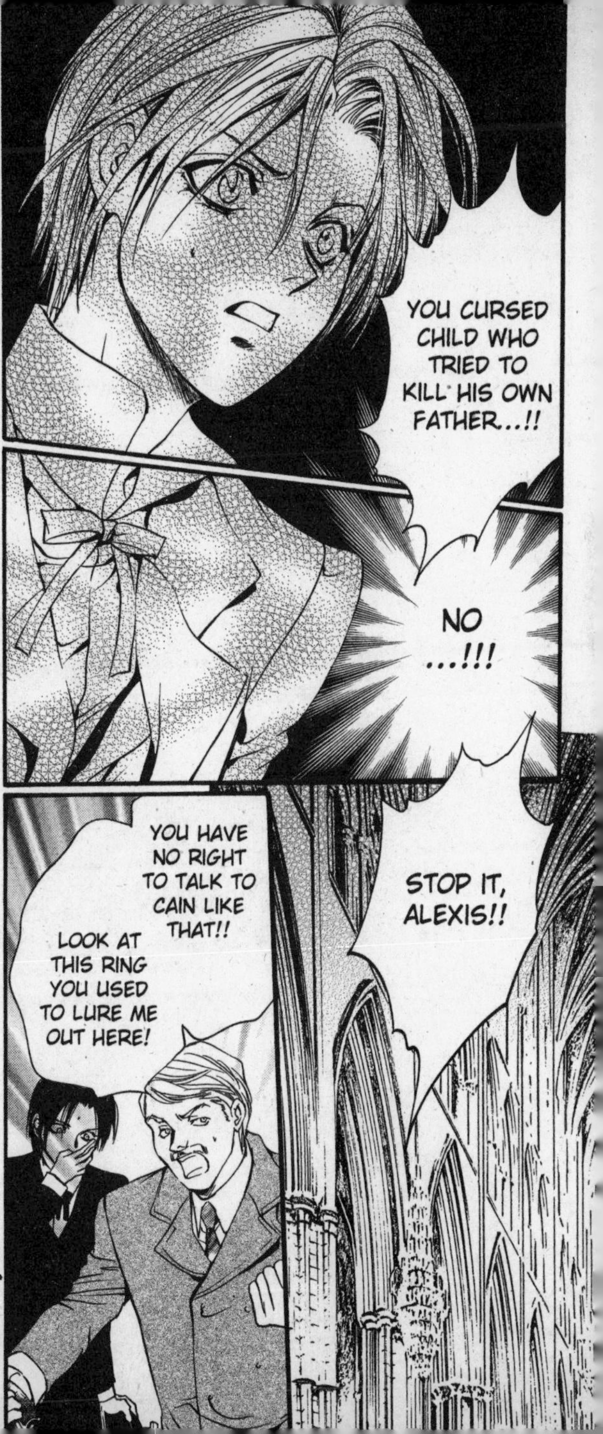
YOU CURSED CHILD WHO TRIED TO KILL HIS OWN FATHER...!!
NO ...!!!
STOP IT, ALEXIS!!
YOU HAVE NO RIGHT TO TALK TO CAIN LIKE THAT!!
LOOK AT THIS RING YOU USED TO LURE ME OUT HERE!

Westminster Cathedral is really a beautiful place. It was built as a tomb to house the remains of the royal family so there must be a lot of caskets in there with kings and other royalty. Hmm...It's pretty amazing to think that there really are those people in there. And now I'm thinking about a certain kind of attire from that time period. Which is... men's underwear. Even proper gentlemen in their dandy looking suits wore thermal underwear underneath everything...(Because England is cold.) But that just doesn't fit the mood of this comic... At the very least Cain never wears any underwear under his shirt. He even sleeps buck-naked. You're gonna catch a cold... Maybe you're actually really healthy? Cain...

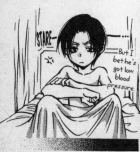

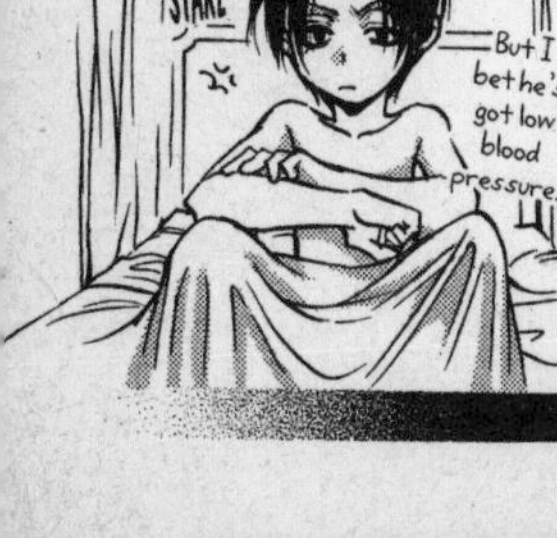
STARE—
...
But I bet he's got low blood pressure.

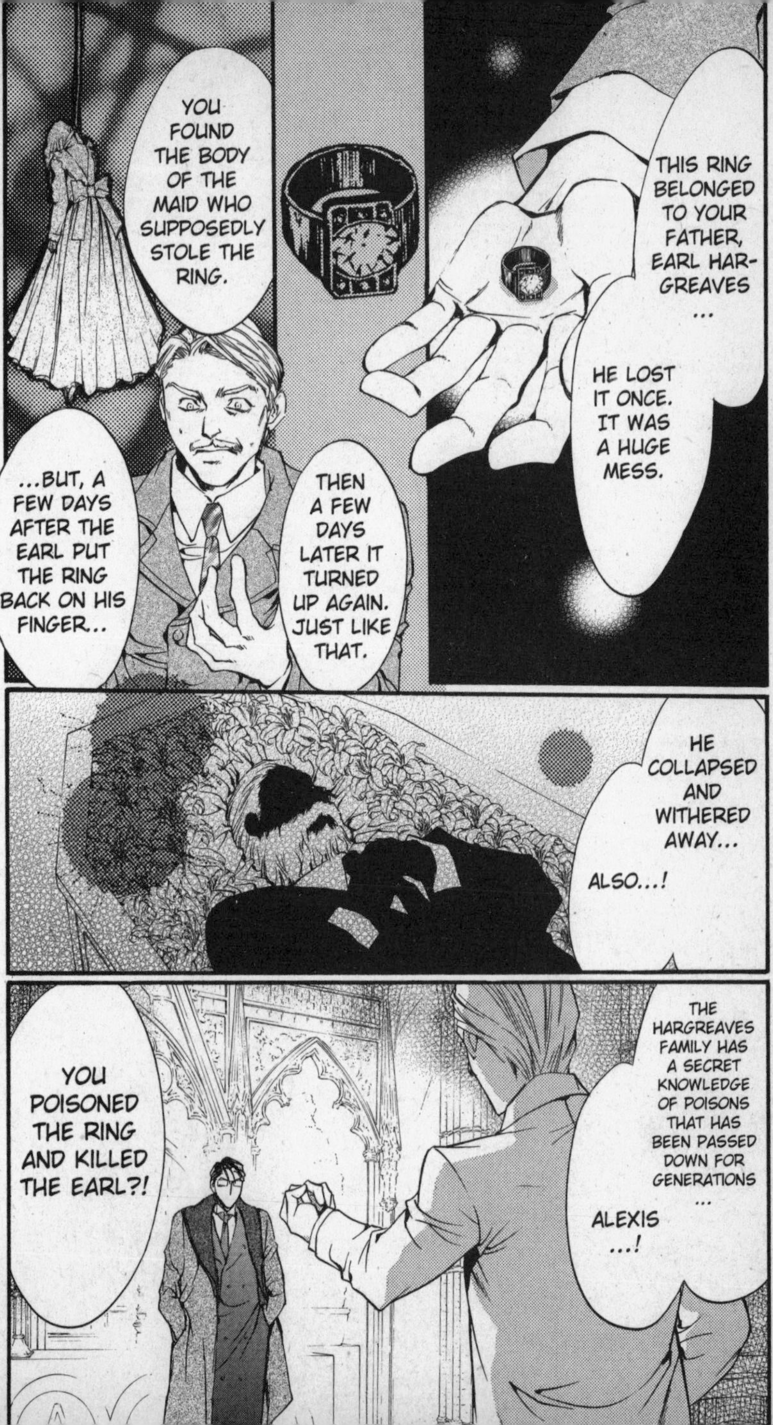
THIS RING BELONGED TO YOUR FATHER, EARL HARGREAVES...
HE LOST IT ONCE. IT WAS A HUGE MESS.
YOU FOUND THE BODY OF THE MAID WHO SUPPOSEDLY STOLE THE RING.
THEN A FEW DAYS LATER IT TURNED UP AGAIN. JUST LIKE THAT.
...BUT, A FEW DAYS AFTER THE EARL PUT THE RING BACK ON HIS FINGER...
HE COLLAPSED AND WITHERED AWAY...
ALSO...!
THE HARGREAVES FAMILY HAS A SECRET KNOWLEDGE OF POISONS THAT HAS BEEN PASSED DOWN FOR GENERATIONS...
ALEXIS...!
YOU POISONED THE RING AND KILLED THE EARL?!

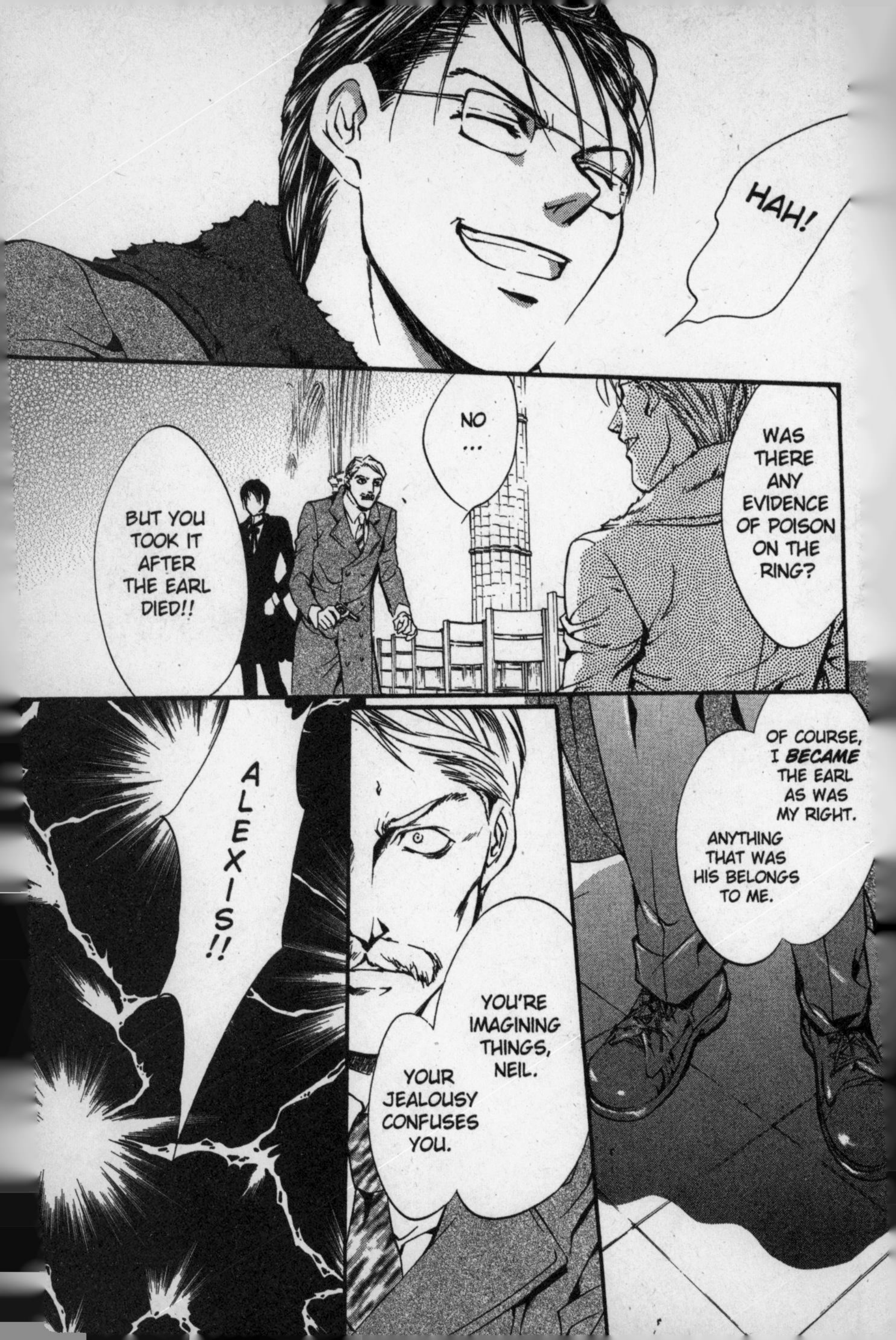
HAH!
WAS THERE ANY EVIDENCE OF POISON ON THE RING?
NO ...
BUT YOU TOOK IT AFTER THE EARL DIED!!
OF COURSE, I **BECAME** THE EARL AS WAS MY RIGHT.
ANYTHING THAT WAS HIS BELONGS TO ME.
YOU'RE IMAGINING THINGS, NEIL.
YOUR JEALOUSY CONFUSES YOU.
ALEXIS!!

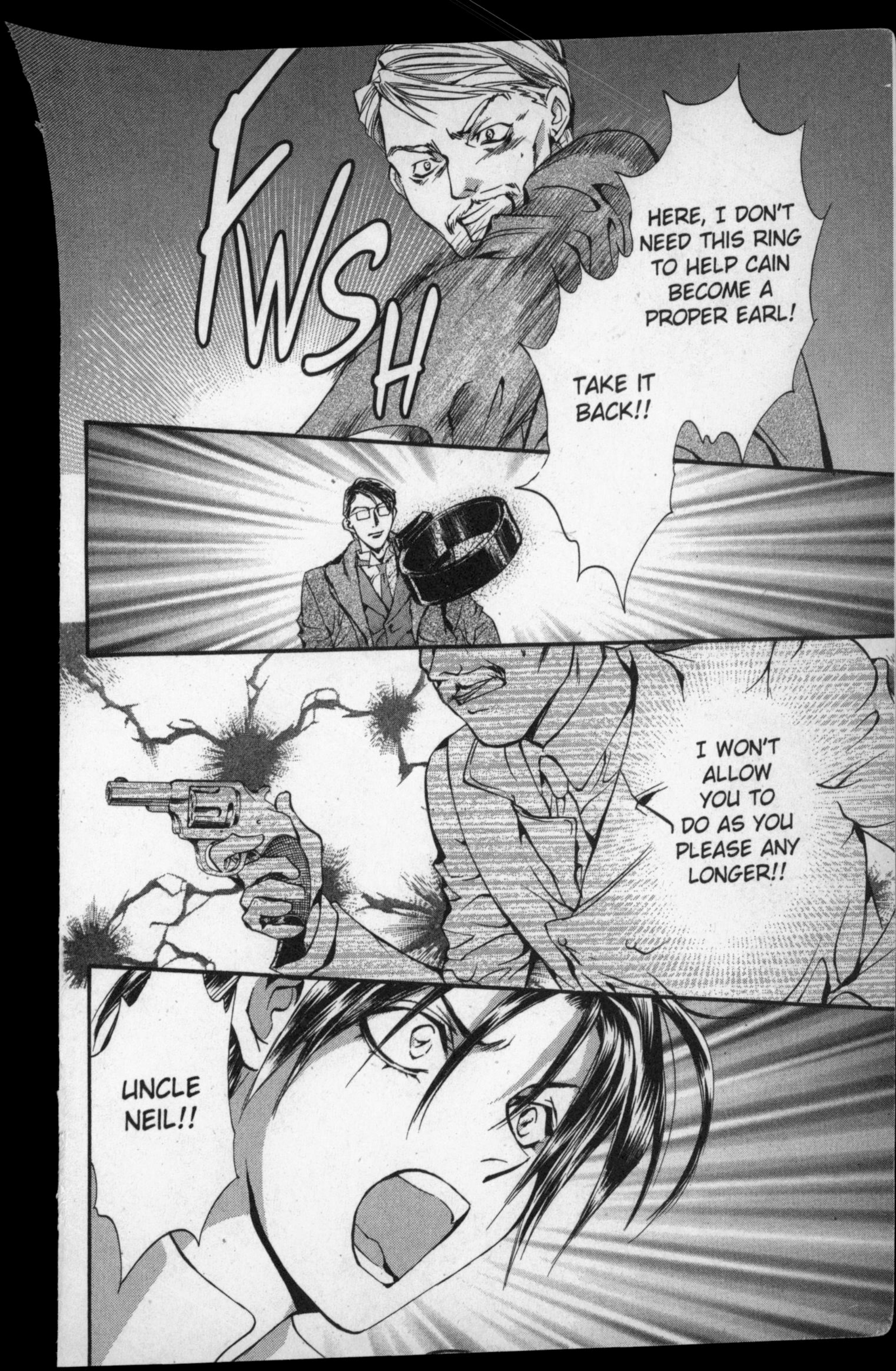
HERE, I DON'T NEED THIS RING TO HELP CAIN BECOME A PROPER EARL!
KWSH
TAKE IT BACK!!
I WON'T ALLOW YOU TO DO AS YOU PLEASE ANY LONGER!!
UNCLE NEIL!!

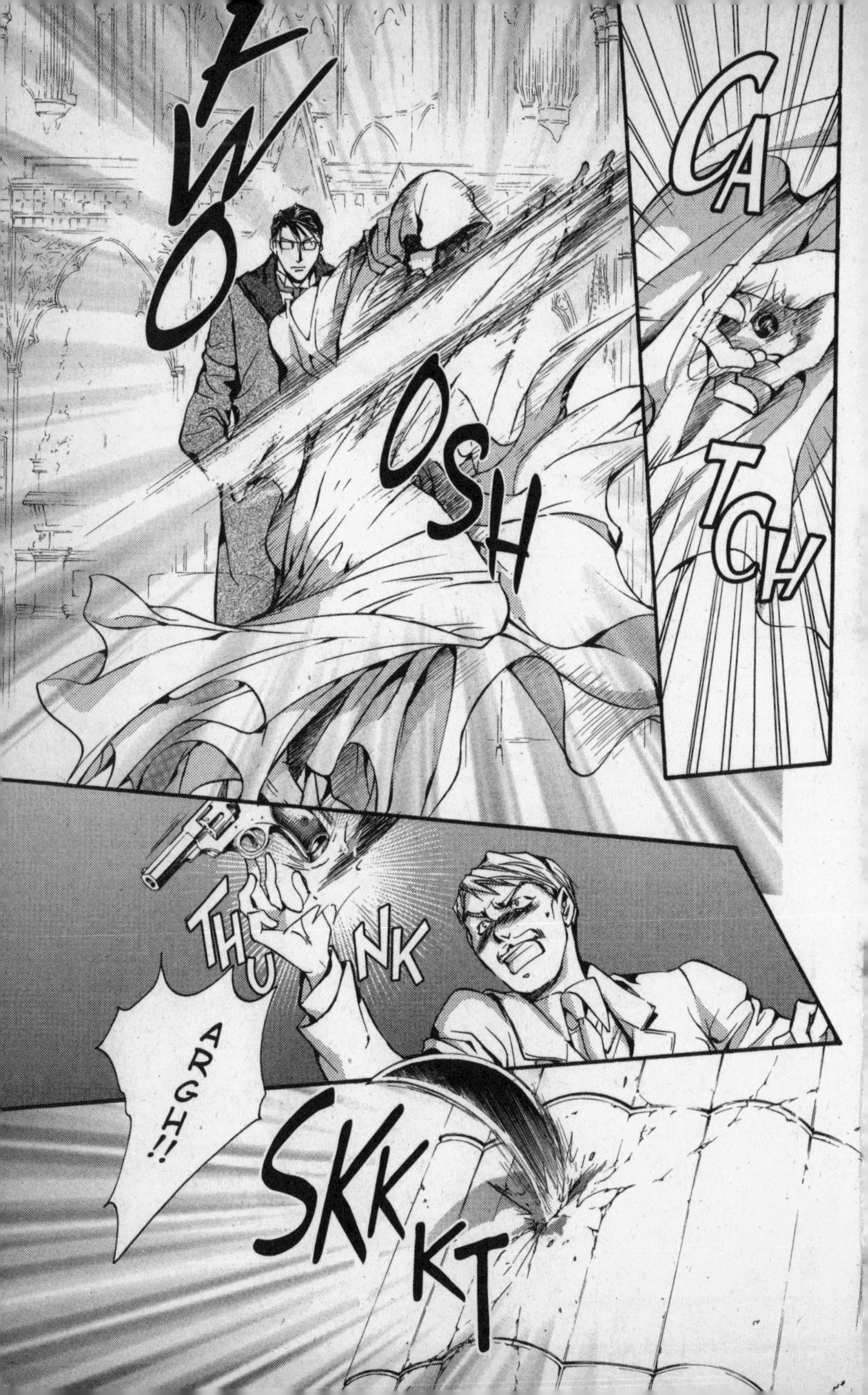
GATCH
FWOOSH
THUNK
ARGH!!
SKKKT

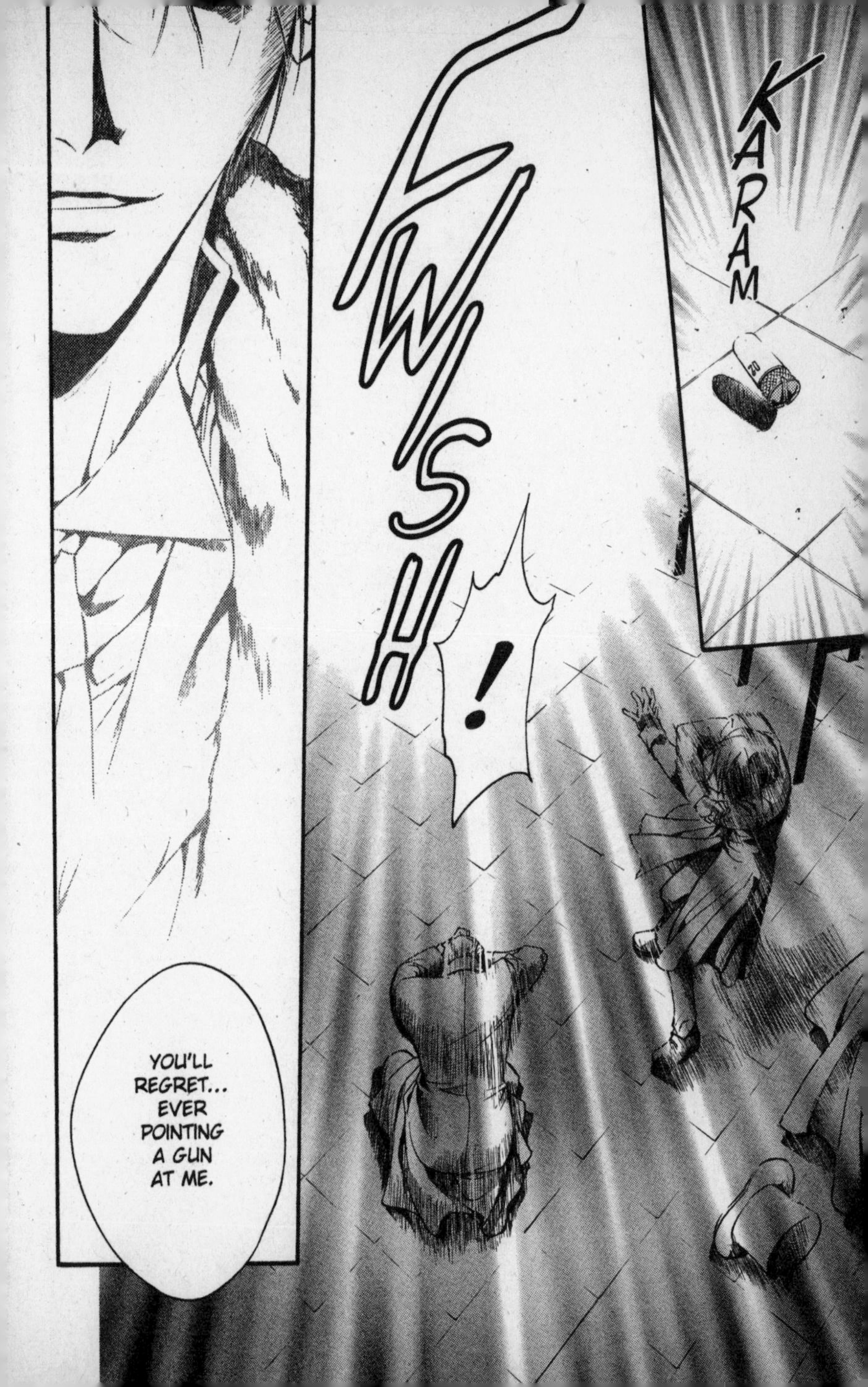
KARAM
WISH
!
YOU'LL REGRET... EVER POINTING A GUN AT ME.

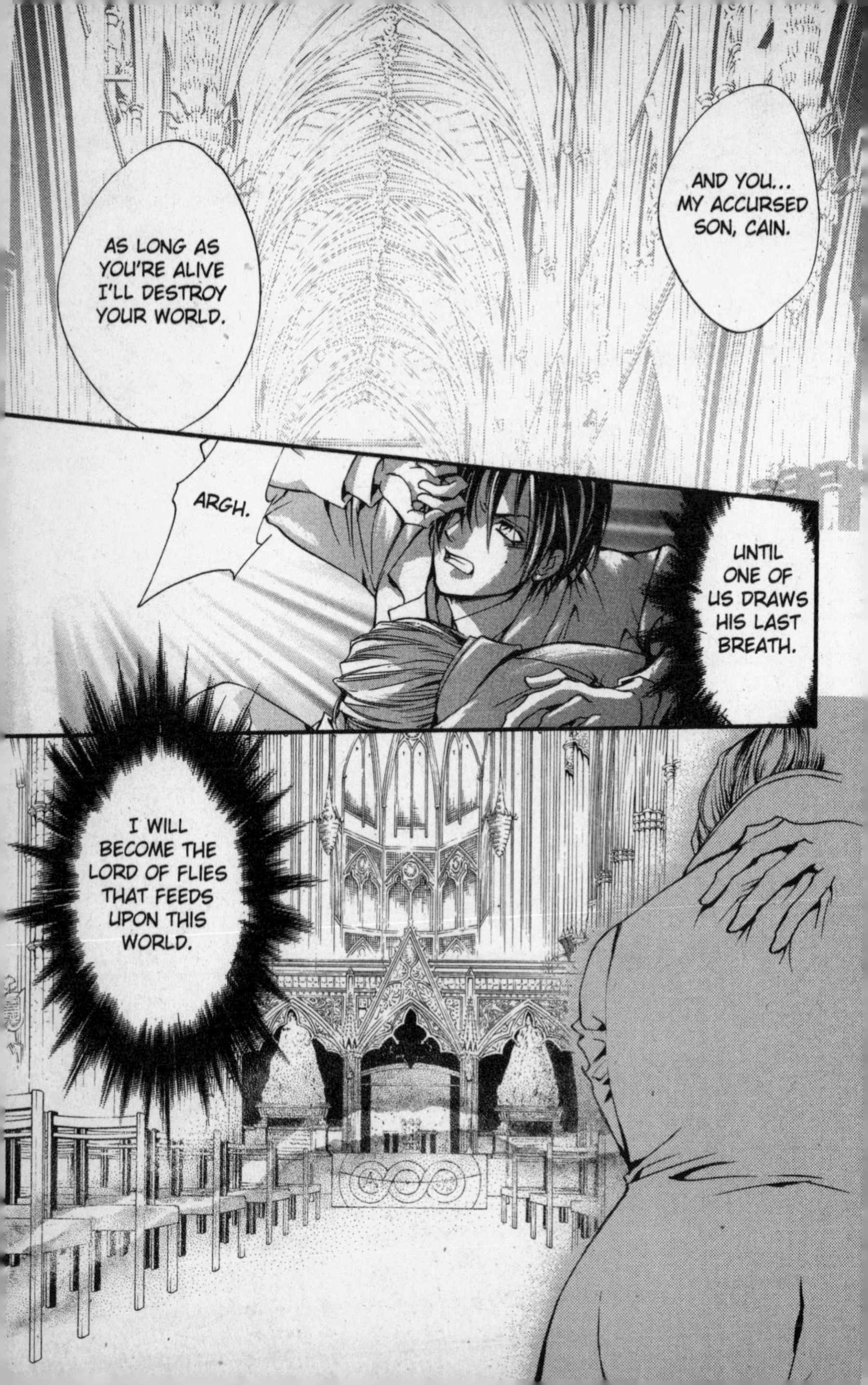
AND YOU... MY ACCURSED SON, CAIN.
AS LONG AS YOU'RE ALIVE I'LL DESTROY YOUR WORLD.
UNTIL ONE OF US DRAWS HIS LAST BREATH.
ARGH.
I WILL BECOME THE LORD OF FLIES THAT FEEDS UPON THIS WORLD.

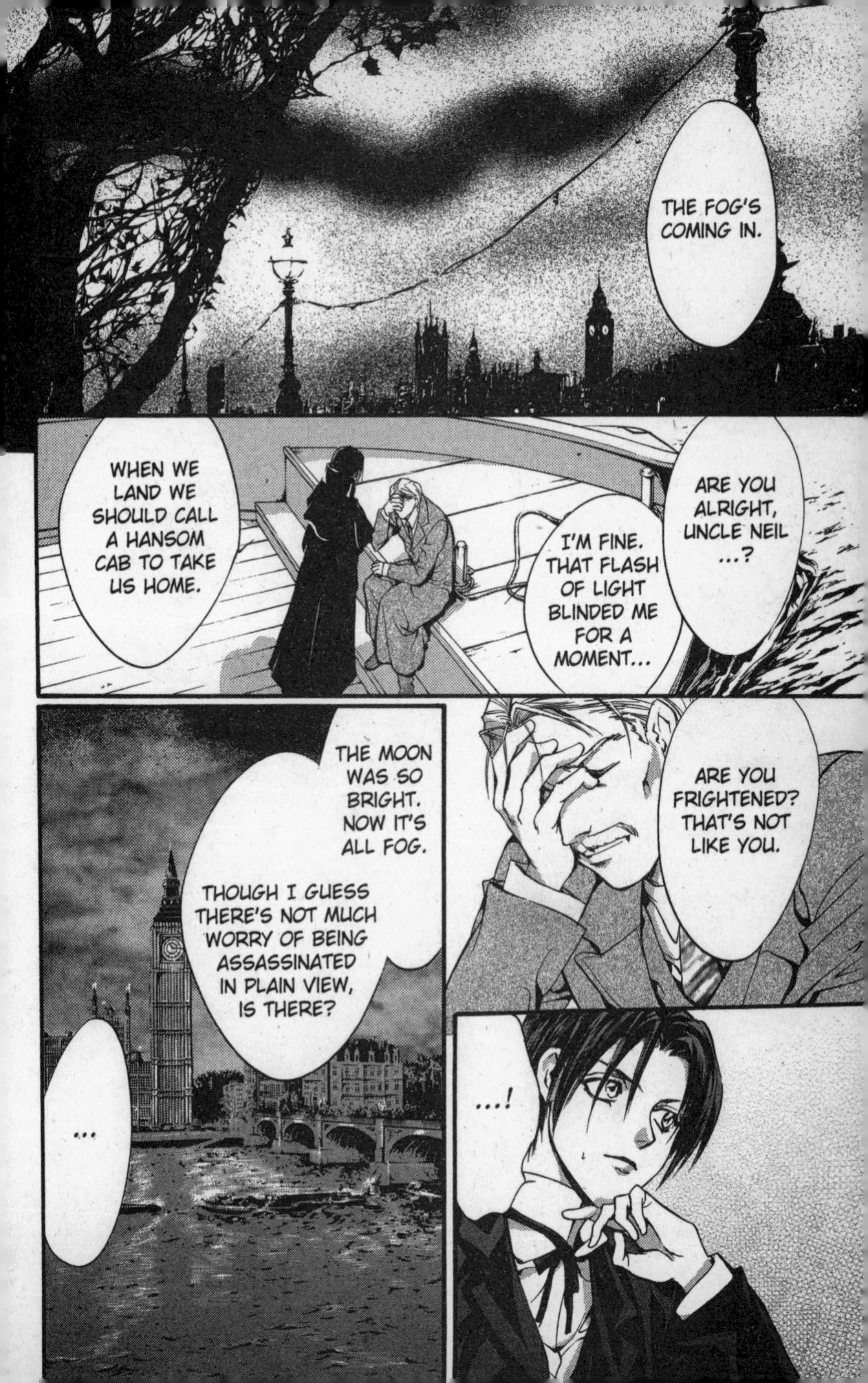
THE FOG'S COMING IN.
ARE YOU ALRIGHT, UNCLE NEIL ...?
I'M FINE. THAT FLASH OF LIGHT BLINDED ME FOR A MOMENT...
WHEN WE LAND WE SHOULD CALL A HANSOM CAB TO TAKE US HOME.
ARE YOU FRIGHTENED? THAT'S NOT LIKE YOU.
...!
THE MOON WAS SO BRIGHT. NOW IT'S ALL FOG.
THOUGH I GUESS THERE'S NOT MUCH WORRY OF BEING ASSASSINATED IN PLAIN VIEW, IS THERE?
...

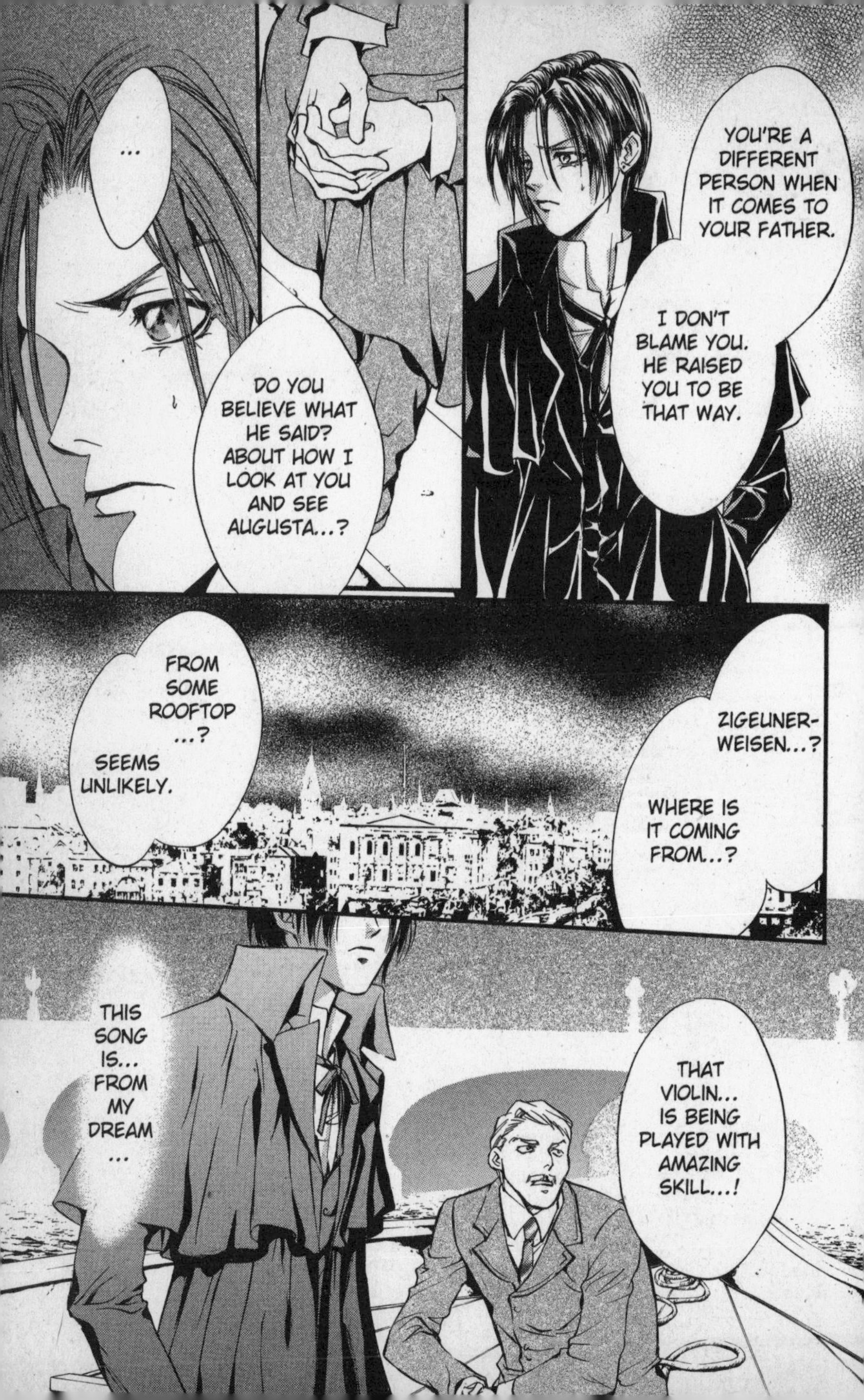
YOU'RE A DIFFERENT PERSON WHEN IT COMES TO YOUR FATHER.
I DON'T BLAME YOU. HE RAISED YOU TO BE THAT WAY.
DO YOU BELIEVE WHAT HE SAID? ABOUT HOW I LOOK AT YOU AND SEE AUGUSTA...?
...
ZIGEUNER-WEISEN...?
WHERE IS IT COMING FROM...?
FROM SOME ROOFTOP ...?
SEEMS UNLIKELY.
THAT VIOLIN... IS BEING PLAYED WITH AMAZING SKILL...!
THIS SONG IS... FROM MY DREAM ...

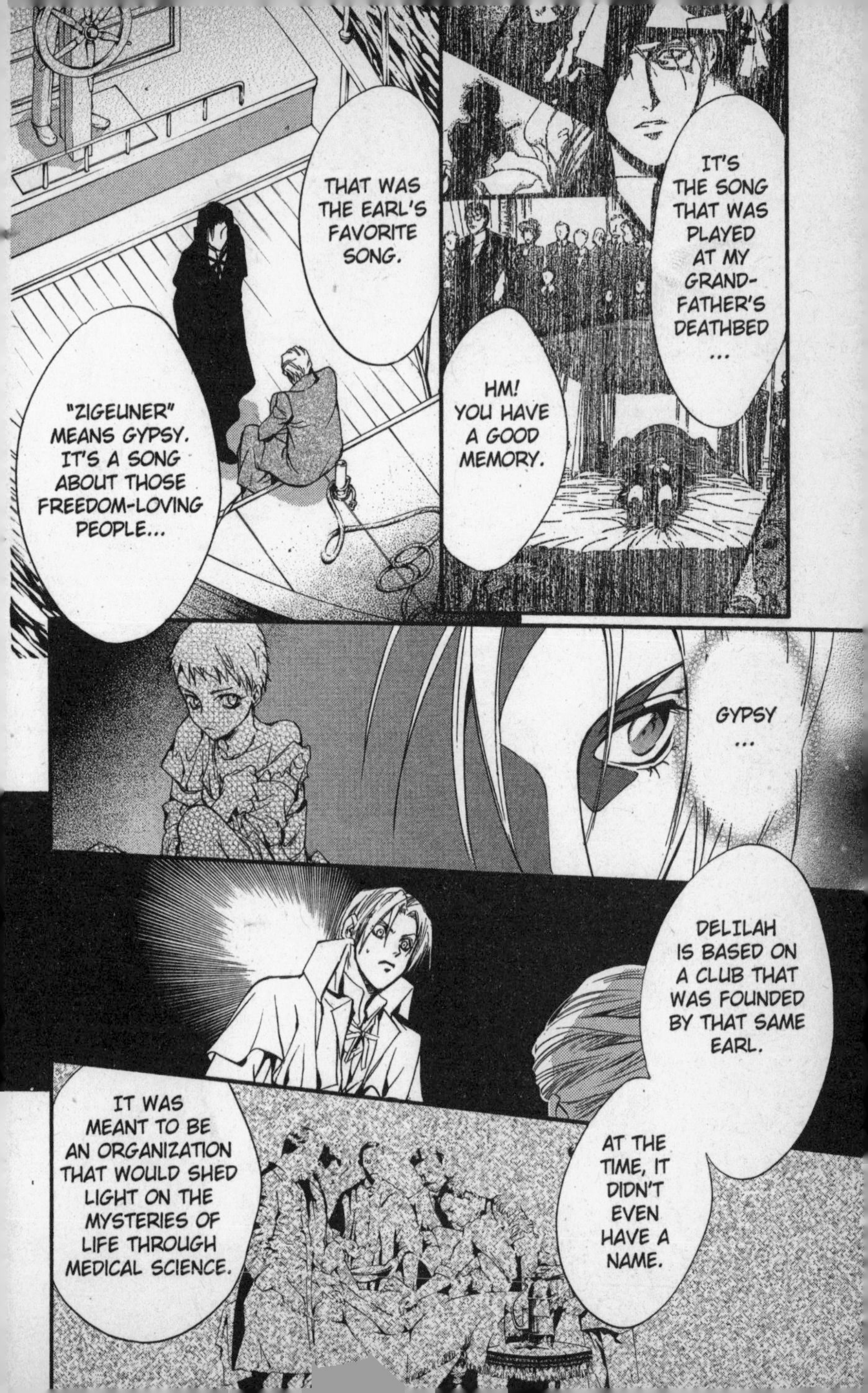
IT'S THE SONG THAT WAS PLAYED AT MY GRAND-FATHER'S DEATHBED ...
HM! YOU HAVE A GOOD MEMORY.
THAT WAS THE EARL'S FAVORITE SONG.
"ZIGEUNER" MEANS GYPSY. IT'S A SONG ABOUT THOSE FREEDOM-LOVING PEOPLE...
GYPSY ...
DELILAH IS BASED ON A CLUB THAT WAS FOUNDED BY THAT SAME EARL.
AT THE TIME, IT DIDN'T EVEN HAVE A NAME.
IT WAS MEANT TO BE AN ORGANIZATION THAT WOULD SHED LIGHT ON THE MYSTERIES OF LIFE THROUGH MEDICAL SCIENCE.

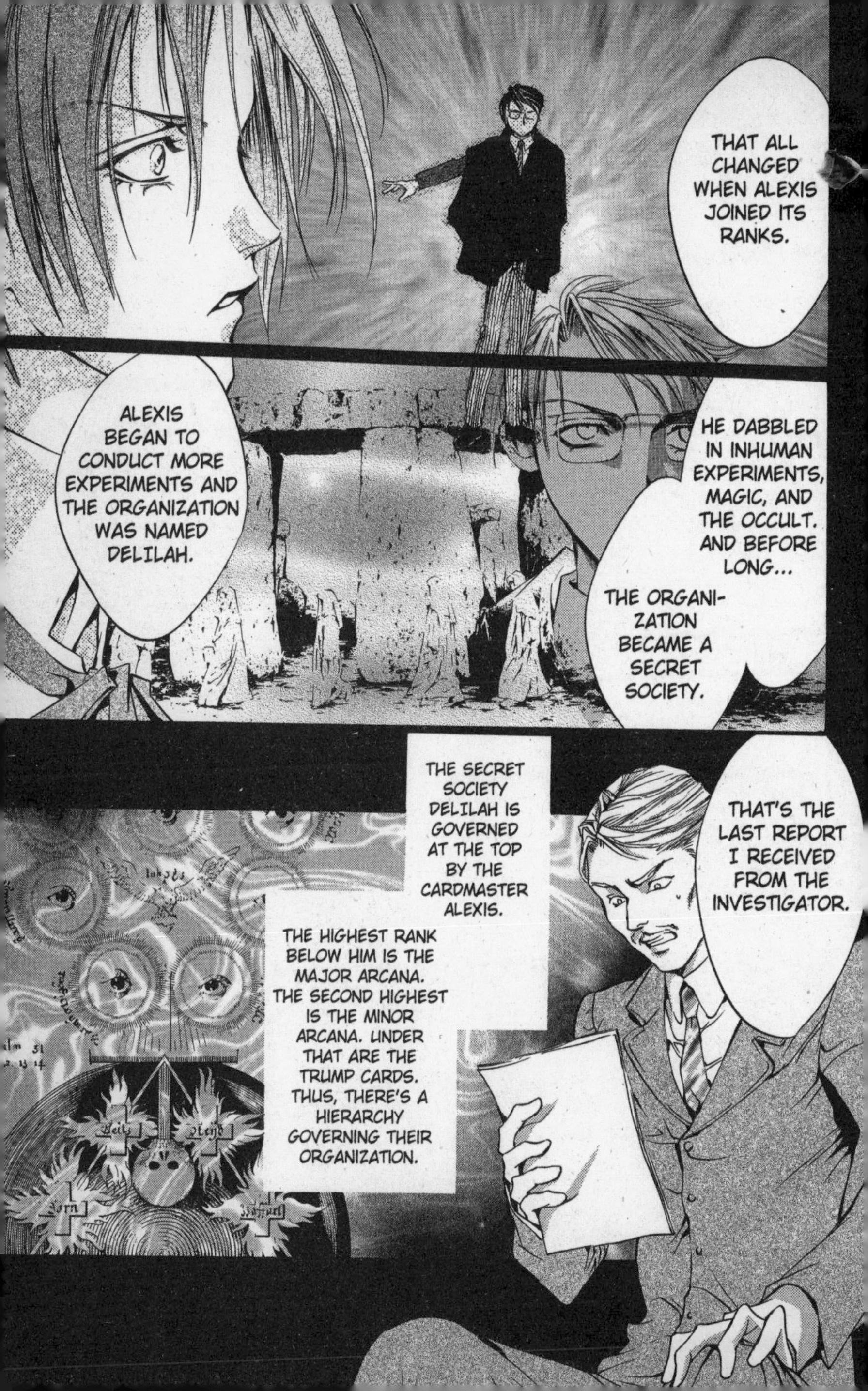
THAT ALL CHANGED WHEN ALEXIS JOINED ITS RANKS.
HE DABBLED IN INHUMAN EXPERIMENTS, MAGIC, AND THE OCCULT. AND BEFORE LONG...
THE ORGANI-ZATION BECAME A SECRET SOCIETY.
ALEXIS BEGAN TO CONDUCT MORE EXPERIMENTS AND THE ORGANIZATION WAS NAMED DELILAH.
THAT'S THE LAST REPORT I RECEIVED FROM THE INVESTIGATOR.
THE SECRET SOCIETY DELILAH IS GOVERNED AT THE TOP BY THE CARDMASTER ALEXIS.
THE HIGHEST RANK BELOW HIM IS THE MAJOR ARCANA. THE SECOND HIGHEST IS THE MINOR ARCANA. UNDER THAT ARE THE TRUMP CARDS. THUS, THERE'S A HIERARCHY GOVERNING THEIR ORGANIZATION.

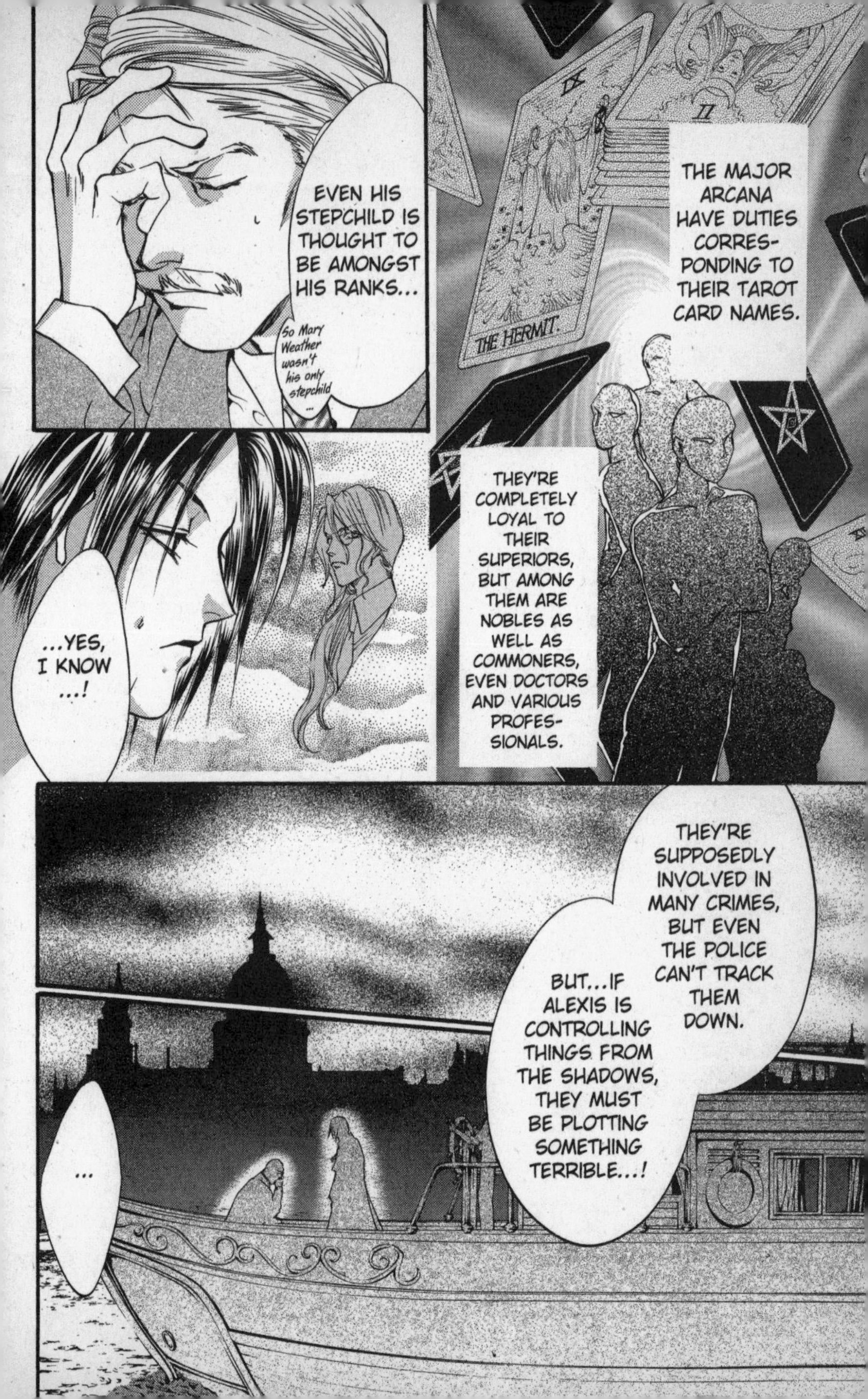
THE MAJOR ARCANA HAVE DUTIES CORRES-PONDING TO THEIR TAROT CARD NAMES.
THE HERMIT.
EVEN HIS STEPCHILD IS THOUGHT TO BE AMONGST HIS RANKS...
So Mary Weather wasn't his only stepchild...
THEY'RE COMPLETELY LOYAL TO THEIR SUPERIORS, BUT AMONG THEM ARE NOBLES AS WELL AS COMMONERS, EVEN DOCTORS AND VARIOUS PROFES-SIONALS.
...YES, I KNOW...!
THEY'RE SUPPOSEDLY INVOLVED IN MANY CRIMES, BUT EVEN THE POLICE CAN'T TRACK THEM DOWN.
BUT...IF ALEXIS IS CONTROLLING THINGS FROM THE SHADOWS, THEY MUST BE PLOTTING SOMETHING TERRIBLE...!
...

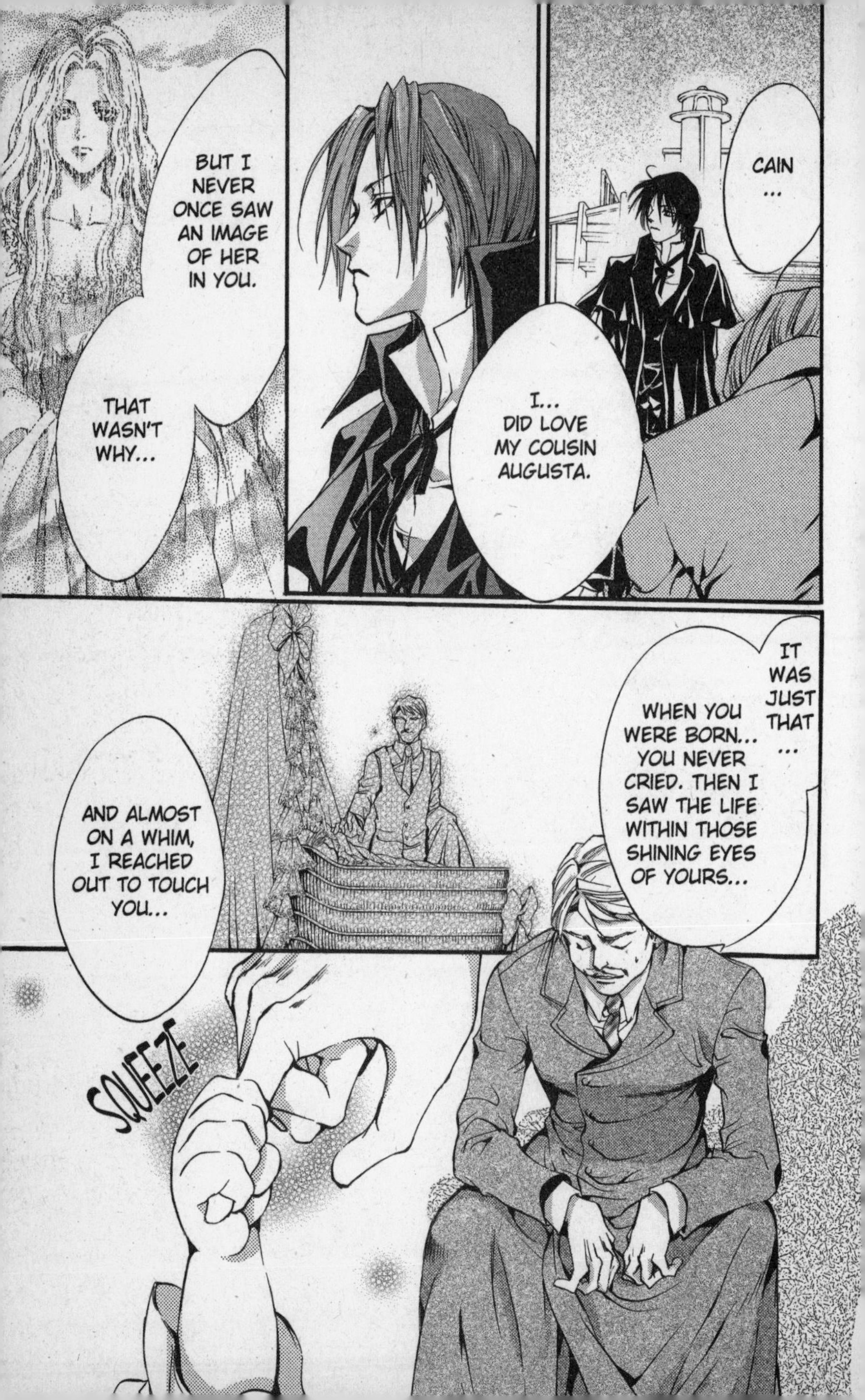
CAIN ...
I... DID LOVE MY COUSIN AUGUSTA.
BUT I NEVER ONCE SAW AN IMAGE OF HER IN YOU.
THAT WASN'T WHY...
IT WAS JUST THAT ...
WHEN YOU WERE BORN... YOU NEVER CRIED. THEN I SAW THE LIFE WITHIN THOSE SHINING EYES OF YOURS...
AND ALMOST ON A WHIM, I REACHED OUT TO TOUCH YOU...
SQUEEZE

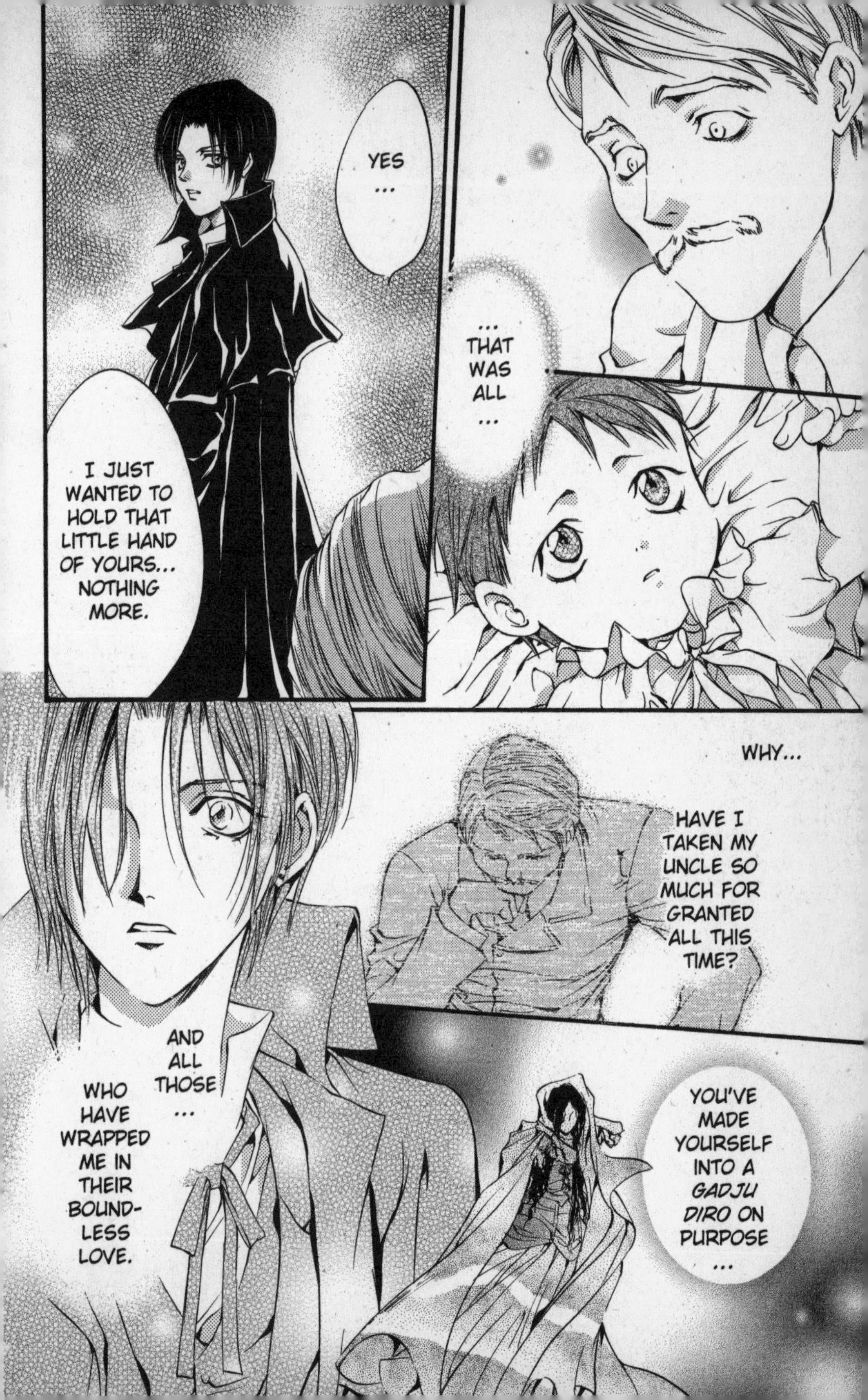
...THAT WAS ALL...
YES...
I JUST WANTED TO HOLD THAT LITTLE HAND OF YOURS... NOTHING MORE.
WHY...
HAVE I TAKEN MY UNCLE SO MUCH FOR GRANTED ALL THIS TIME?
YOU'VE MADE YOURSELF INTO A *GADJU DIRO* ON PURPOSE...
AND ALL THOSE...
WHO HAVE WRAPPED ME IN THEIR BOUNDLESS LOVE.

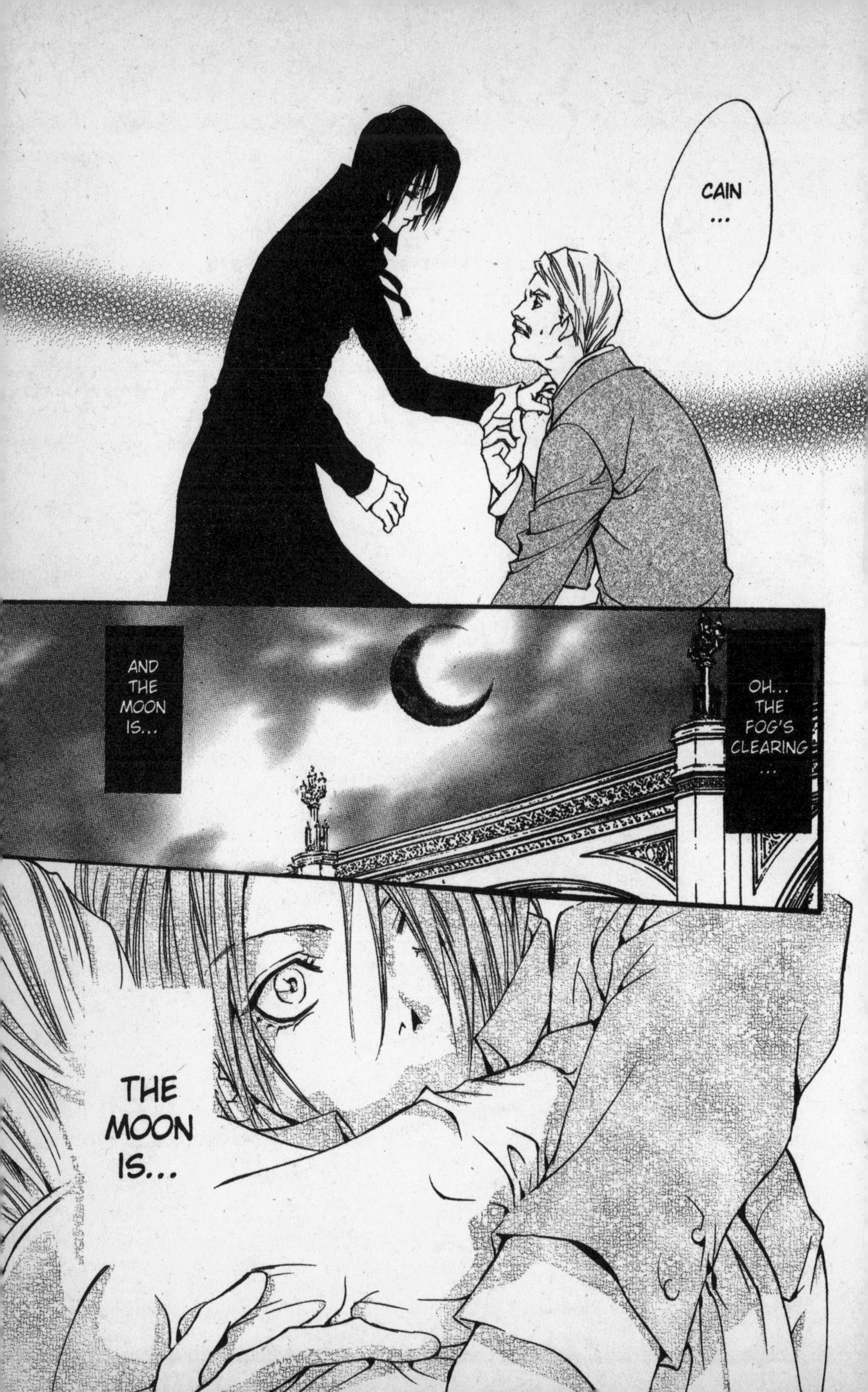
CAIN ...
OH... THE FOG'S CLEARING ...
AND THE MOON IS...
THE MOON IS...

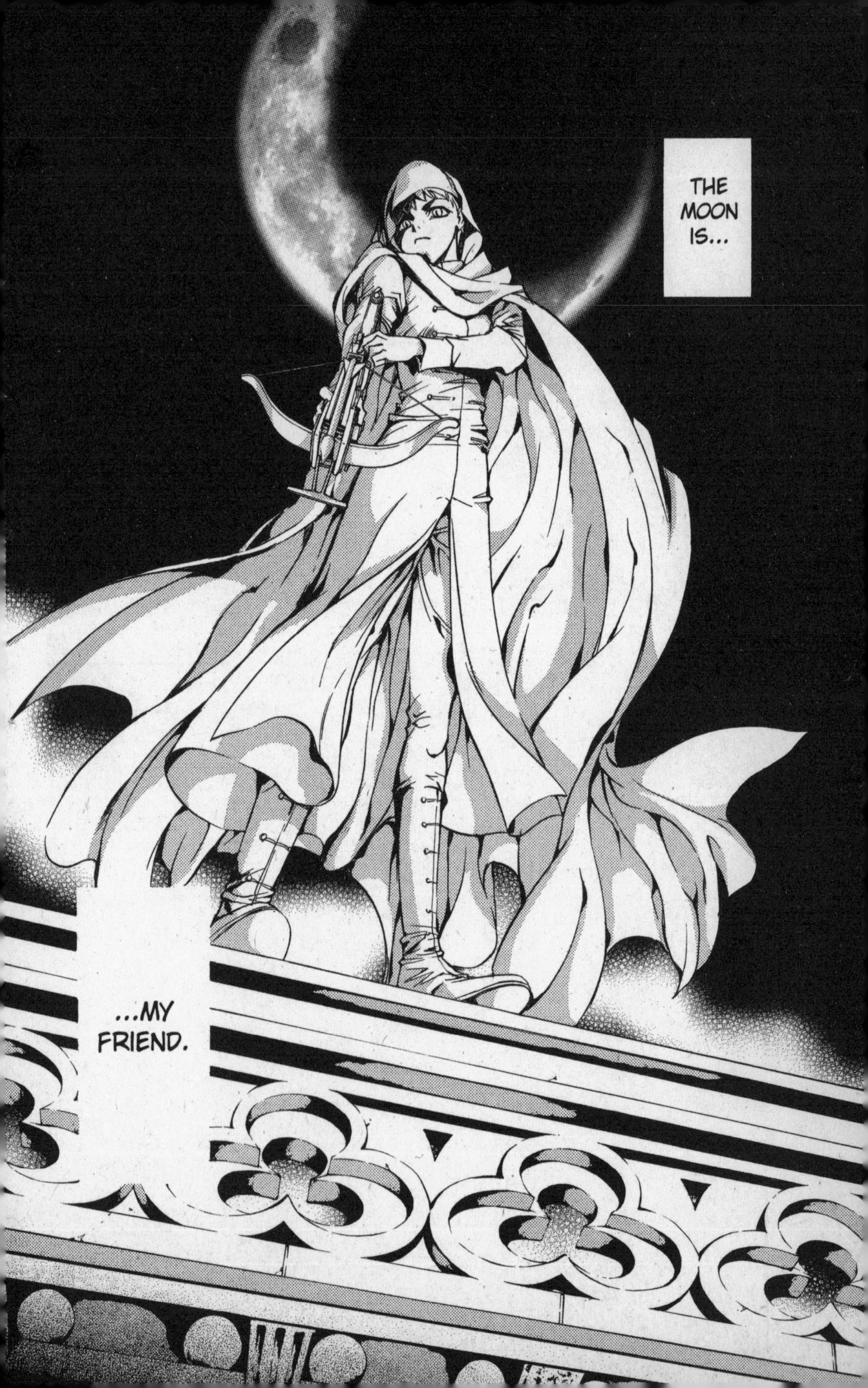
THE MOON IS...
...MY FRIEND.

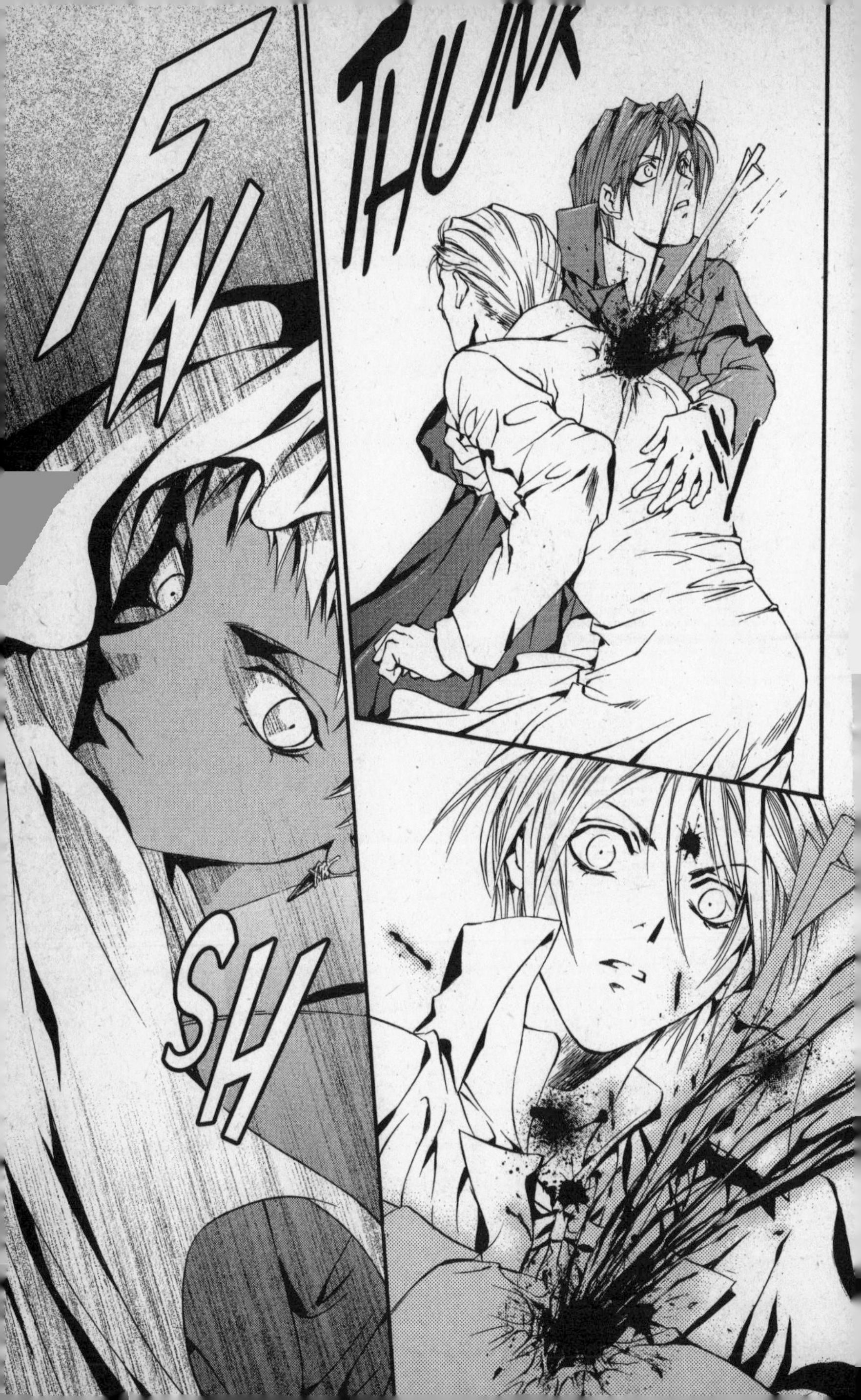
THUNK
FWSH

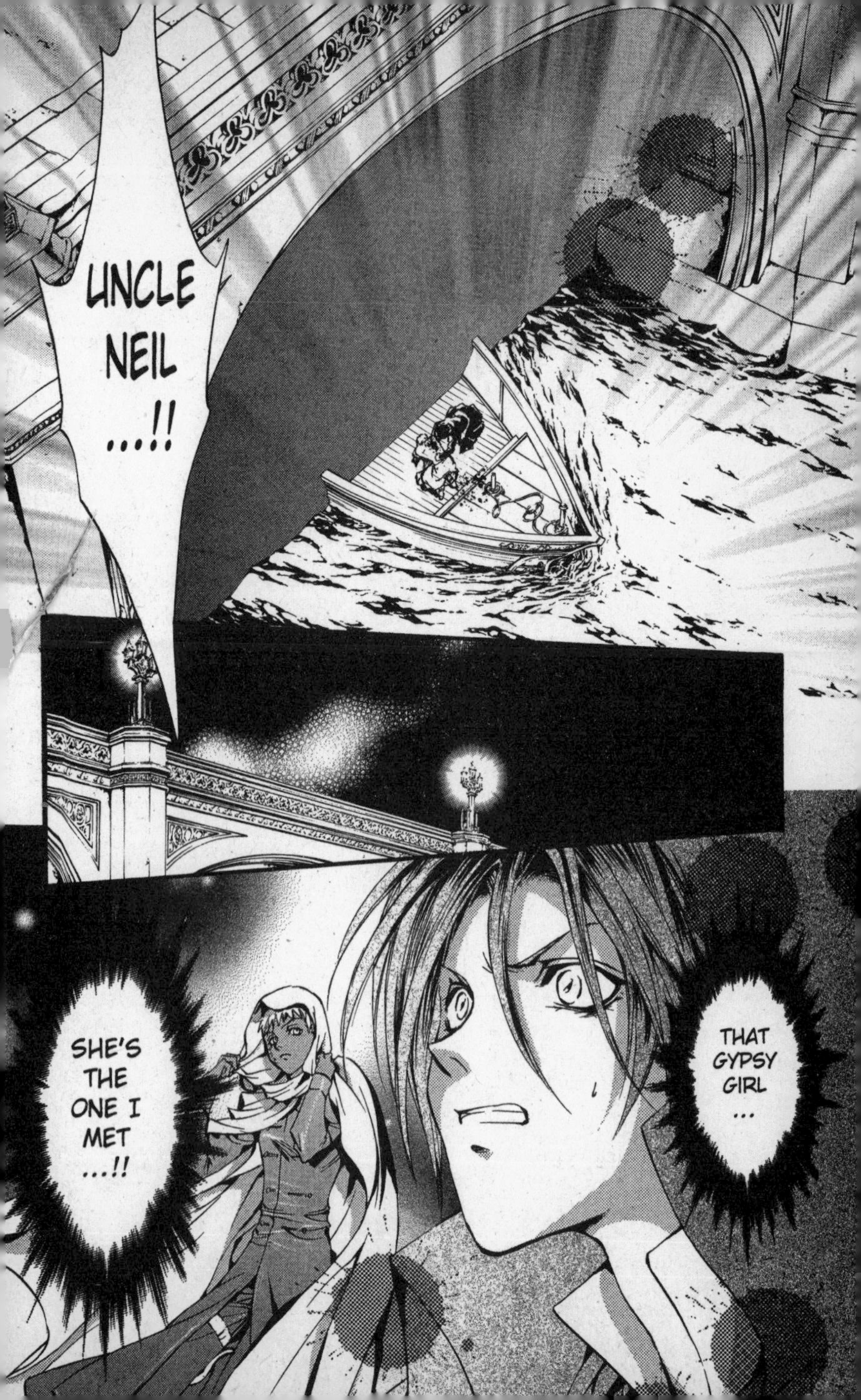
UNCLE NEIL ...!!
THAT GYPSY GIRL ...
SHE'S THE ONE I MET ...!!

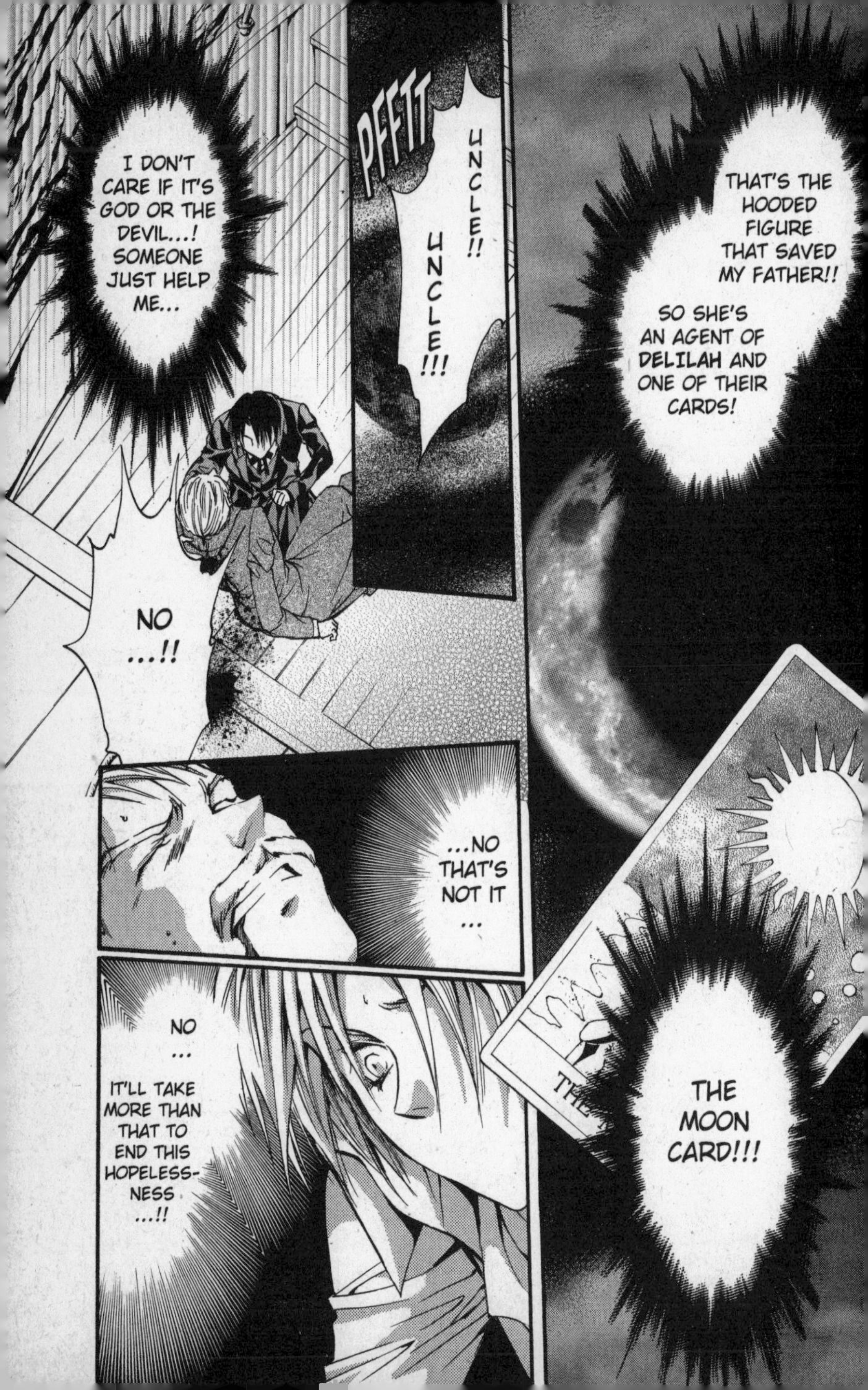

THAT'S THE HOODED FIGURE THAT SAVED MY FATHER!!
SO SHE'S AN AGENT OF DELILAH AND ONE OF THEIR CARDS!
THE
THE MOON CARD!!!
PFFTT
UNCLE!!
UNCLE!!!
I DON'T CARE IF IT'S GOD OR THE DEVIL...! SOMEONE JUST HELP ME...
NO ...!!
...NO THAT'S NOT IT ...
NO ...
IT'LL TAKE MORE THAN THAT TO END THIS HOPELESS-NESS ...!!

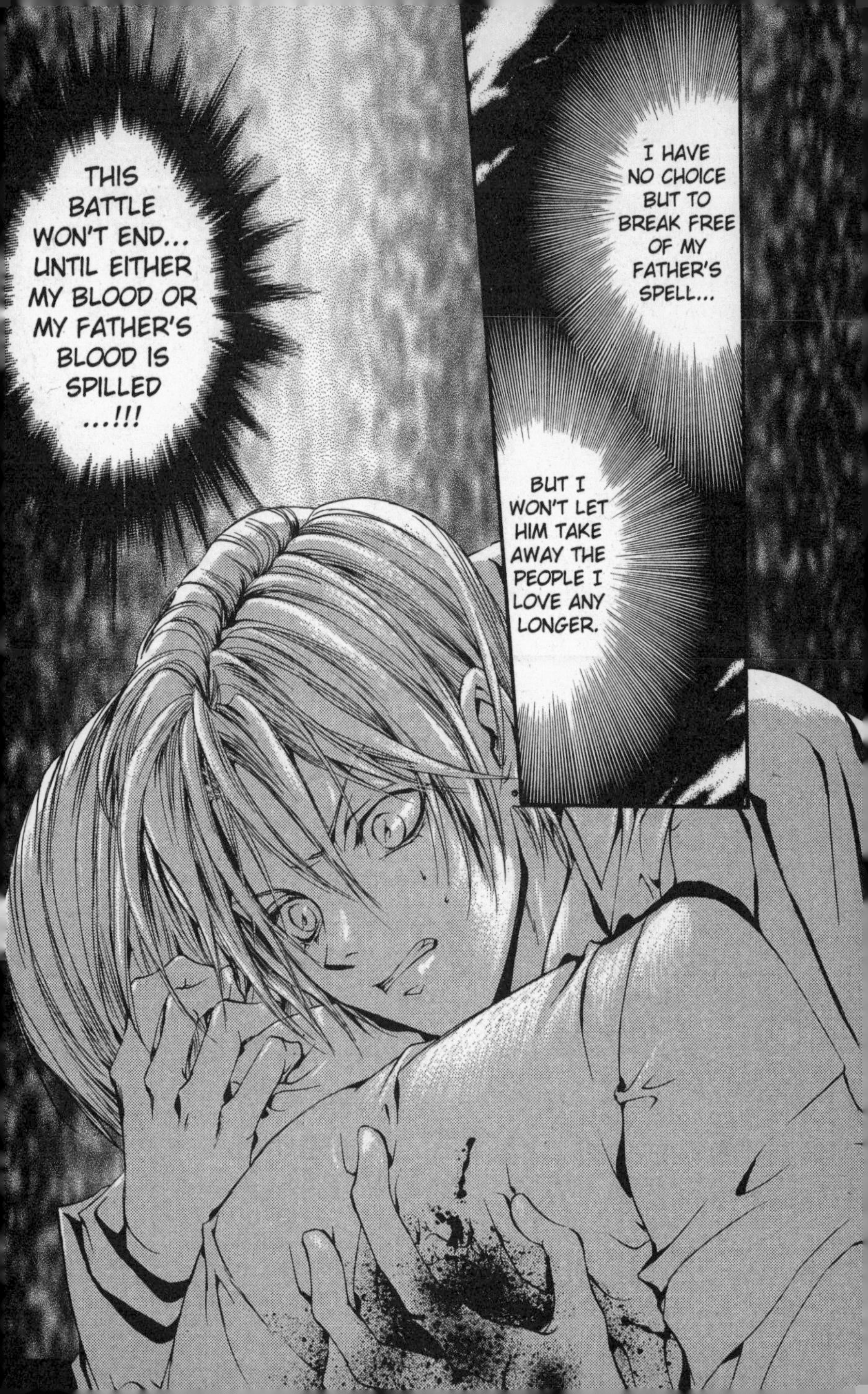
I HAVE NO CHOICE BUT TO BREAK FREE OF MY FATHER'S SPELL...
BUT I WON'T LET HIM TAKE AWAY THE PEOPLE I LOVE ANY LONGER.
THIS BATTLE WON'T END... UNTIL EITHER MY BLOOD OR MY FATHER'S BLOOD IS SPILLED ...!!!

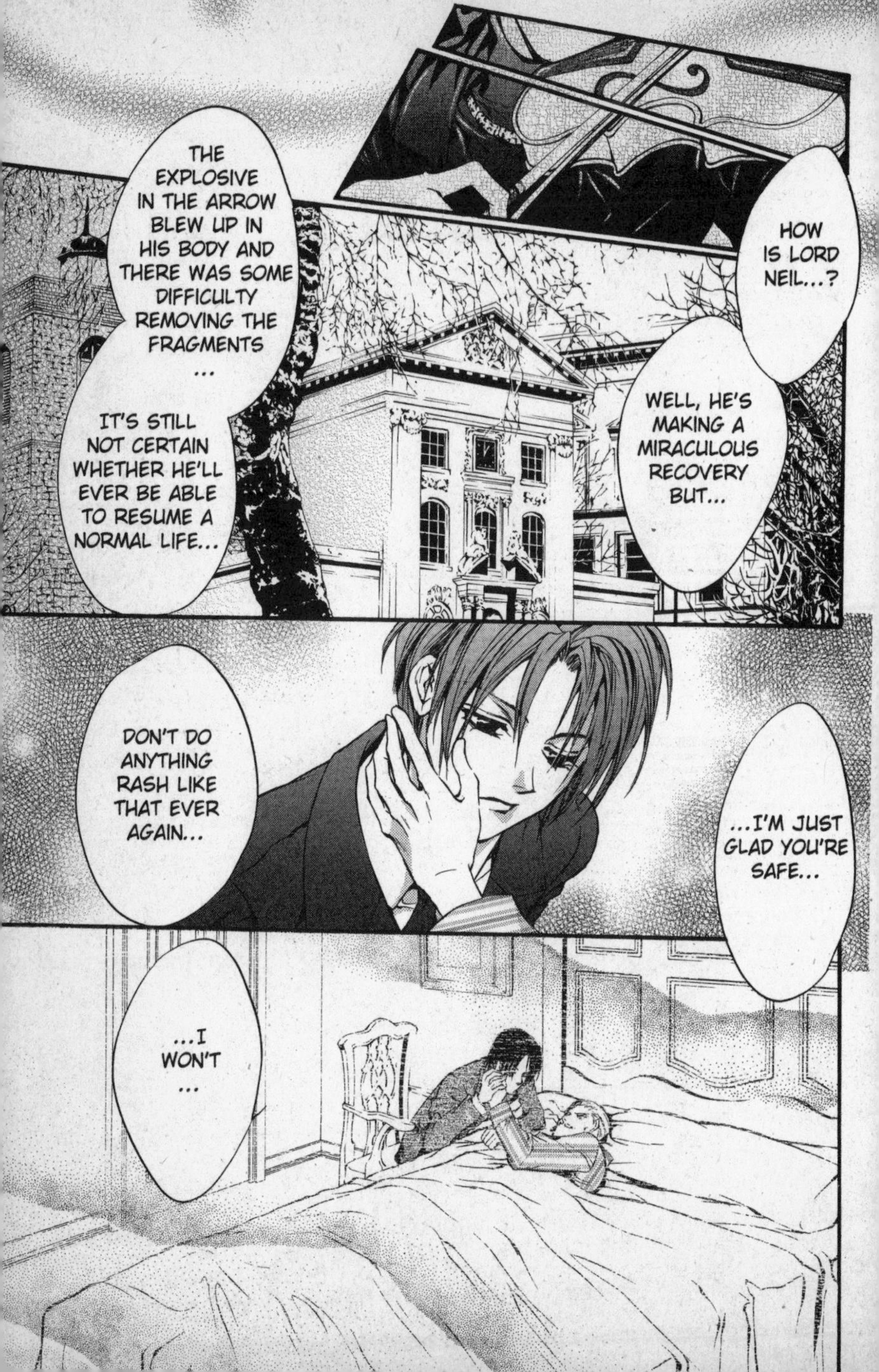
HOW IS LORD NEIL...?
WELL, HE'S MAKING A MIRACULOUS RECOVERY BUT...
THE EXPLOSIVE IN THE ARROW BLEW UP IN HIS BODY AND THERE WAS SOME DIFFICULTY REMOVING THE FRAGMENTS ...
IT'S STILL NOT CERTAIN WHETHER HE'LL EVER BE ABLE TO RESUME A NORMAL LIFE...
...I'M JUST GLAD YOU'RE SAFE...
DON'T DO ANYTHING RASH LIKE THAT EVER AGAIN...
...I WON'T ...

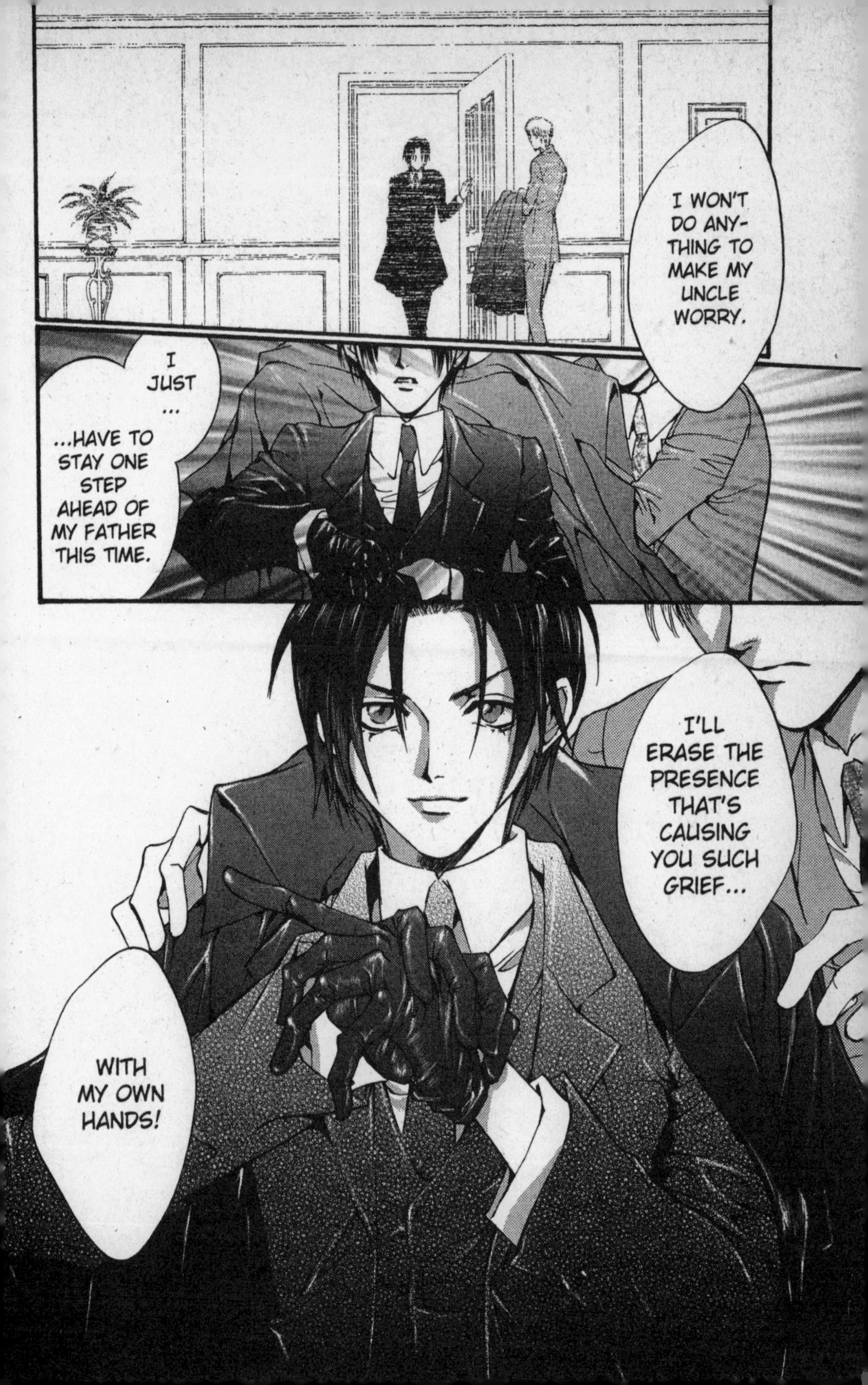
I WON'T DO ANY-THING TO MAKE MY UNCLE WORRY.
I JUST ...
...HAVE TO STAY ONE STEP AHEAD OF MY FATHER THIS TIME.
I'LL ERASE THE PRESENCE THAT'S CAUSING YOU SUCH GRIEF...
WITH MY OWN HANDS!

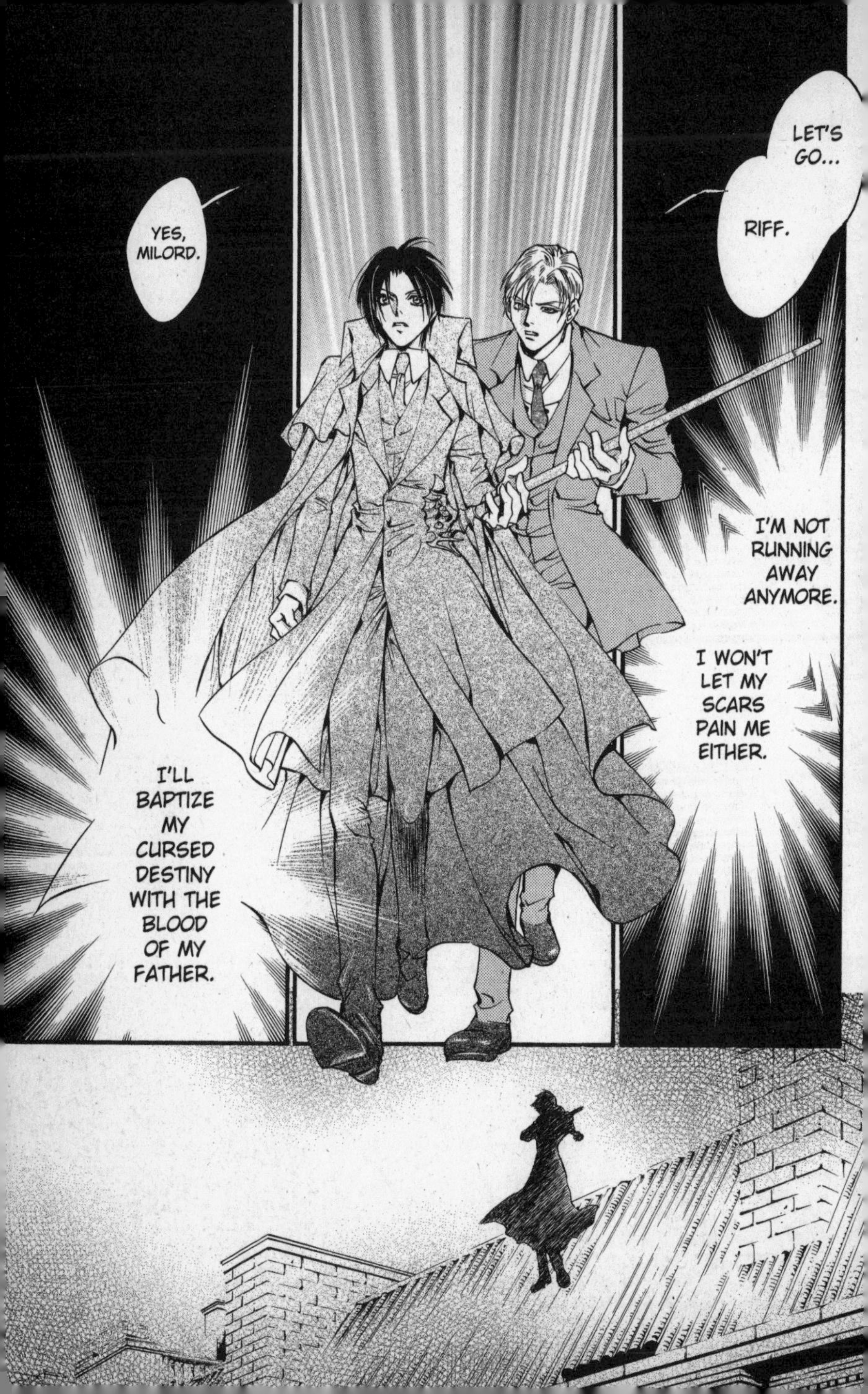
LET'S GO...
RIFF.
YES, MILORD.
I'M NOT RUNNING AWAY ANYMORE.
I WON'T LET MY SCARS PAIN ME EITHER.
I'LL BAPTIZE MY CURSED DESTINY WITH THE BLOOD OF MY FATHER.

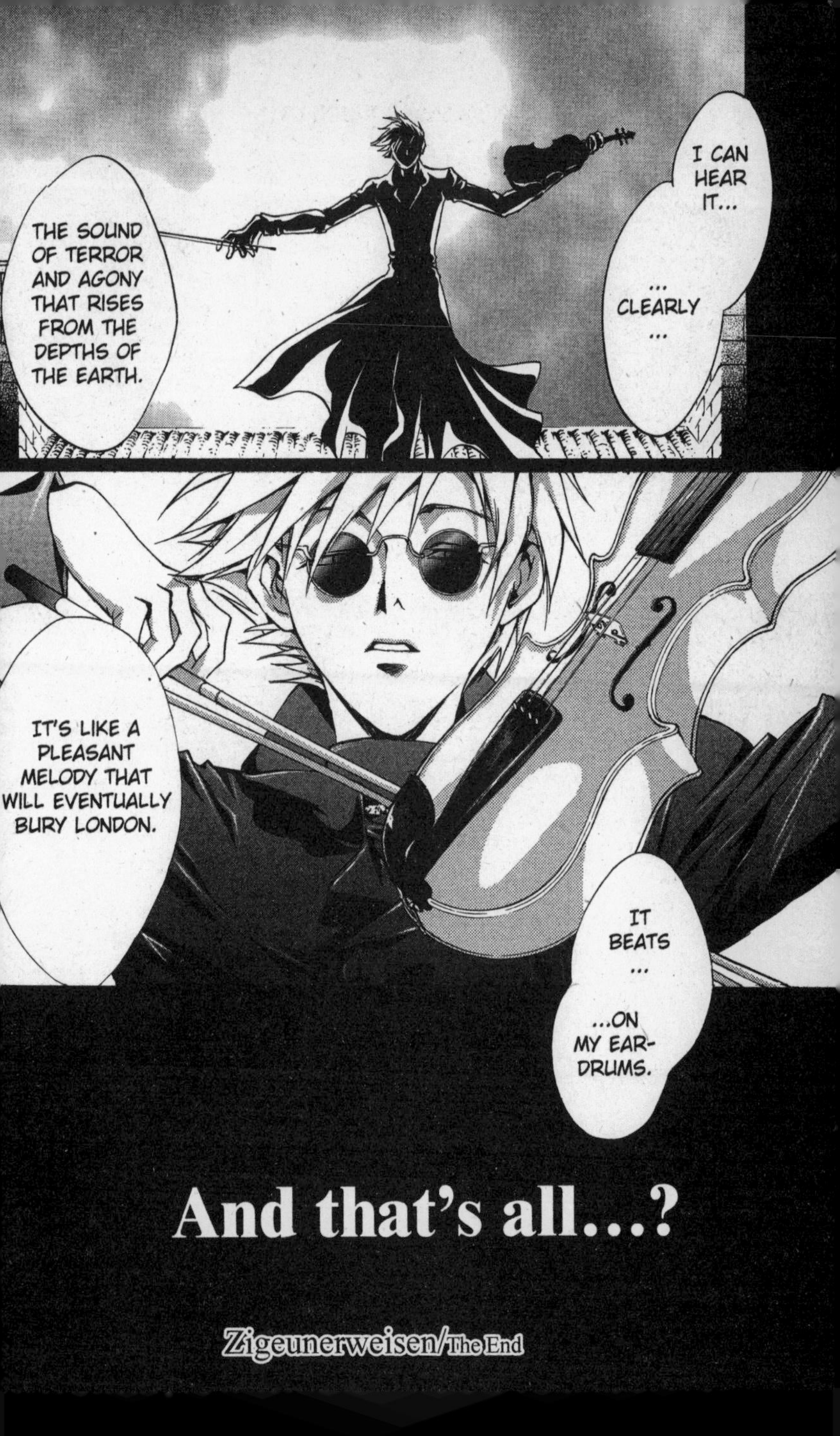
I CAN HEAR IT...
...CLEARLY...
THE SOUND OF TERROR AND AGONY THAT RISES FROM THE DEPTHS OF THE EARTH.
IT BEATS...
...ON MY EAR-DRUMS.
IT'S LIKE A PLEASANT MELODY THAT WILL EVENTUALLY BURY LONDON.
And that's all...?
Zigeunerweisen/The End

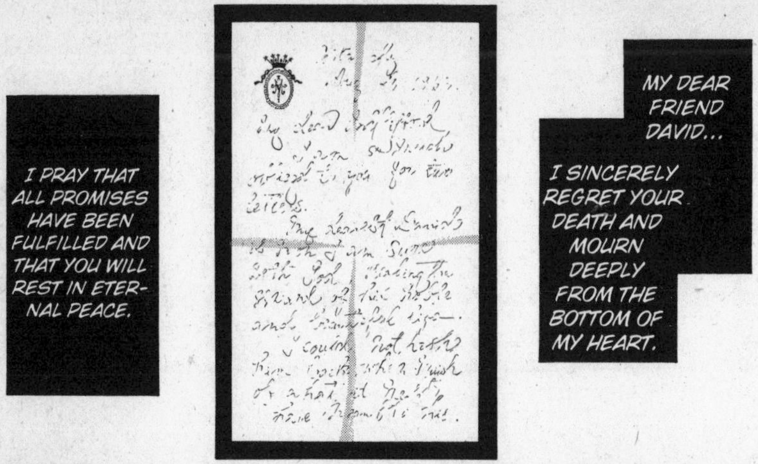
MY DEAR FRIEND DAVID...
I SINCERELY REGRET YOUR DEATH AND MOURN DEEPLY FROM THE BOTTOM OF MY HEART.
I PRAY THAT ALL PROMISES HAVE BEEN FULFILLED AND THAT YOU WILL REST IN ETERNAL PEACE.

Mortician's Daughter

(Scene 1)

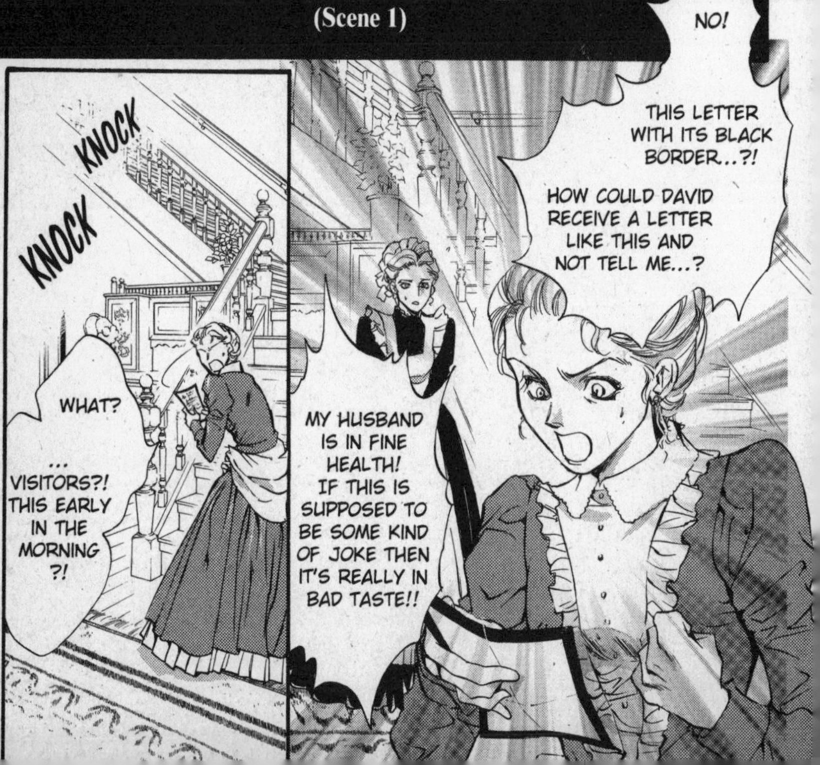
NO!
THIS LETTER WITH ITS BLACK BORDER..?!
HOW COULD DAVID RECEIVE A LETTER LIKE THIS AND NOT TELL ME...?
MY HUSBAND IS IN FINE HEALTH! IF THIS IS SUPPOSED TO BE SOME KIND OF JOKE THEN IT'S REALLY IN BAD TASTE!!
KNOCK
KNOCK
WHAT?
... VISITORS?! THIS EARLY IN THE MORNING?!

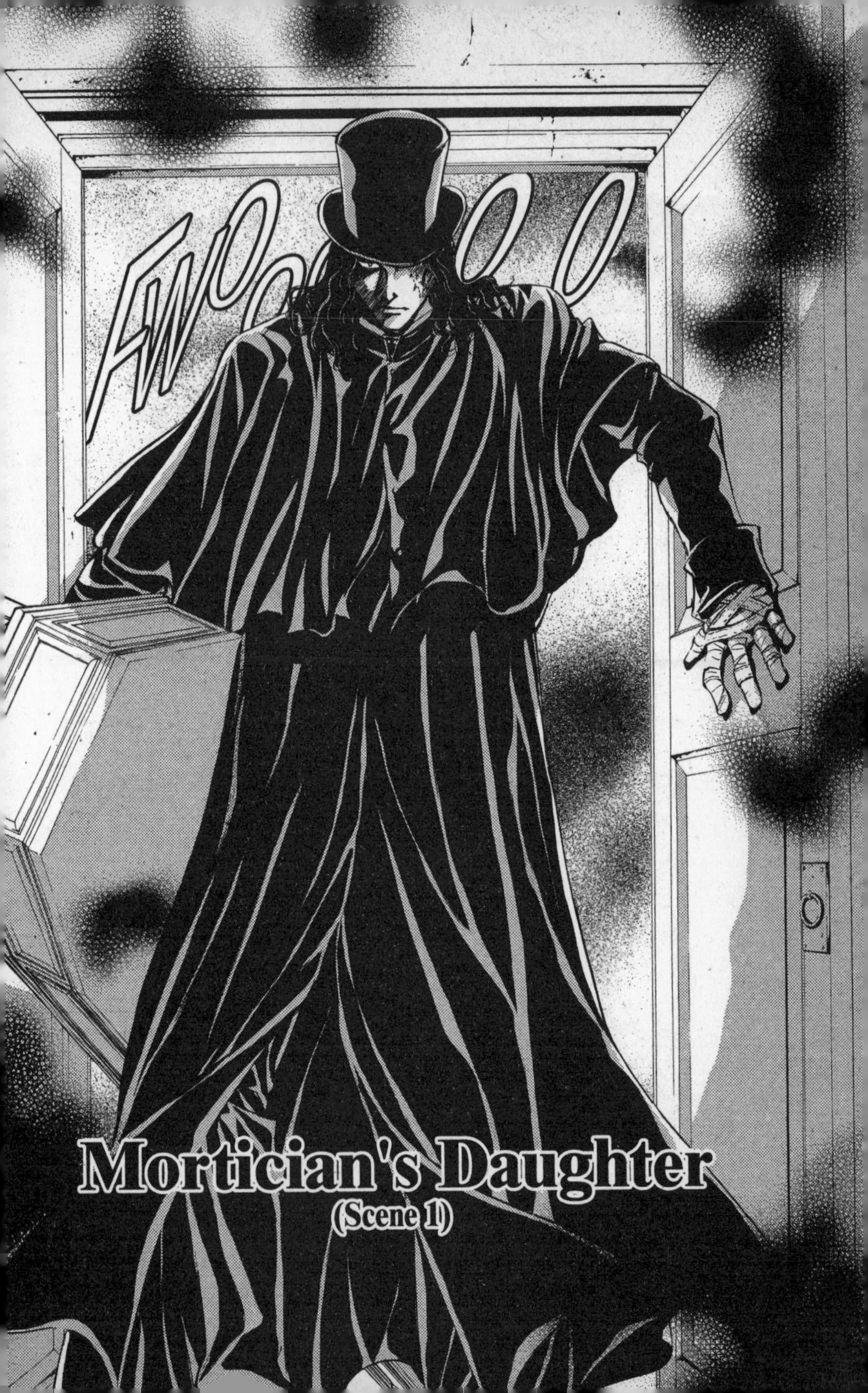
FWOOOOOO
Mortician's Daughter
(Scene 1)

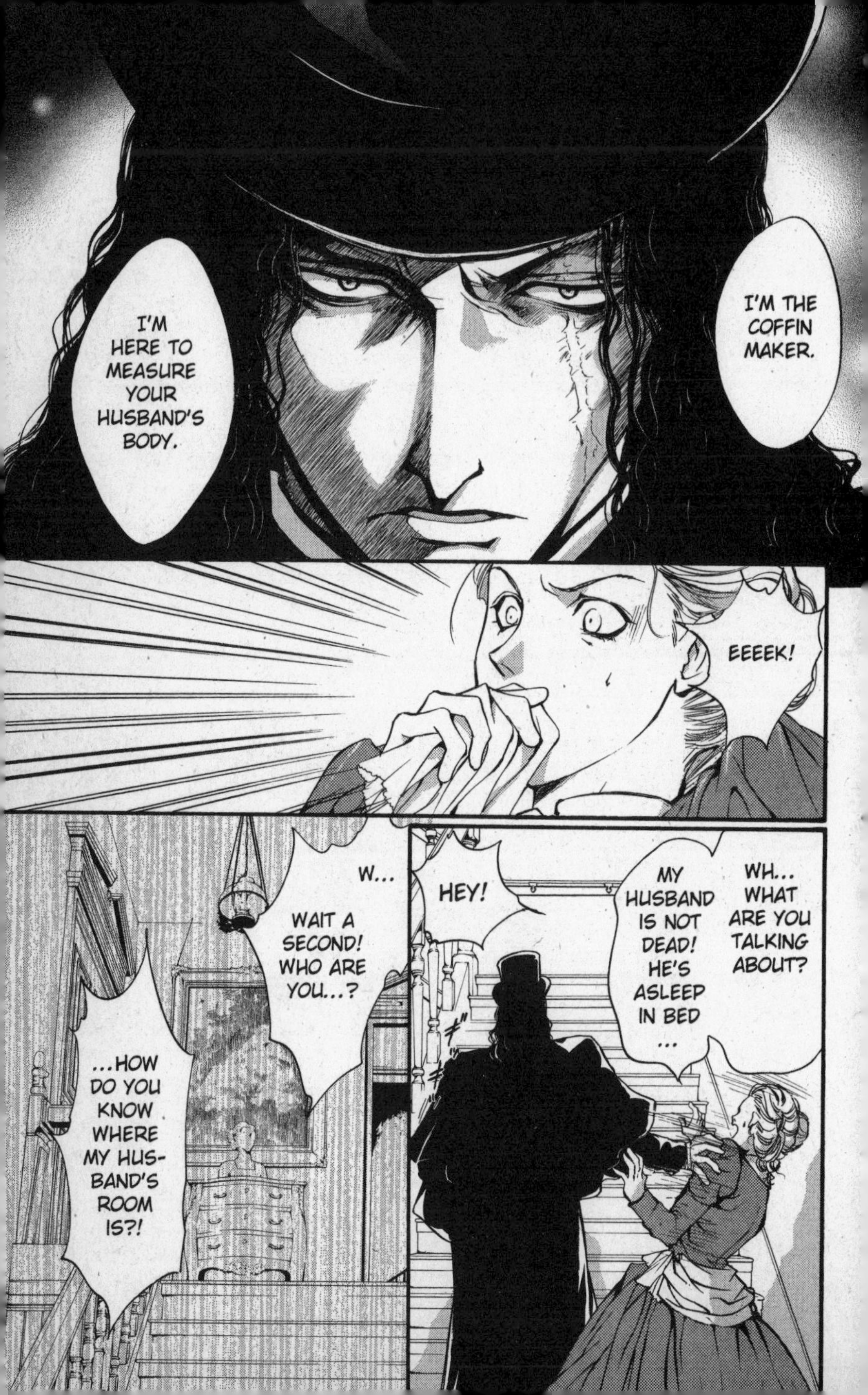
I'M THE COFFIN MAKER.
I'M HERE TO MEASURE YOUR HUSBAND'S BODY.
EEEEK!
WH... WHAT ARE YOU TALKING ABOUT?
MY HUSBAND IS NOT DEAD! HE'S ASLEEP IN BED ...
HEY!
W... WAIT A SECOND! WHO ARE YOU...?
...HOW DO YOU KNOW WHERE MY HUSBAND'S ROOM IS?!

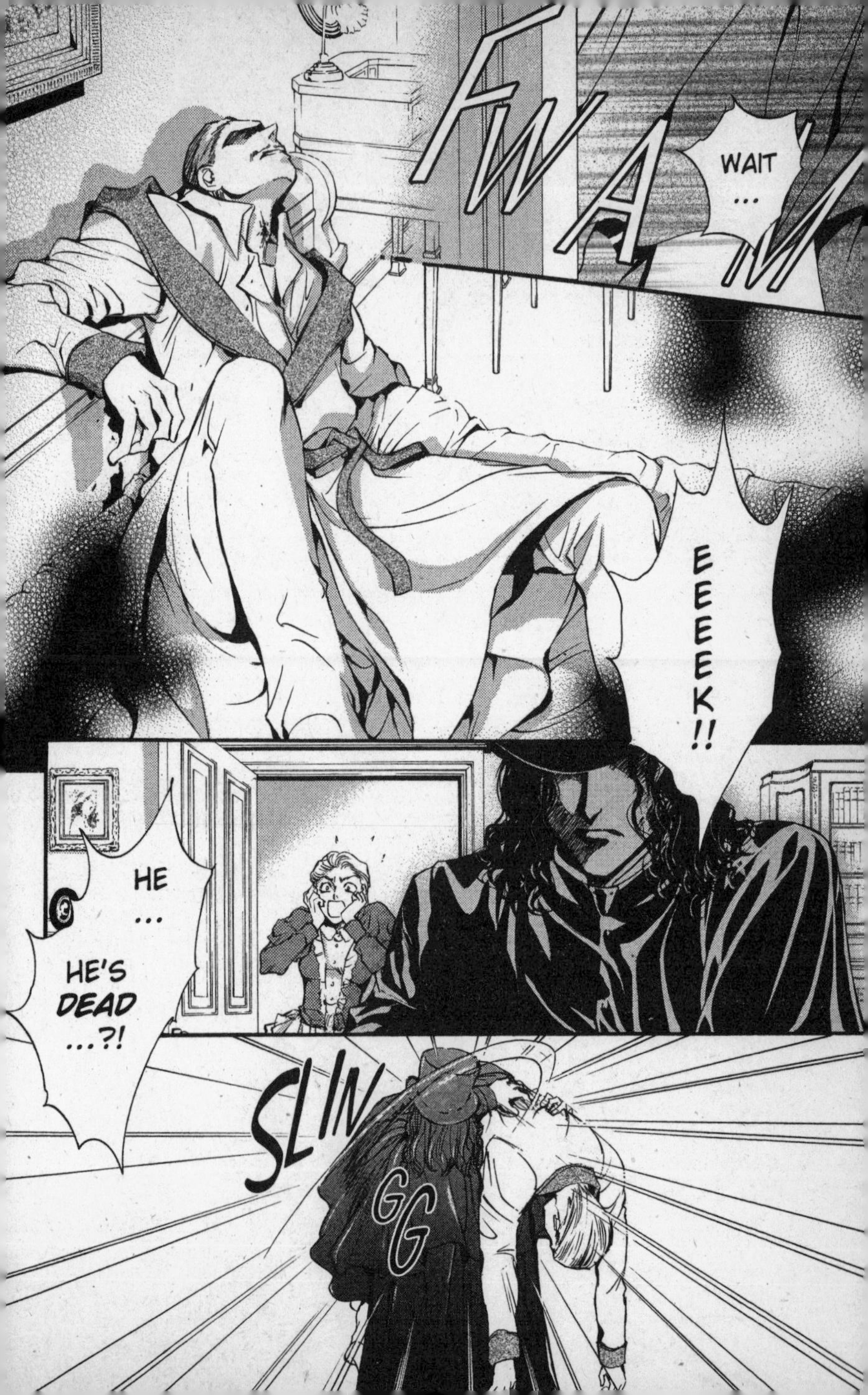
WAIT ...
FWAM
EEEEEK!!
HE ... HE'S DEAD ...?!
SLINGG

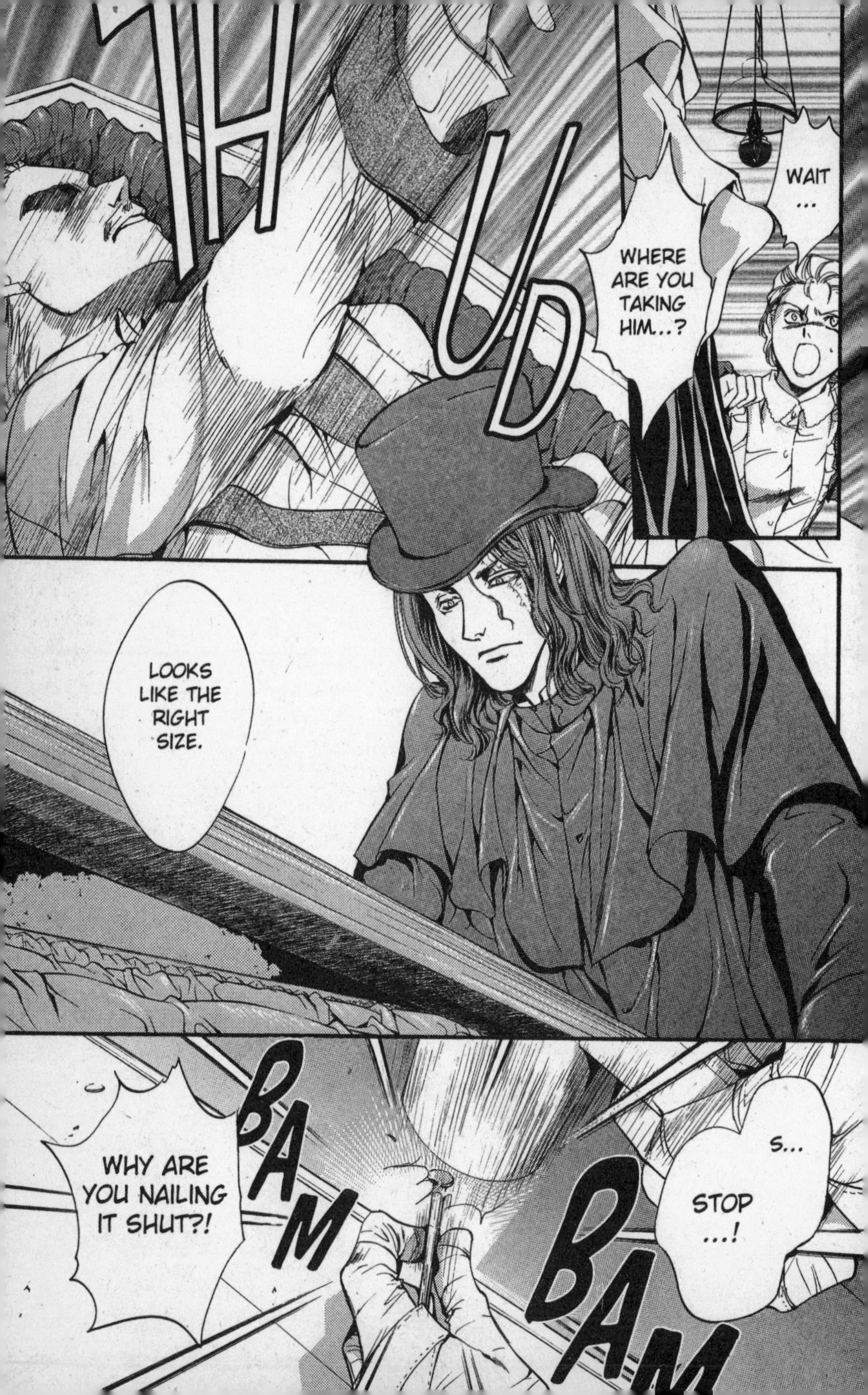
WAIT ...
WHERE ARE YOU TAKING HIM..?
HUD
LOOKS LIKE THE RIGHT SIZE.
S...
STOP ...!
BAM
BAM
WHY ARE YOU NAILING IT SHUT?!

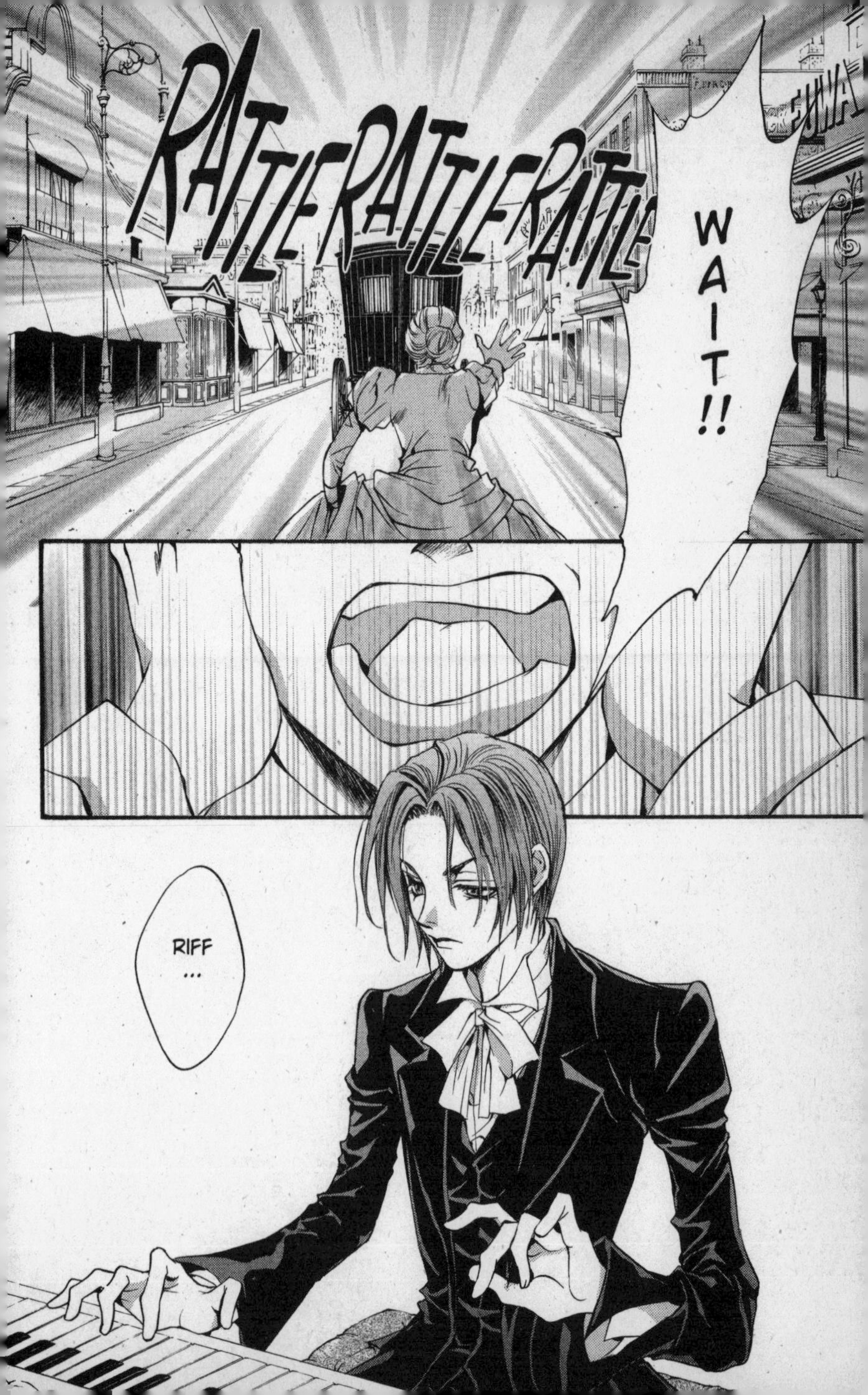
WAIT!!
RATTLE RATTLE RATTLE
RIFF ...

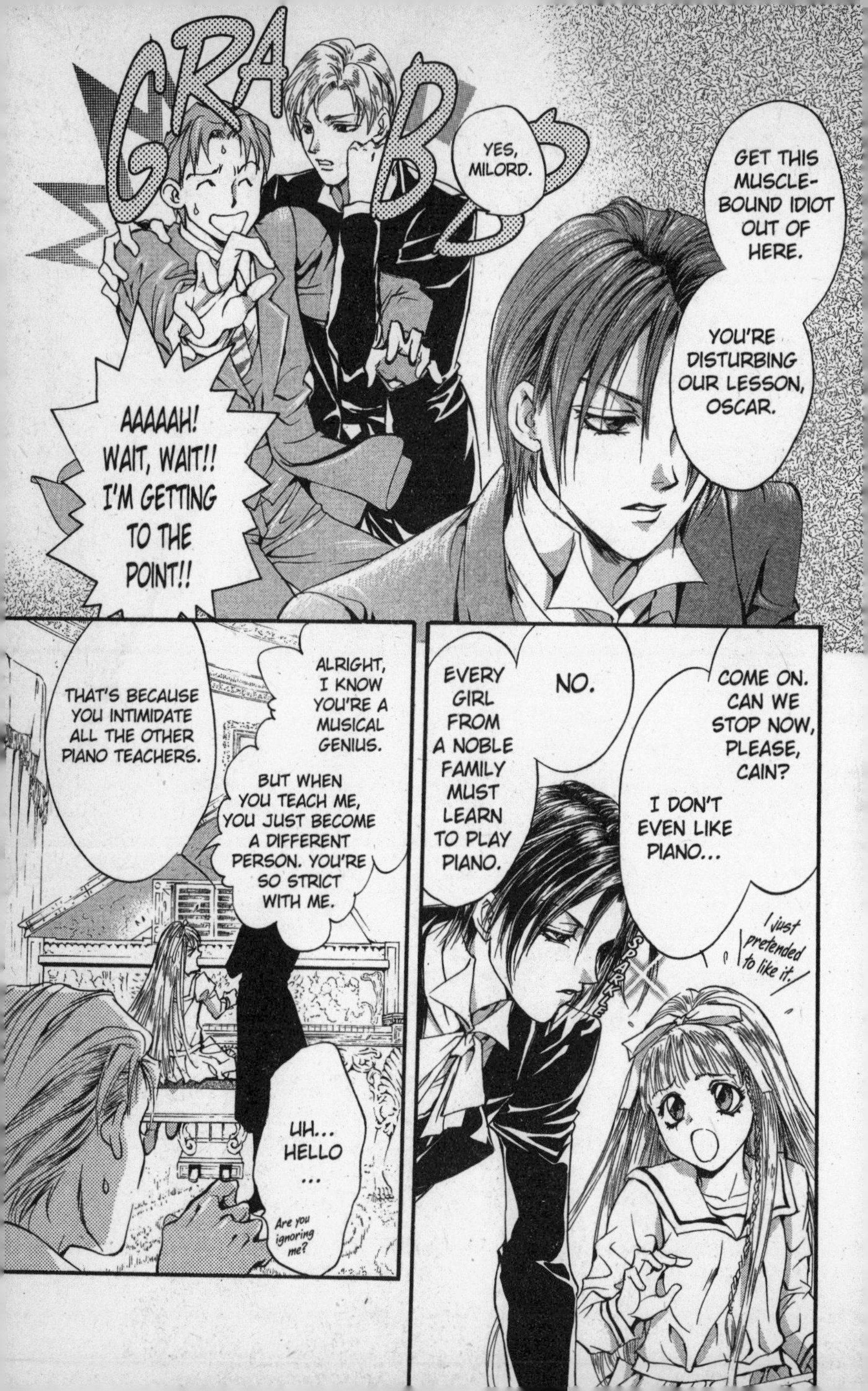
GET THIS MUSCLE-BOUND IDIOT OUT OF HERE.
YOU'RE DISTURBING OUR LESSON, OSCAR.
YES, MILORD.
GRABB
AAAAAH! WAIT, WAIT!! I'M GETTING TO THE POINT!!
COME ON. CAN WE STOP NOW, PLEASE, CAIN?
I DON'T EVEN LIKE PIANO...
I just pretended to like it.
NO.
EVERY GIRL FROM A NOBLE FAMILY MUST LEARN TO PLAY PIANO.
SPARKLE
ALRIGHT, I KNOW YOU'RE A MUSICAL GENIUS.
BUT WHEN YOU TEACH ME, YOU JUST BECOME A DIFFERENT PERSON. YOU'RE SO STRICT WITH ME.
THAT'S BECAUSE YOU INTIMIDATE ALL THE OTHER PIANO TEACHERS.
UH... HELLO ...
Are you ignoring me?

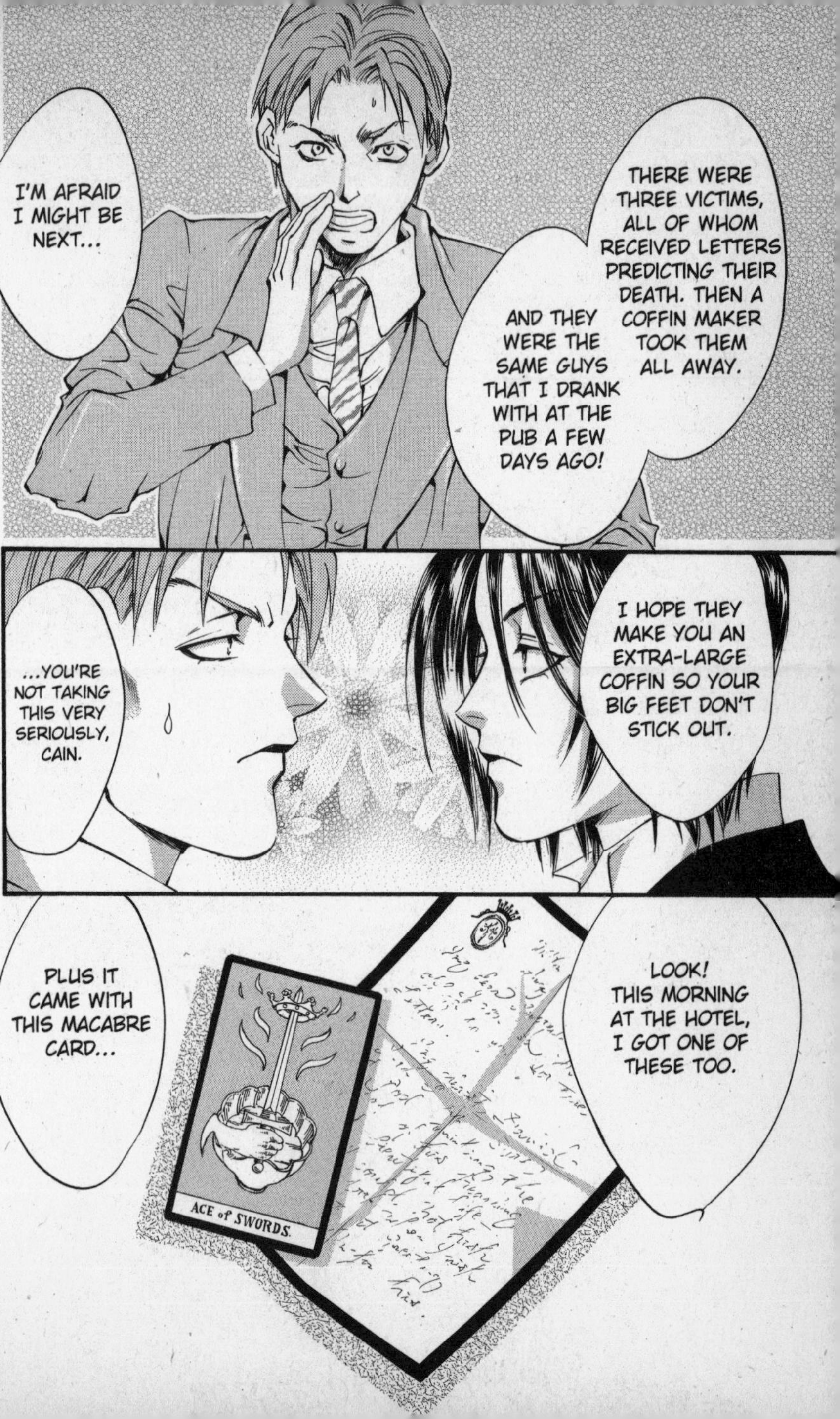
THERE WERE THREE VICTIMS, ALL OF WHOM RECEIVED LETTERS PREDICTING THEIR DEATH. THEN A COFFIN MAKER TOOK THEM ALL AWAY.
AND THEY WERE THE SAME GUYS THAT I DRANK WITH AT THE PUB A FEW DAYS AGO!
I'M AFRAID I MIGHT BE NEXT...
I HOPE THEY MAKE YOU AN EXTRA-LARGE COFFIN SO YOUR BIG FEET DON'T STICK OUT.
...YOU'RE NOT TAKING THIS VERY SERIOUSLY, CAIN.
LOOK! THIS MORNING AT THE HOTEL, I GOT ONE OF THESE TOO.
PLUS IT CAME WITH THIS MACABRE CARD...
ACE of SWORDS

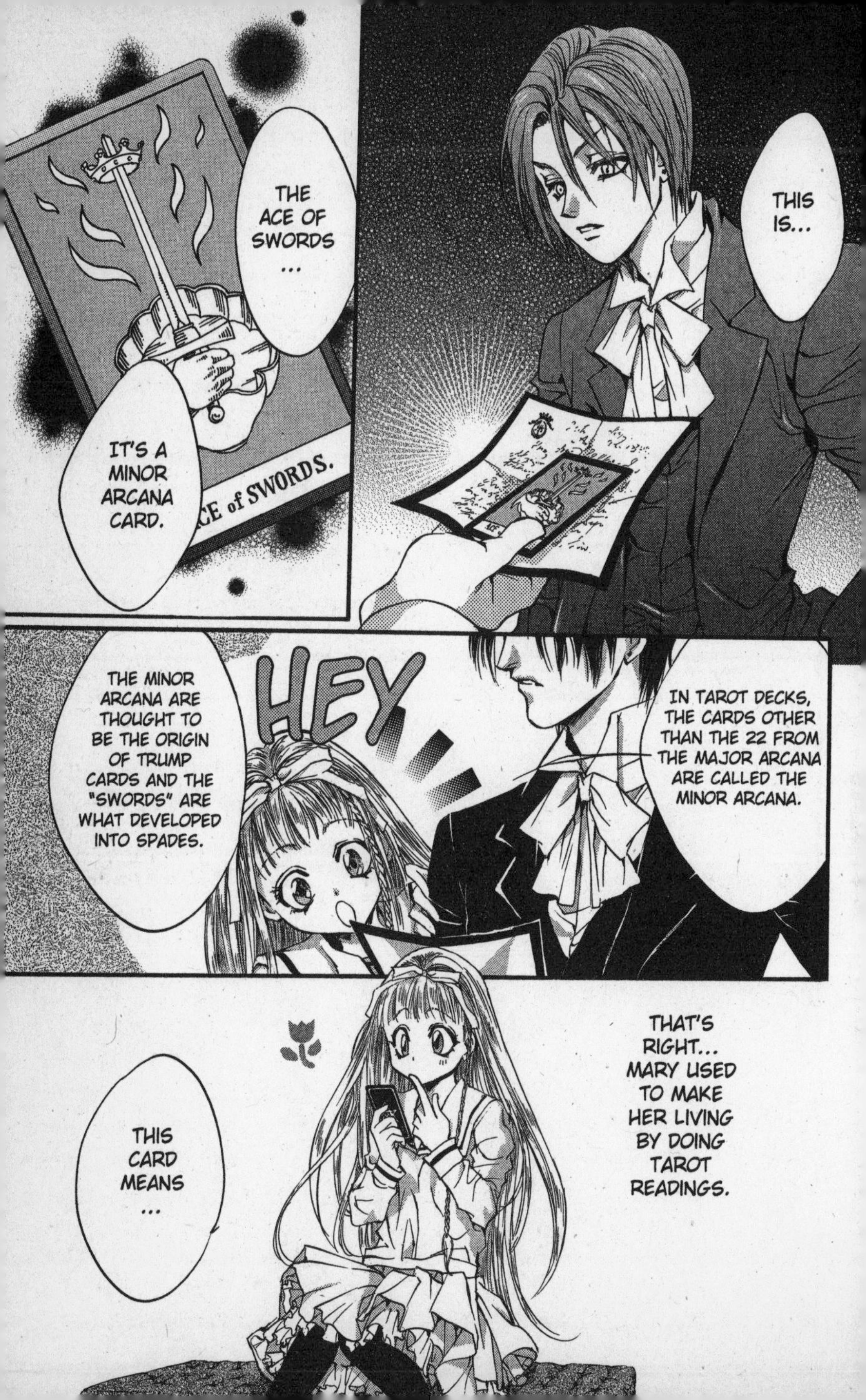
THIS IS...
THE ACE OF SWORDS ...
IT'S A MINOR ARCANA CARD.
IN TAROT DECKS, THE CARDS OTHER THAN THE 22 FROM THE MAJOR ARCANA ARE CALLED THE MINOR ARCANA.
HEY
THE MINOR ARCANA ARE THOUGHT TO BE THE ORIGIN OF TRUMP CARDS AND THE "SWORDS" ARE WHAT DEVELOPED INTO SPADES.
THAT'S RIGHT... MARY USED TO MAKE HER LIVING BY DOING TAROT READINGS.
THIS CARD MEANS ...

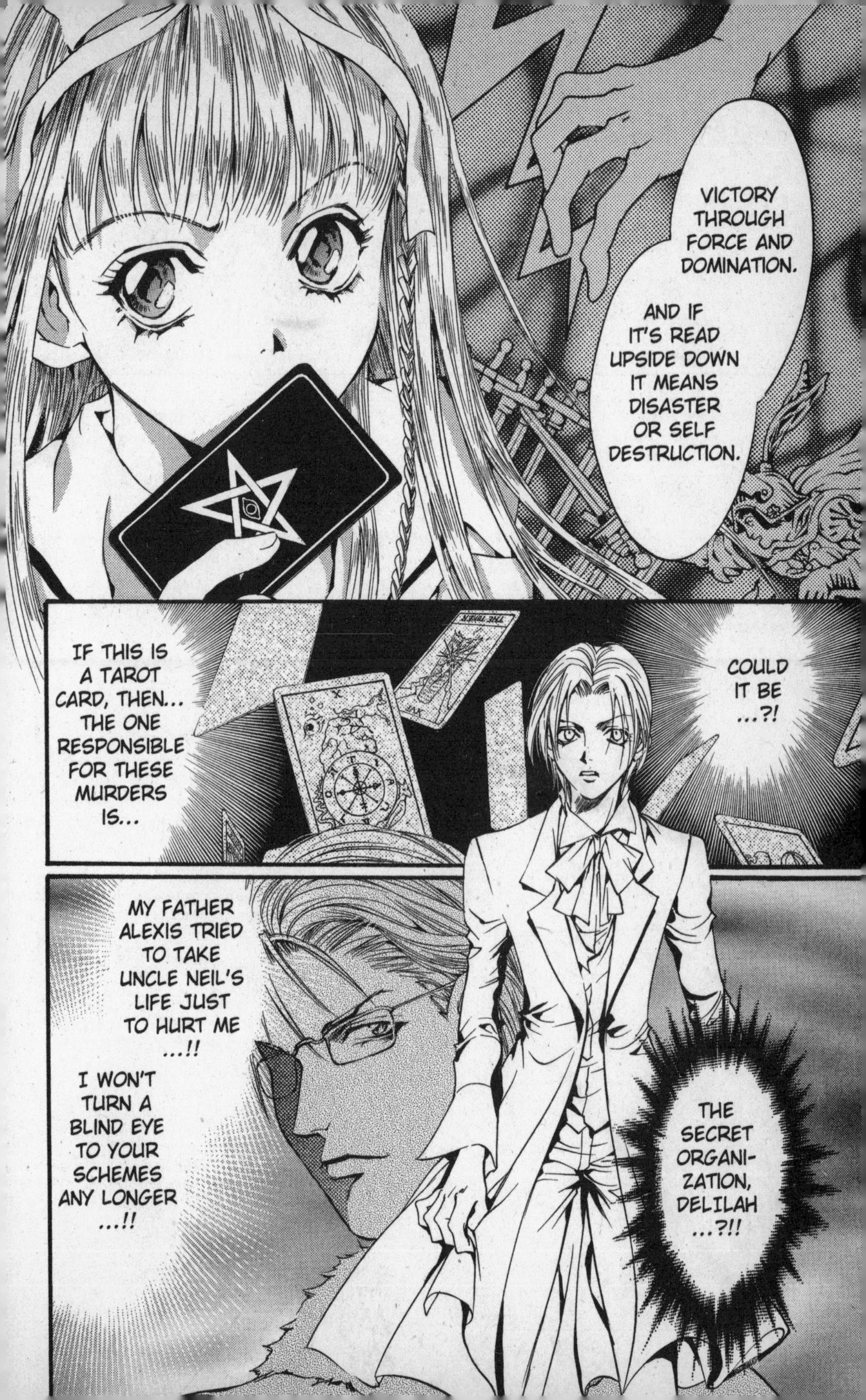
VICTORY THROUGH FORCE AND DOMINATION.
AND IF IT'S READ UPSIDE DOWN IT MEANS DISASTER OR SELF DESTRUCTION.
IF THIS IS A TAROT CARD, THEN... THE ONE RESPONSIBLE FOR THESE MURDERS IS...
COULD IT BE ...?!
THE SECRET ORGANIZATION, DELILAH ...?!!
MY FATHER ALEXIS TRIED TO TAKE UNCLE NEIL'S LIFE JUST TO HURT ME ...!!
I WON'T TURN A BLIND EYE TO YOUR SCHEMES ANY LONGER ...!!

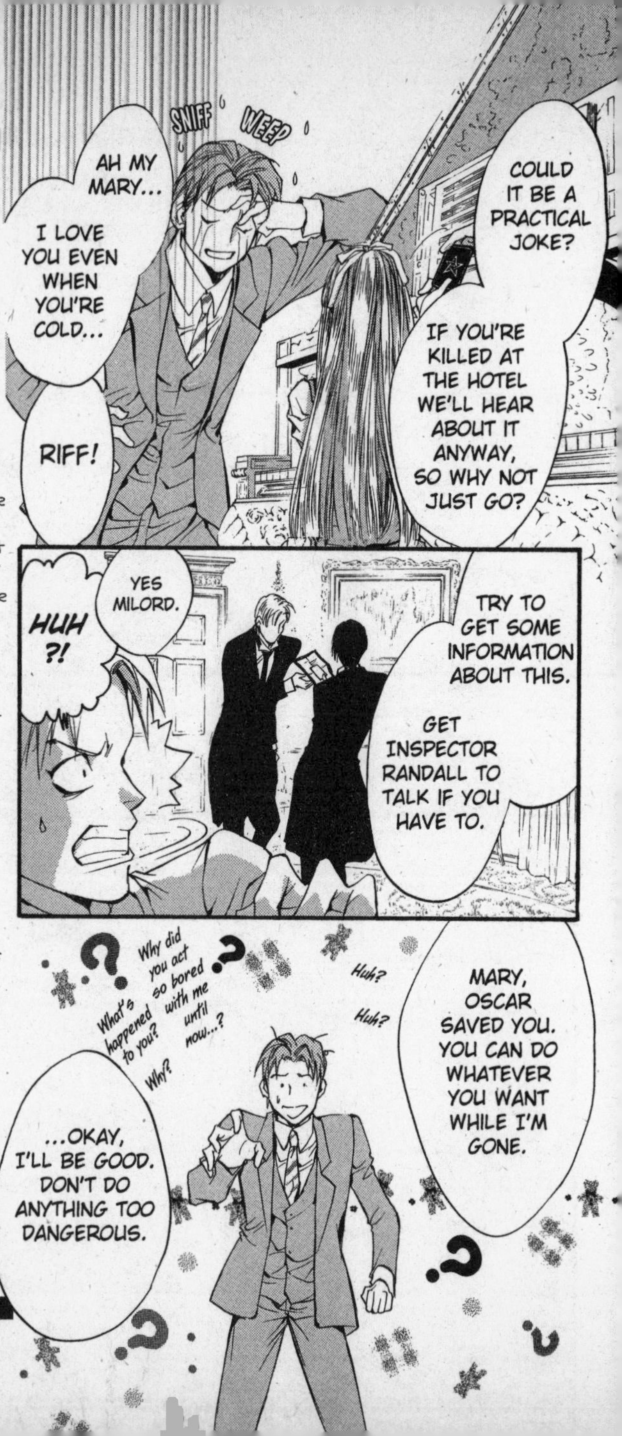
COULD IT BE A PRACTICAL JOKE?
IF YOU'RE KILLED AT THE HOTEL WE'LL HEAR ABOUT IT ANYWAY, SO WHY NOT JUST GO?
WEEP
SNIFF
AH MY MARY...
I LOVE YOU EVEN WHEN YOU'RE COLD...
RIFF!
TRY TO GET SOME INFORMATION ABOUT THIS.
GET INSPECTOR RANDALL TO TALK IF YOU HAVE TO.
YES MILORD.
HUH ?!
MARY, OSCAR SAVED YOU. YOU CAN DO WHATEVER YOU WANT WHILE I'M GONE.
Huh?
Huh?
Why did you act so bored with me until now...?
What's happened to you?
Why?
...OKAY, I'LL BE GOOD. DON'T DO ANYTHING TOO DANGEROUS.

Mortician's Daughter... I really liked this story. Madame Flemming seemed to think Mary was good at every subject but actually she's not very good at playing the piano. I'd planned Cain's piano scene a while ago but it kept getting cut because it had nothing to do with the story, but now I can finally include it... It's rare for the main character to be a girl with glasses like Marjorie but I was running out of character variations. I don't usually like drawing girls with glasses but once I got started it was actually fun. I liked the coffin maker too, but he was a pain to draw. The claws he sometimes wears as weapons are really hard to get right. ——

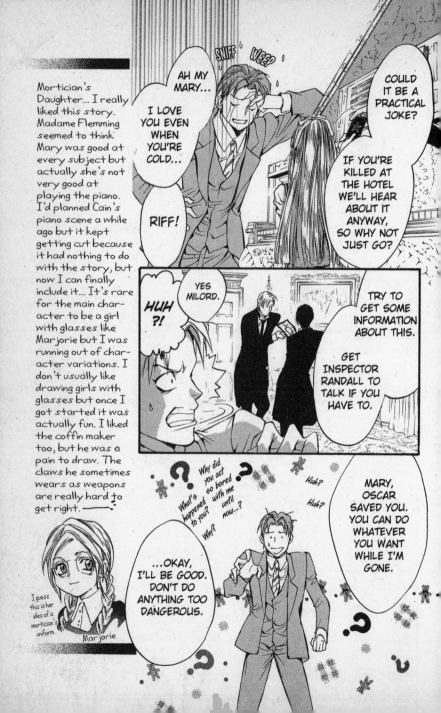

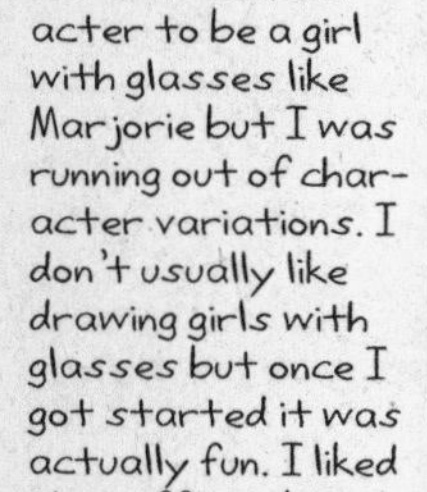
I guess this is her idea of a mortician's uniform.
Marjorie

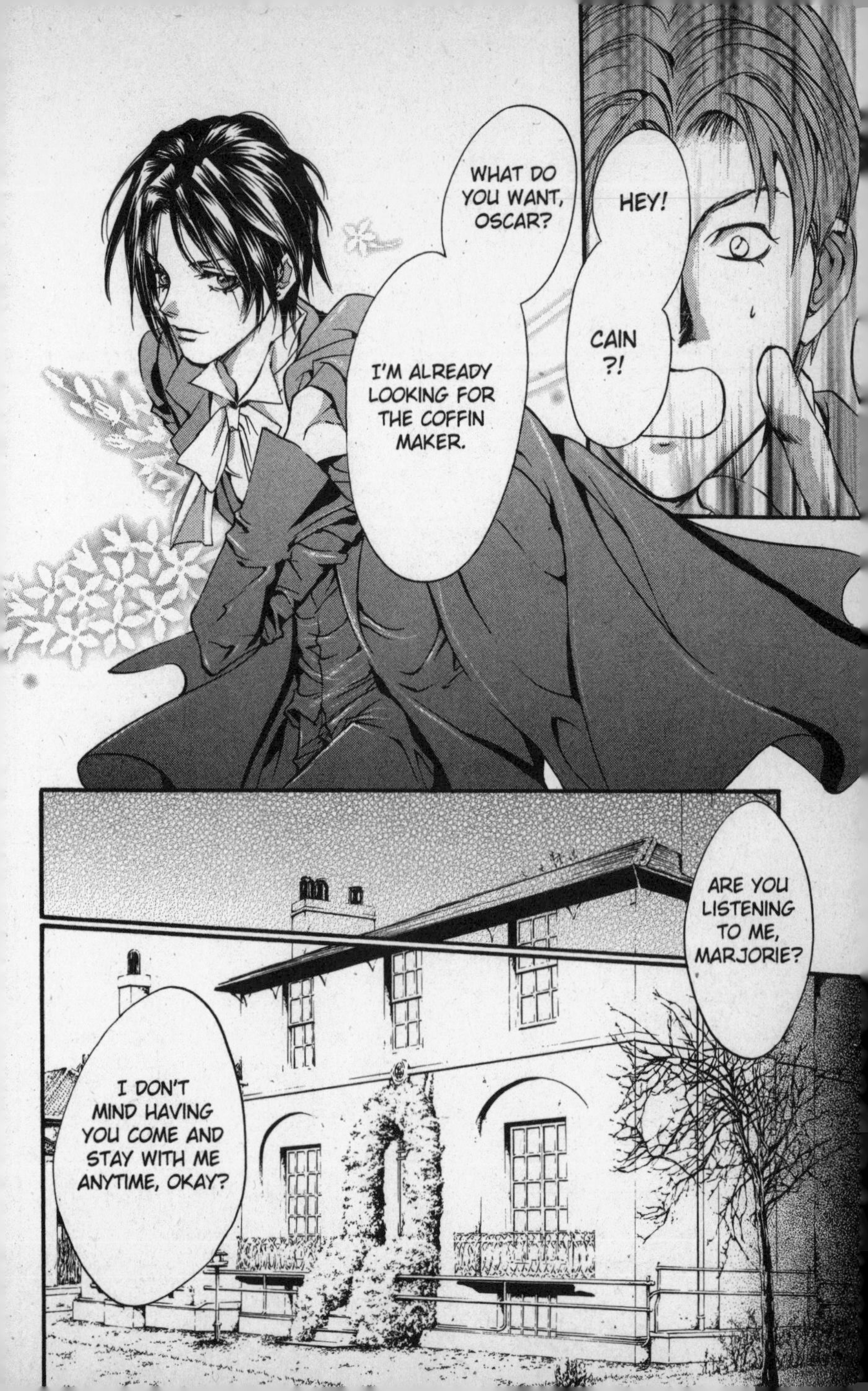
HEY!
CAIN ?!
WHAT DO YOU WANT, OSCAR?
I'M ALREADY LOOKING FOR THE COFFIN MAKER.
ARE YOU LISTENING TO ME, MARJORIE?
I DON'T MIND HAVING YOU COME AND STAY WITH ME ANYTIME, OKAY?

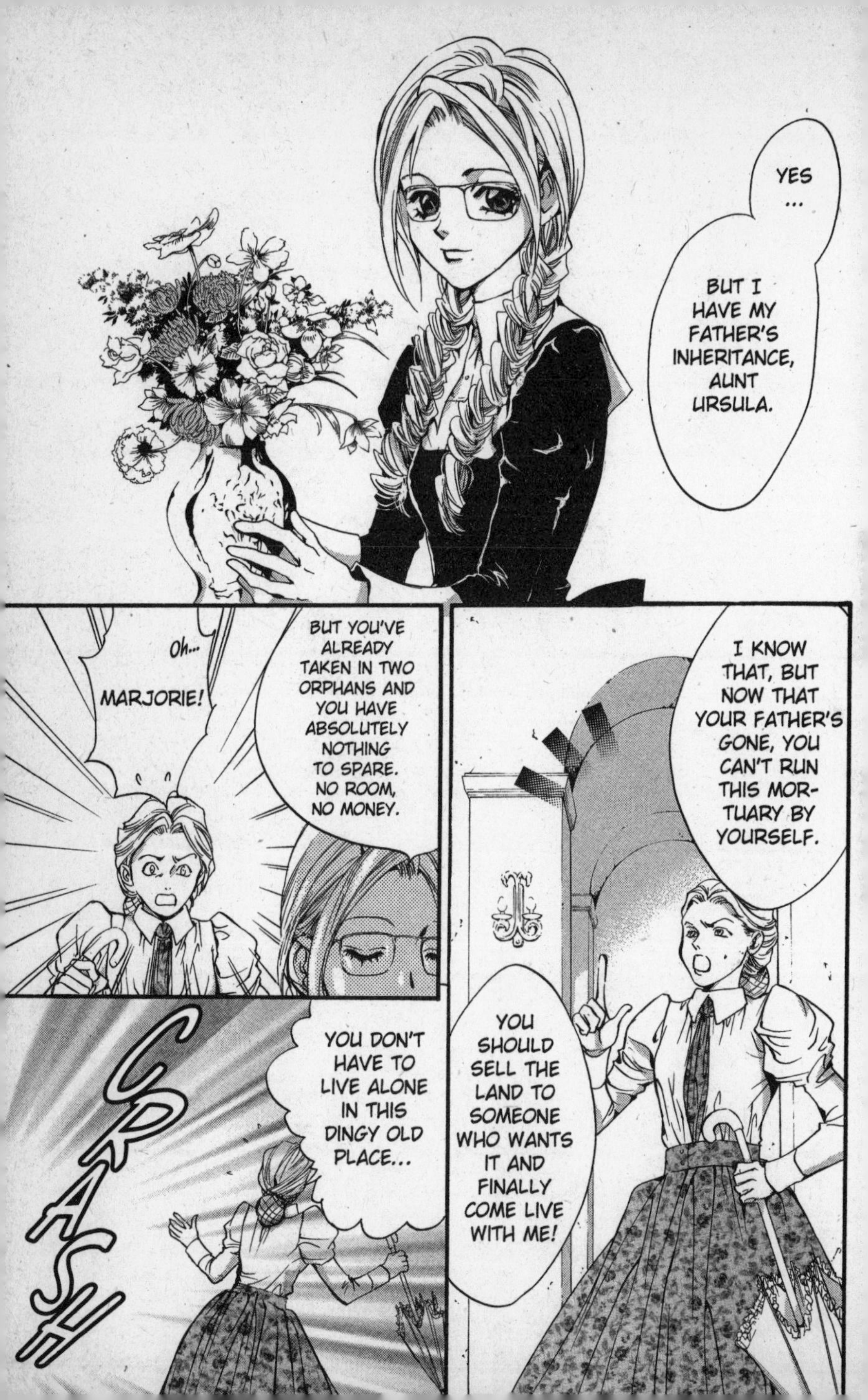
YES ...
BUT I HAVE MY FATHER'S INHERITANCE, AUNT URSULA.
I KNOW THAT, BUT NOW THAT YOUR FATHER'S GONE, YOU CAN'T RUN THIS MOR-TUARY BY YOURSELF.
YOU SHOULD SELL THE LAND TO SOMEONE WHO WANTS IT AND FINALLY COME LIVE WITH ME!
BUT YOU'VE ALREADY TAKEN IN TWO ORPHANS AND YOU HAVE ABSOLUTELY NOTHING TO SPARE. NO ROOM, NO MONEY.
Oh...
MARJORIE!
YOU DON'T HAVE TO LIVE ALONE IN THIS DINGY OLD PLACE...
CRASH

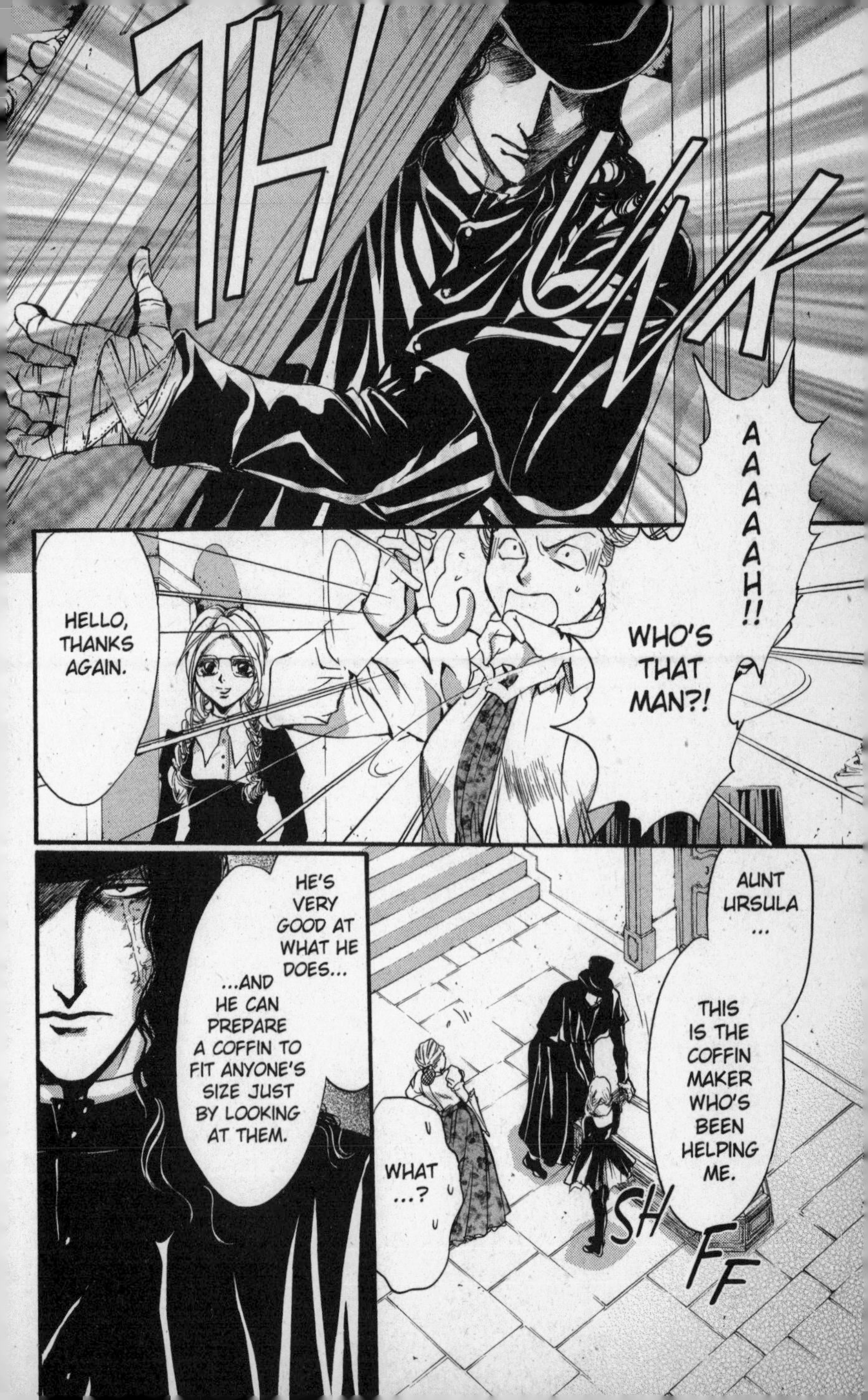
THUNK
AAAAAAH!!
WHO'S THAT MAN?!
HELLO, THANKS AGAIN.
AUNT URSULA ...
THIS IS THE COFFIN MAKER WHO'S BEEN HELPING ME.
SHFF
WHAT ...?
HE'S VERY GOOD AT WHAT HE DOES...
...AND HE CAN PREPARE A COFFIN TO FIT ANYONE'S SIZE JUST BY LOOKING AT THEM.

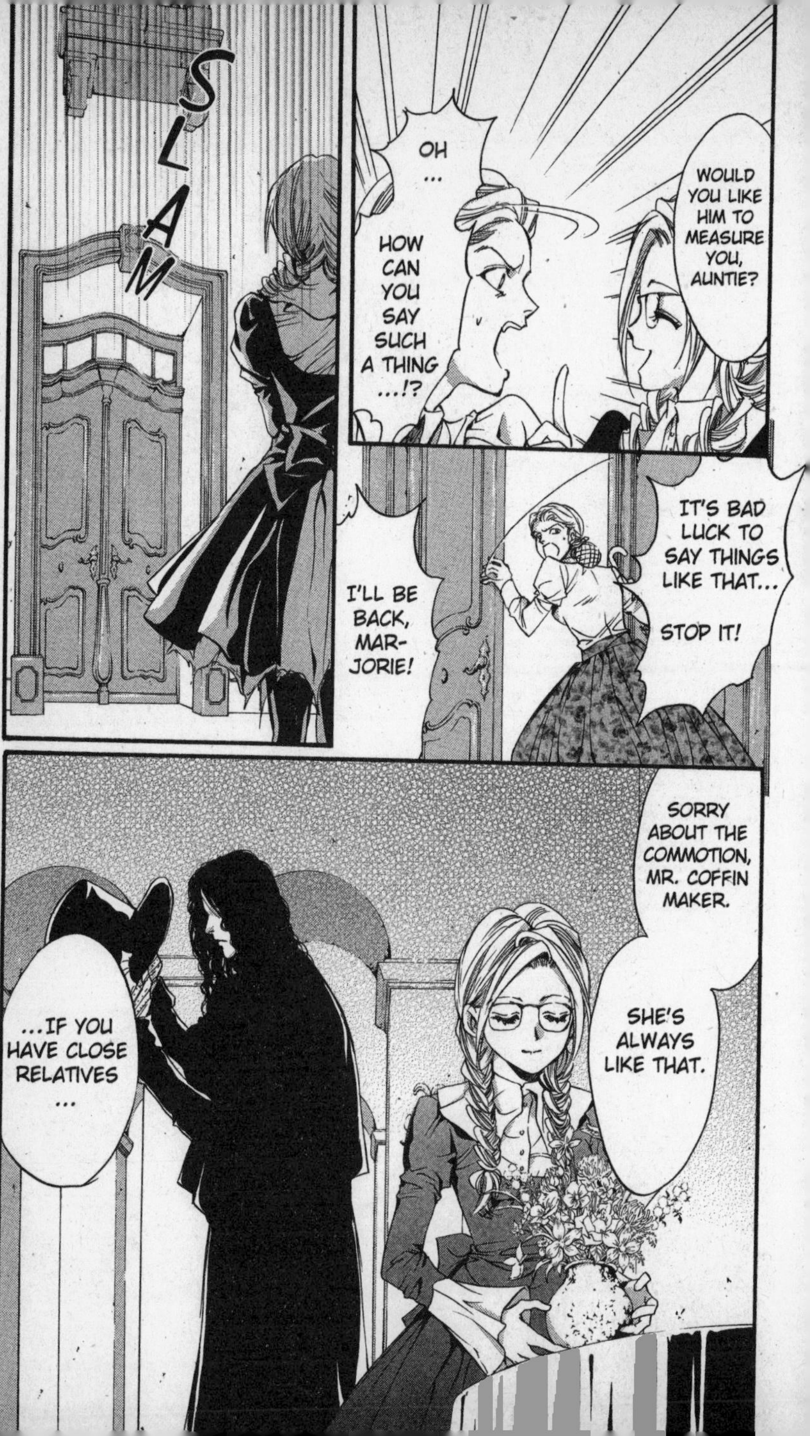
WOULD YOU LIKE HIM TO MEASURE YOU, AUNTIE?
OH ...
HOW CAN YOU SAY SUCH A THING ...!?
IT'S BAD LUCK TO SAY THINGS LIKE THAT...
STOP IT!
I'LL BE BACK, MAR-JORIE!
SLAM
SORRY ABOUT THE COMMOTION, MR. COFFIN MAKER.
SHE'S ALWAYS LIKE THAT.
...IF YOU HAVE CLOSE RELATIVES ...

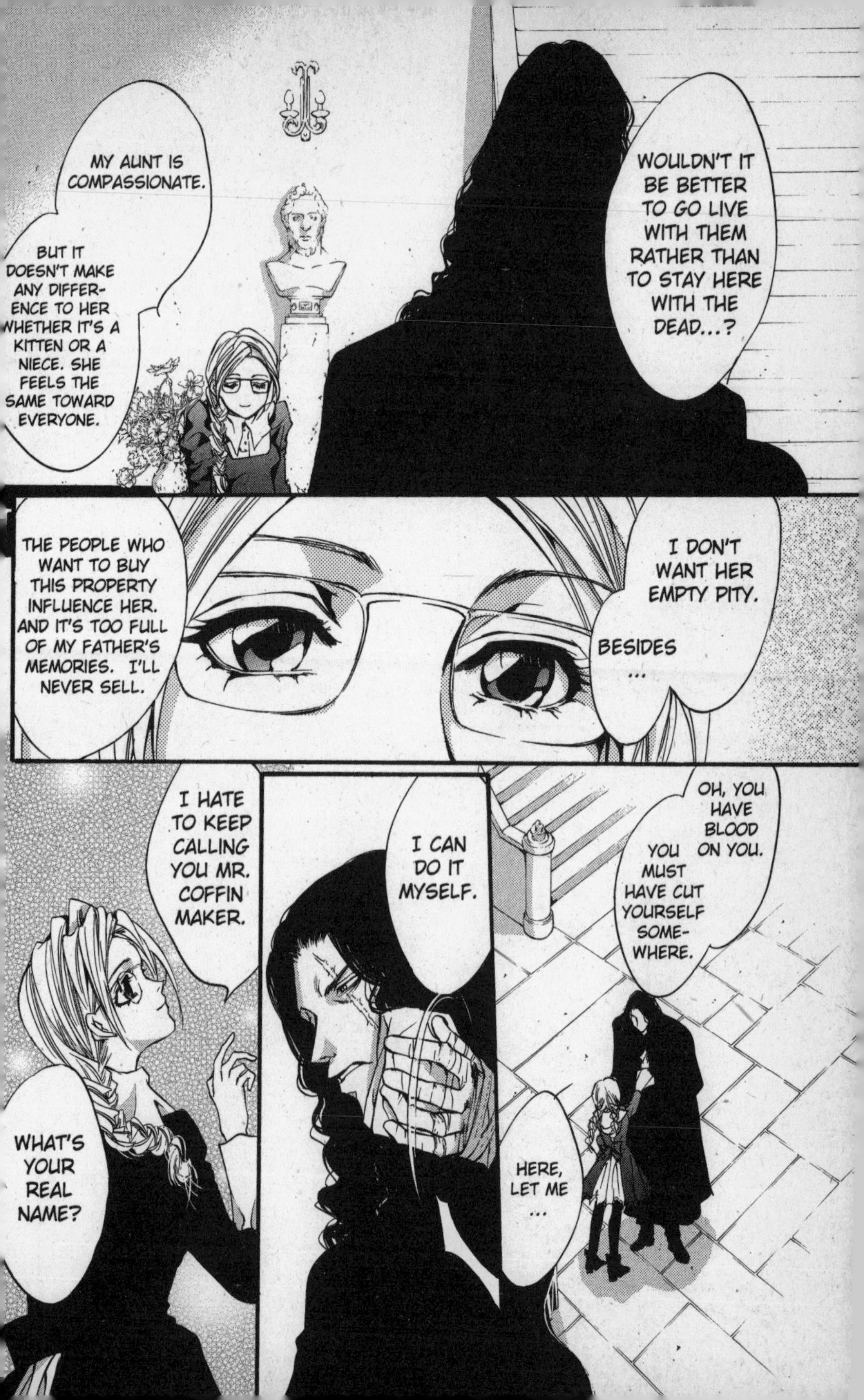
WOULDN'T IT BE BETTER TO GO LIVE WITH THEM RATHER THAN TO STAY HERE WITH THE DEAD...?
MY AUNT IS COMPASSIONATE.
BUT IT DOESN'T MAKE ANY DIFFERENCE TO HER WHETHER IT'S A KITTEN OR A NIECE. SHE FEELS THE SAME TOWARD EVERYONE.
I DON'T WANT HER EMPTY PITY.
BESIDES ...
THE PEOPLE WHO WANT TO BUY THIS PROPERTY INFLUENCE HER. AND IT'S TOO FULL OF MY FATHER'S MEMORIES. I'LL NEVER SELL.
OH, YOU HAVE BLOOD ON YOU.
YOU MUST HAVE CUT YOURSELF SOMEWHERE.
HERE, LET ME ...
I CAN DO IT MYSELF.
I HATE TO KEEP CALLING YOU MR. COFFIN MAKER.
WHAT'S YOUR REAL NAME?

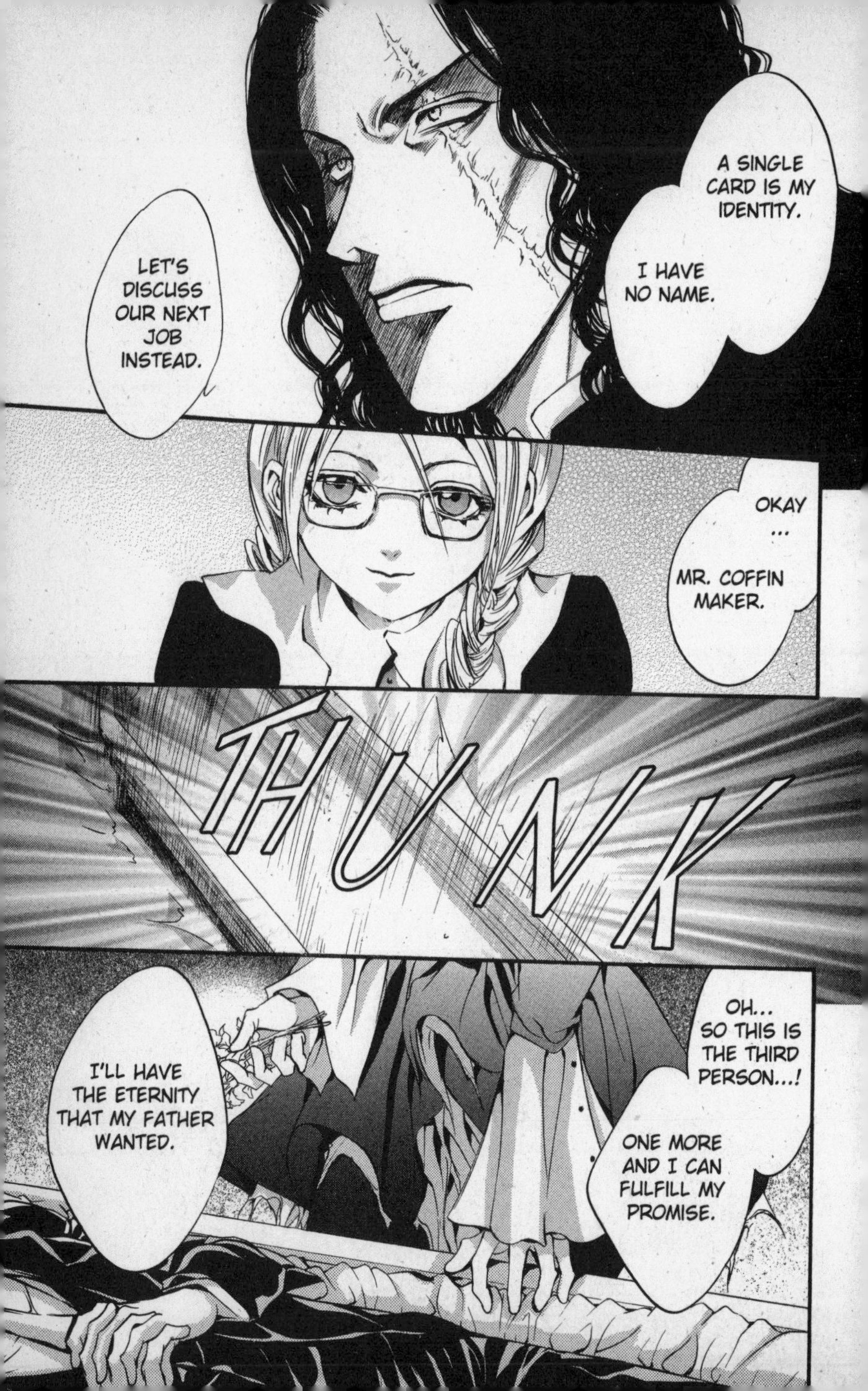
A SINGLE CARD IS MY IDENTITY.
I HAVE NO NAME.
LET'S DISCUSS OUR NEXT JOB INSTEAD.
OKAY ... MR. COFFIN MAKER.
THUNK
OH... SO THIS IS THE THIRD PERSON...!
ONE MORE AND I CAN FULFILL MY PROMISE.
I'LL HAVE THE ETERNITY THAT MY FATHER WANTED.

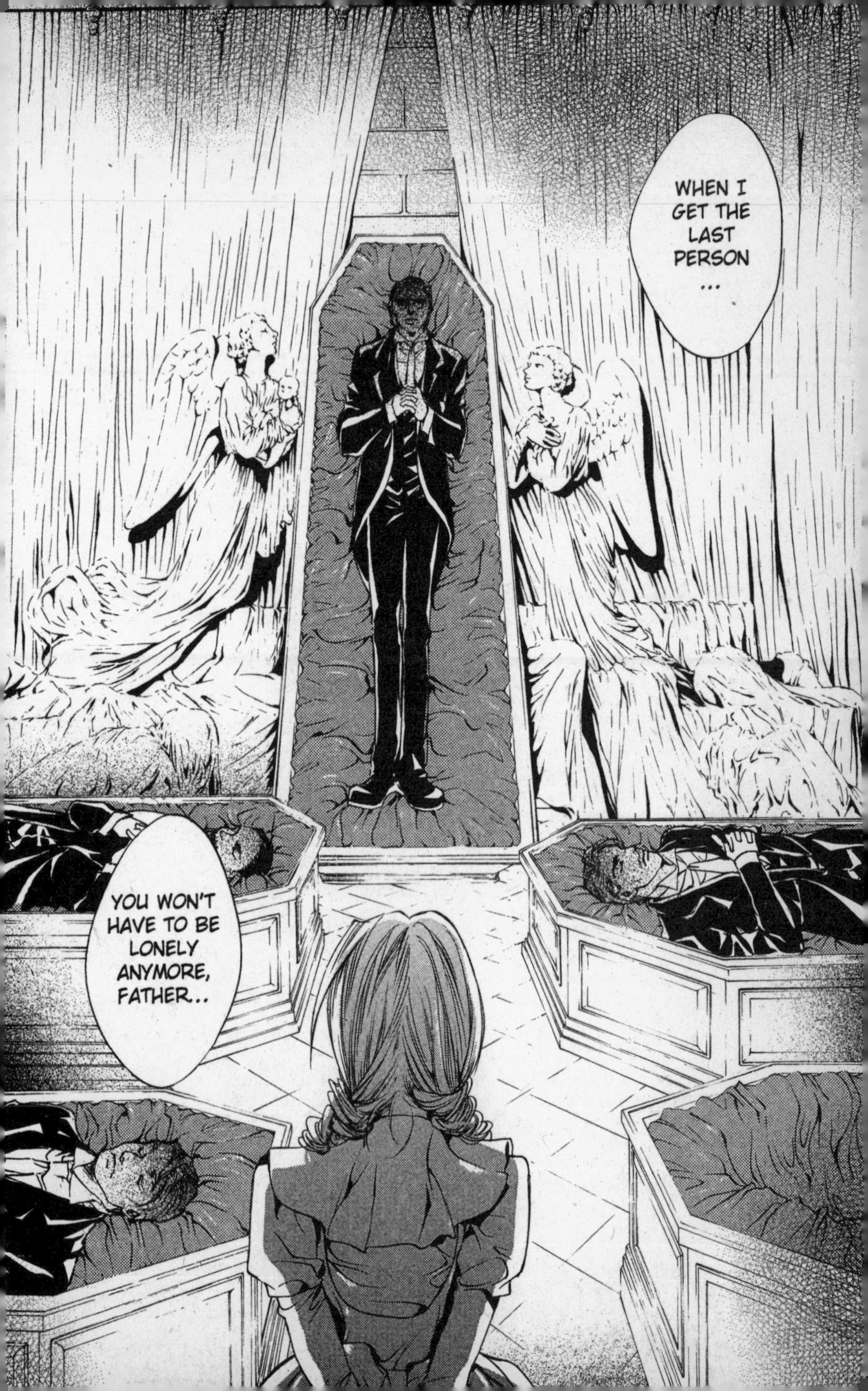
WHEN I GET THE LAST PERSON ...
YOU WON'T HAVE TO BE LONELY ANYMORE, FATHER..

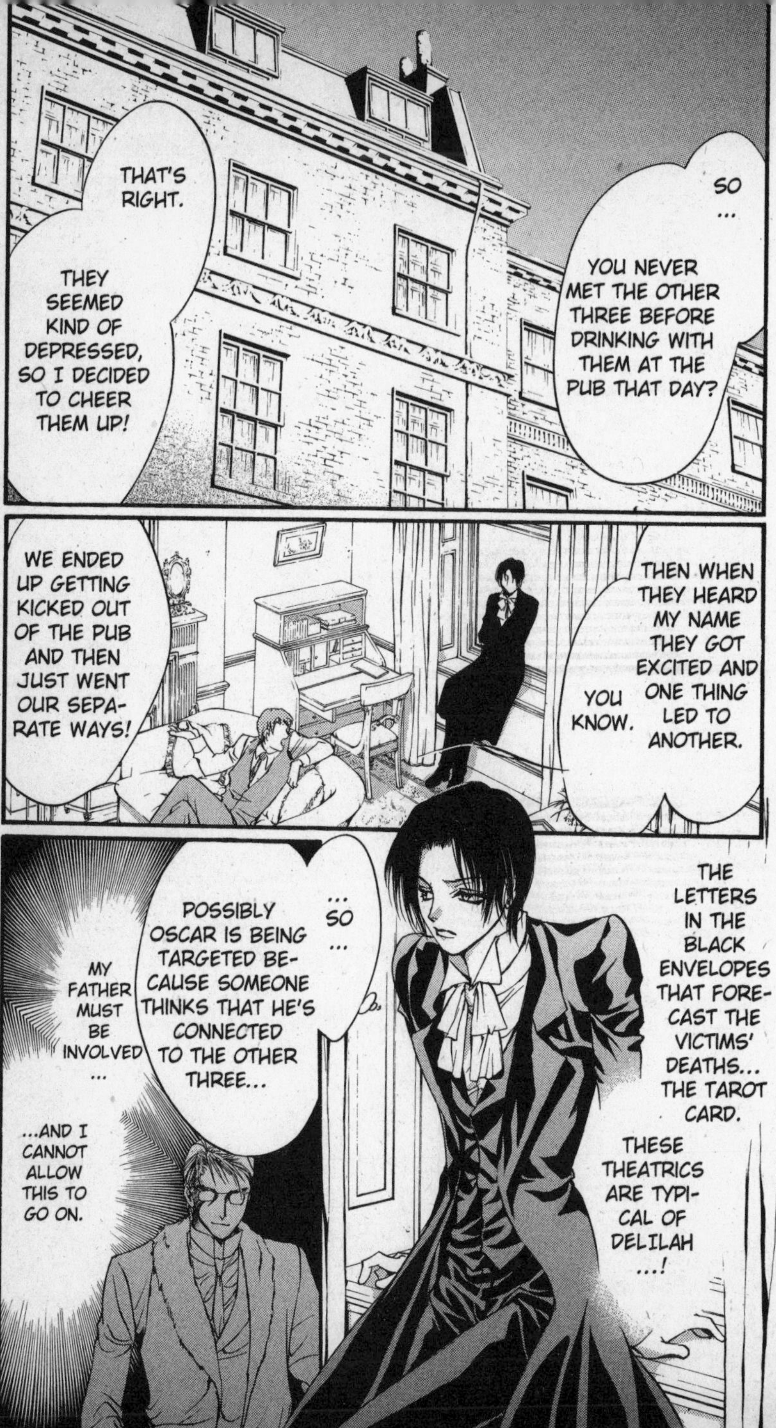
SO ...
YOU NEVER MET THE OTHER THREE BEFORE DRINKING WITH THEM AT THE PUB THAT DAY?
THAT'S RIGHT.
THEY SEEMED KIND OF DEPRESSED, SO I DECIDED TO CHEER THEM UP!
THEN WHEN THEY HEARD MY NAME THEY GOT EXCITED AND ONE THING LED TO ANOTHER.
YOU KNOW.
WE ENDED UP GETTING KICKED OUT OF THE PUB AND THEN JUST WENT OUR SEPA-RATE WAYS!
THE LETTERS IN THE BLACK ENVELOPES THAT FORE-CAST THE VICTIMS' DEATHS... THE TAROT CARD.
THESE THEATRICS ARE TYPI-CAL OF DELILAH ...!
... SO ...
POSSIBLY OSCAR IS BEING TARGETED BE-CAUSE SOMEONE THINKS THAT HE'S CONNECTED TO THE OTHER THREE...
MY FATHER MUST BE INVOLVED ...
...AND I CANNOT ALLOW THIS TO GO ON.

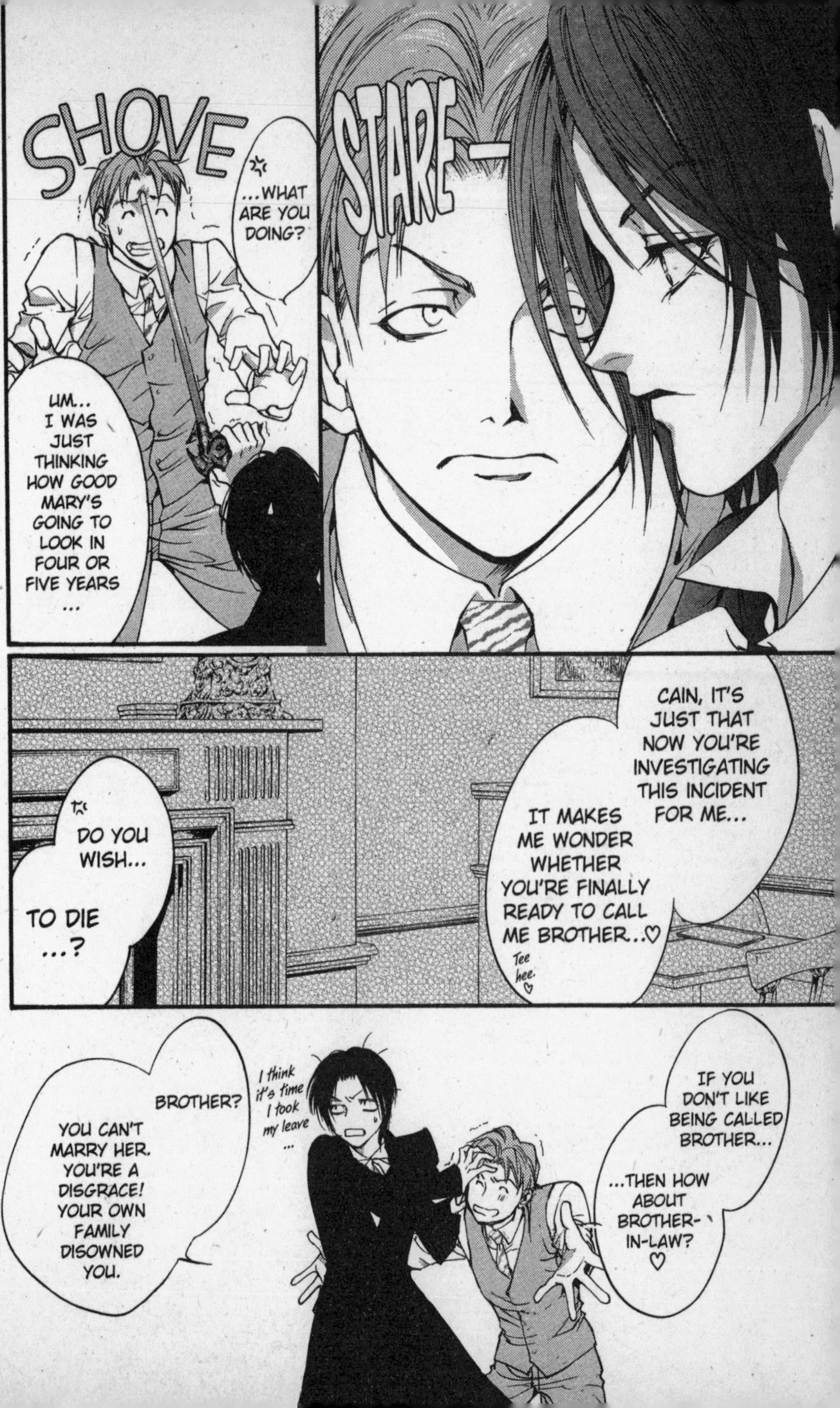
STARE—
...WHAT ARE YOU DOING?
SHOVE
UM... I WAS JUST THINKING HOW GOOD MARY'S GOING TO LOOK IN FOUR OR FIVE YEARS...
CAIN, IT'S JUST THAT NOW YOU'RE INVESTIGATING THIS INCIDENT FOR ME...
IT MAKES ME WONDER WHETHER YOU'RE FINALLY READY TO CALL ME BROTHER..♡
Tee hee.♡
DO YOU WISH...
TO DIE...?
IF YOU DON'T LIKE BEING CALLED BROTHER...
...THEN HOW ABOUT BROTHER-IN-LAW? ♡
I think it's time I took my leave...
BROTHER?
YOU CAN'T MARRY HER. YOU'RE A DISGRACE! YOUR OWN FAMILY DISOWNED YOU.

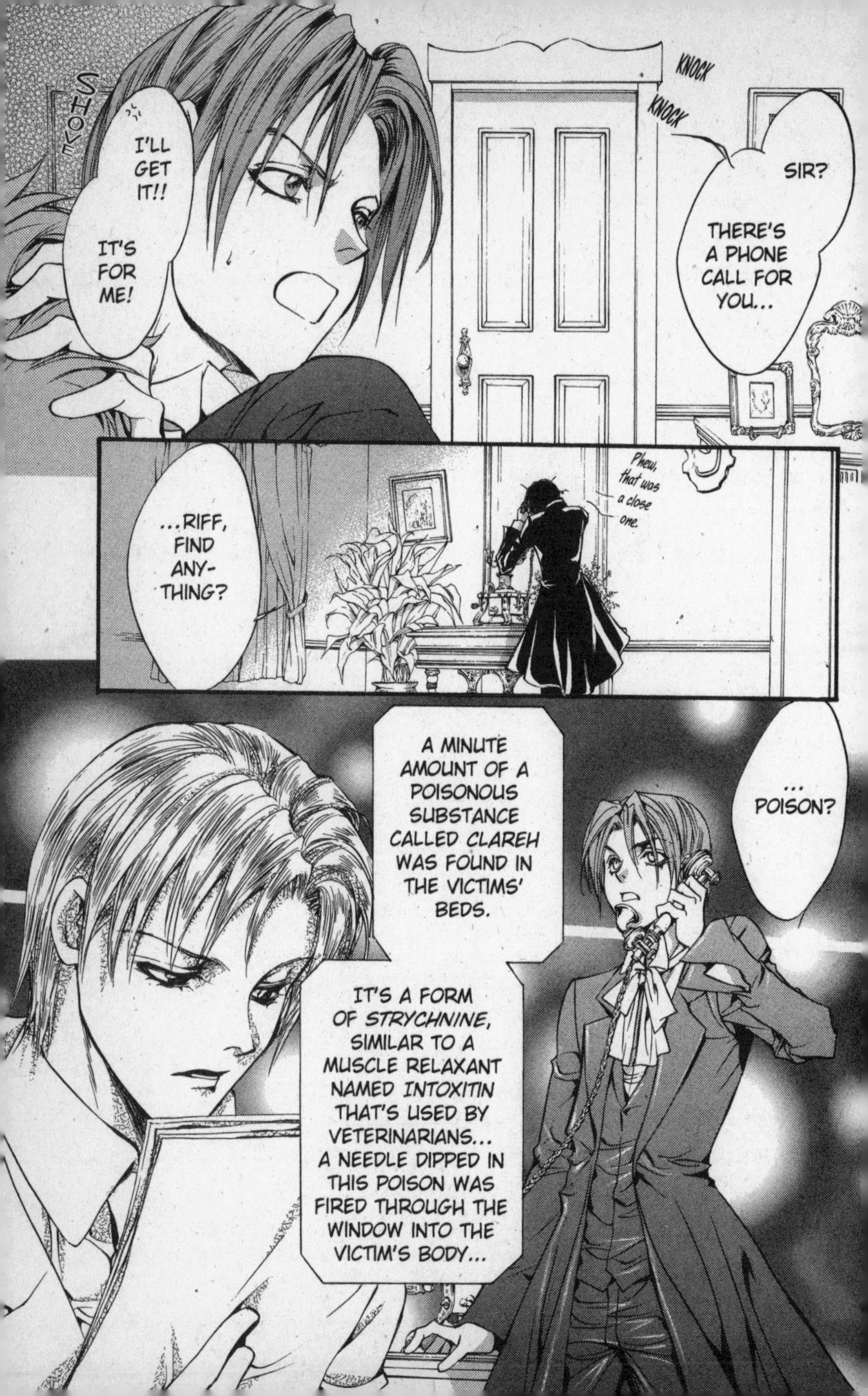
KNOCK
KNOCK
SIR? THERE'S A PHONE CALL FOR YOU...
SHOVE
I'LL GET IT!!
IT'S FOR ME!
Phew, that was a close one.
...RIFF, FIND ANYTHING?
... POISON?
A MINUTE AMOUNT OF A POISONOUS SUBSTANCE CALLED *CLAREH* WAS FOUND IN THE VICTIMS' BEDS.
IT'S A FORM OF *STRYCHNINE*, SIMILAR TO A MUSCLE RELAXANT NAMED *INTOXITIN* THAT'S USED BY VETERINARIANS... A NEEDLE DIPPED IN THIS POISON WAS FIRED THROUGH THE WINDOW INTO THE VICTIM'S BODY...

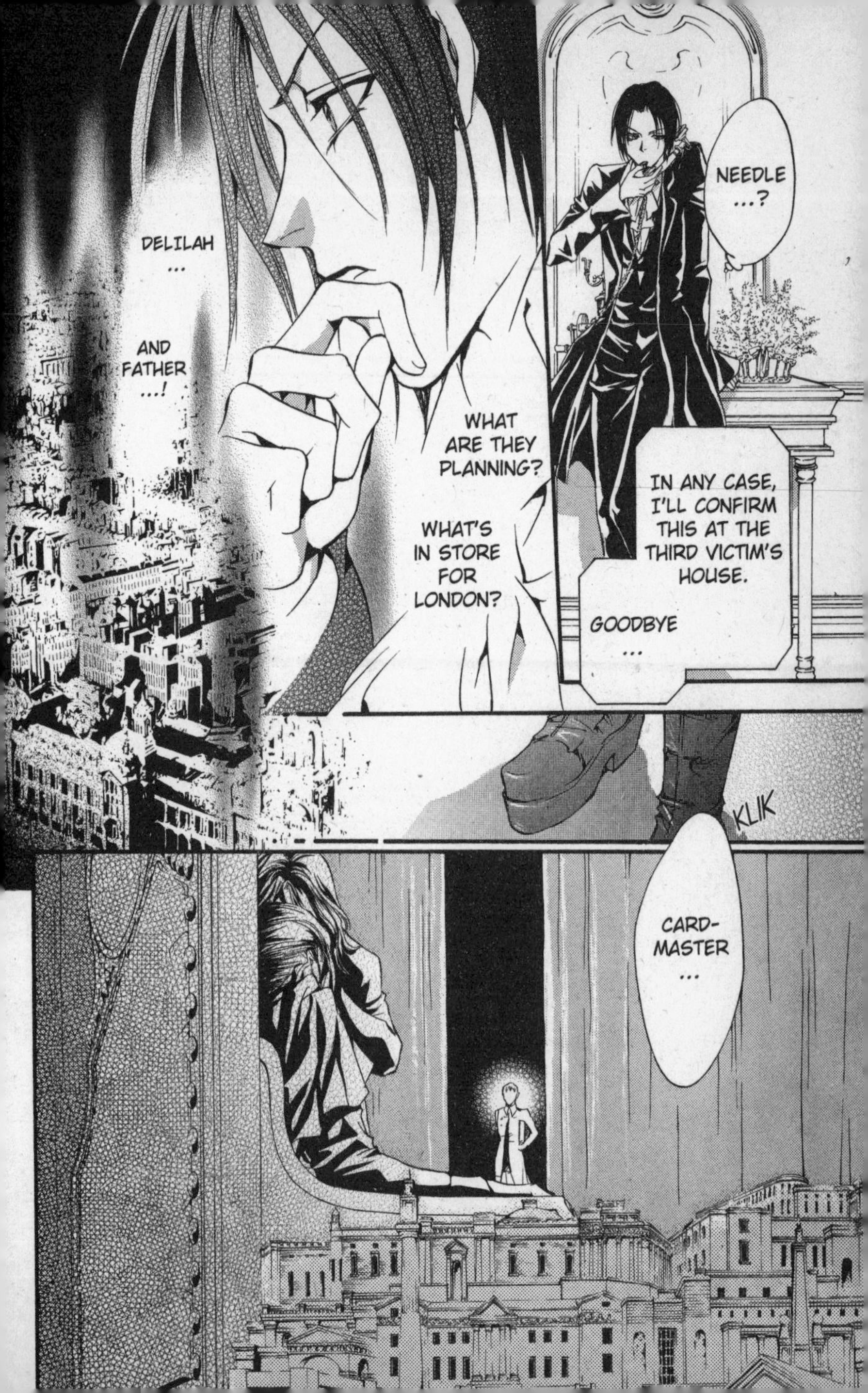
NEEDLE ...?
IN ANY CASE, I'LL CONFIRM THIS AT THE THIRD VICTIM'S HOUSE.
GOODBYE ...
KLIK
DELILAH ...
AND FATHER ...!
WHAT ARE THEY PLANNING?
WHAT'S IN STORE FOR LONDON?
CARD-MASTER ...

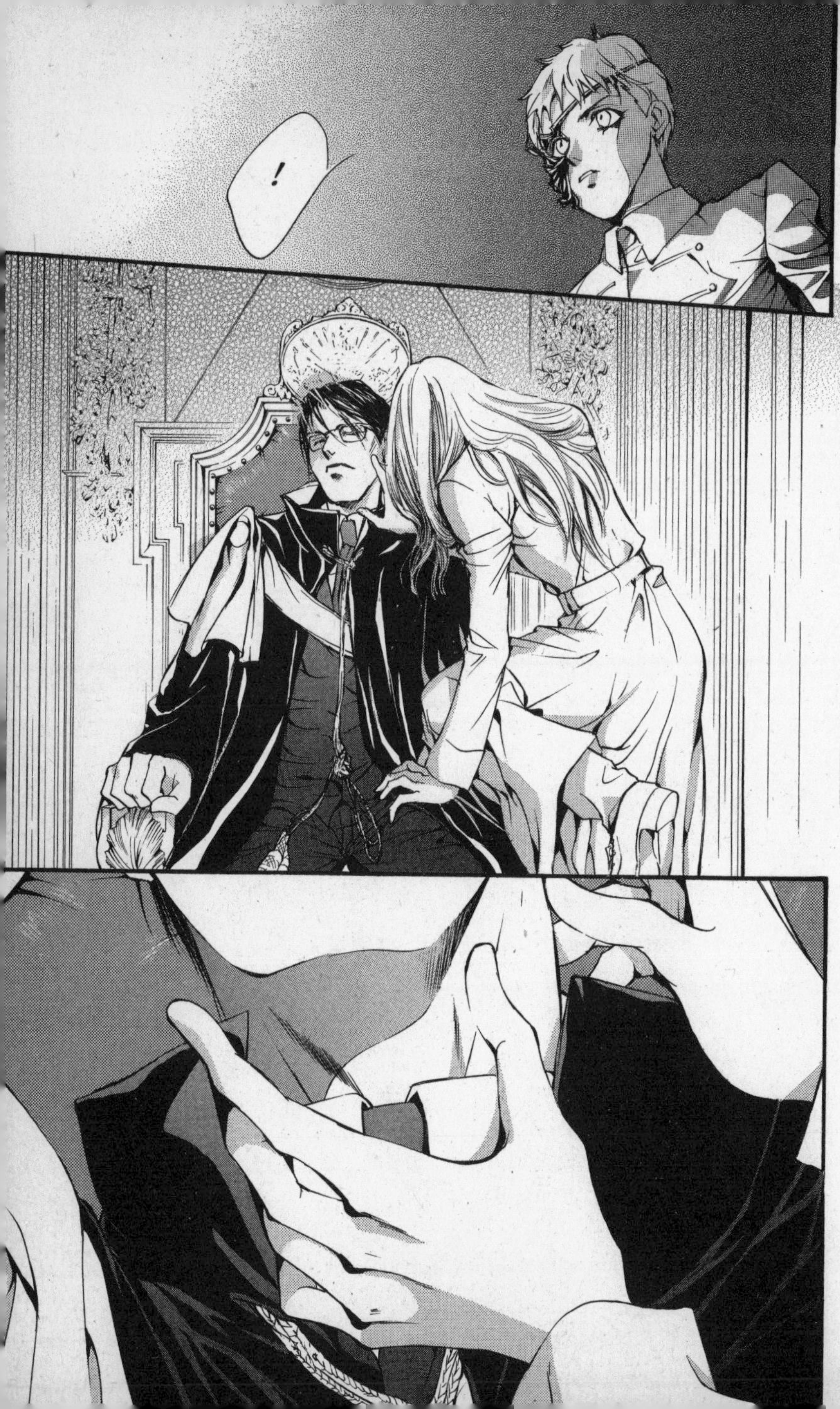
!

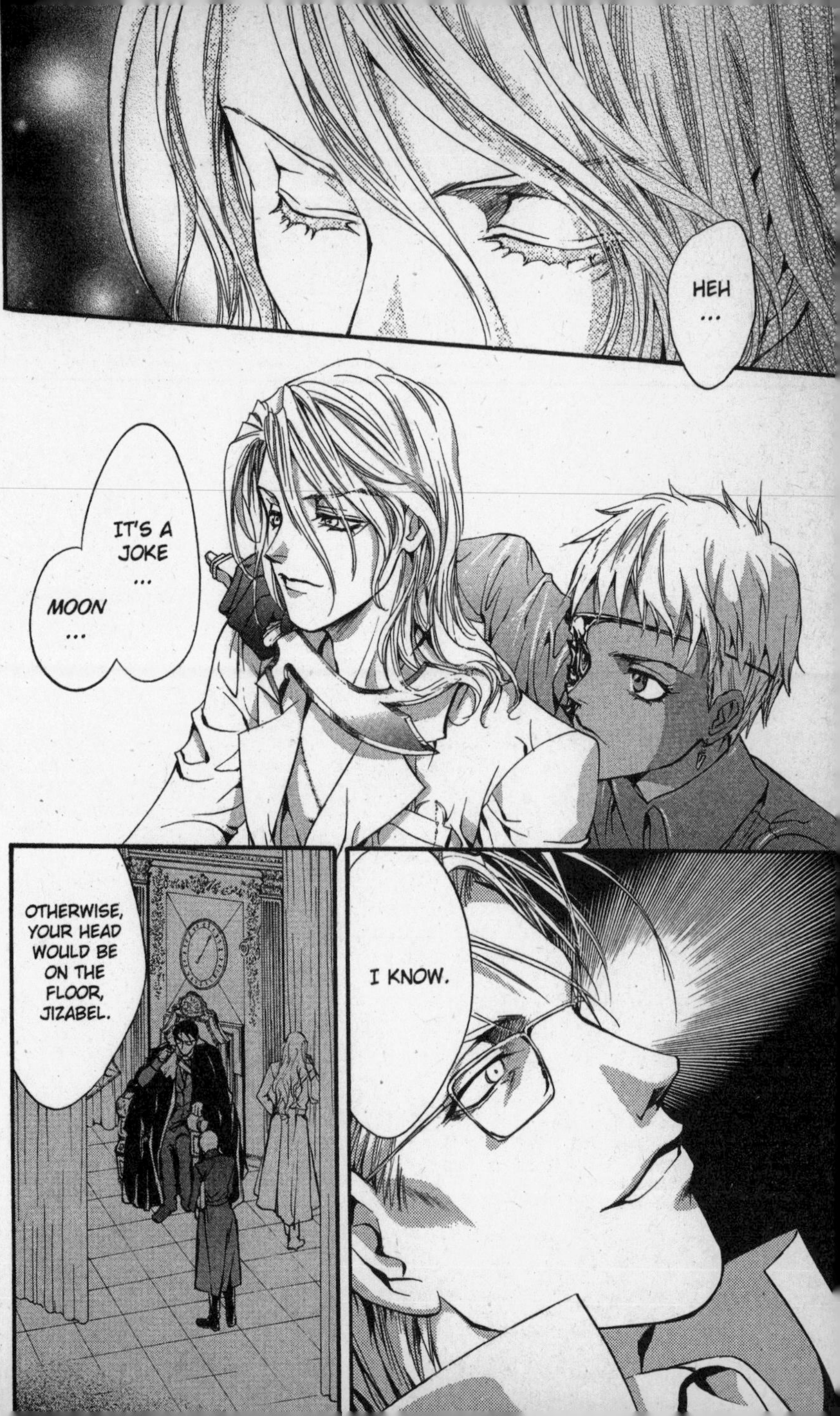
HEH ...
IT'S A JOKE ... MOON ...
I KNOW.
OTHERWISE, YOUR HEAD WOULD BE ON THE FLOOR, JIZABEL.

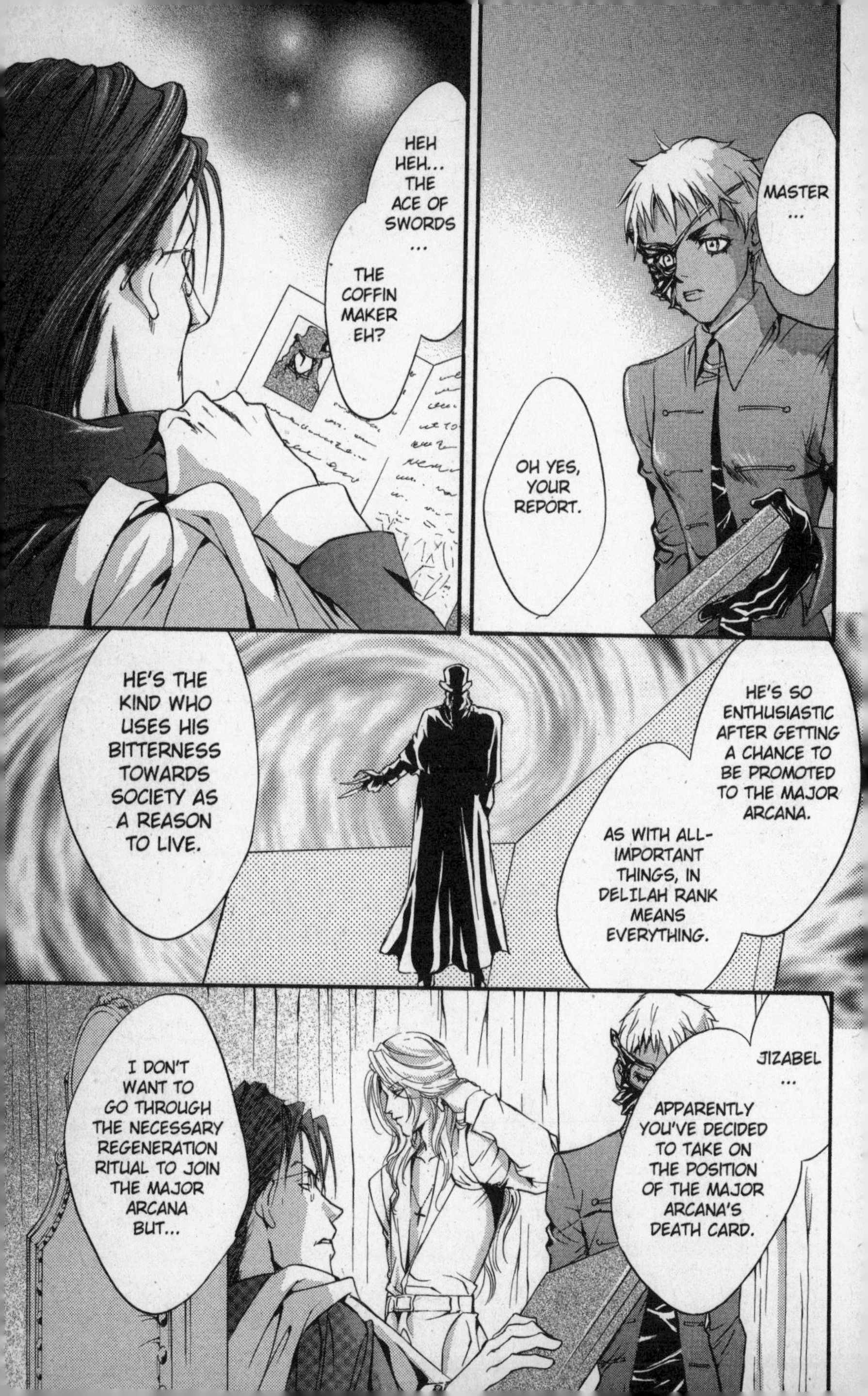
MASTER ...
OH YES, YOUR REPORT.
HEH HEH... THE ACE OF SWORDS ...
THE COFFIN MAKER EH?
HE'S SO ENTHUSIASTIC AFTER GETTING A CHANCE TO BE PROMOTED TO THE MAJOR ARCANA.
AS WITH ALL-IMPORTANT THINGS, IN DELILAH RANK MEANS EVERYTHING.
HE'S THE KIND WHO USES HIS BITTERNESS TOWARDS SOCIETY AS A REASON TO LIVE.
JIZABEL ...
APPARENTLY YOU'VE DECIDED TO TAKE ON THE POSITION OF THE MAJOR ARCANA'S DEATH CARD.
I DON'T WANT TO GO THROUGH THE NECESSARY REGENERATION RITUAL TO JOIN THE MAJOR ARCANA BUT...

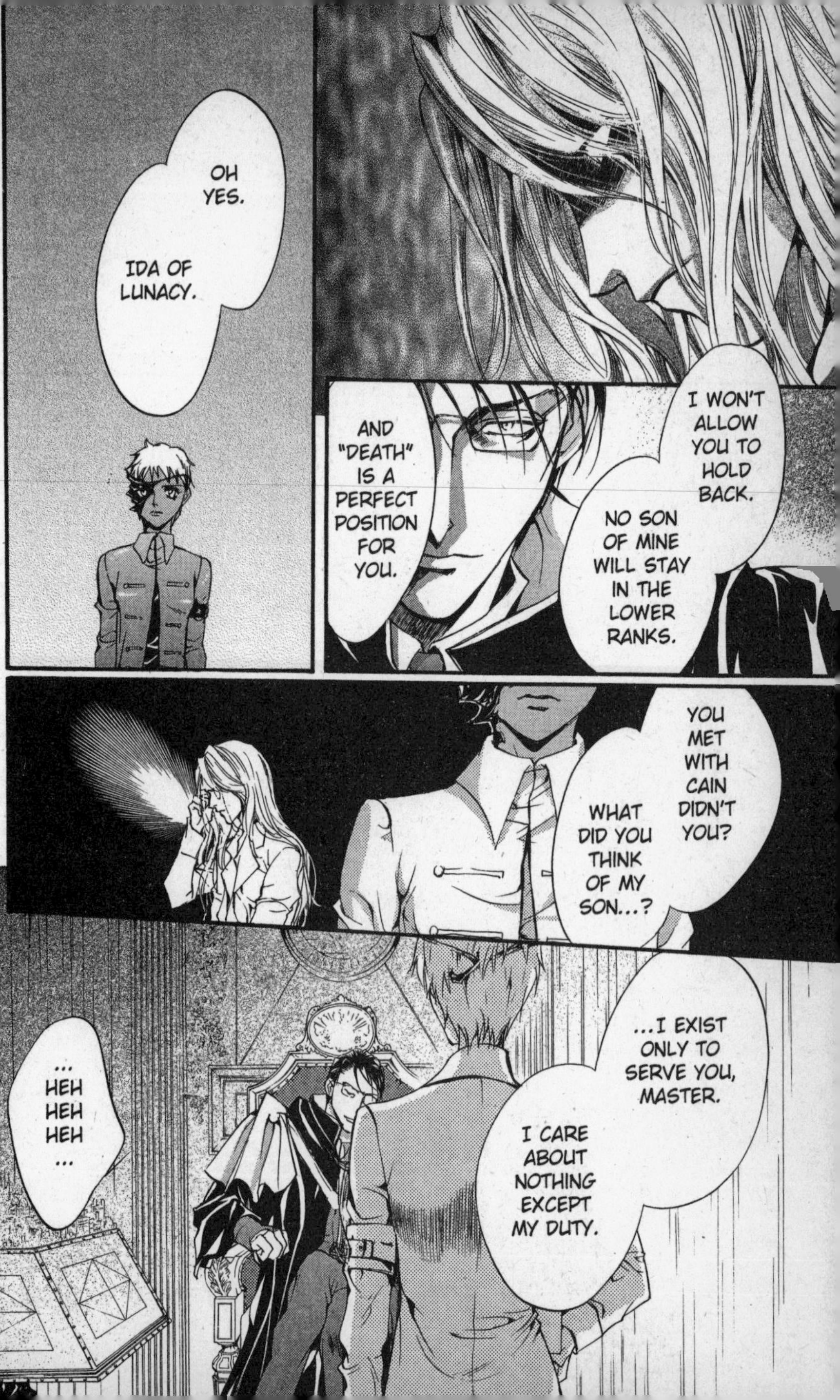
I WON'T ALLOW YOU TO HOLD BACK.
NO SON OF MINE WILL STAY IN THE LOWER RANKS.
AND "DEATH" IS A PERFECT POSITION FOR YOU.
OH YES.
IDA OF LUNACY.
YOU MET WITH CAIN DIDN'T YOU?
WHAT DID YOU THINK OF MY SON...?
...I EXIST ONLY TO SERVE YOU, MASTER.
I CARE ABOUT NOTHING EXCEPT MY DUTY.
...HEH HEH HEH...

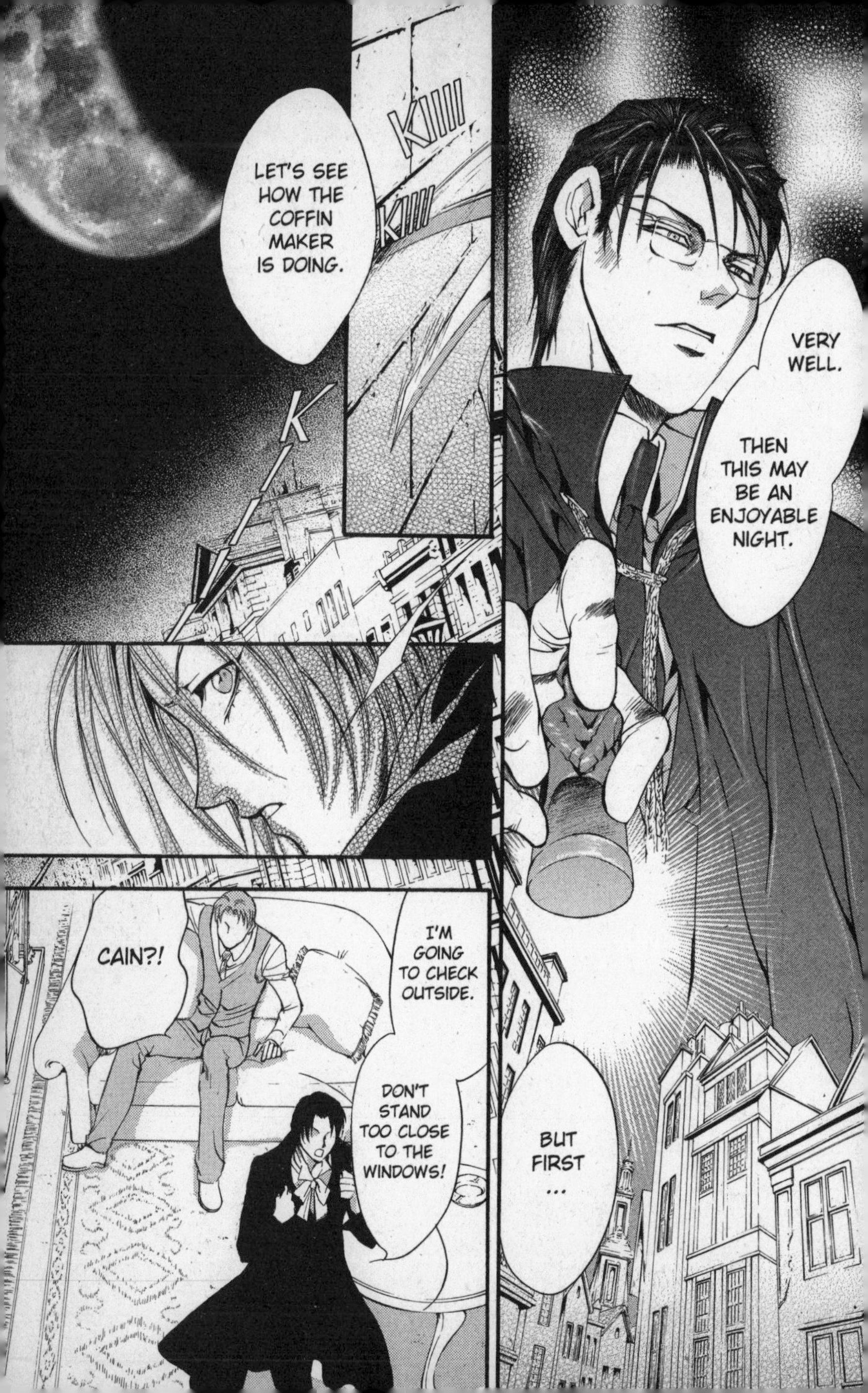
VERY WELL.
THEN THIS MAY BE AN ENJOYABLE NIGHT.
BUT FIRST ...
KIIII
KIIII
K
LET'S SEE HOW THE COFFIN MAKER IS DOING.
I'M GOING TO CHECK OUTSIDE.
DON'T STAND TOO CLOSE TO THE WINDOWS!
CAIN?!

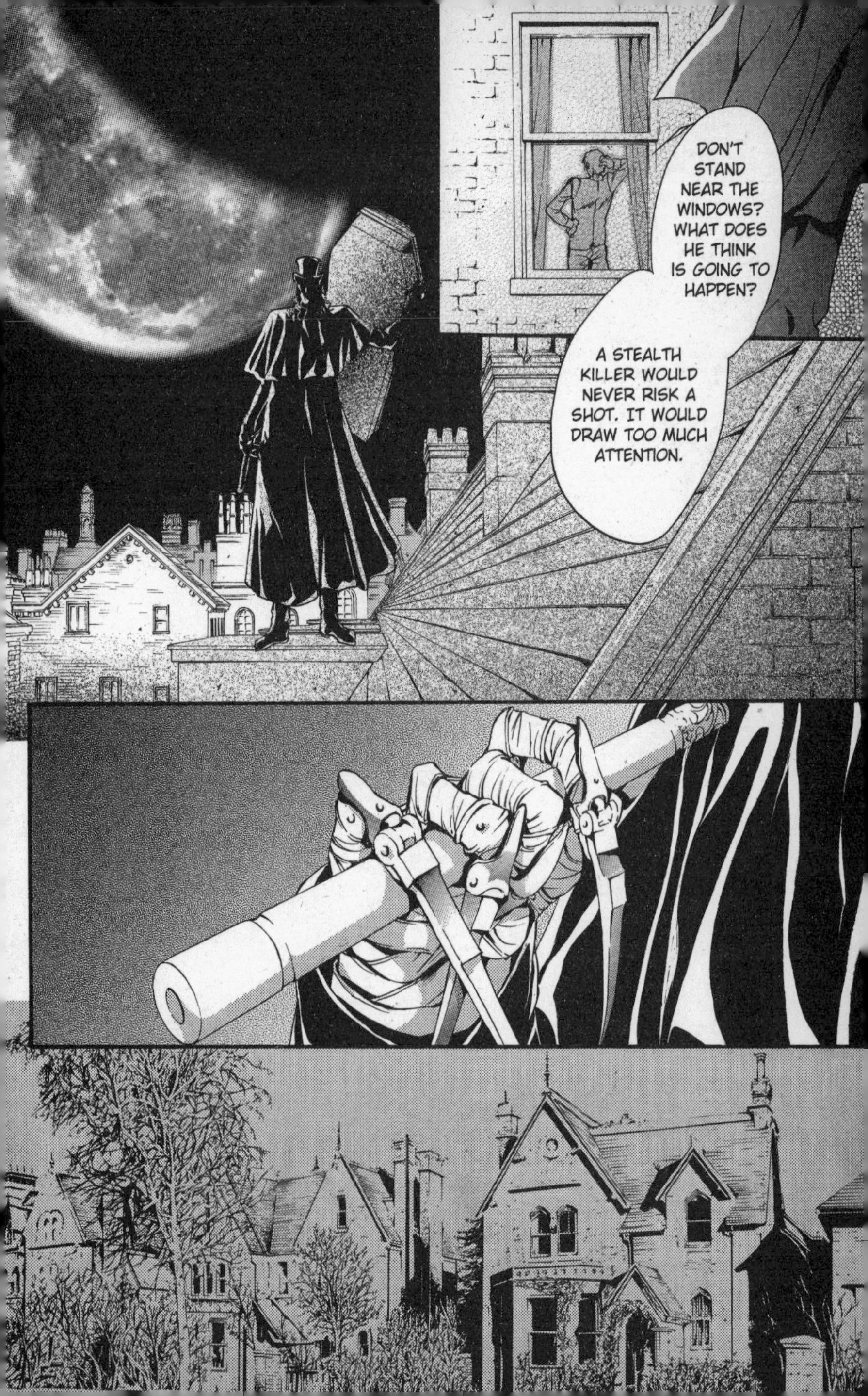
DON'T STAND NEAR THE WINDOWS? WHAT DOES HE THINK IS GOING TO HAPPEN?
A STEALTH KILLER WOULD NEVER RISK A SHOT. IT WOULD DRAW TOO MUCH ATTENTION.

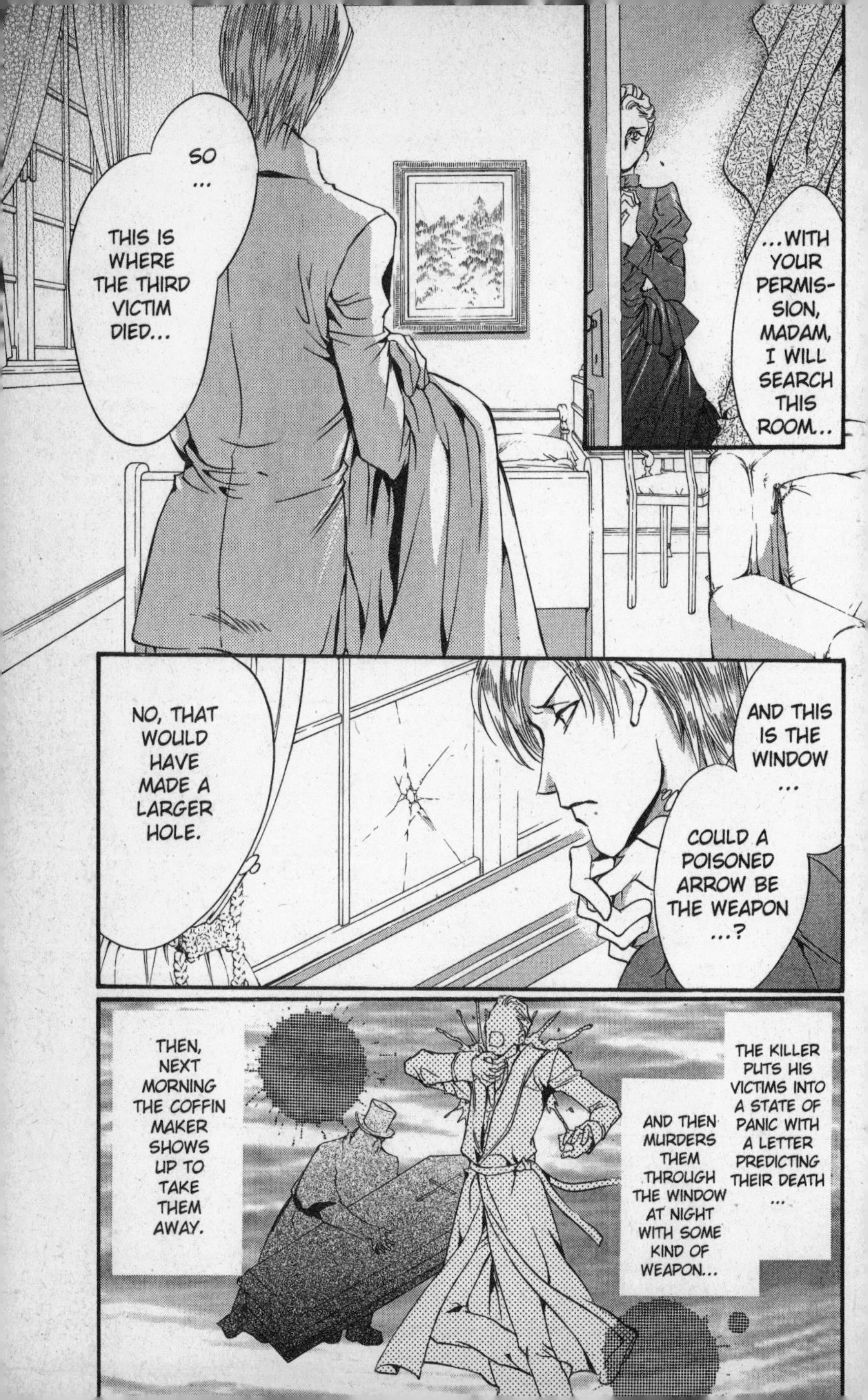
...WITH YOUR PERMISSION, MADAM, I WILL SEARCH THIS ROOM...
SO ...
THIS IS WHERE THE THIRD VICTIM DIED...
AND THIS IS THE WINDOW ...
COULD A POISONED ARROW BE THE WEAPON ...?
NO, THAT WOULD HAVE MADE A LARGER HOLE.
THE KILLER PUTS HIS VICTIMS INTO A STATE OF PANIC WITH A LETTER PREDICTING THEIR DEATH ...
AND THEN MURDERS THEM THROUGH THE WINDOW AT NIGHT WITH SOME KIND OF WEAPON...
THEN, NEXT MORNING THE COFFIN MAKER SHOWS UP TO TAKE THEM AWAY.

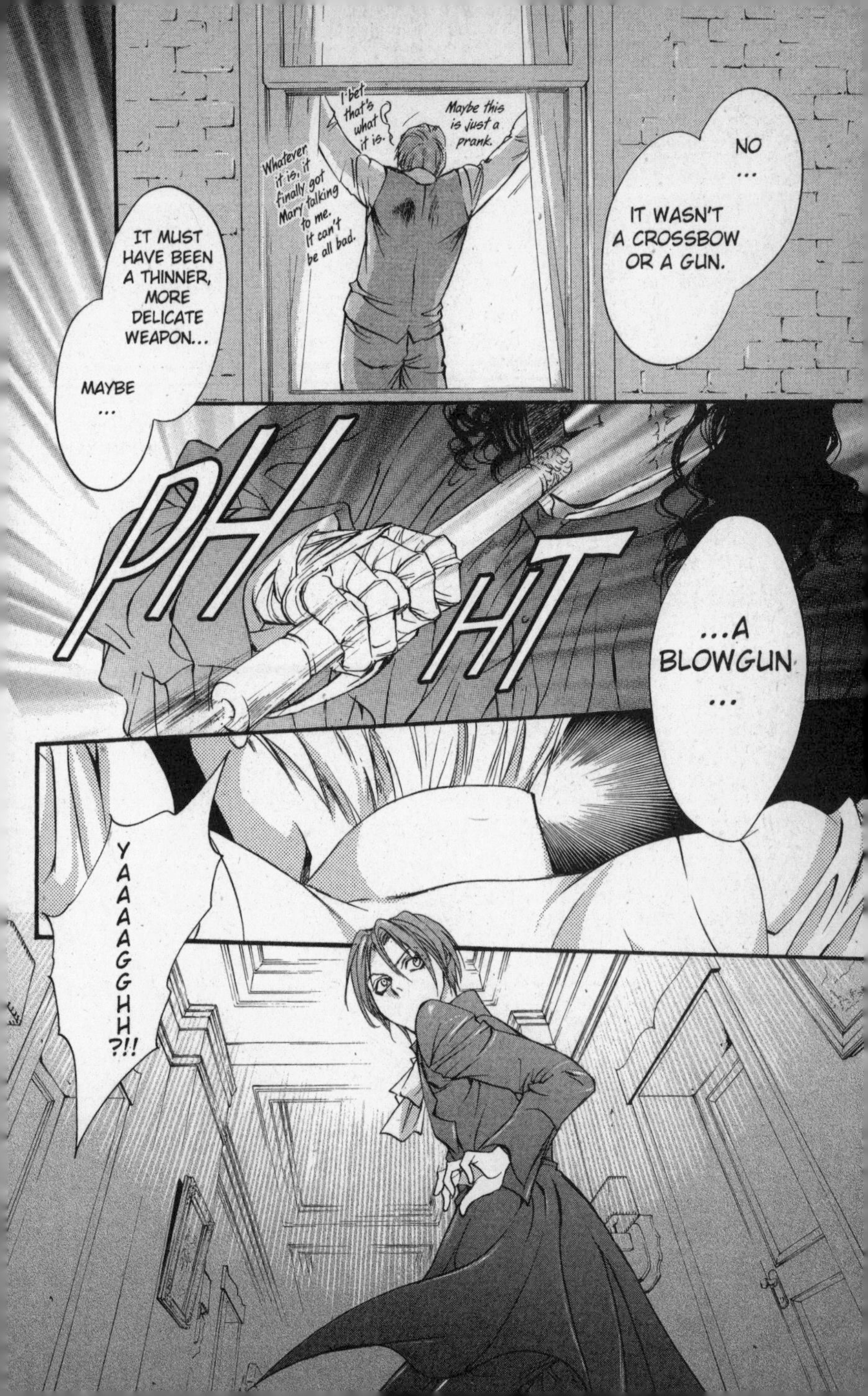
NO ...
IT WASN'T A CROSSBOW OR A GUN.
Maybe this is just a prank.
I bet that's what it is.
Whatever it is, it finally got Mary talking to me. It can't be all bad.
IT MUST HAVE BEEN A THINNER, MORE DELICATE WEAPON...
MAYBE ...
...A BLOWGUN ...
PHHT
YAAAAAGGHH?!!

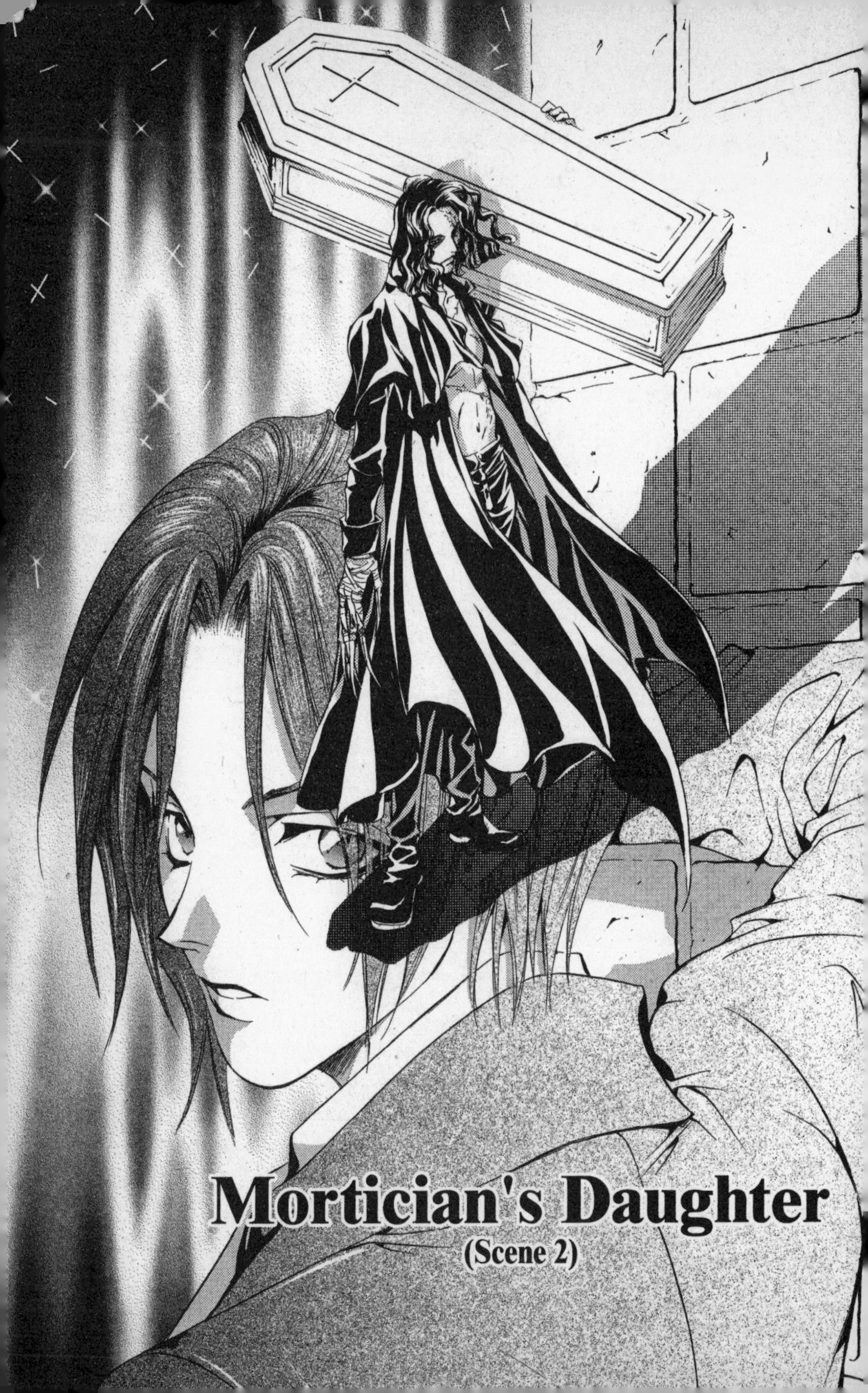
Mortician's Daughter
(Scene 2)

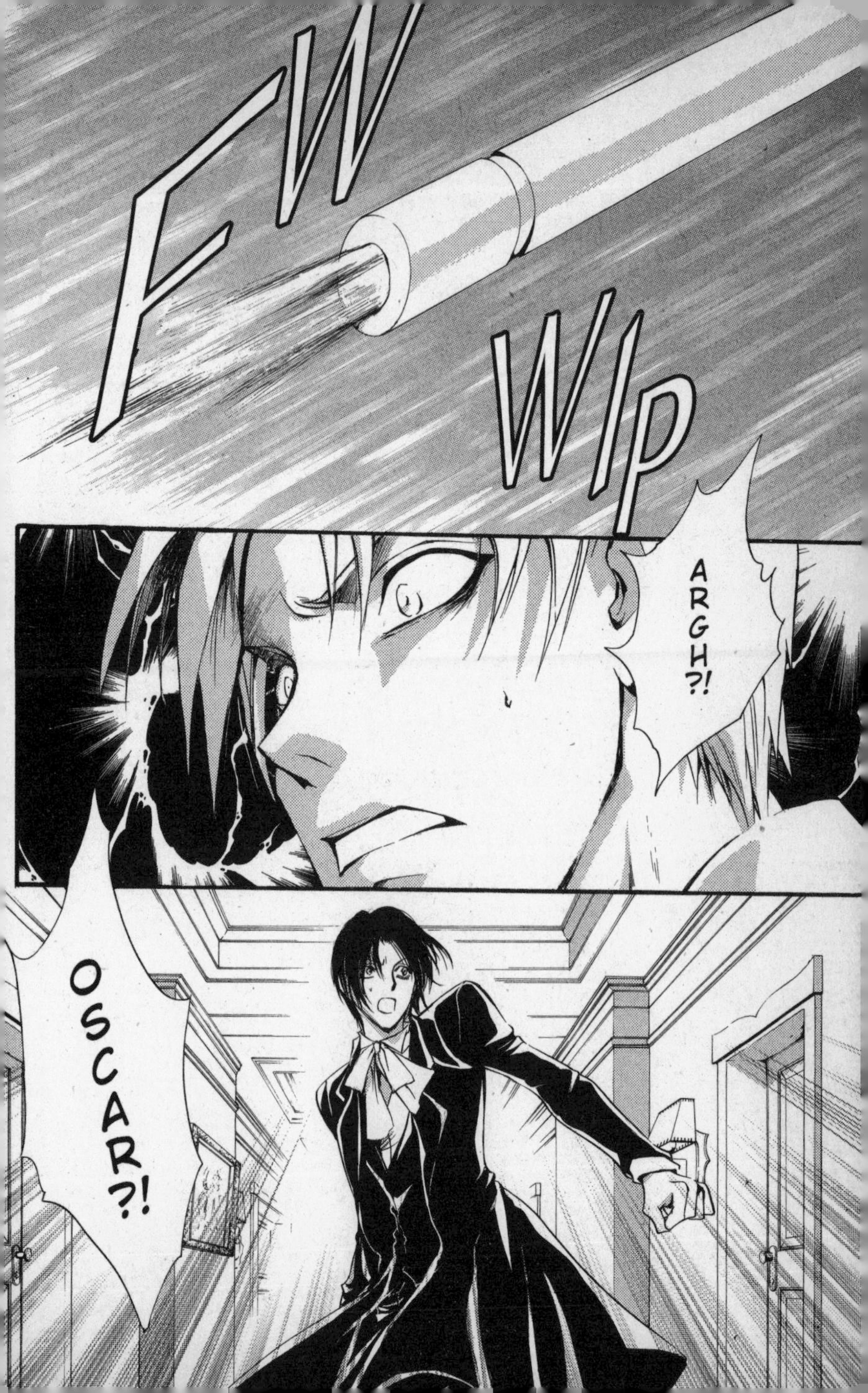
FWWIP
ARGH?!
OSCAR?!

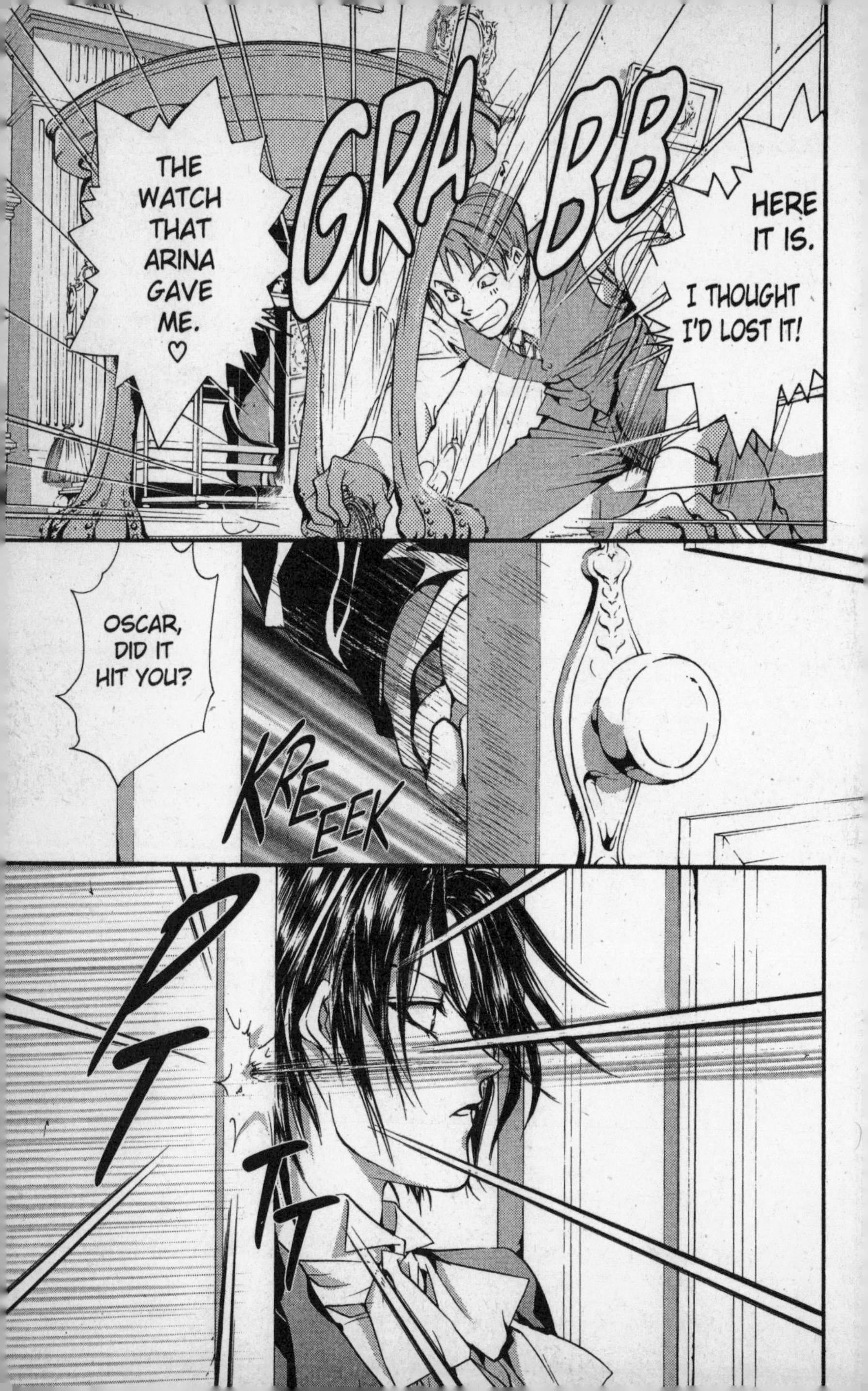
HERE IT IS.
I THOUGHT I'D LOST IT!
GRABB
THE WATCH THAT ARINA GAVE ME. ♡
KREEEK
OSCAR, DID IT HIT YOU?
PTTT

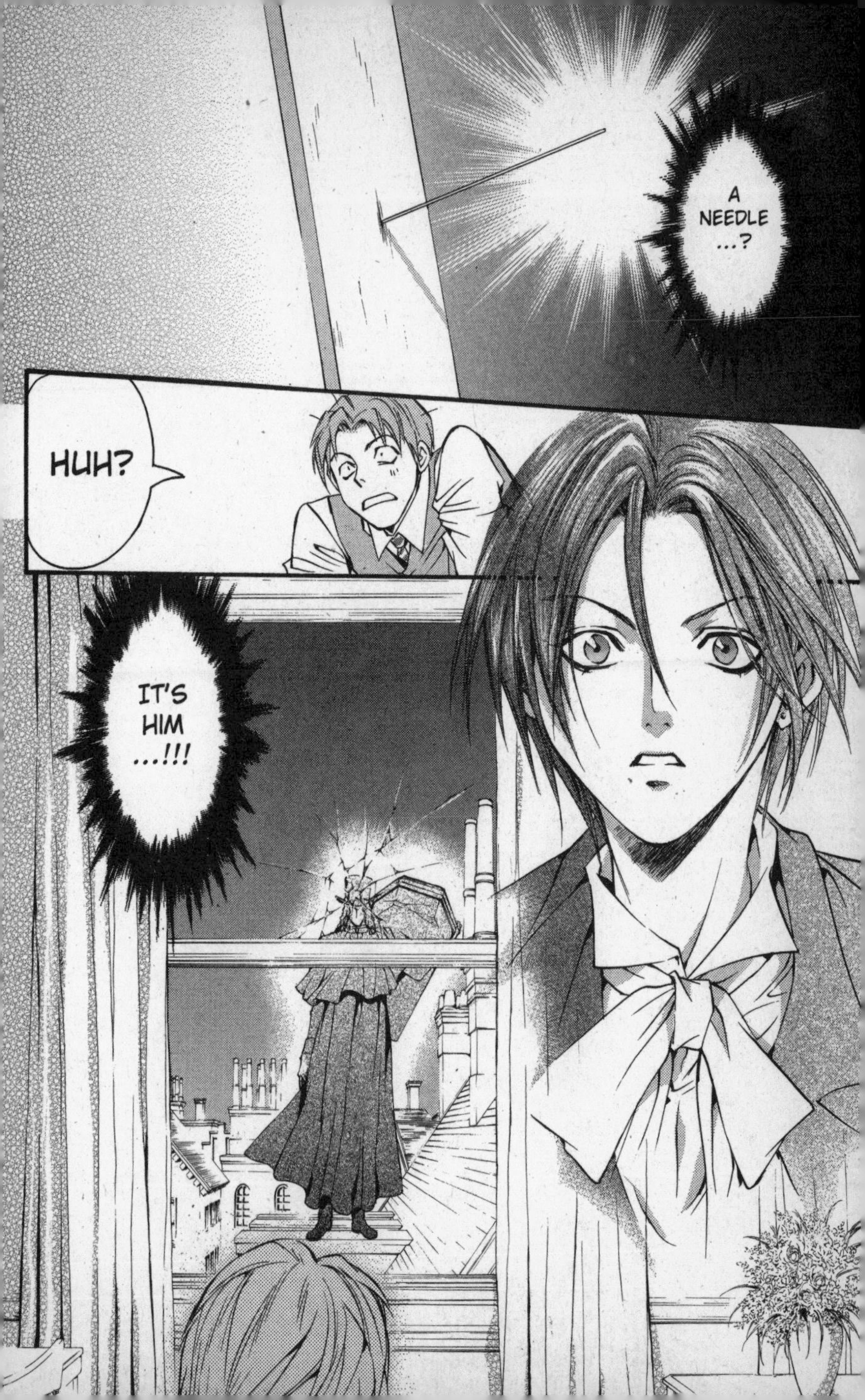
A NEEDLE ...?
HUH?
IT'S HIM ...!!!

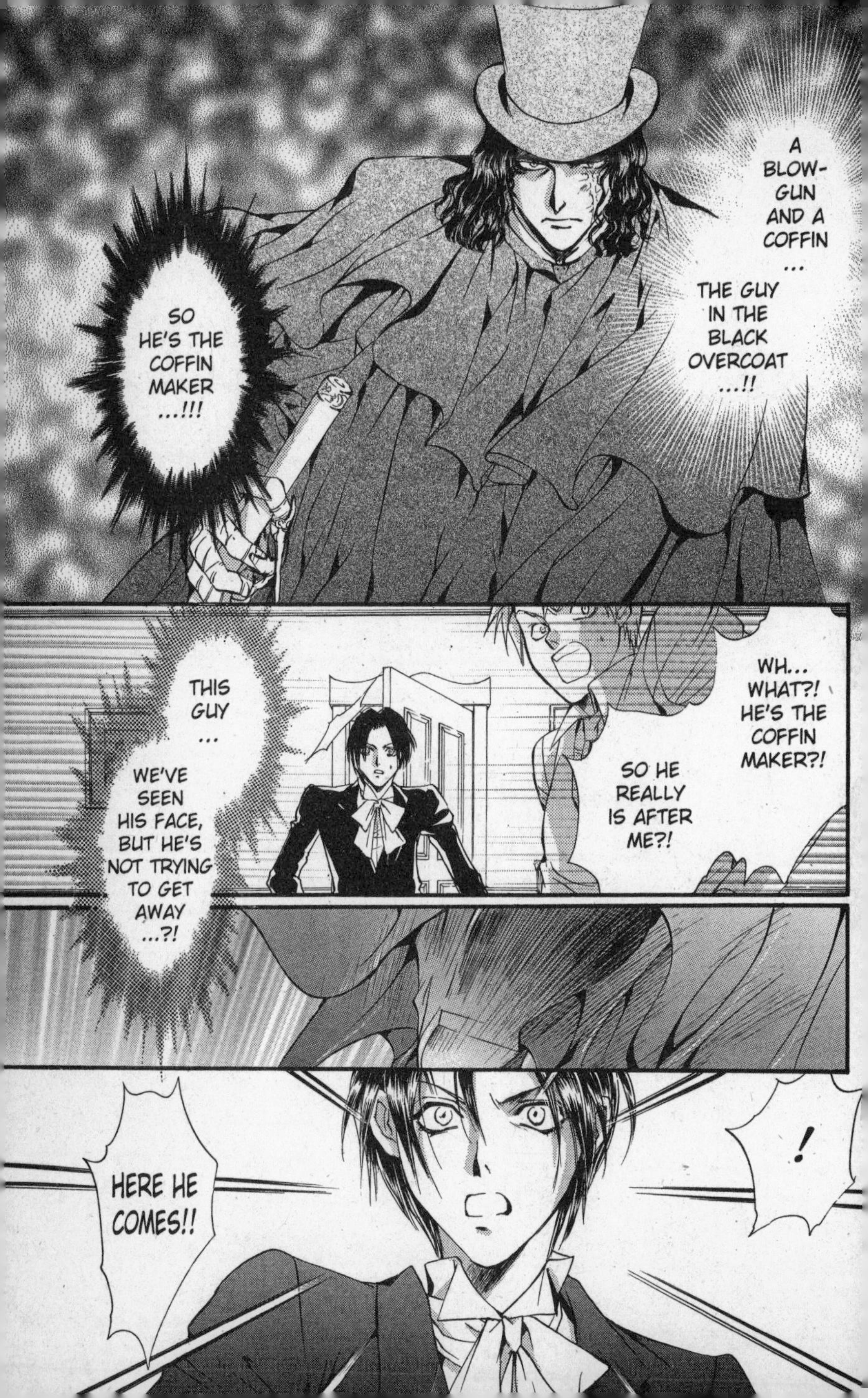
A BLOW-GUN AND A COFFIN ...
THE GUY IN THE BLACK OVERCOAT ...!!
SO HE'S THE COFFIN MAKER ...!!!
WH... WHAT?! HE'S THE COFFIN MAKER?!
SO HE REALLY IS AFTER ME?!
THIS GUY ...
WE'VE SEEN HIS FACE, BUT HE'S NOT TRYING TO GET AWAY ...?!
!
HERE HE COMES!!

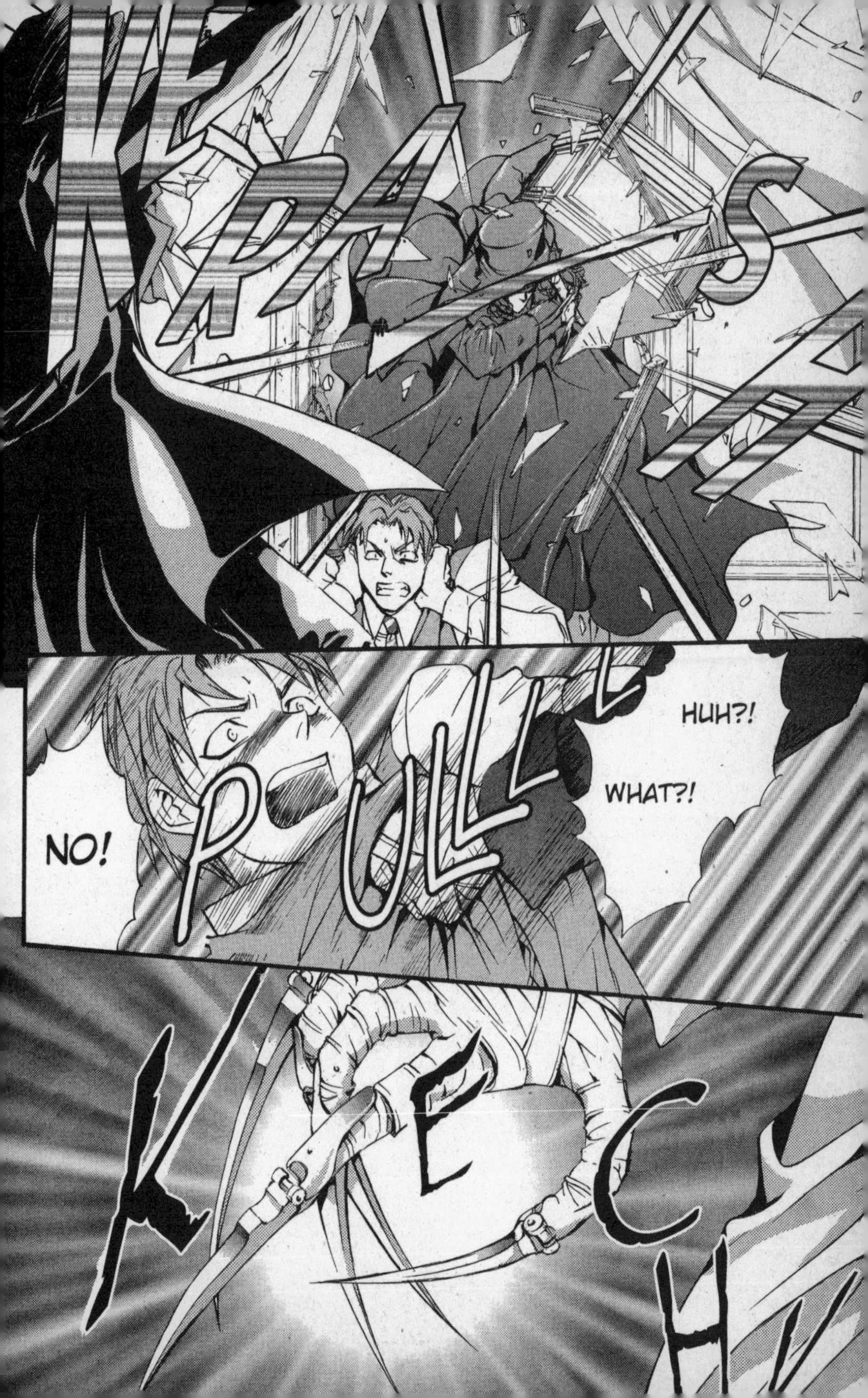
HUH?!
WHAT?!
PULL
NO!

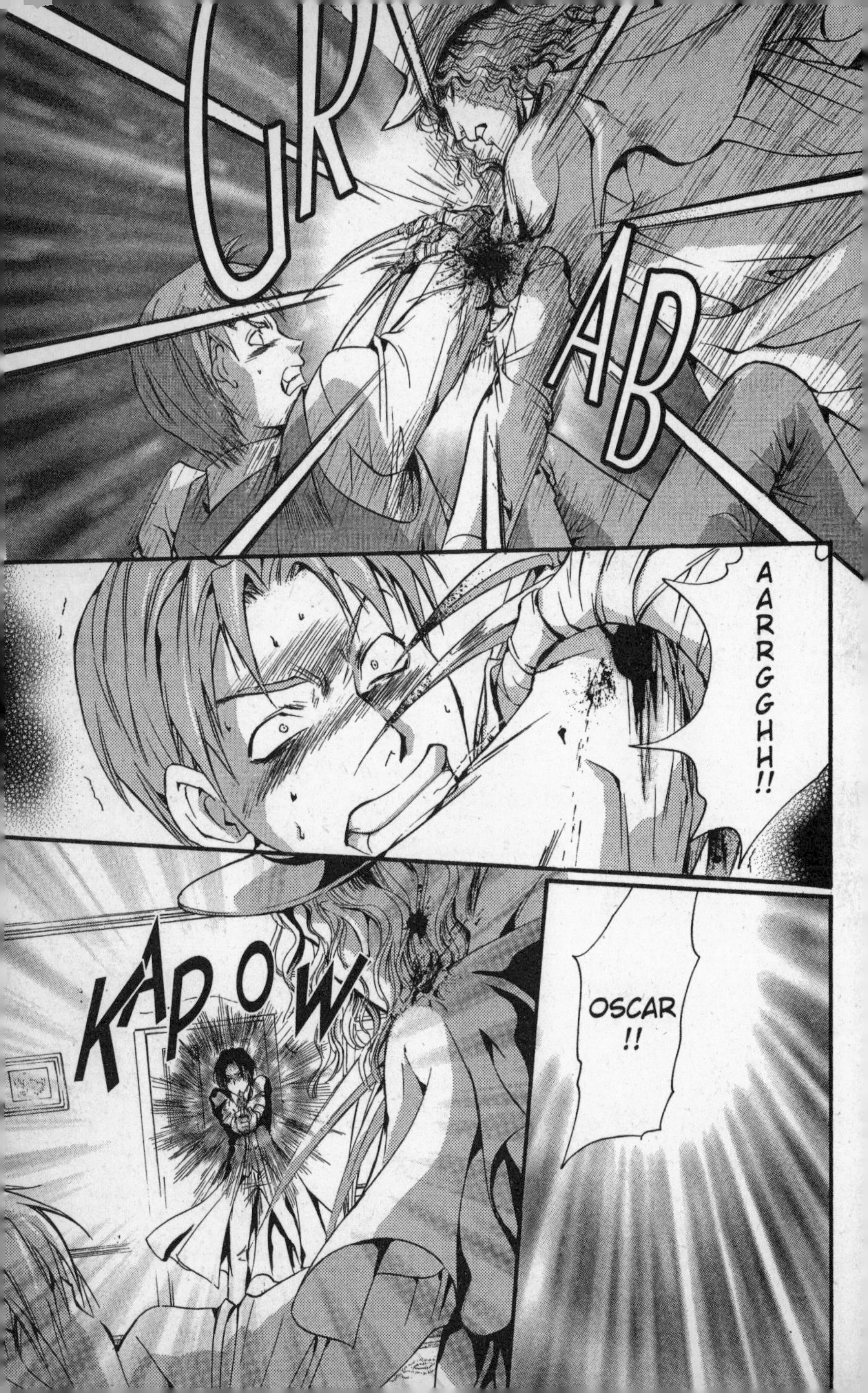
GRAB
AARRGGHH!!
OSCAR!!
KAPOW

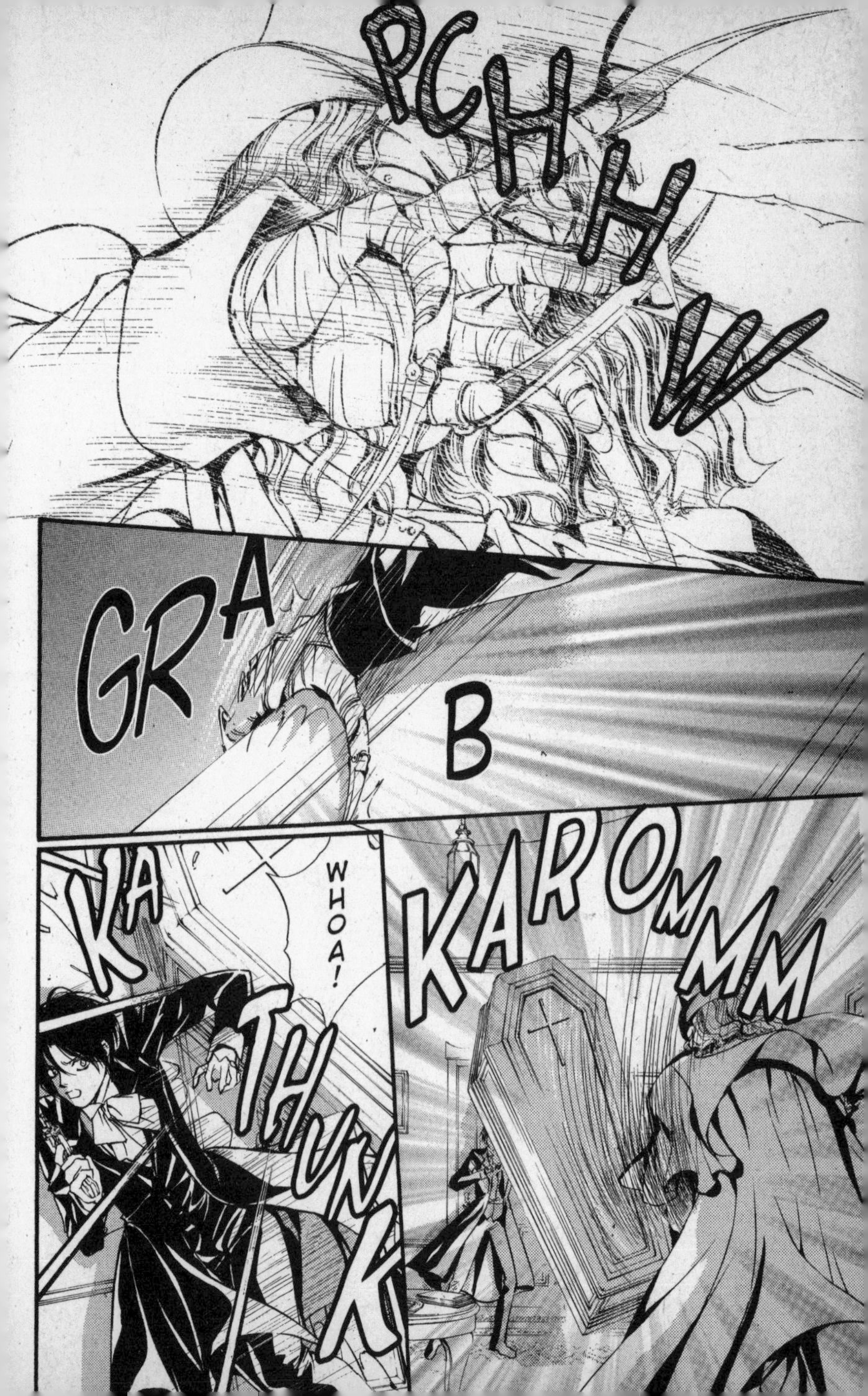
PCHHHW
GRAB
KAROMMM
WHOA!
KATHUNK

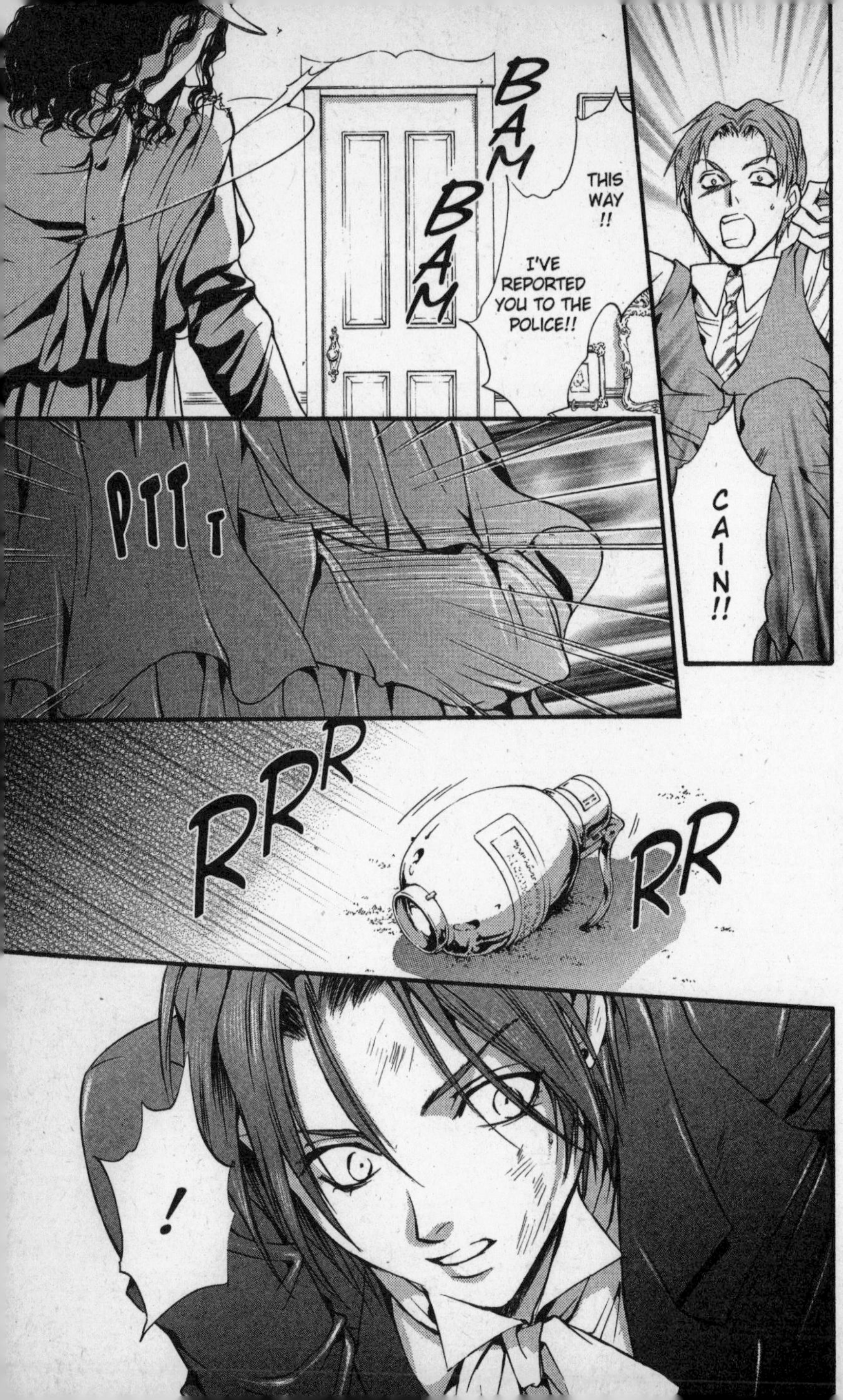
CAIN!!
THIS WAY!!
BAM BAM
I'VE REPORTED YOU TO THE POLICE!!
PTTT T
RRR
RR
!

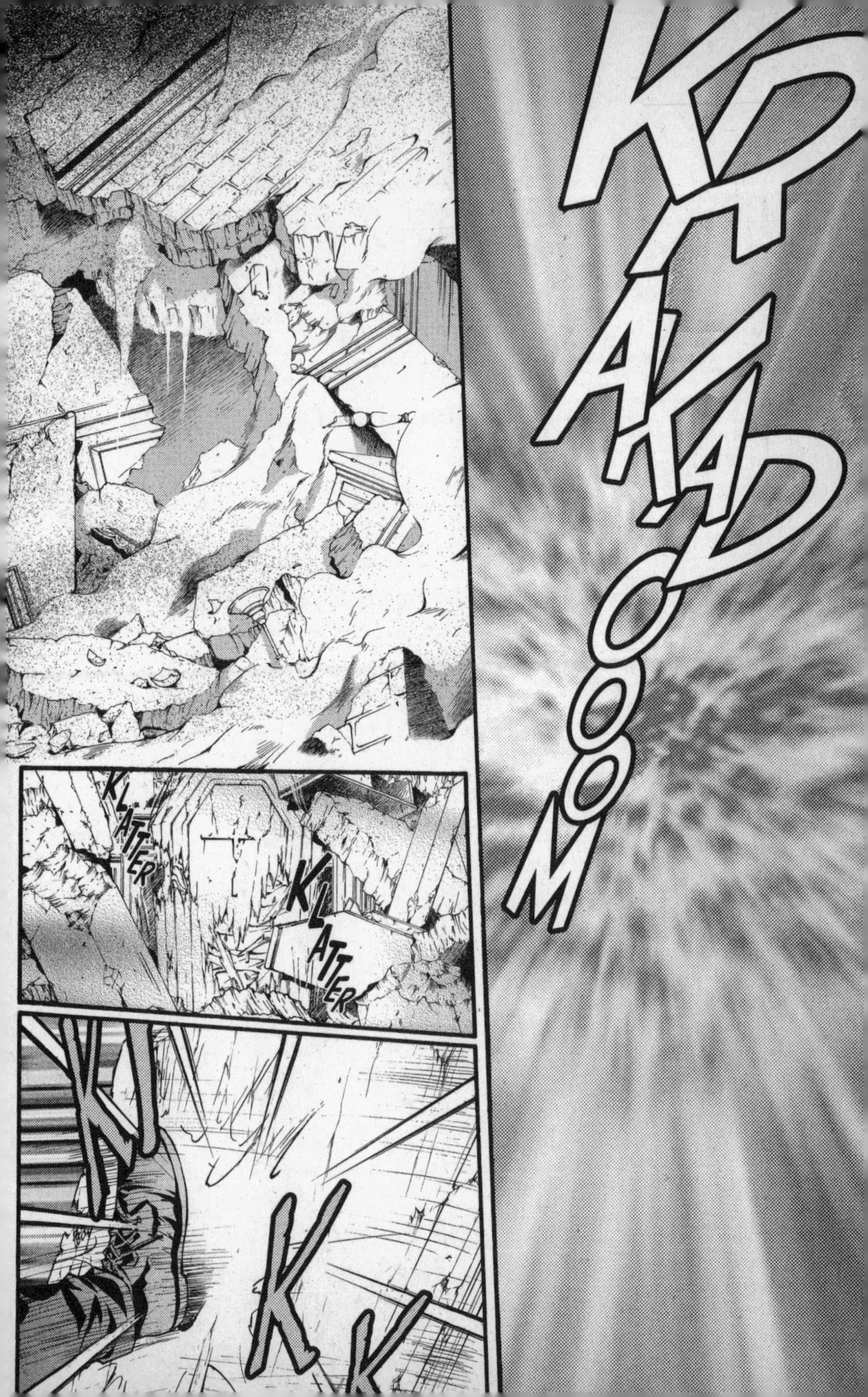
KRAKADOOOOM
KLATTER
KLATTER
K K K K

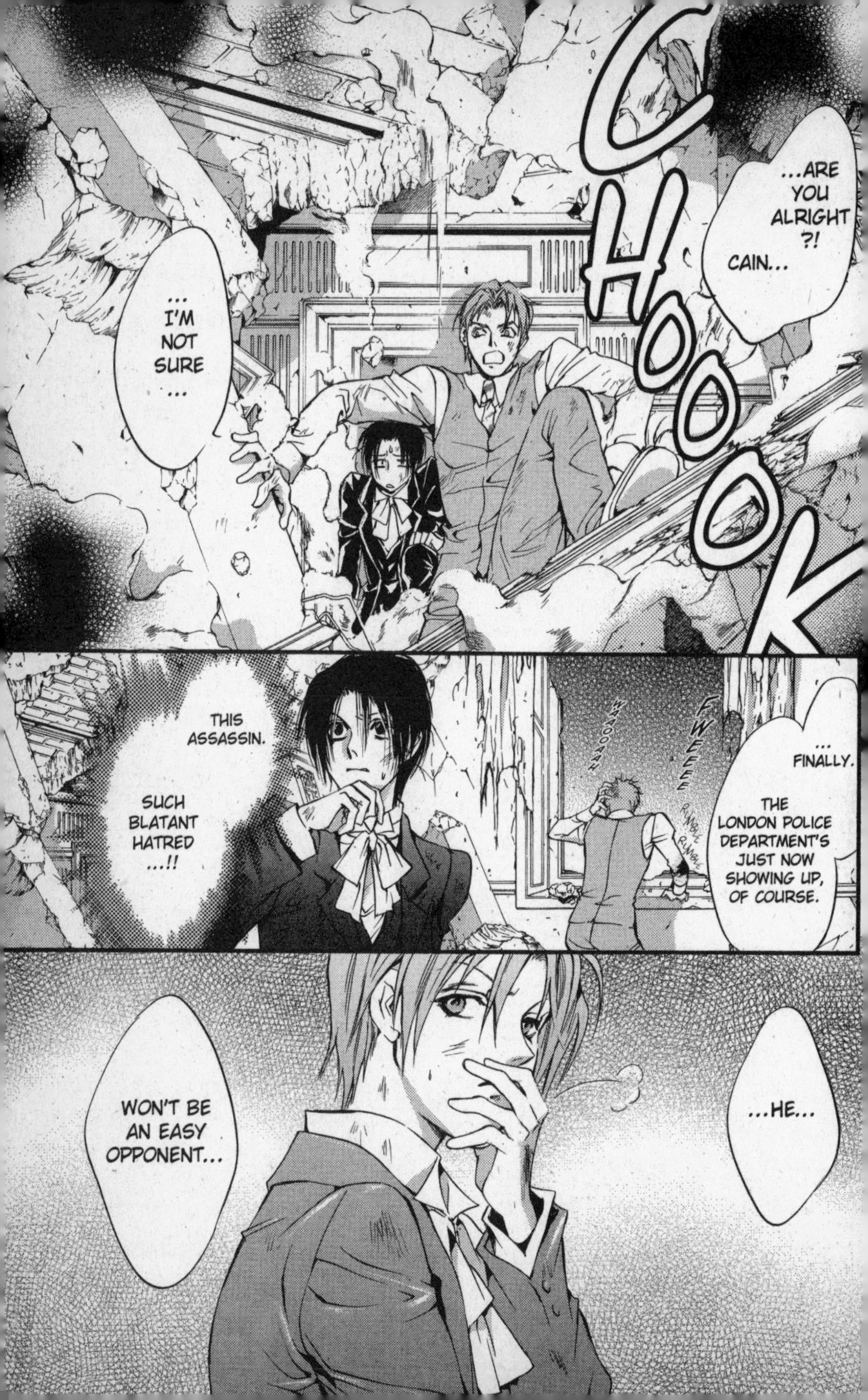
CHOOOOK
...ARE YOU ALRIGHT ?! CAIN...
... I'M NOT SURE ...
... FINALLY. THE LONDON POLICE DEPARTMENT'S JUST NOW SHOWING UP, OF COURSE.
FWEEEEE
RUMBLE RUMBLE
THIS ASSASSIN.
SUCH BLATANT HATRED ...!!
...HE...
WON'T BE AN EASY OPPONENT...

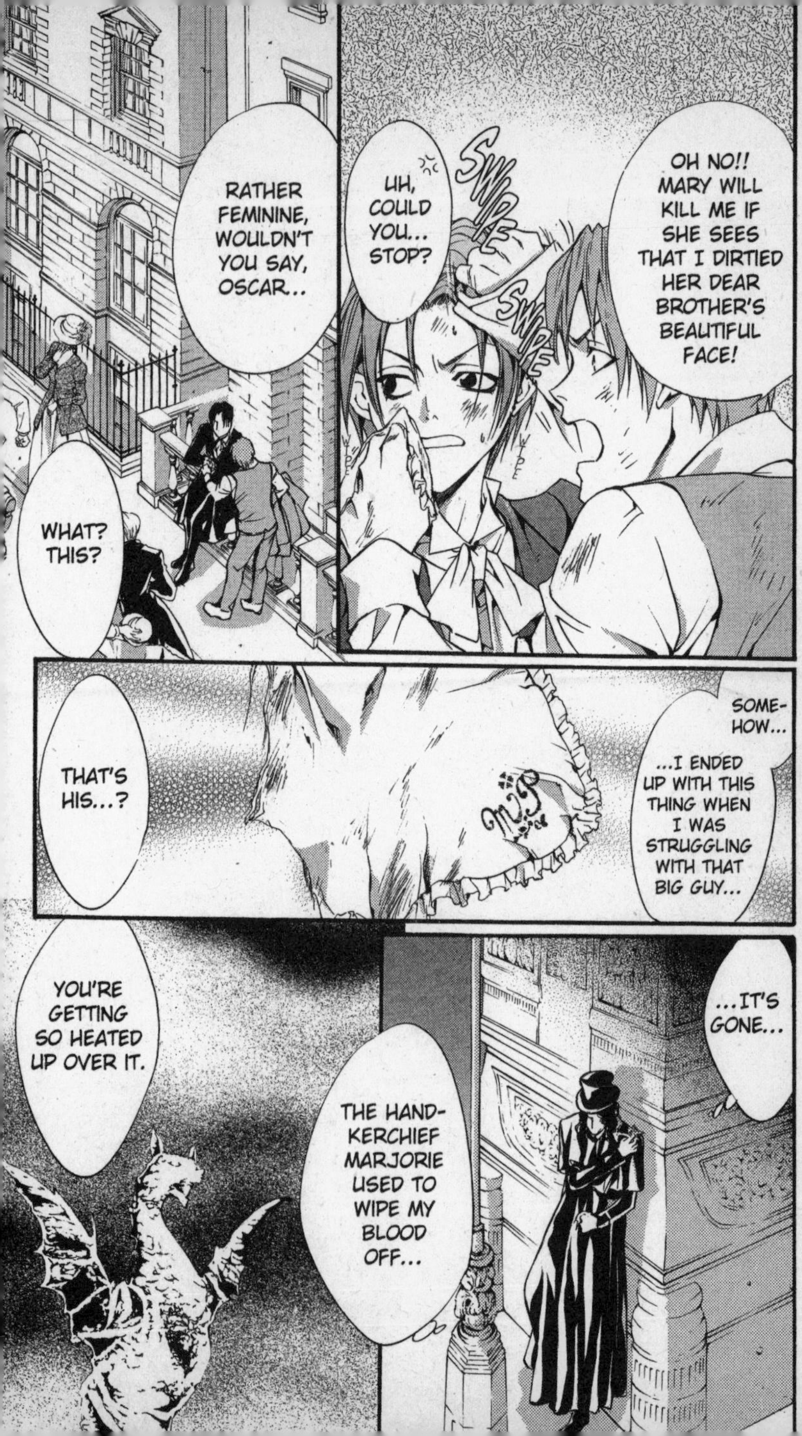
OH NO!! MARY WILL KILL ME IF SHE SEES THAT I DIRTIED HER DEAR BROTHER'S BEAUTIFUL FACE!
SWIPE
SWIPE
UH, COULD YOU... STOP?
WIPE
WIPE
RATHER FEMININE, WOULDN'T YOU SAY, OSCAR...
WHAT? THIS?
SOME-HOW...
...I ENDED UP WITH THIS THING WHEN I WAS STRUGGLING WITH THAT BIG GUY...
THAT'S HIS...?
...IT'S GONE...
THE HAND-KERCHIEF MARJORIE USED TO WIPE MY BLOOD OFF...
YOU'RE GETTING SO HEATED UP OVER IT.

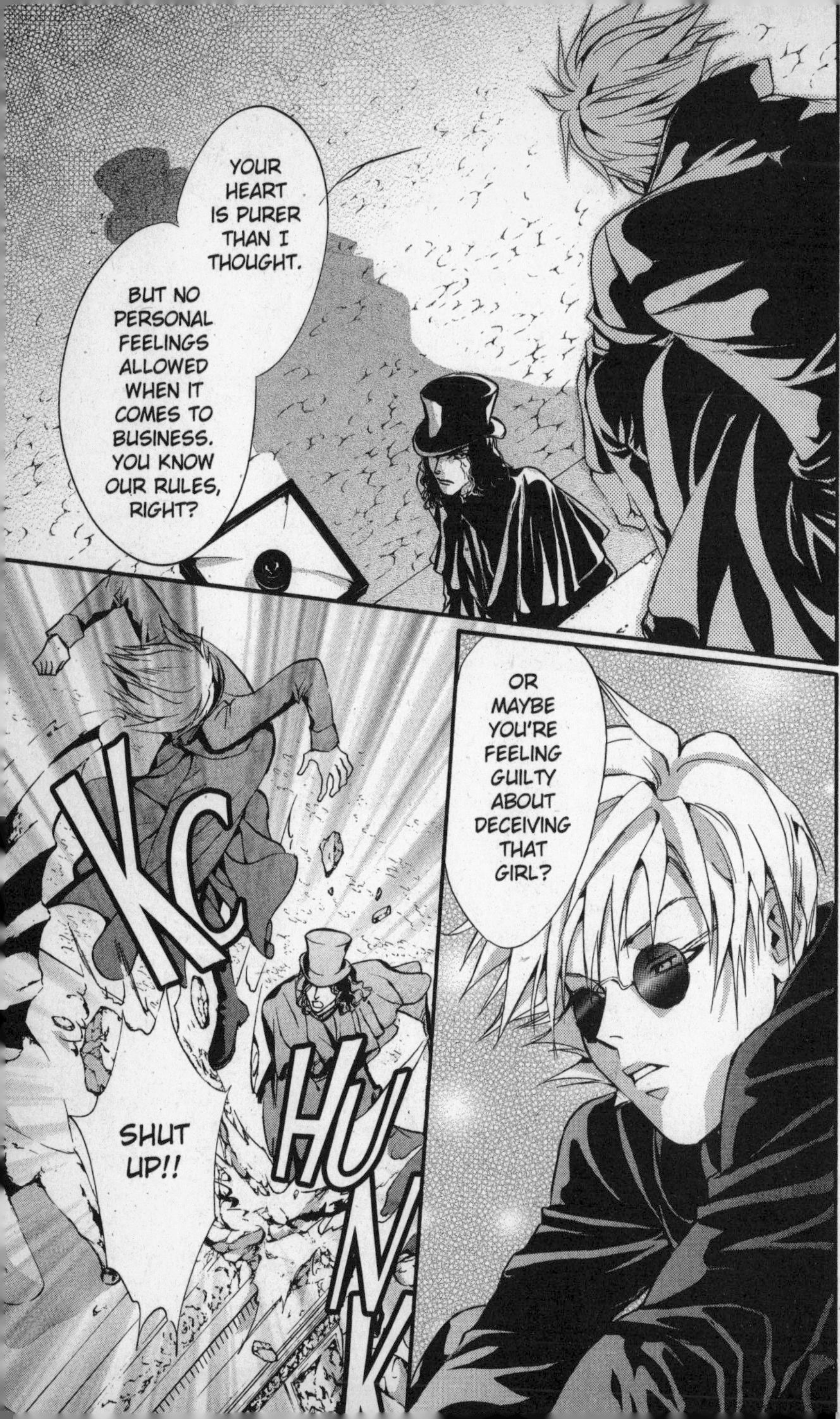
YOUR HEART IS PURER THAN I THOUGHT.
BUT NO PERSONAL FEELINGS ALLOWED WHEN IT COMES TO BUSINESS. YOU KNOW OUR RULES, RIGHT?
OR MAYBE YOU'RE FEELING GUILTY ABOUT DECEIVING THAT GIRL?
KC
HUNK
SHUT UP!!

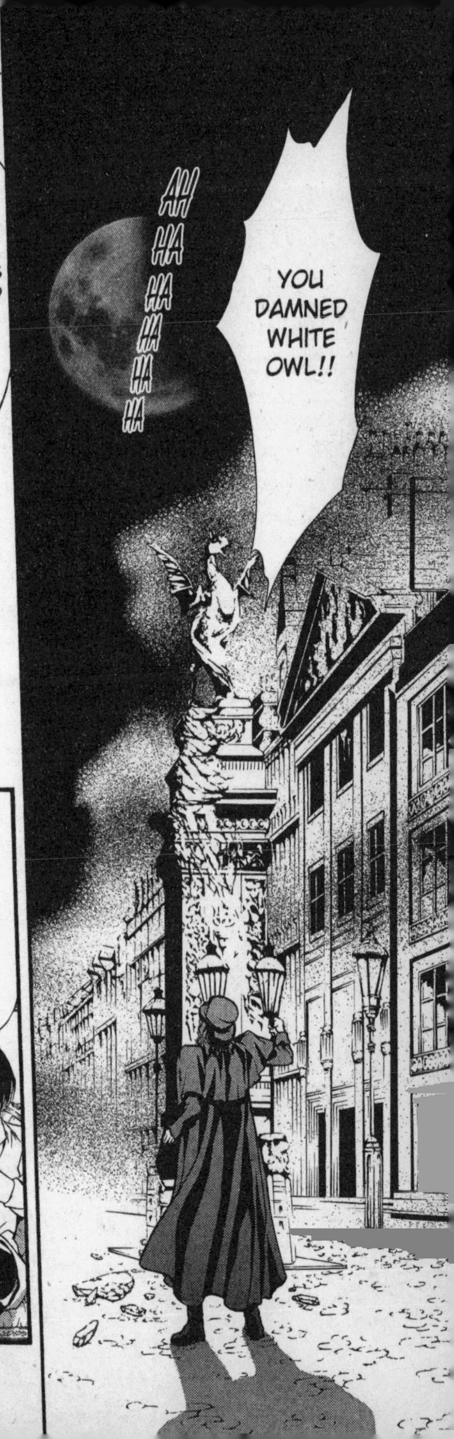
YOU DAMNED WHITE OWL!!
AH HA HA HA HA HA HA

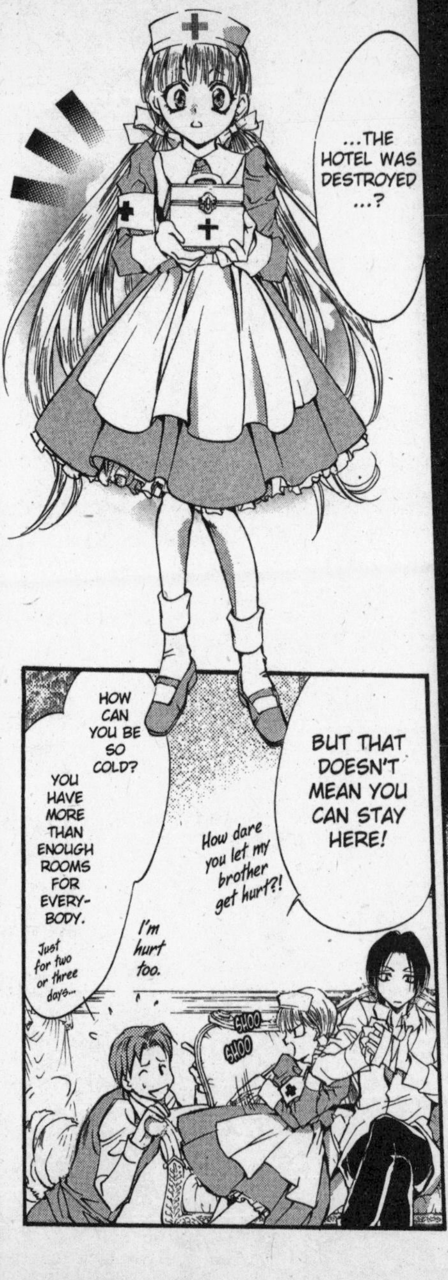
...THE HOTEL WAS DESTROYED ...?
BUT THAT DOESN'T MEAN YOU CAN STAY HERE!
How dare you let my brother get hurt?!
HOW CAN YOU BE SO COLD?
YOU HAVE MORE THAN ENOUGH ROOMS FOR EVERY-BODY.
I'm hurt too.
Just for two or three days...
SHOO
SHOO

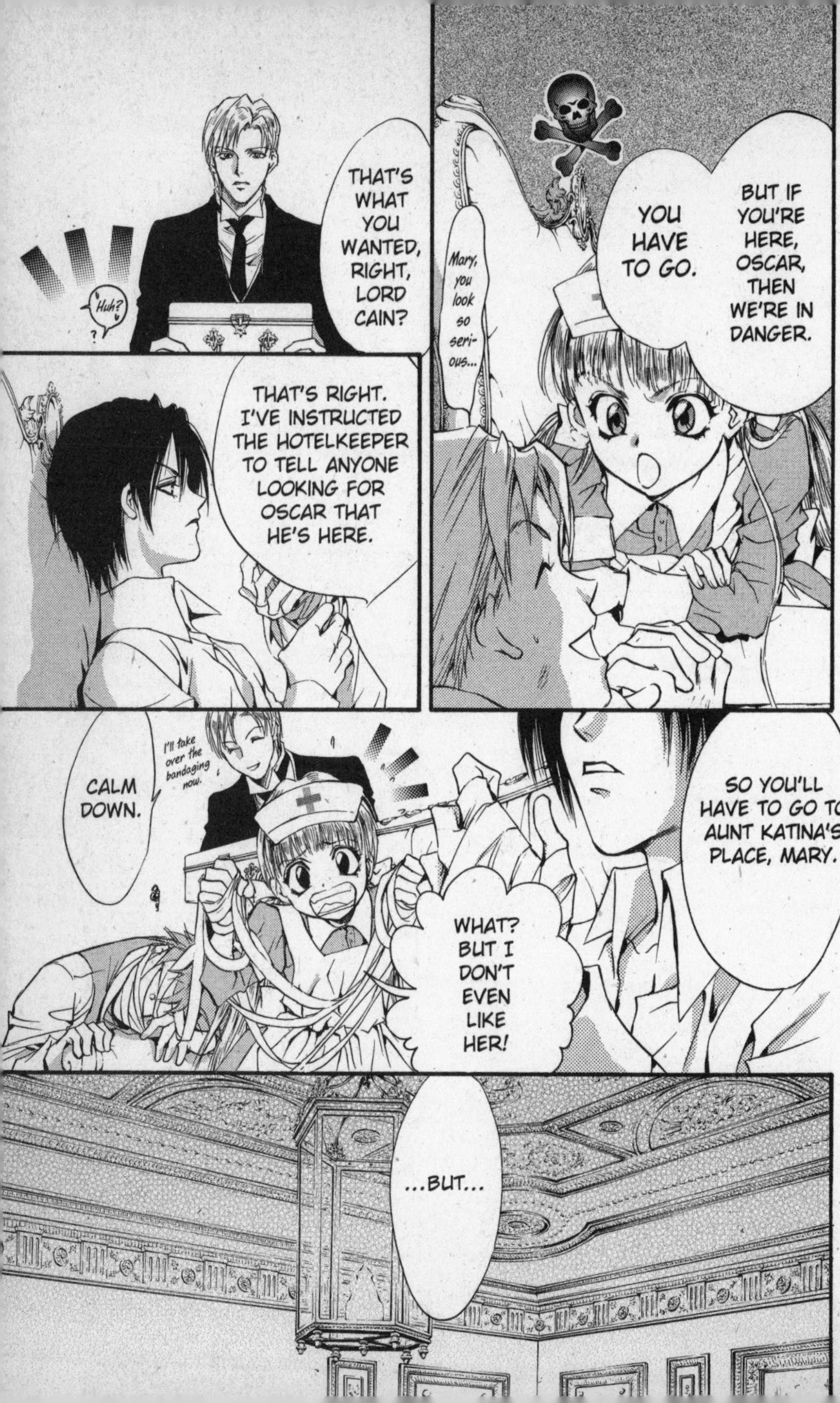
BUT IF YOU'RE HERE, OSCAR, THEN WE'RE IN DANGER.
YOU HAVE TO GO.
Mary, you look so seri-ous...
THAT'S WHAT YOU WANTED, RIGHT, LORD CAIN?
Huh?
THAT'S RIGHT. I'VE INSTRUCTED THE HOTELKEEPER TO TELL ANYONE LOOKING FOR OSCAR THAT HE'S HERE.
SO YOU'LL HAVE TO GO TO AUNT KATINA'S PLACE, MARY.
WHAT? BUT I DON'T EVEN LIKE HER!
I'll take over the bandaging now.
CALM DOWN.
...BUT...

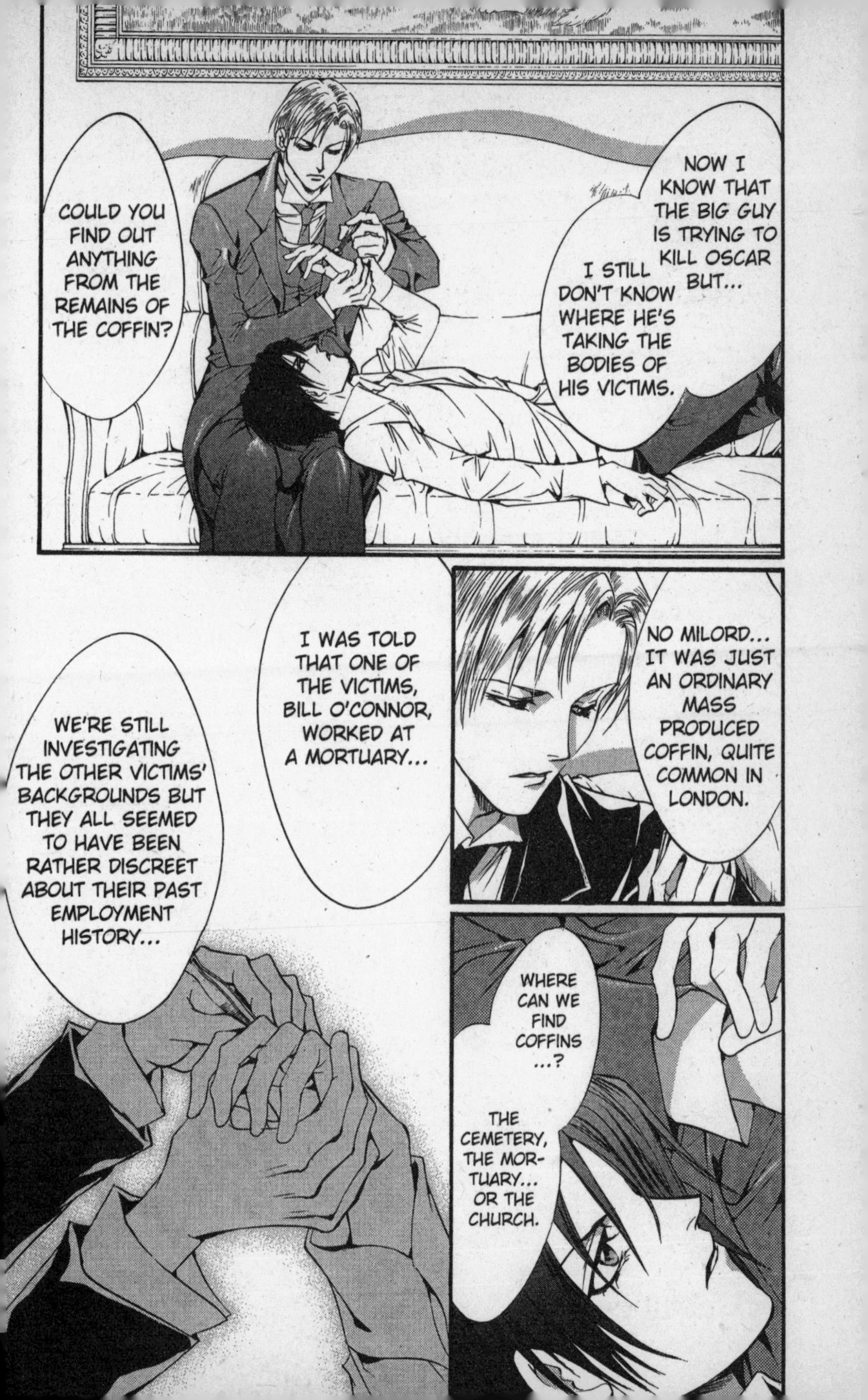
NOW I KNOW THAT THE BIG GUY IS TRYING TO KILL OSCAR BUT...
I STILL DON'T KNOW WHERE HE'S TAKING THE BODIES OF HIS VICTIMS.
COULD YOU FIND OUT ANYTHING FROM THE REMAINS OF THE COFFIN?
NO MILORD... IT WAS JUST AN ORDINARY MASS PRODUCED COFFIN, QUITE COMMON IN LONDON.
WHERE CAN WE FIND COFFINS ...?
THE CEMETERY, THE MOR-TUARY... OR THE CHURCH.
I WAS TOLD THAT ONE OF THE VICTIMS, BILL O'CONNOR, WORKED AT A MORTUARY...
WE'RE STILL INVESTIGATING THE OTHER VICTIMS' BACKGROUNDS BUT THEY ALL SEEMED TO HAVE BEEN RATHER DISCREET ABOUT THEIR PAST EMPLOYMENT HISTORY...

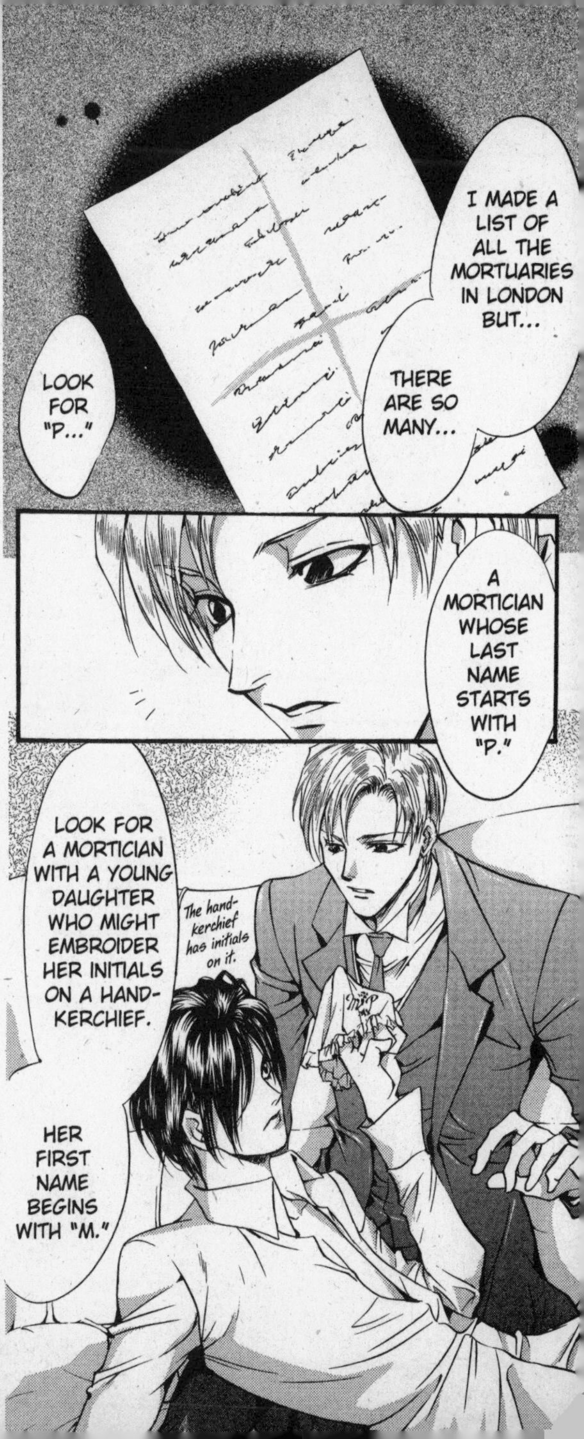

I MADE A LIST OF ALL THE MORTUARIES IN LONDON BUT...
THERE ARE SO MANY...
LOOK FOR "P..."
A MORTICIAN WHOSE LAST NAME STARTS WITH "P."
LOOK FOR A MORTICIAN WITH A YOUNG DAUGHTER WHO MIGHT EMBROIDER HER INITIALS ON A HAND-KERCHIEF.
The hand-kerchief has initials on it.
HER FIRST NAME BEGINS WITH "M."

I bought a pet robot dog around the time I was working on this story. I can't have any pets, plus they're so hard to take care of... The robot I bought is called Macaron and it has a cute black face. It's so cute when it cocks its head to the side! And it's the type that has to be trained but lately I've been so busy that I haven't been giving it any attention at all... sorry. Also, I've been collecting Alice dolls but lately they haven't been in stock at any stores... I still don't have Humpty Dumpty or Tisha... it's really making me sad. I got the collection from a longtime fan of mine and then I started collecting on my own... (Thanks for everything Haruka!) But the chance of getting the same one again is getting kind of tough. Before that I used to collect action figures but I don't by any means "love" action figures... It's just that I kind of like the ones that look like miniatures... Maybe that's because I do love doll-houses... I especially like the shiny little ones.

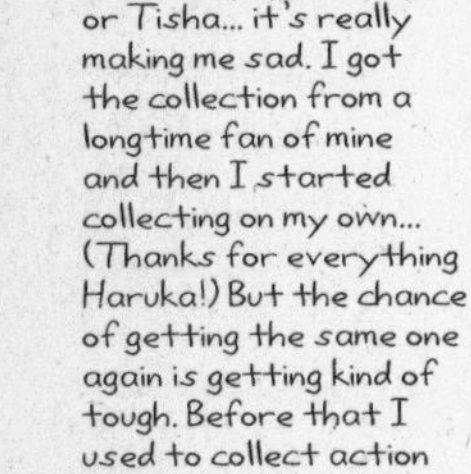

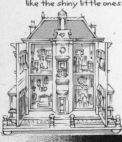

But only the cheap dollhouses... the others are too expensive.

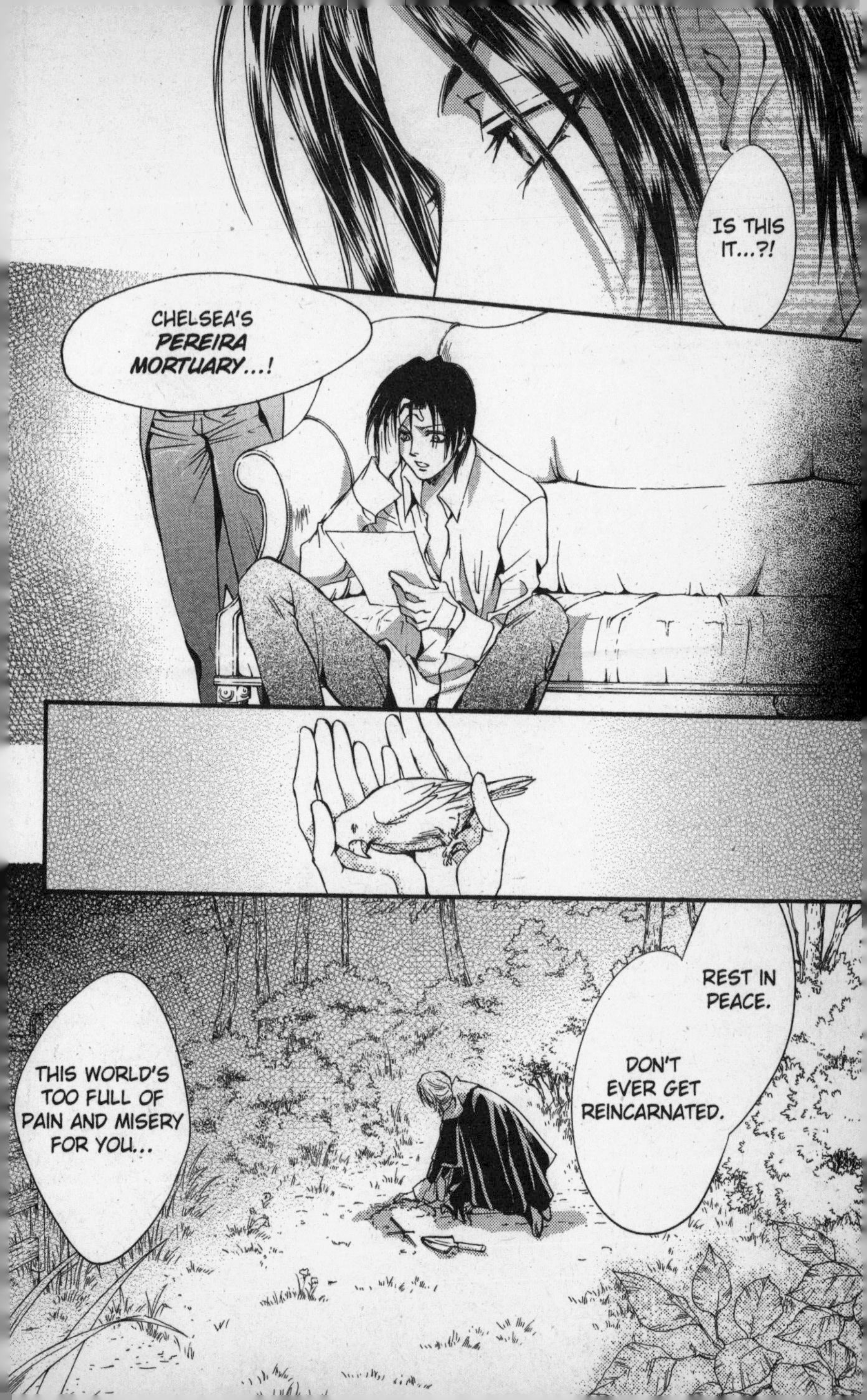
IS THIS IT...?!
CHELSEA'S *PEREIRA MORTUARY*...!
REST IN PEACE.
DON'T EVER GET REINCARNATED.
THIS WORLD'S TOO FULL OF PAIN AND MISERY FOR YOU...

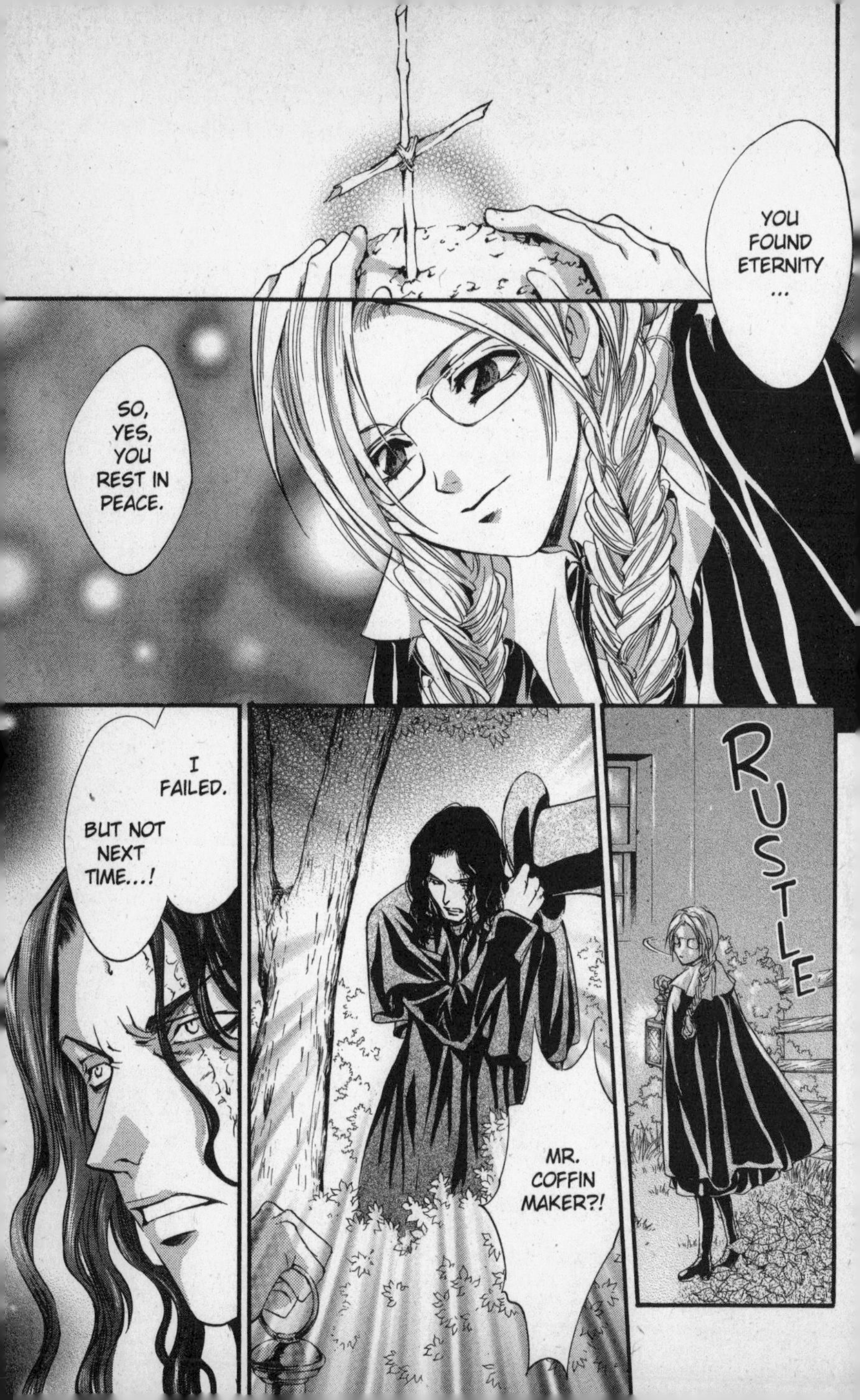
YOU FOUND ETERNITY ...
SO, YES, YOU REST IN PEACE.
RUSTLE
MR. COFFIN MAKER?!
I FAILED.
BUT NOT NEXT TIME...!

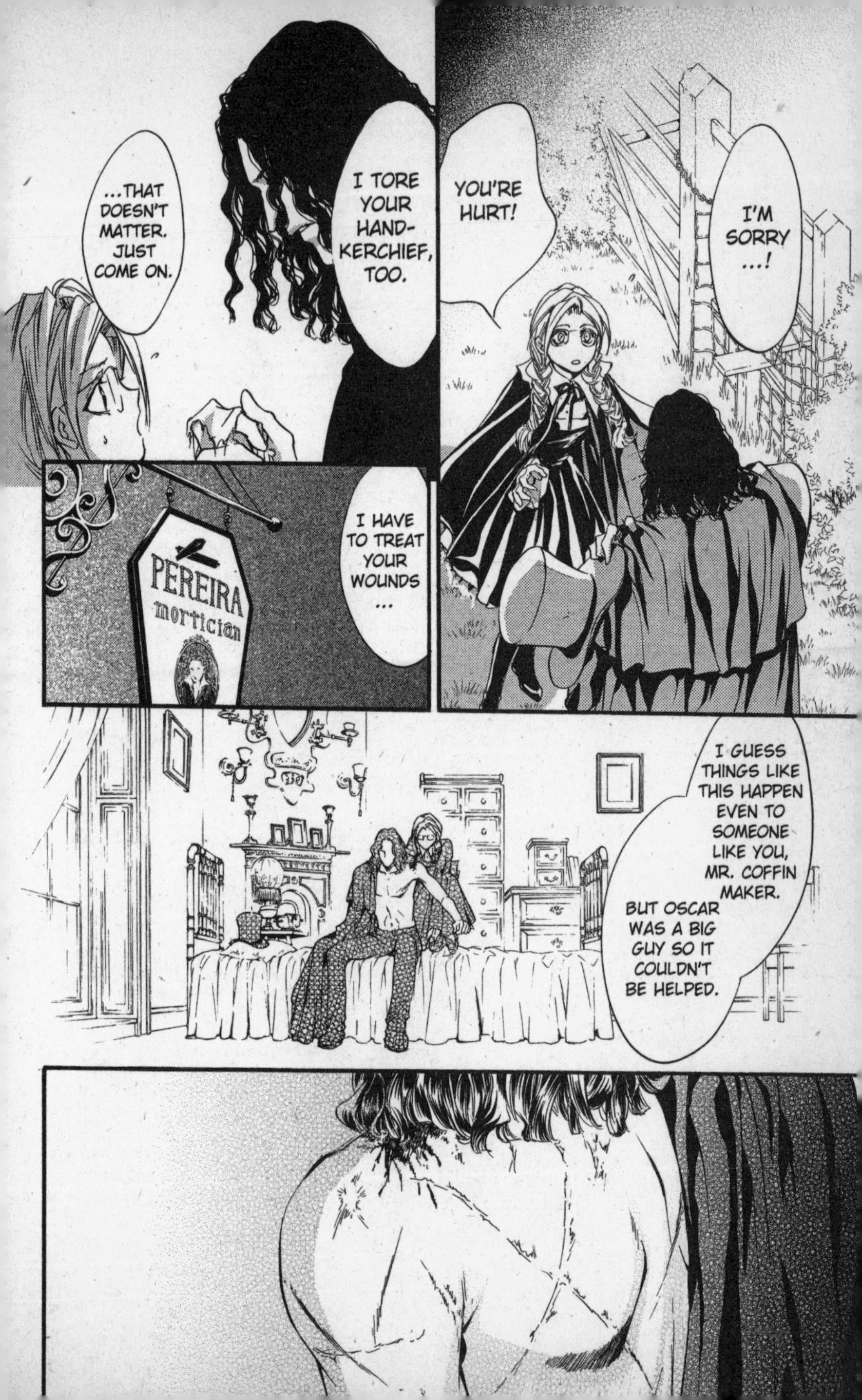
I'M SORRY ...!
YOU'RE HURT!
I TORE YOUR HAND-KERCHIEF, TOO.
...THAT DOESN'T MATTER. JUST COME ON.
I HAVE TO TREAT YOUR WOUNDS ...
PEREIRA mortician
I GUESS THINGS LIKE THIS HAPPEN EVEN TO SOMEONE LIKE YOU, MR. COFFIN MAKER.
BUT OSCAR WAS A BIG GUY SO IT COULDN'T BE HELPED.

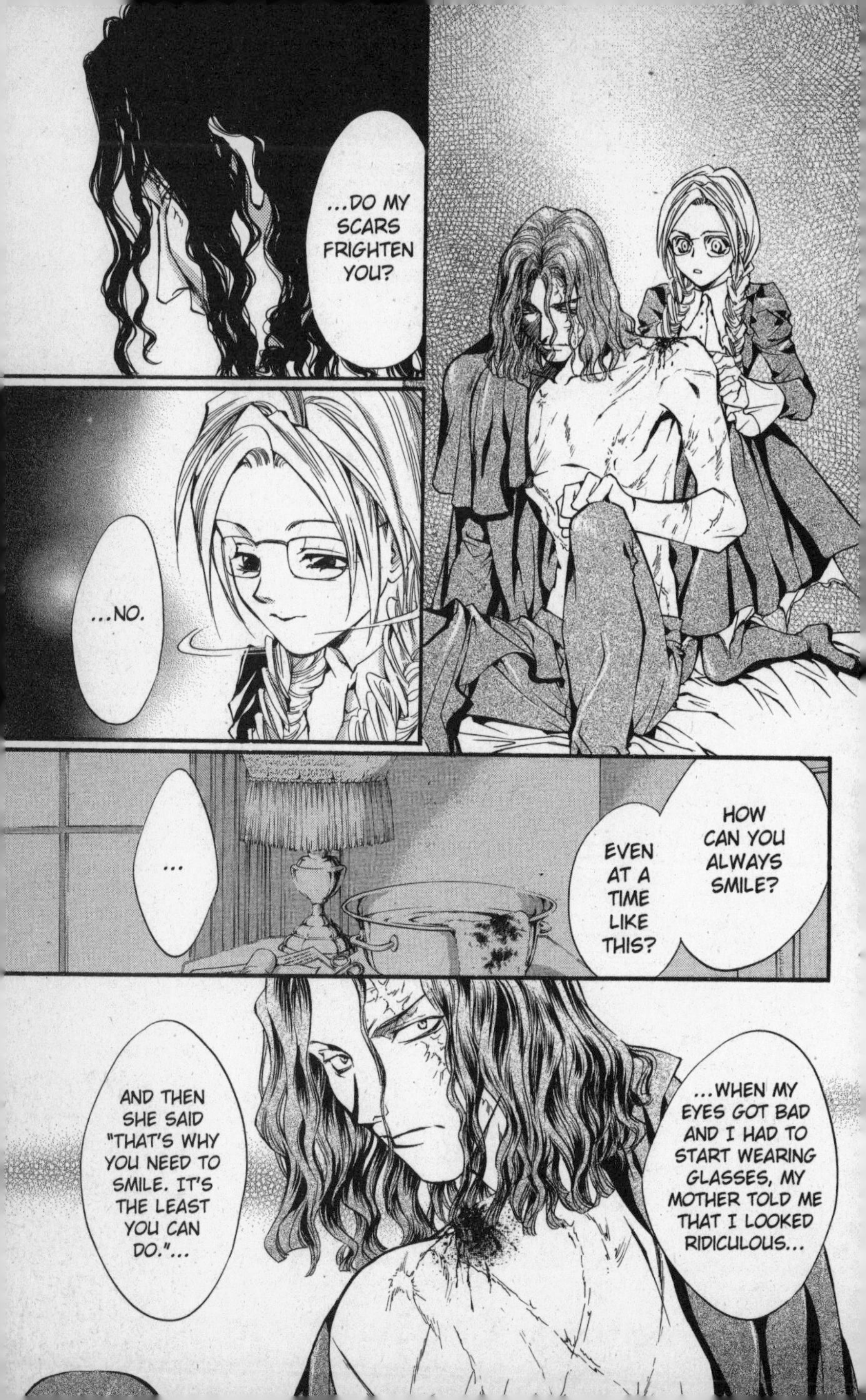
...DO MY SCARS FRIGHTEN YOU?
...NO.
HOW CAN YOU ALWAYS SMILE?
EVEN AT A TIME LIKE THIS?
...
...WHEN MY EYES GOT BAD AND I HAD TO START WEARING GLASSES, MY MOTHER TOLD ME THAT I LOOKED RIDICULOUS...
AND THEN SHE SAID "THAT'S WHY YOU NEED TO SMILE. IT'S THE LEAST YOU CAN DO."...

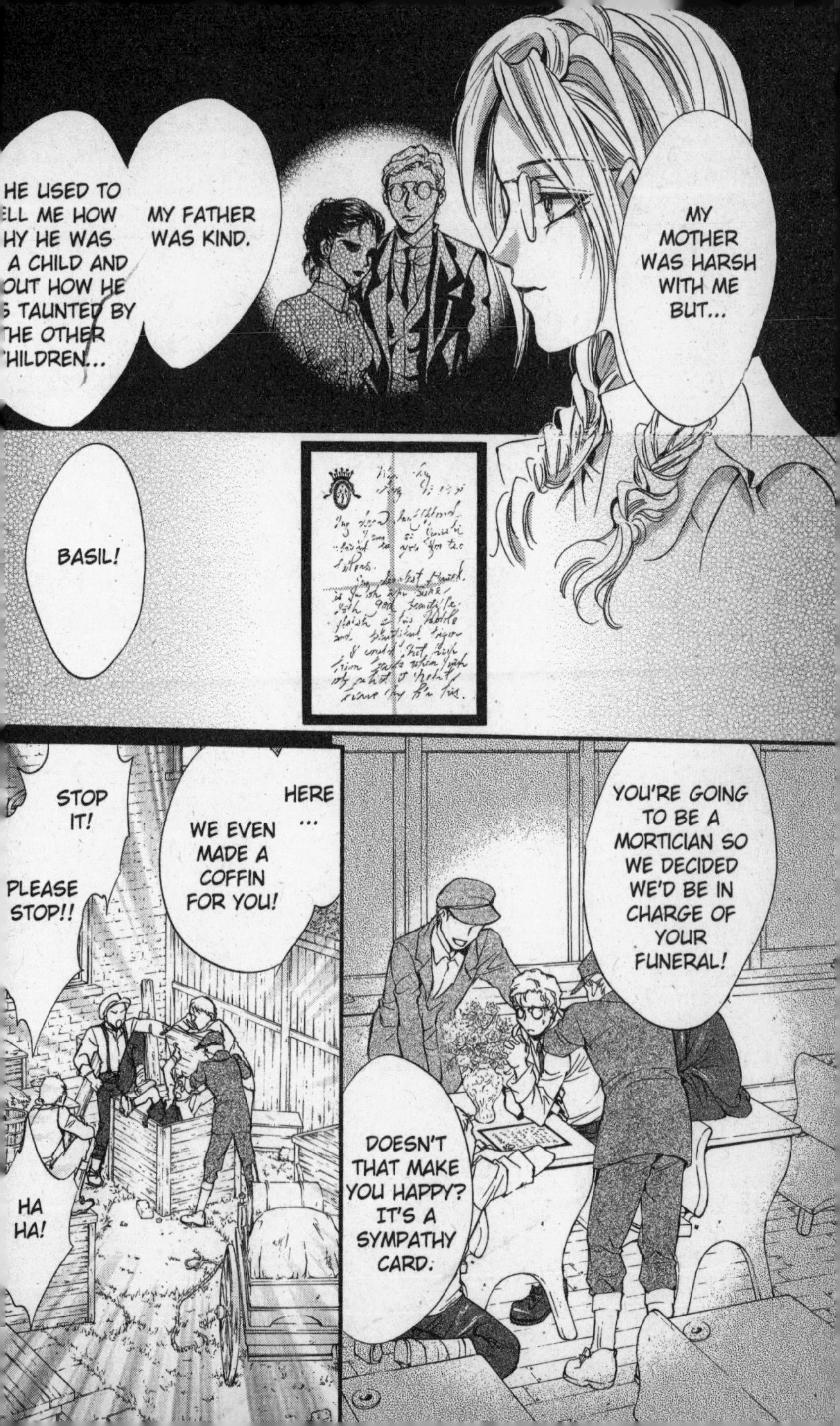

MY MOTHER WAS HARSH WITH ME BUT...
MY FATHER WAS KIND.
HE USED TO ELL ME HOW HY HE WAS A CHILD AND OUT HOW HE S TAUNTED BY THE OTHER HILDREN...
BASIL!
YOU'RE GOING TO BE A MORTICIAN SO WE DECIDED WE'D BE IN CHARGE OF YOUR FUNERAL!
DOESN'T THAT MAKE YOU HAPPY? IT'S A SYMPATHY CARD.
HERE...
WE EVEN MADE A COFFIN FOR YOU!
STOP IT!
PLEASE STOP!!
HA HA!

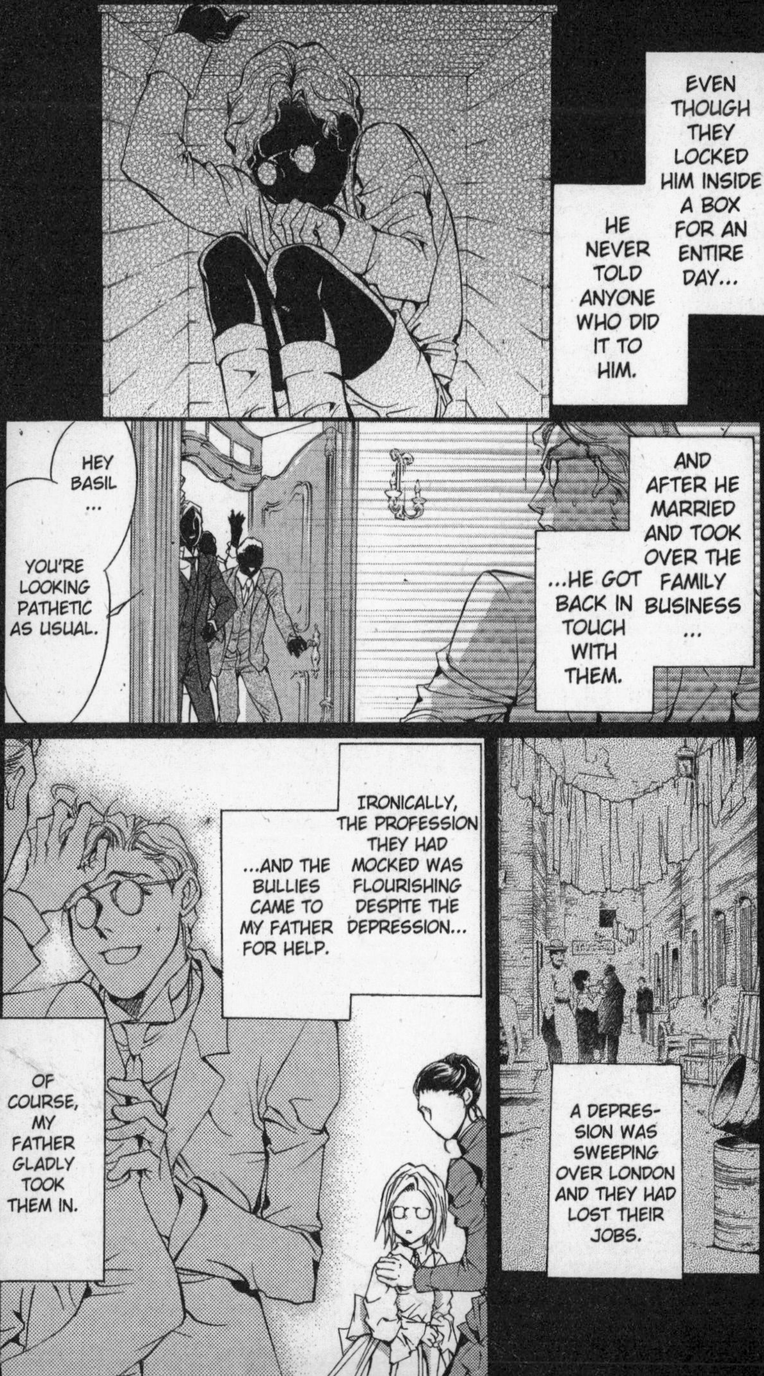
EVEN THOUGH THEY LOCKED HIM INSIDE A BOX FOR AN ENTIRE DAY...
HE NEVER TOLD ANYONE WHO DID IT TO HIM.
AND AFTER HE MARRIED AND TOOK OVER THE FAMILY BUSINESS...
...HE GOT BACK IN TOUCH WITH THEM.
HEY BASIL...
YOU'RE LOOKING PATHETIC AS USUAL.
A DEPRESSION WAS SWEEPING OVER LONDON AND THEY HAD LOST THEIR JOBS.
IRONICALLY, THE PROFESSION THEY HAD MOCKED WAS FLOURISHING DESPITE THE DEPRESSION...
...AND THE BULLIES CAME TO MY FATHER FOR HELP.
OF COURSE, MY FATHER GLADLY TOOK THEM IN.

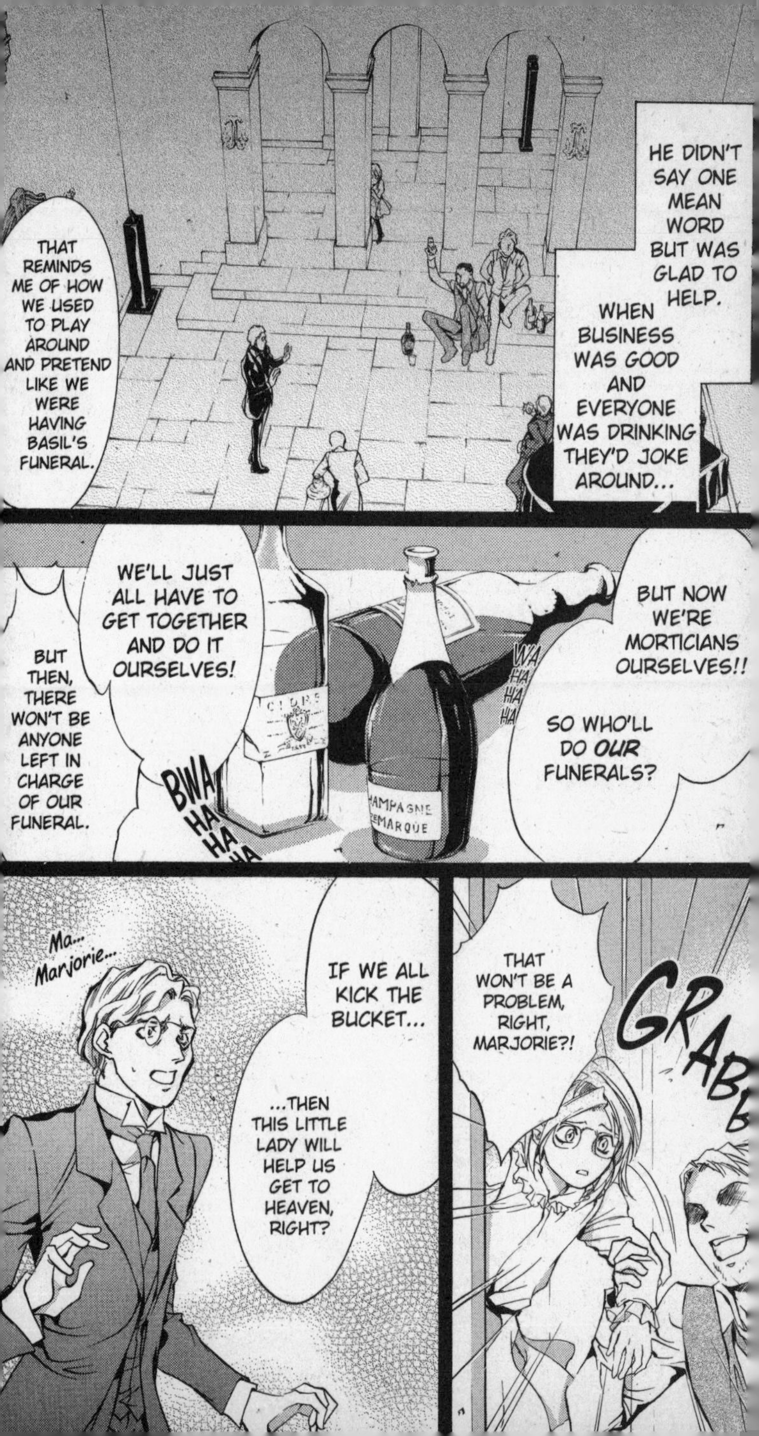
HE DIDN'T SAY ONE MEAN WORD BUT WAS GLAD TO HELP.
WHEN BUSINESS WAS GOOD AND EVERYONE WAS DRINKING THEY'D JOKE AROUND...
THAT REMINDS ME OF HOW WE USED TO PLAY AROUND AND PRETEND LIKE WE WERE HAVING BASIL'S FUNERAL.
BUT NOW WE'RE MORTICIANS OURSELVES!!
SO WHO'LL DO OUR FUNERALS?
WA HA HA HA
WE'LL JUST ALL HAVE TO GET TOGETHER AND DO IT OURSELVES!
BUT THEN, THERE WON'T BE ANYONE LEFT IN CHARGE OF OUR FUNERAL.
BWA HA HA HA
THAT WON'T BE A PROBLEM, RIGHT, MARJORIE?!
GRAB
IF WE ALL KICK THE BUCKET...
...THEN THIS LITTLE LADY WILL HELP US GET TO HEAVEN, RIGHT?
Ma... Marjorie...

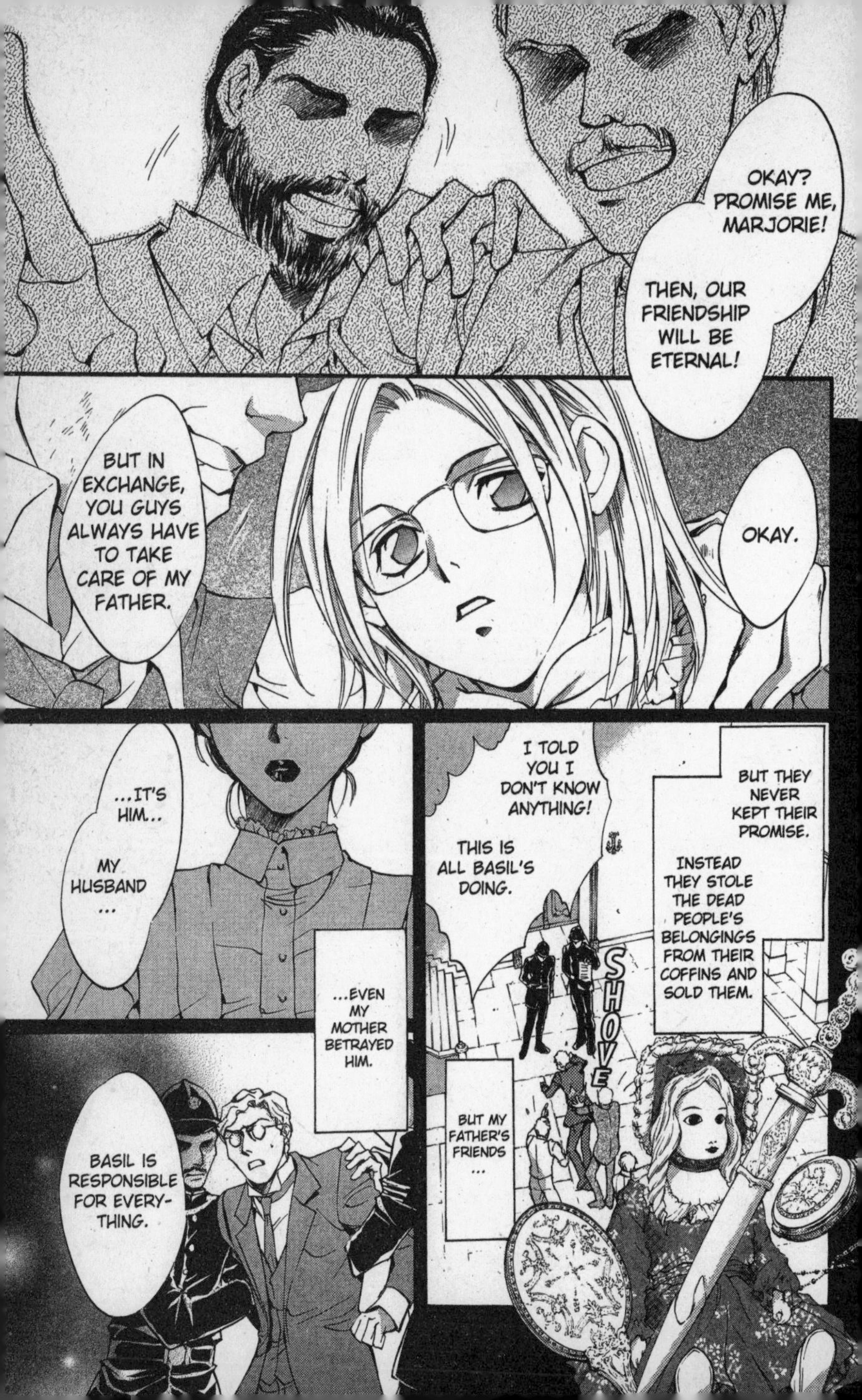

OKAY? PROMISE ME, MARJORIE!
THEN, OUR FRIENDSHIP WILL BE ETERNAL!
BUT IN EXCHANGE, YOU GUYS ALWAYS HAVE TO TAKE CARE OF MY FATHER.
OKAY.
BUT THEY NEVER KEPT THEIR PROMISE.
INSTEAD THEY STOLE THE DEAD PEOPLE'S BELONGINGS FROM THEIR COFFINS AND SOLD THEM.
I TOLD YOU I DON'T KNOW ANYTHING!
THIS IS ALL BASIL'S DOING.
SHOVE
BUT MY FATHER'S FRIENDS ...
...IT'S HIM...
MY HUSBAND ...
...EVEN MY MOTHER BETRAYED HIM.
BASIL IS RESPONSIBLE FOR EVERY-THING.

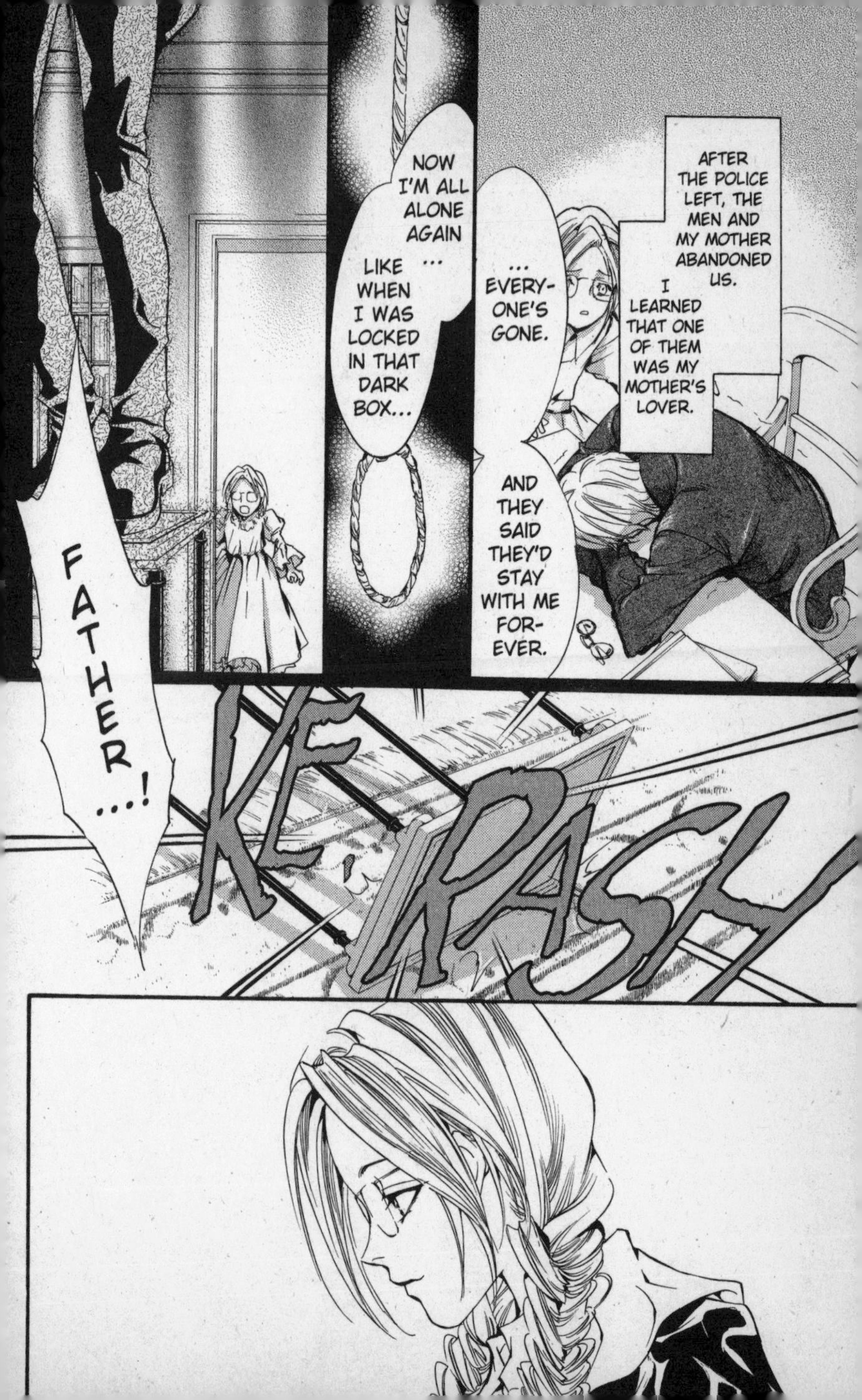
AFTER THE POLICE LEFT, THE MEN AND MY MOTHER ABANDONED US.
I LEARNED THAT ONE OF THEM WAS MY MOTHER'S LOVER.
...EVERYONE'S GONE.
AND THEY SAID THEY'D STAY WITH ME FOREVER.
NOW I'M ALL ALONE AGAIN...
LIKE WHEN I WAS LOCKED IN THAT DARK BOX...
KE-RASH
FATHER...!

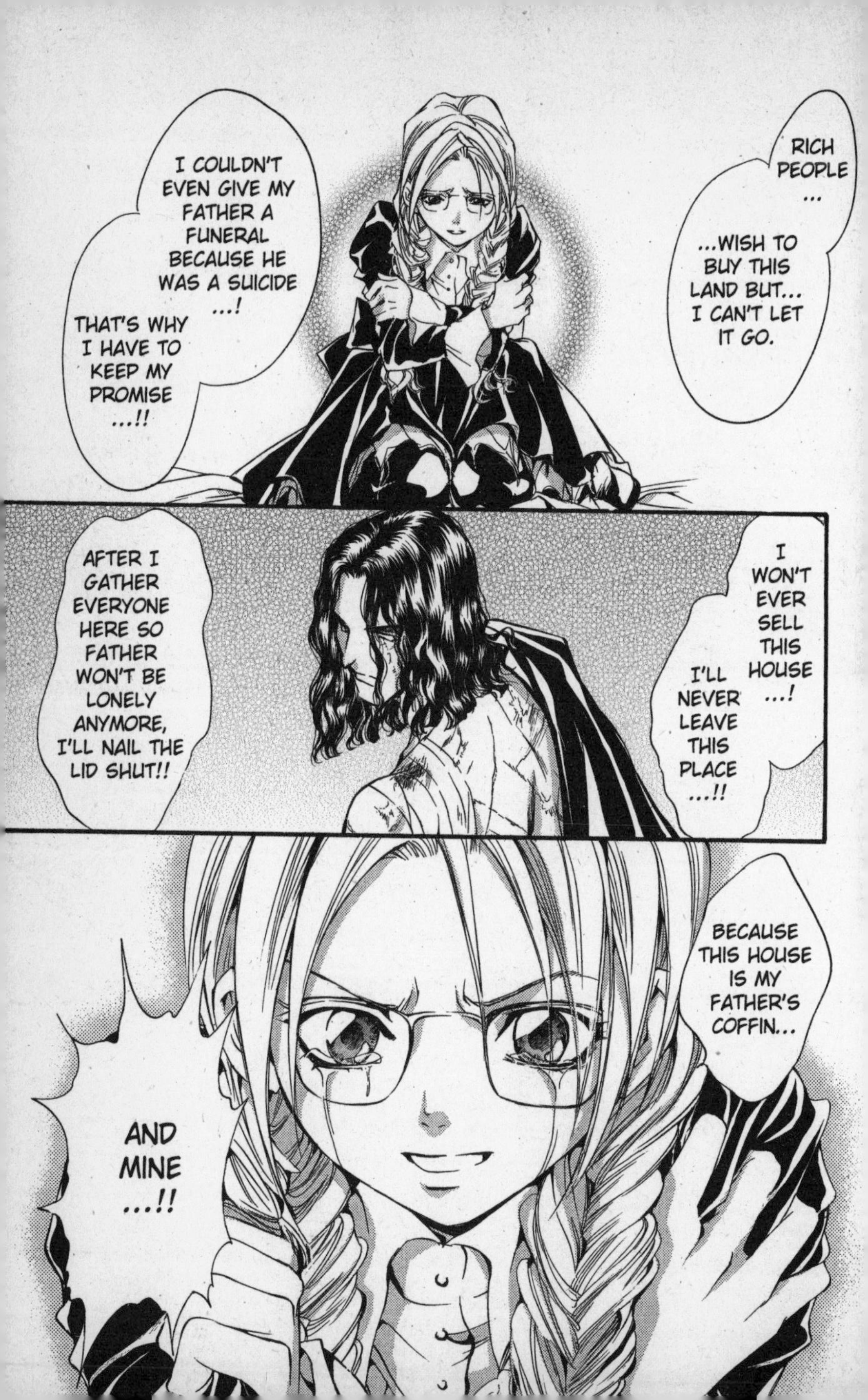
RICH PEOPLE ...
...WISH TO BUY THIS LAND BUT... I CAN'T LET IT GO.
I COULDN'T EVEN GIVE MY FATHER A FUNERAL BECAUSE HE WAS A SUICIDE ...!
THAT'S WHY I HAVE TO KEEP MY PROMISE ...!!
I WON'T EVER SELL THIS HOUSE ...!
I'LL NEVER LEAVE THIS PLACE ...!!
AFTER I GATHER EVERYONE HERE SO FATHER WON'T BE LONELY ANYMORE, I'LL NAIL THE LID SHUT!!
BECAUSE THIS HOUSE IS MY FATHER'S COFFIN...
AND MINE ...!!

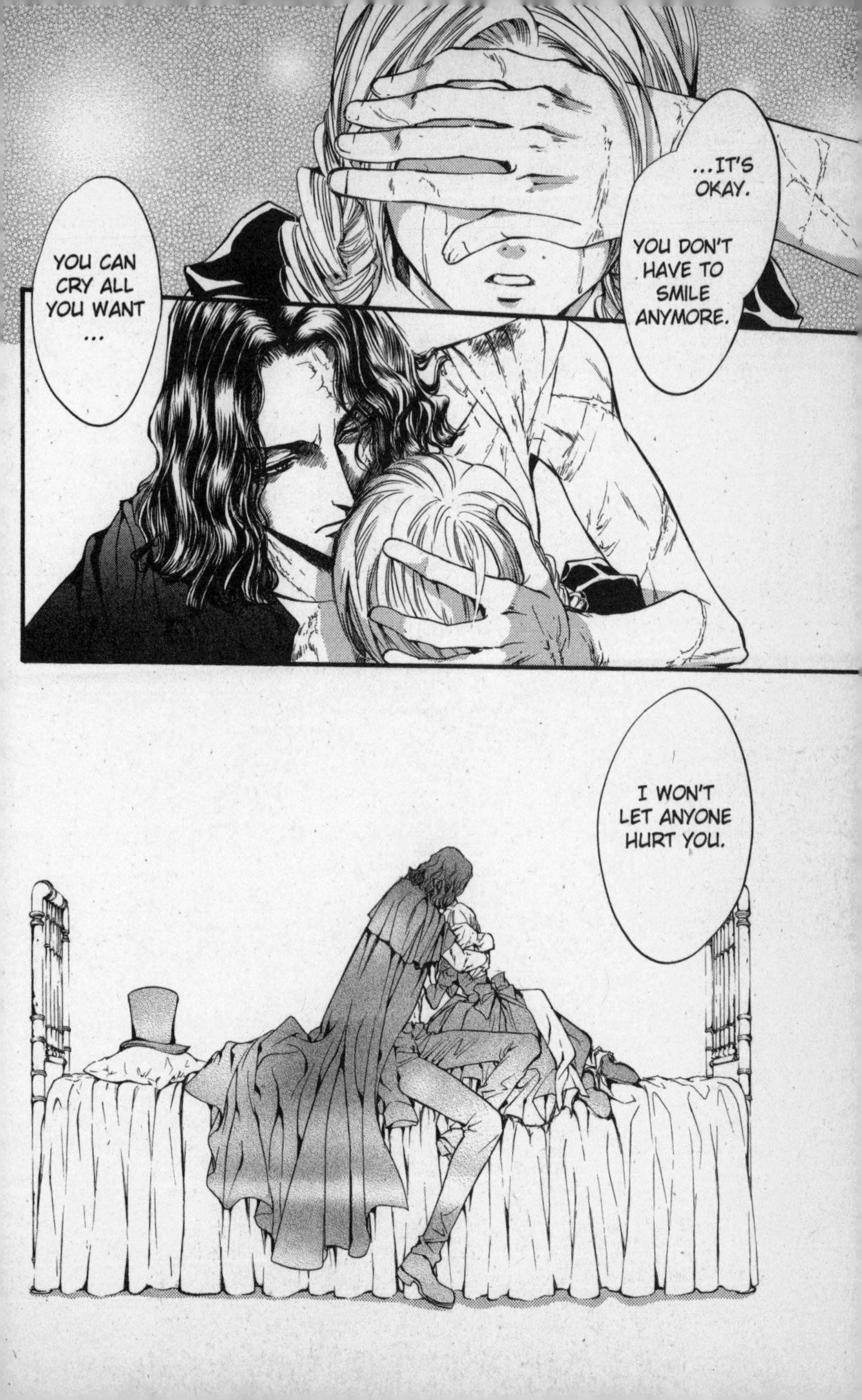
...IT'S OKAY.
YOU DON'T HAVE TO SMILE ANYMORE.
YOU CAN CRY ALL YOU WANT ...
I WON'T LET ANYONE HURT YOU.

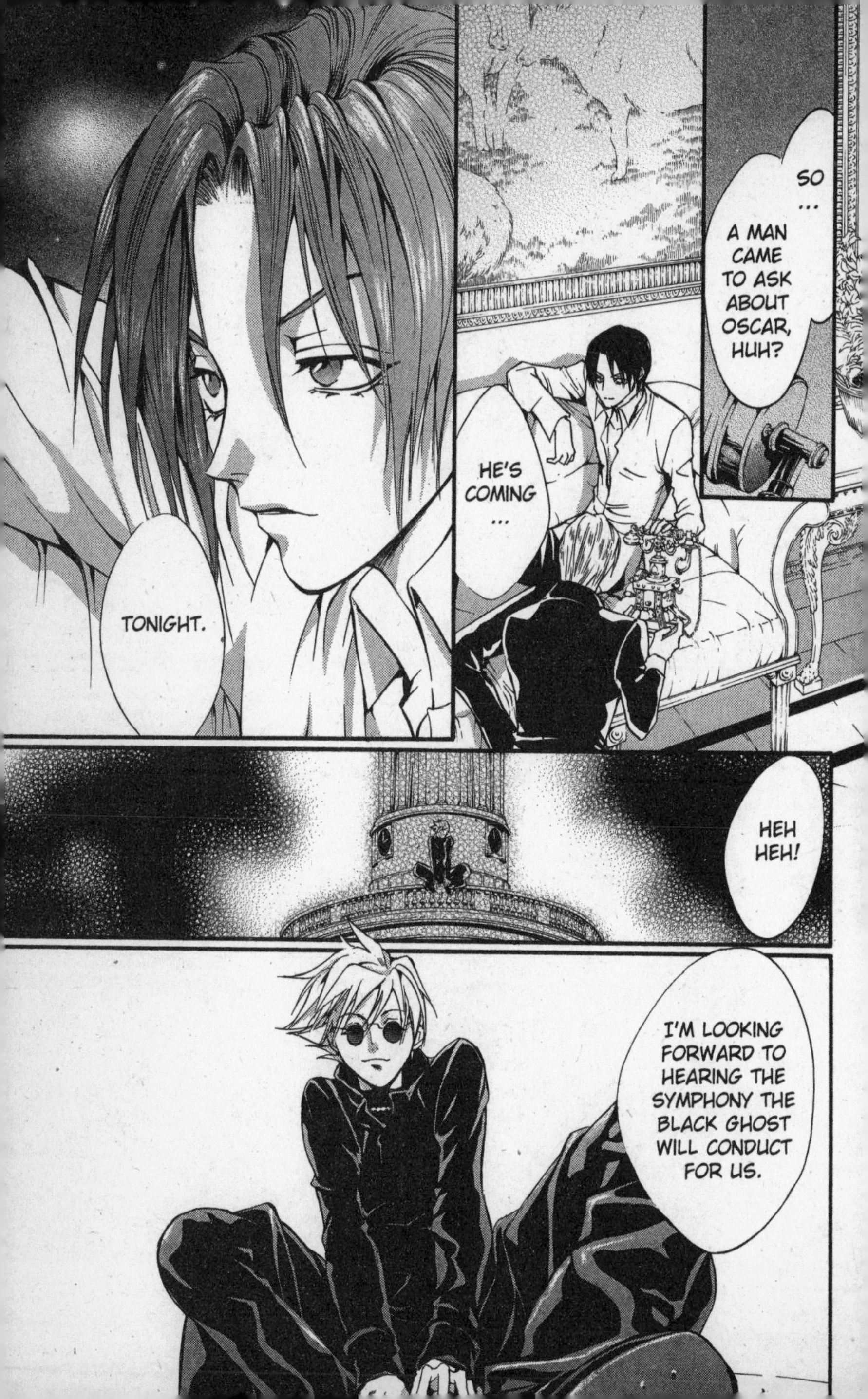
SO ... A MAN CAME TO ASK ABOUT OSCAR, HUH?
HE'S COMING ...
TONIGHT.
HEH HEH!
I'M LOOKING FORWARD TO HEARING THE SYMPHONY THE BLACK GHOST WILL CONDUCT FOR US.

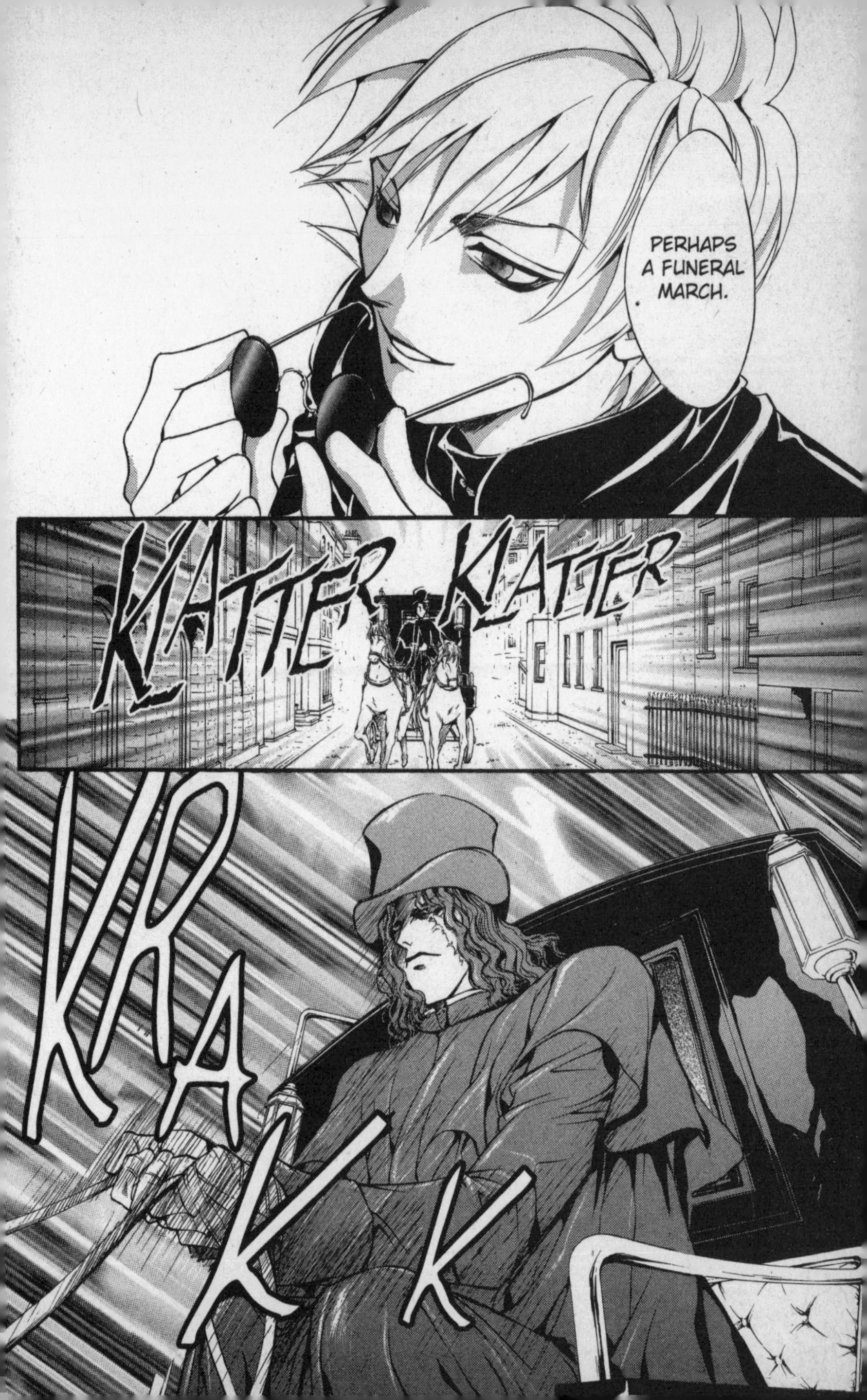
PERHAPS A FUNERAL MARCH.
KLATTER KLATTER
KRAKK

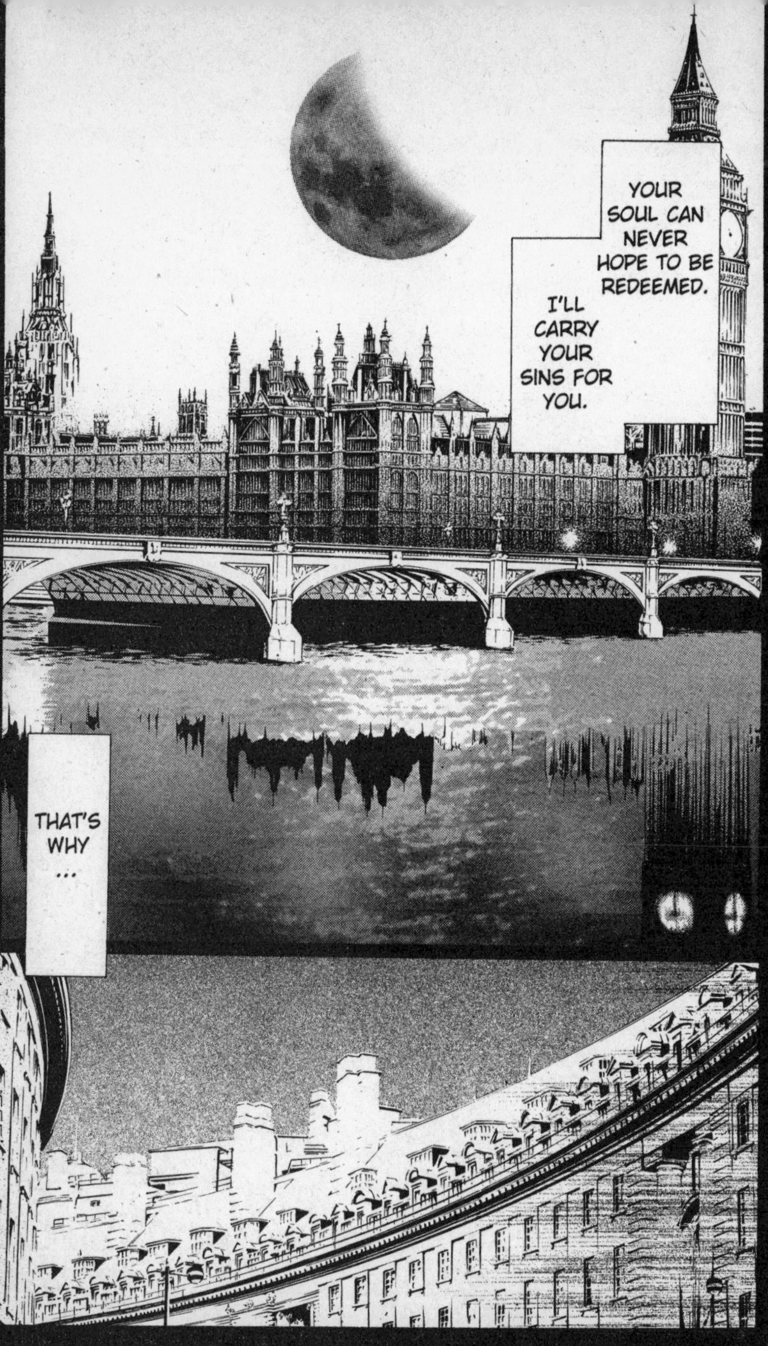
YOUR SOUL CAN NEVER HOPE TO BE REDEEMED.
I'LL CARRY YOUR SINS FOR YOU.
THAT'S WHY ...

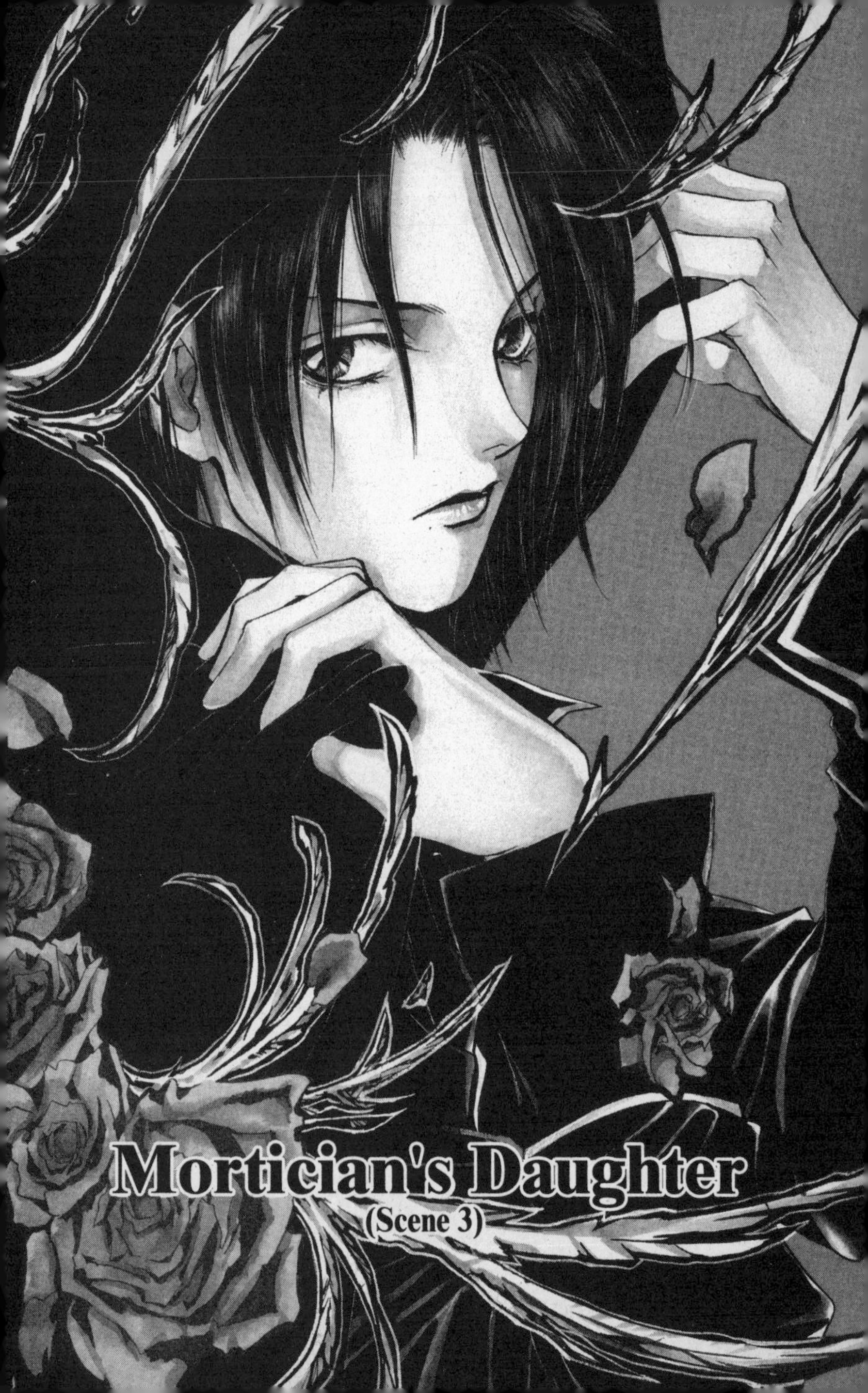
Mortician's Daughter
(Scene 3)

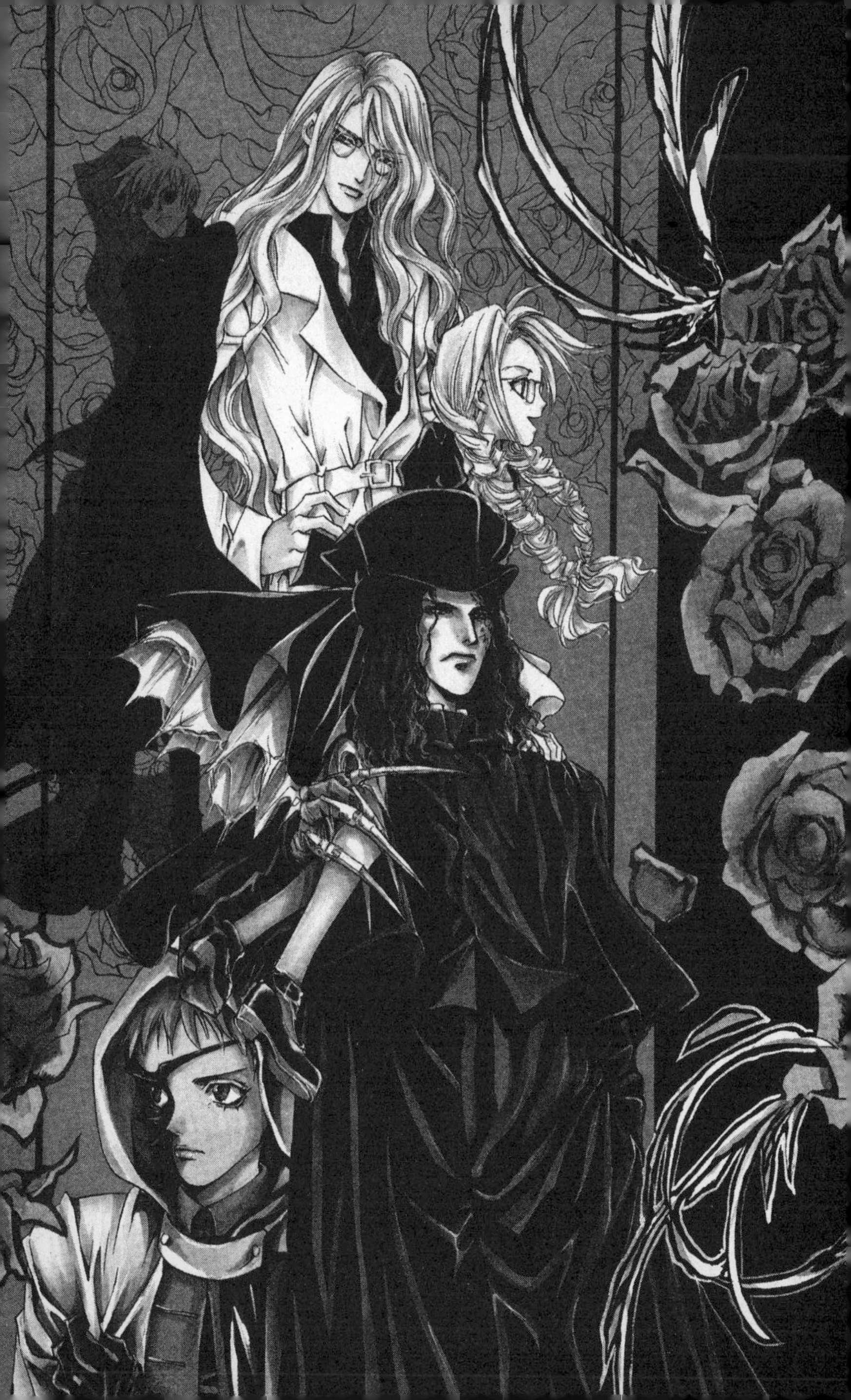

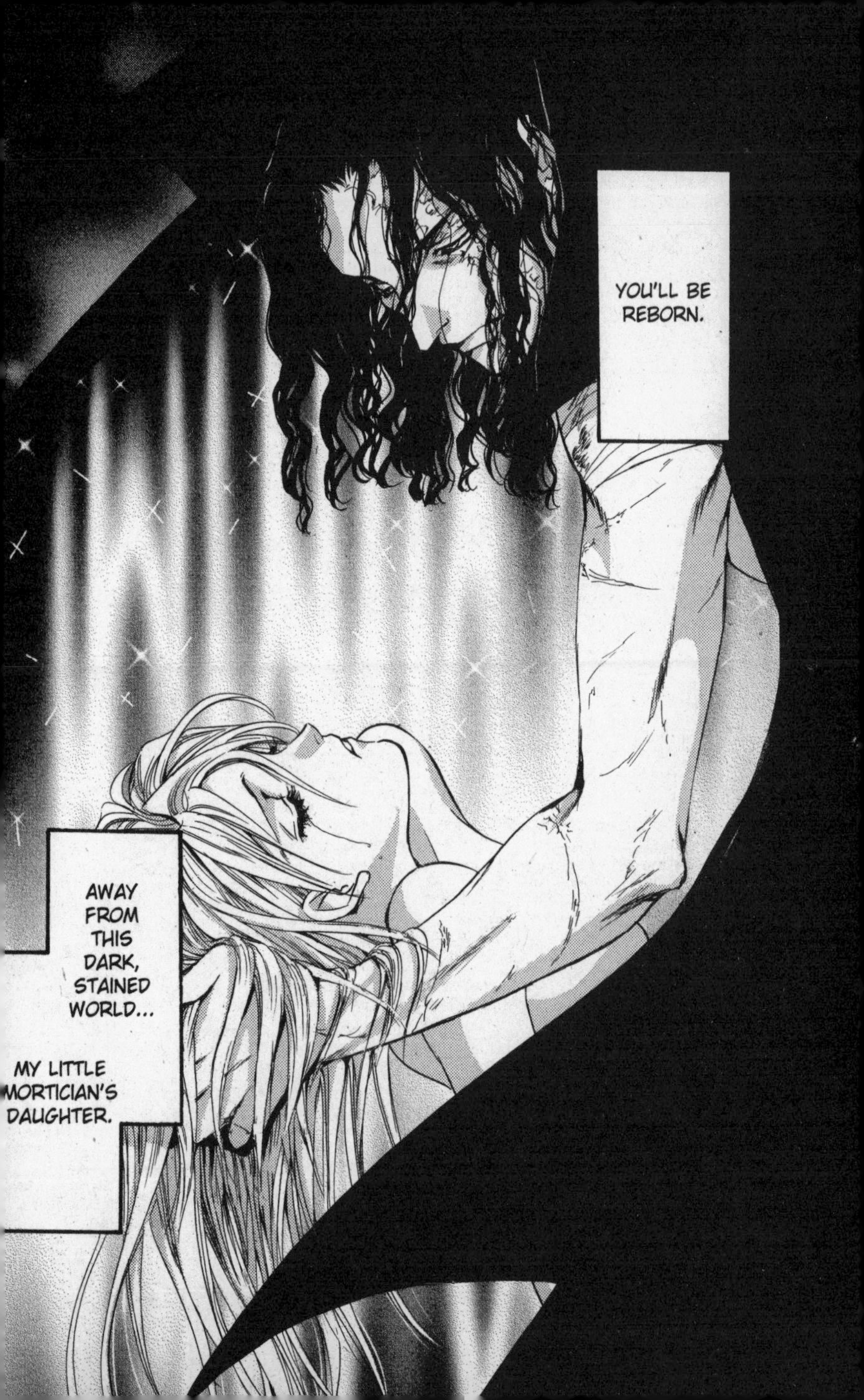
YOU'LL BE REBORN.
AWAY FROM THIS DARK, STAINED WORLD...
MY LITTLE MORTICIAN'S DAUGHTER.

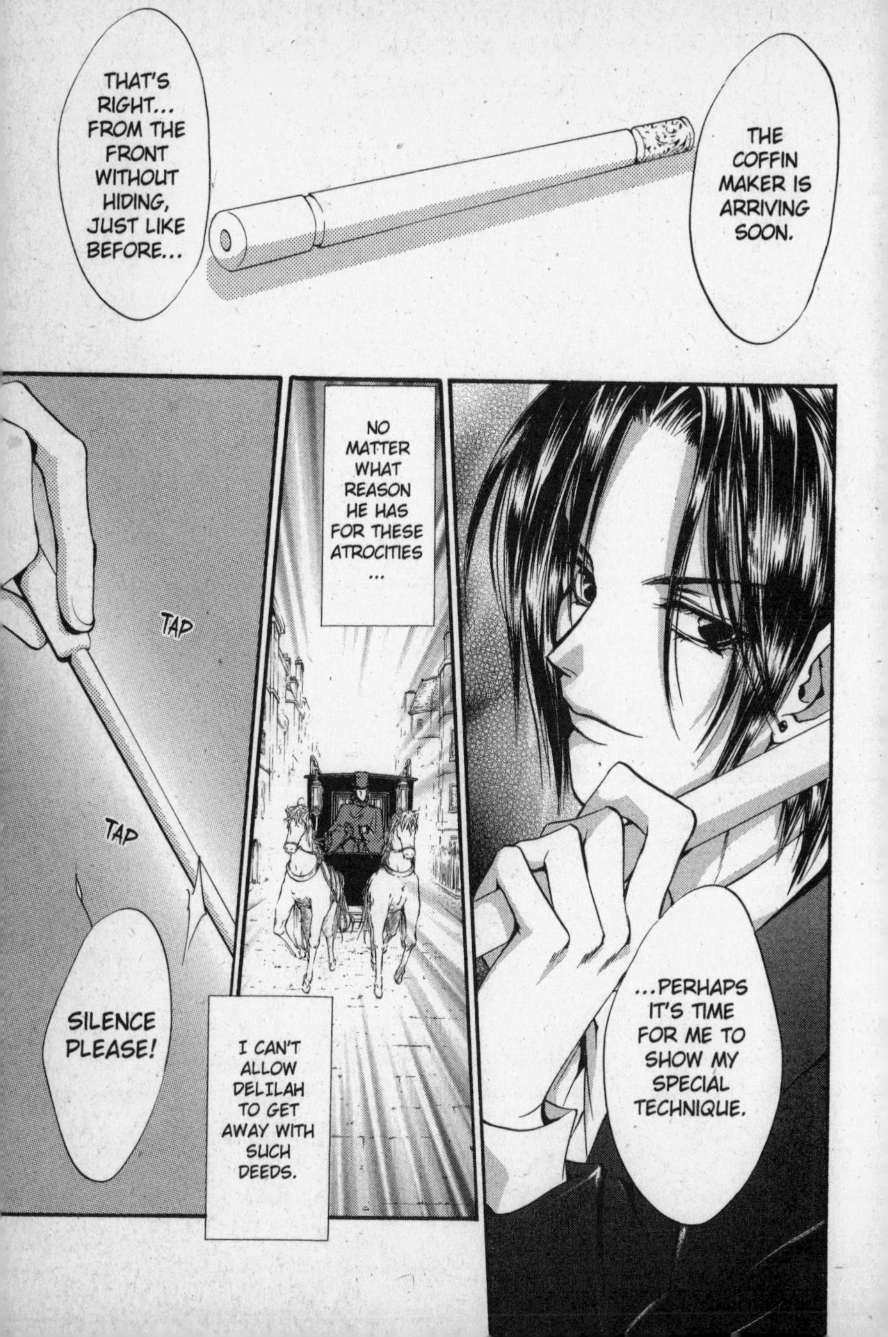
THE COFFIN MAKER IS ARRIVING SOON.
THAT'S RIGHT... FROM THE FRONT WITHOUT HIDING, JUST LIKE BEFORE...
...PERHAPS IT'S TIME FOR ME TO SHOW MY SPECIAL TECHNIQUE.
NO MATTER WHAT REASON HE HAS FOR THESE ATROCITIES...
I CAN'T ALLOW DELILAH TO GET AWAY WITH SUCH DEEDS.
TAP
TAP
SILENCE PLEASE!

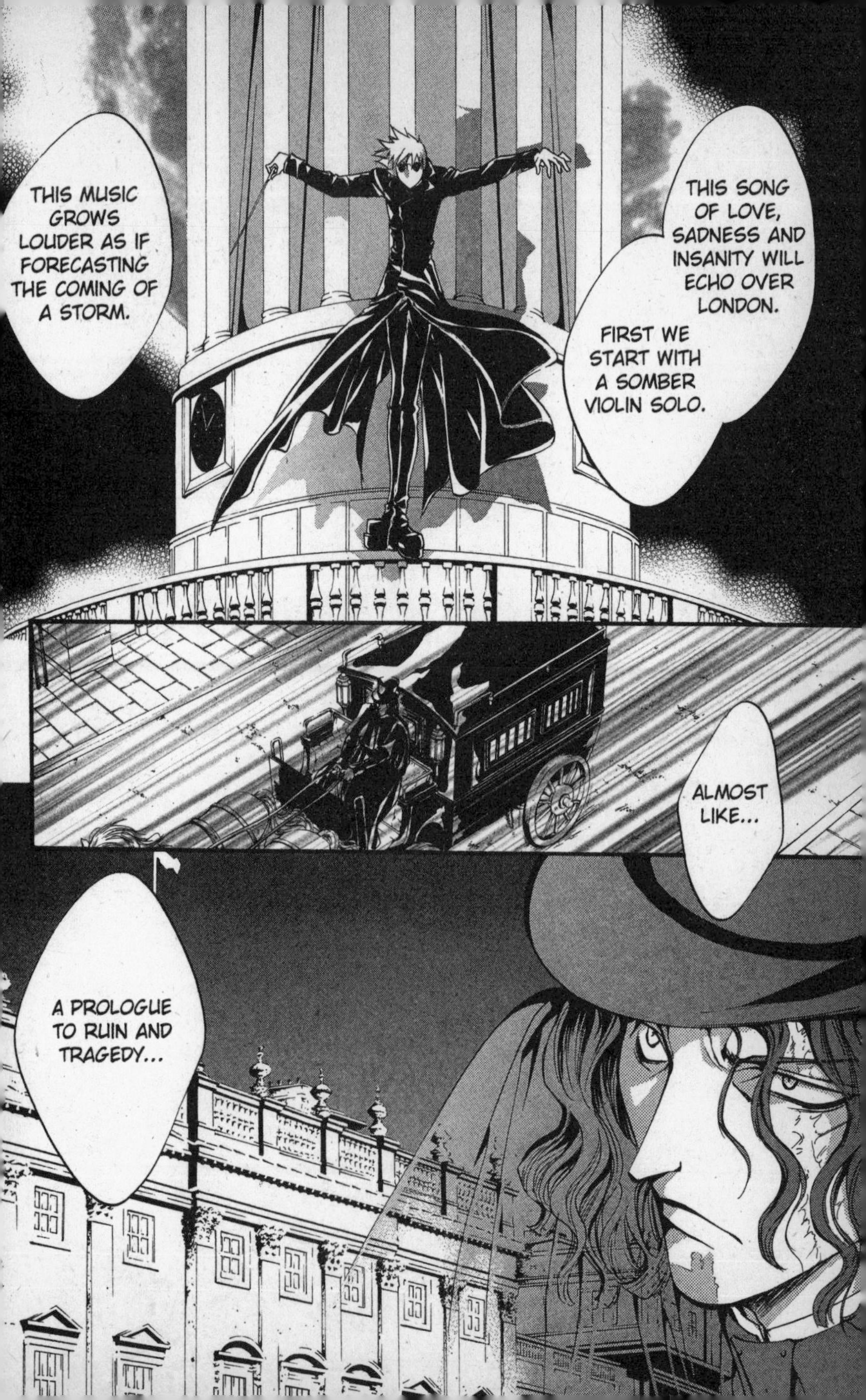
THIS SONG OF LOVE, SADNESS AND INSANITY WILL ECHO OVER LONDON.
FIRST WE START WITH A SOMBER VIOLIN SOLO.
THIS MUSIC GROWS LOUDER AS IF FORECASTING THE COMING OF A STORM.
ALMOST LIKE...
A PROLOGUE TO RUIN AND TRAGEDY...

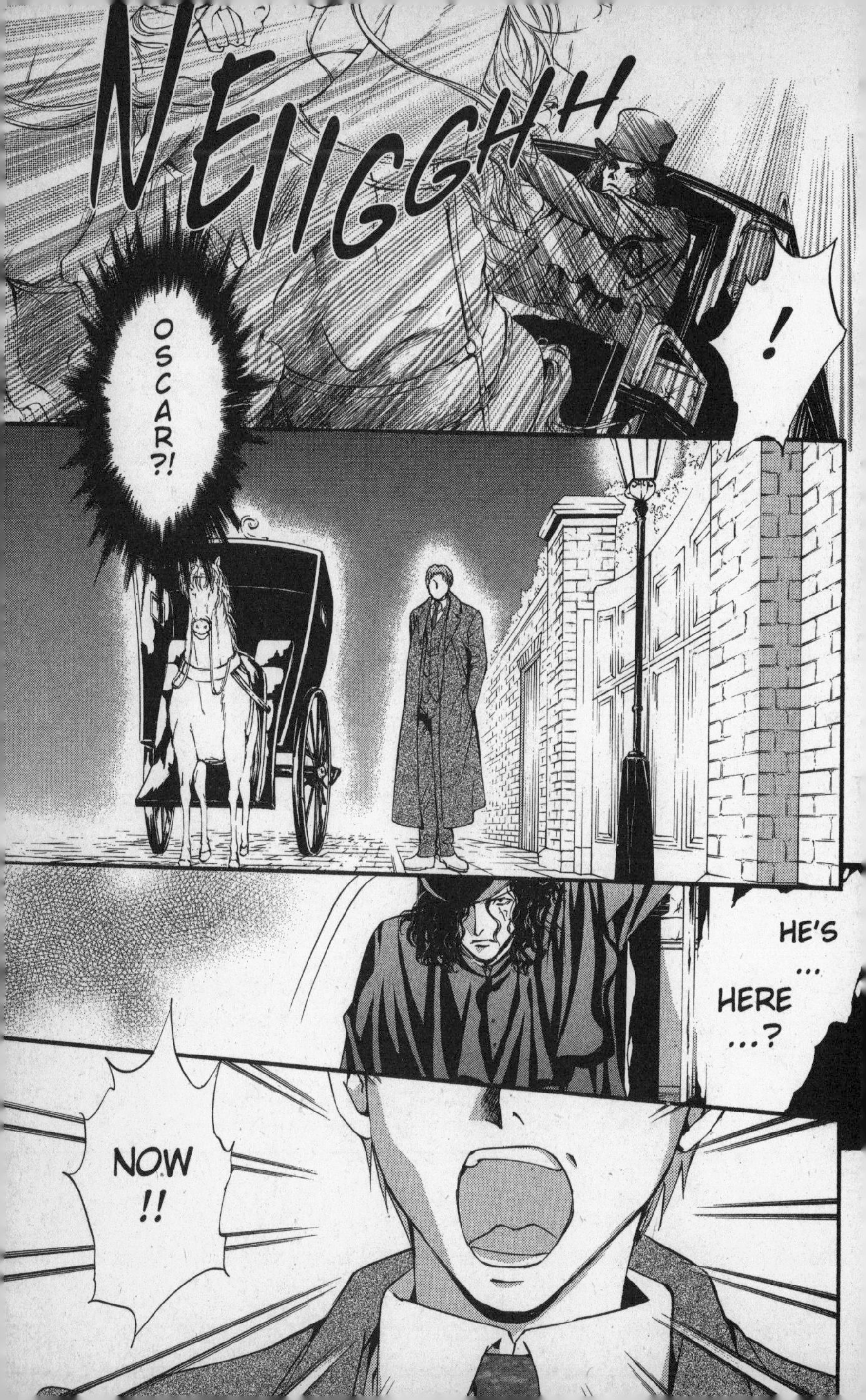
NEIIGGHH
!
OSCAR?!
HE'S ... HERE ...?
NOW!!

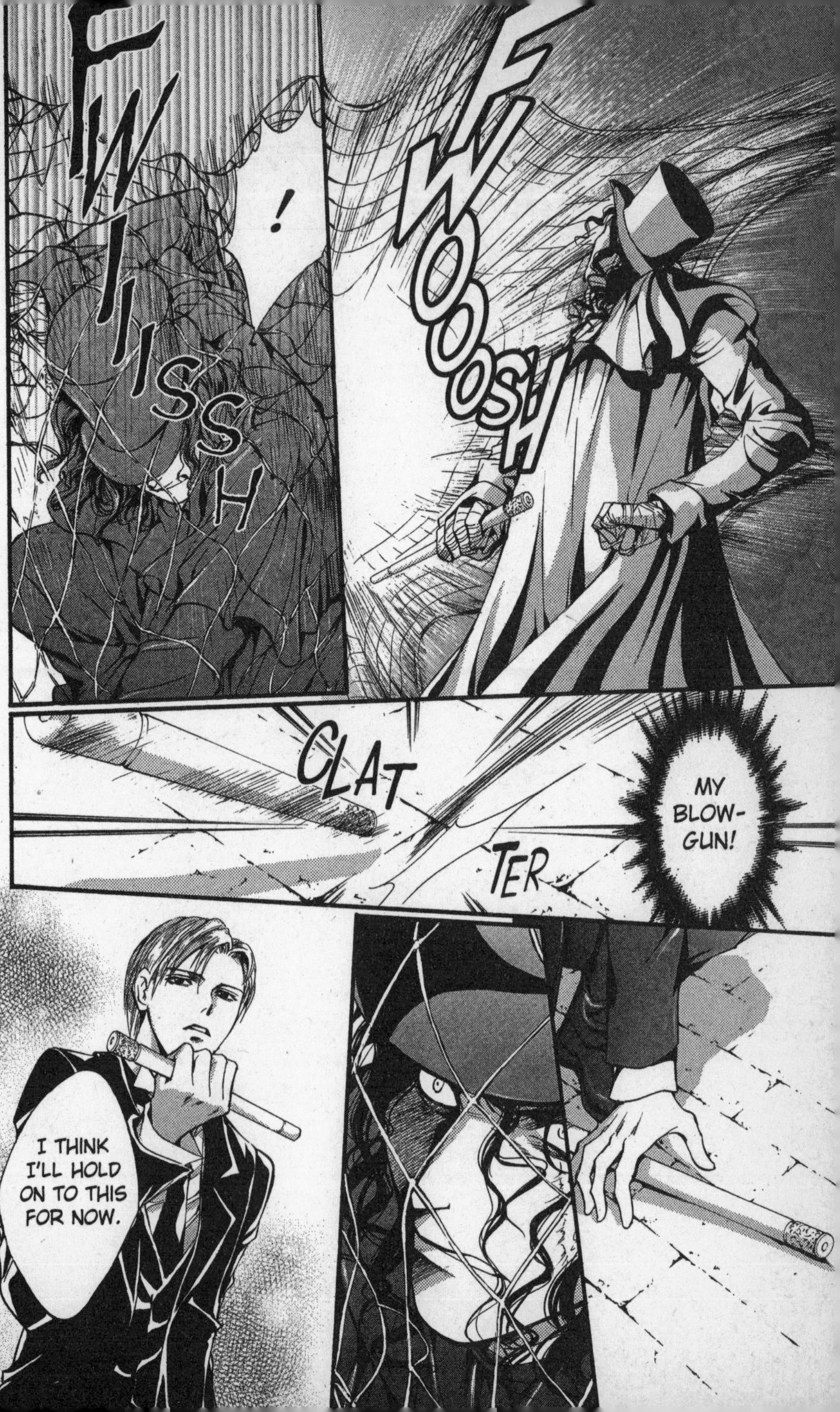
FWOOOSH
FWIISSH
!
MY BLOW-GUN!
CLATTER
I THINK I'LL HOLD ON TO THIS FOR NOW.

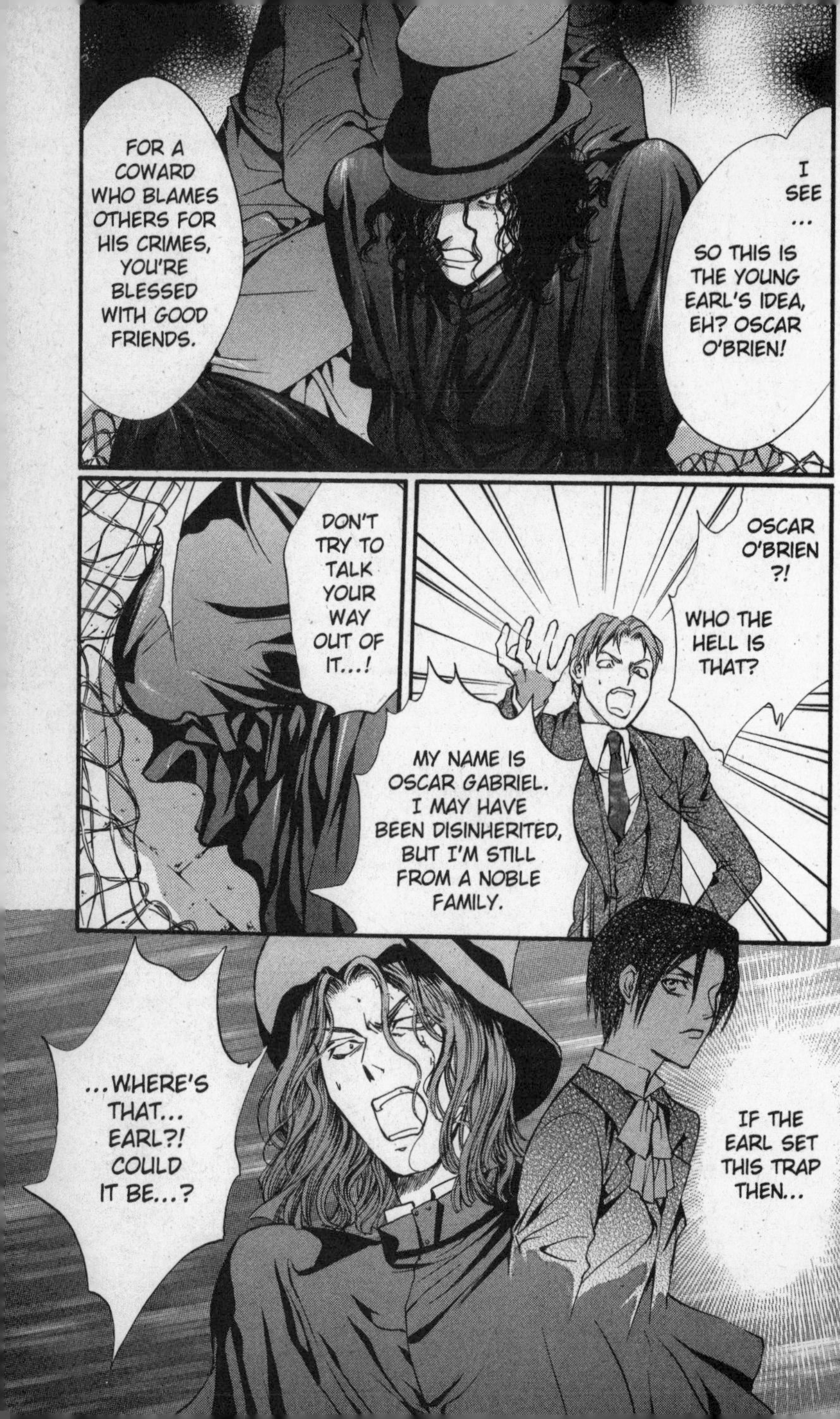
I SEE ... SO THIS IS THE YOUNG EARL'S IDEA, EH? OSCAR O'BRIEN!
FOR A COWARD WHO BLAMES OTHERS FOR HIS CRIMES, YOU'RE BLESSED WITH GOOD FRIENDS.
OSCAR O'BRIEN ?!
WHO THE HELL IS THAT?
MY NAME IS OSCAR GABRIEL. I MAY HAVE BEEN DISINHERITED, BUT I'M STILL FROM A NOBLE FAMILY.
DON'T TRY TO TALK YOUR WAY OUT OF IT...!
IF THE EARL SET THIS TRAP THEN...
...WHERE'S THAT... EARL?! COULD IT BE...?

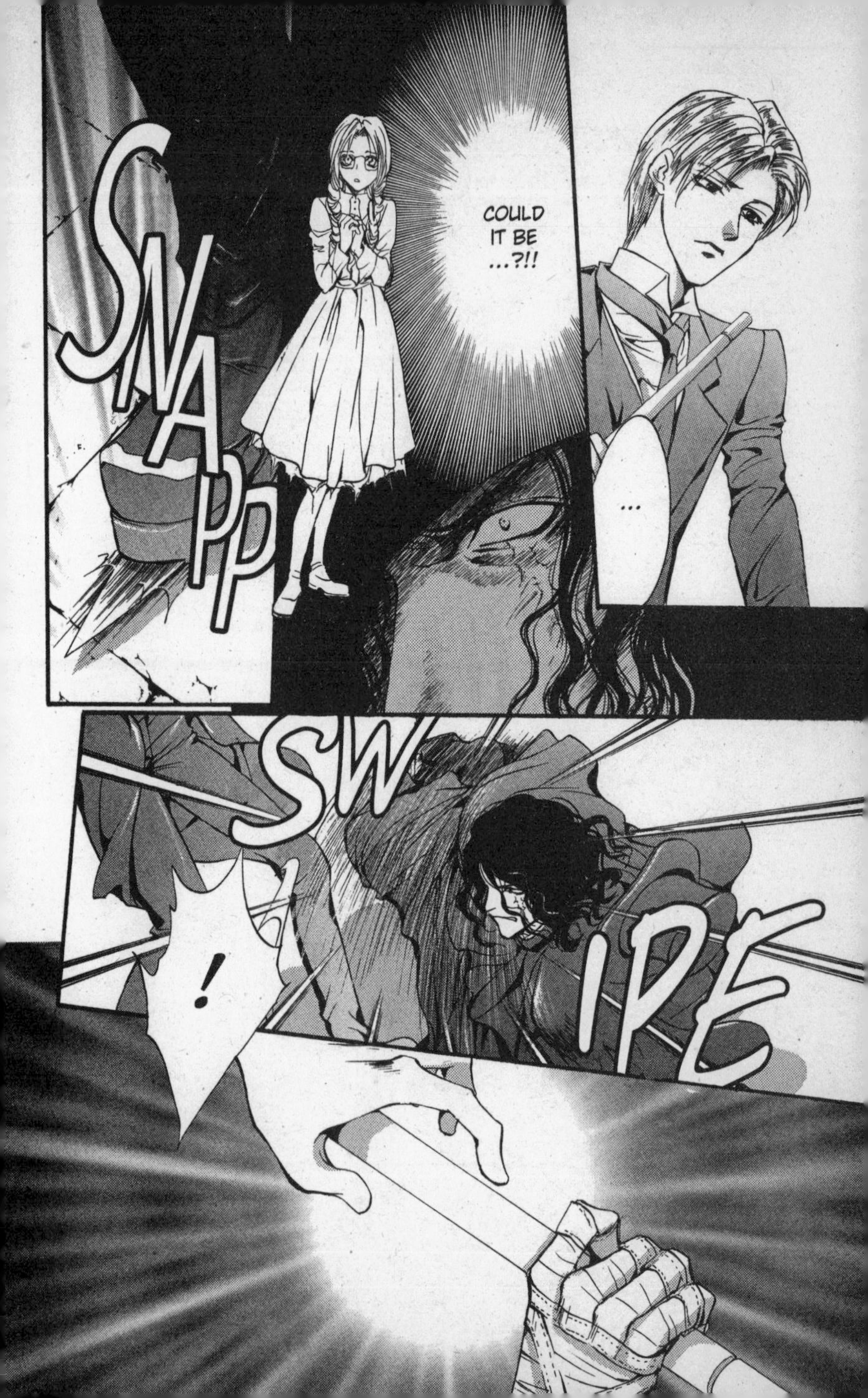
...
COULD IT BE ...?!!
SNAPP!
SWIPE
!

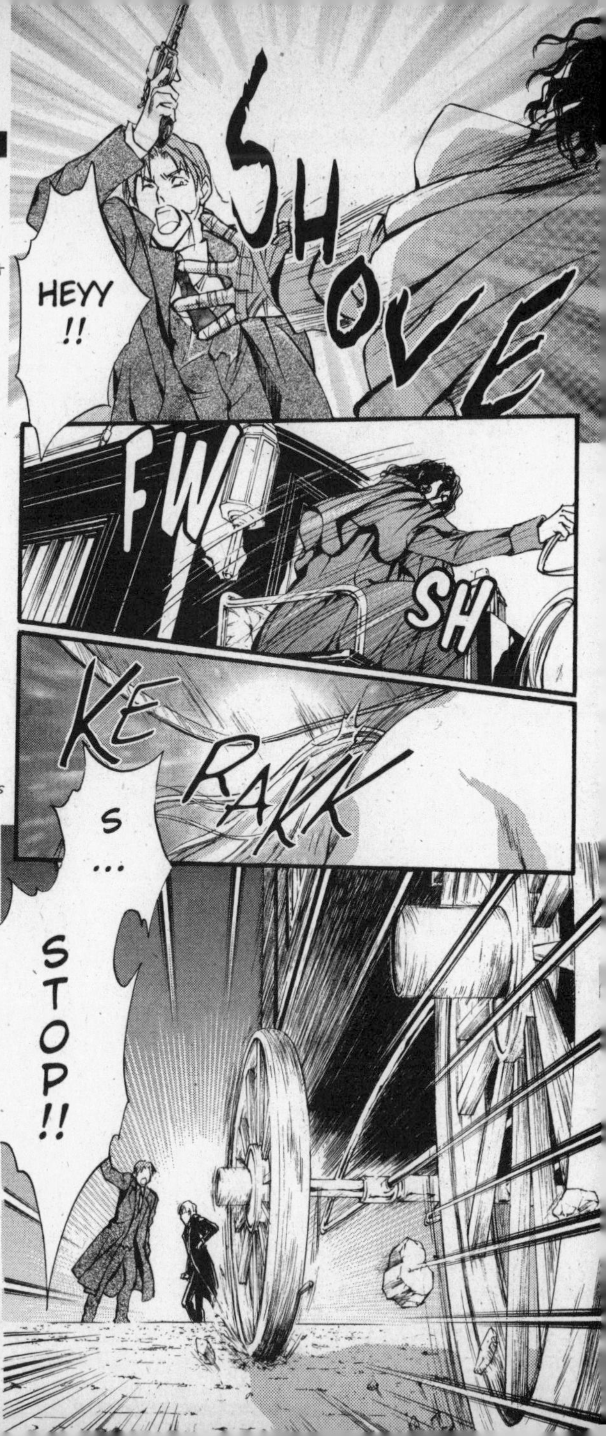
SHOVE
HEYY!!
FW
SH
KERAKK
S...
STOP!!

Oh yeah that's right, after *God-child Volume 2* when I mentioned that I'd like to see Saint Lukia's picture... someone actually sent it to me! Is this a color copy? It was much more laid back than I'd imagined. It shows two eyes on a tray with a sleepy gaze. Quite an unusual painting...

↓Like this.

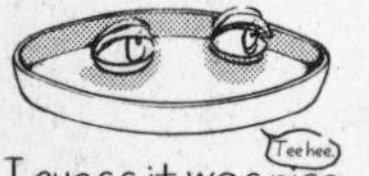
Teehee

I guess it was nice because it wasn't so graphic... Not only that but afterwards she puts her eyes back in her face so that's quite a miracle... Well thank you so much for satisfying my curiosity. (She bows) The most amazing painting that I've seen recently is in a book of Dante's songs in which a bird's entire body is covered with human faces. It's supposedly a bird of righteousness filled with human souls but... Huh? No, I'm way too scared to draw it... Even the wings and feet were all covered with faces... Meow!

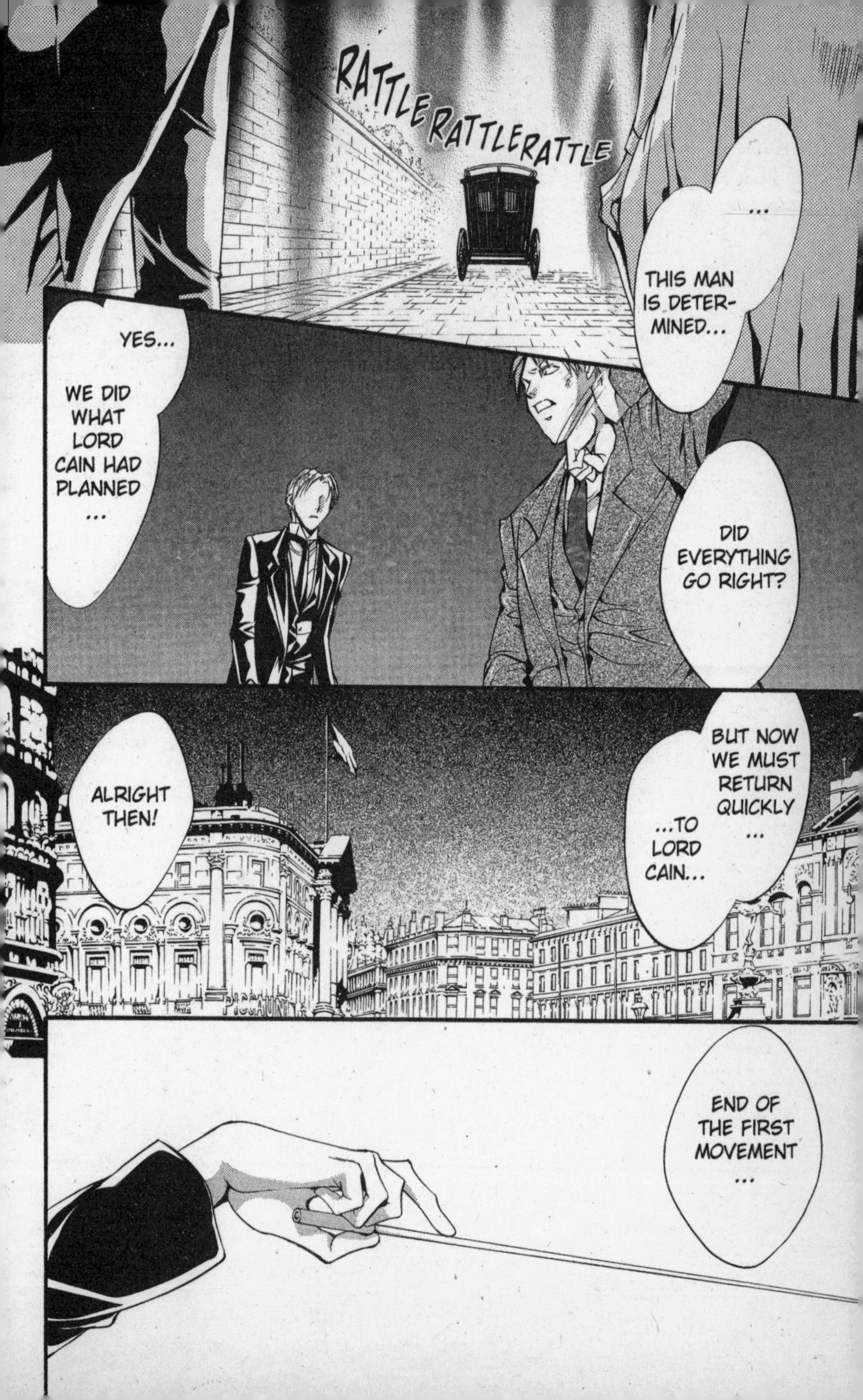
...
THIS MAN IS DETERMINED...
RATTLE RATTLE RATTLE
DID EVERYTHING GO RIGHT?
YES...
WE DID WHAT LORD CAIN HAD PLANNED...
BUT NOW WE MUST RETURN QUICKLY...
...TO LORD CAIN...
ALRIGHT THEN!
END OF THE FIRST MOVEMENT...

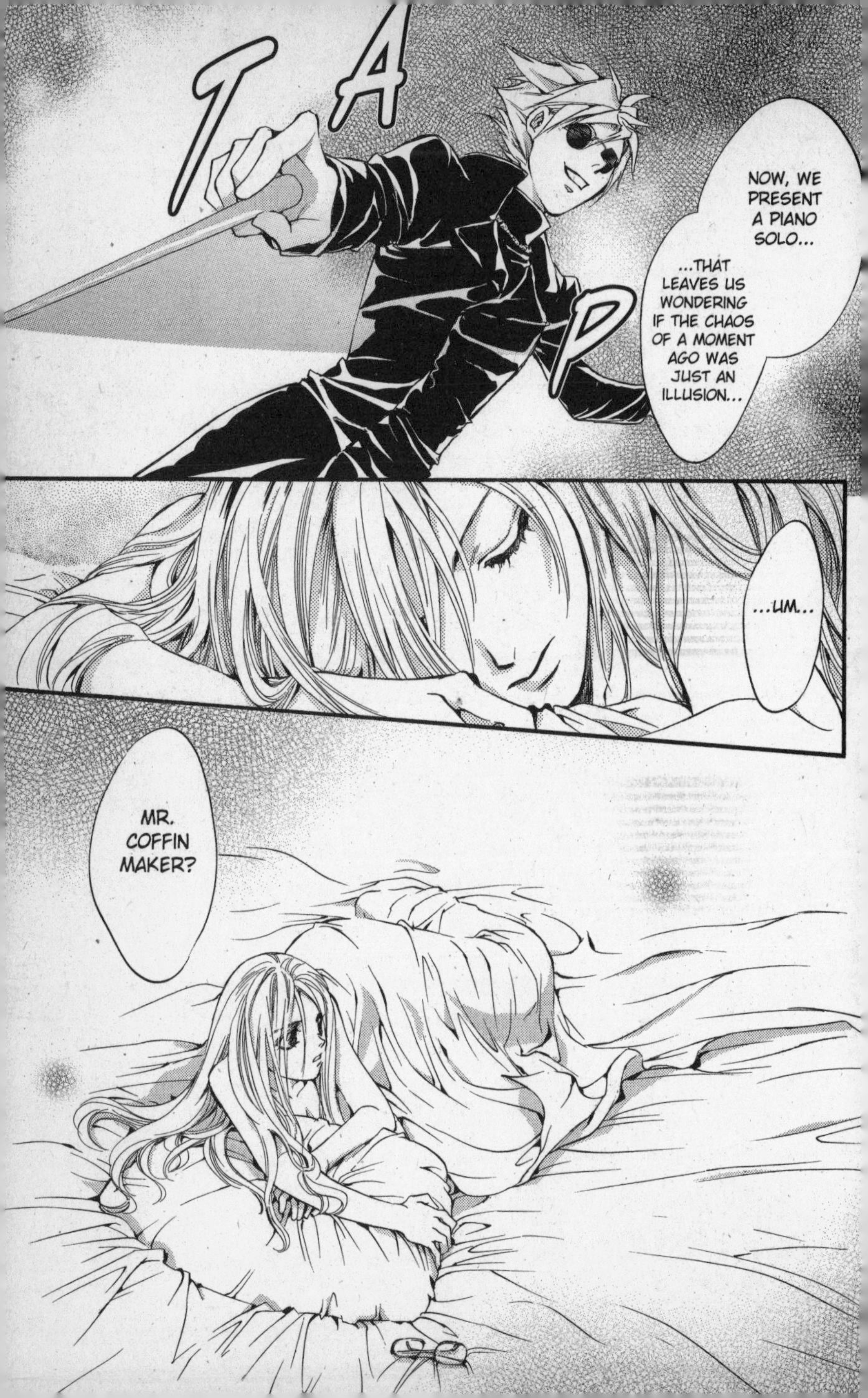
TAP
NOW, WE PRESENT A PIANO SOLO...
...THAT LEAVES US WONDERING IF THE CHAOS OF A MOMENT AGO WAS JUST AN ILLUSION...
...UM...
MR. COFFIN MAKER?

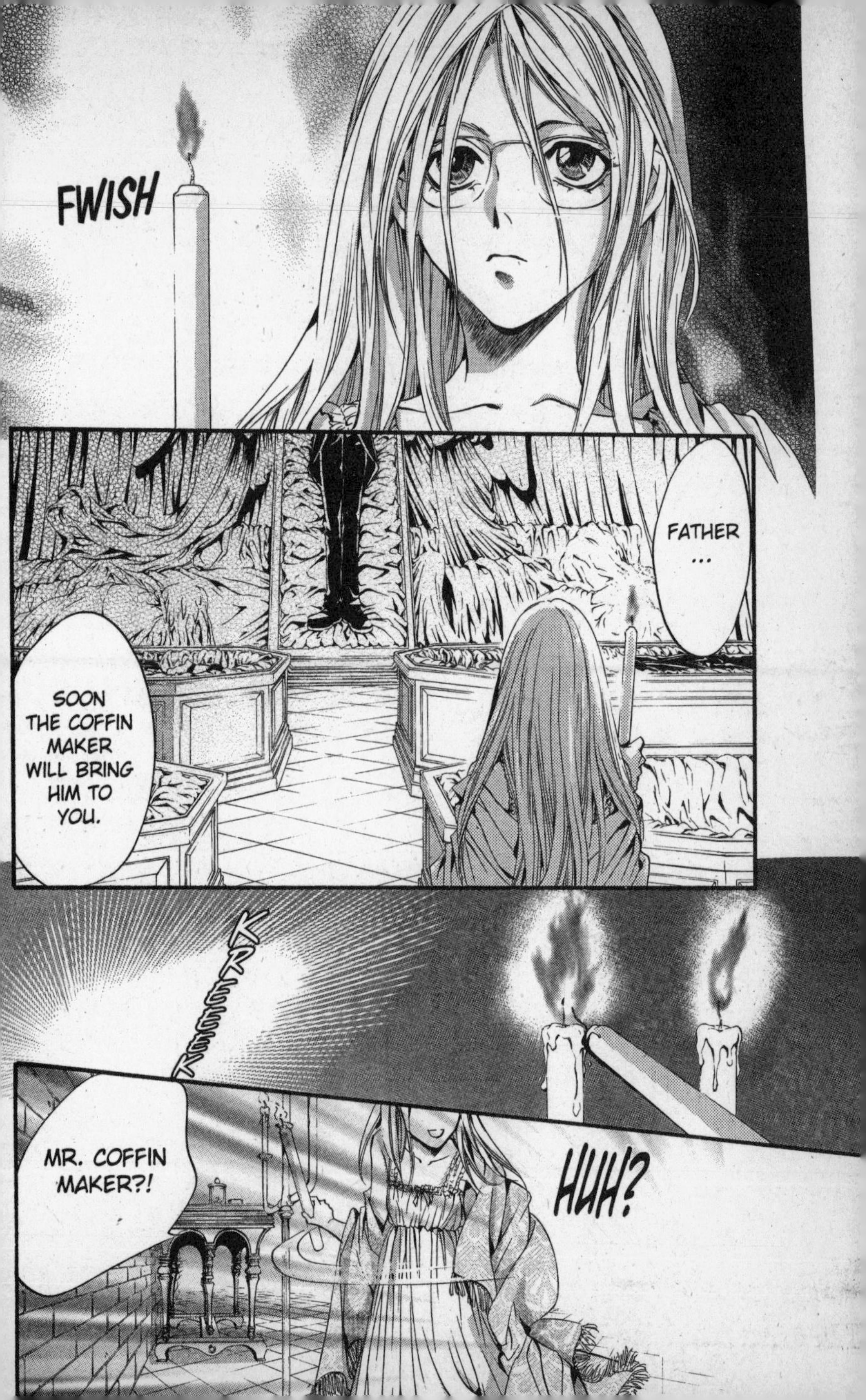
FWISH
FATHER ...
SOON THE COFFIN MAKER WILL BRING HIM TO YOU.
KREEEEEK
HUH?
MR. COFFIN MAKER?!

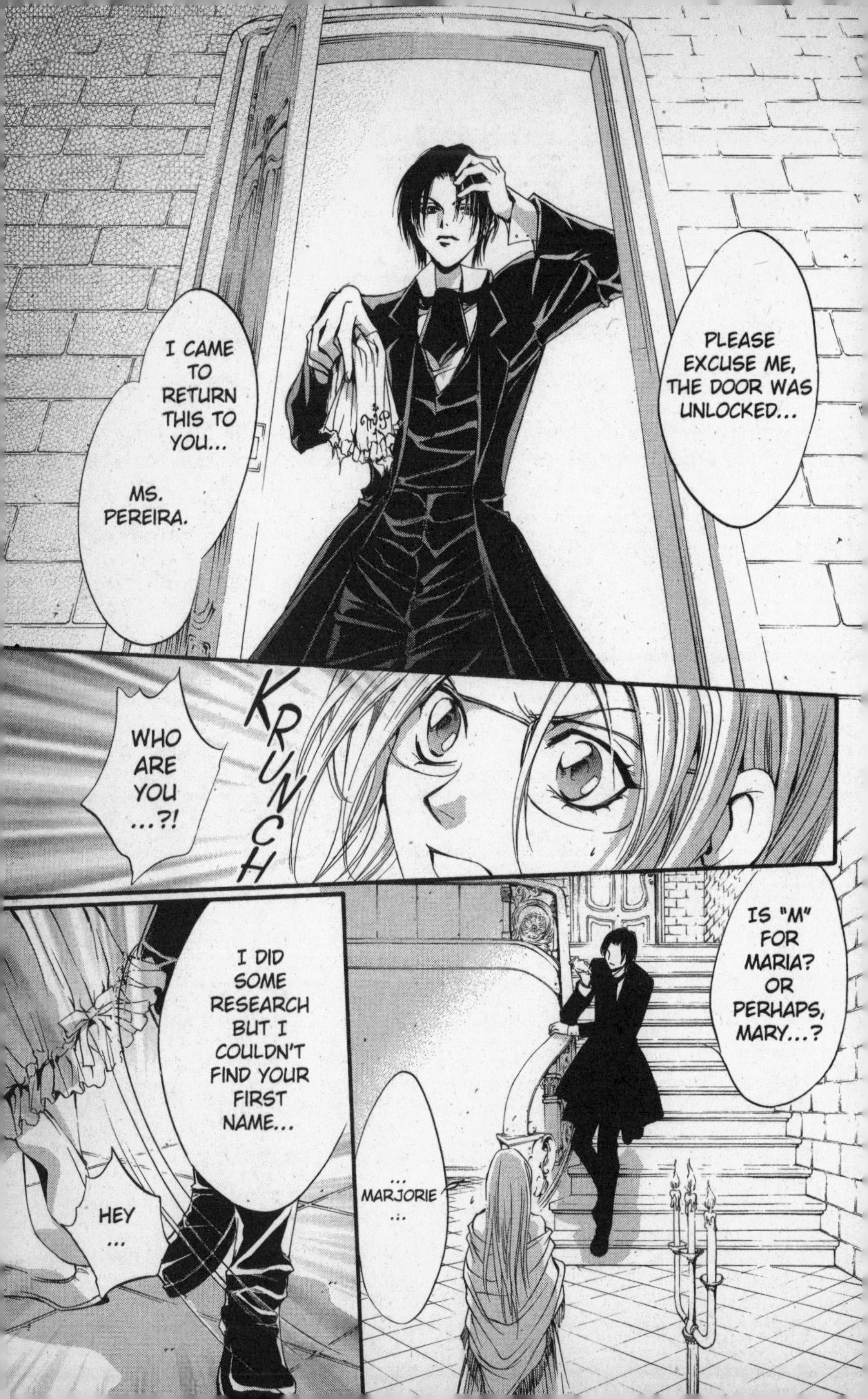
PLEASE EXCUSE ME, THE DOOR WAS UNLOCKED...
I CAME TO RETURN THIS TO YOU...
MS. PEREIRA.
KRUNCH
WHO ARE YOU ...?!
IS "M" FOR MARIA? OR PERHAPS, MARY...?
I DID SOME RESEARCH BUT I COULDN'T FIND YOUR FIRST NAME...
... MARJORIE ...
HEY ...

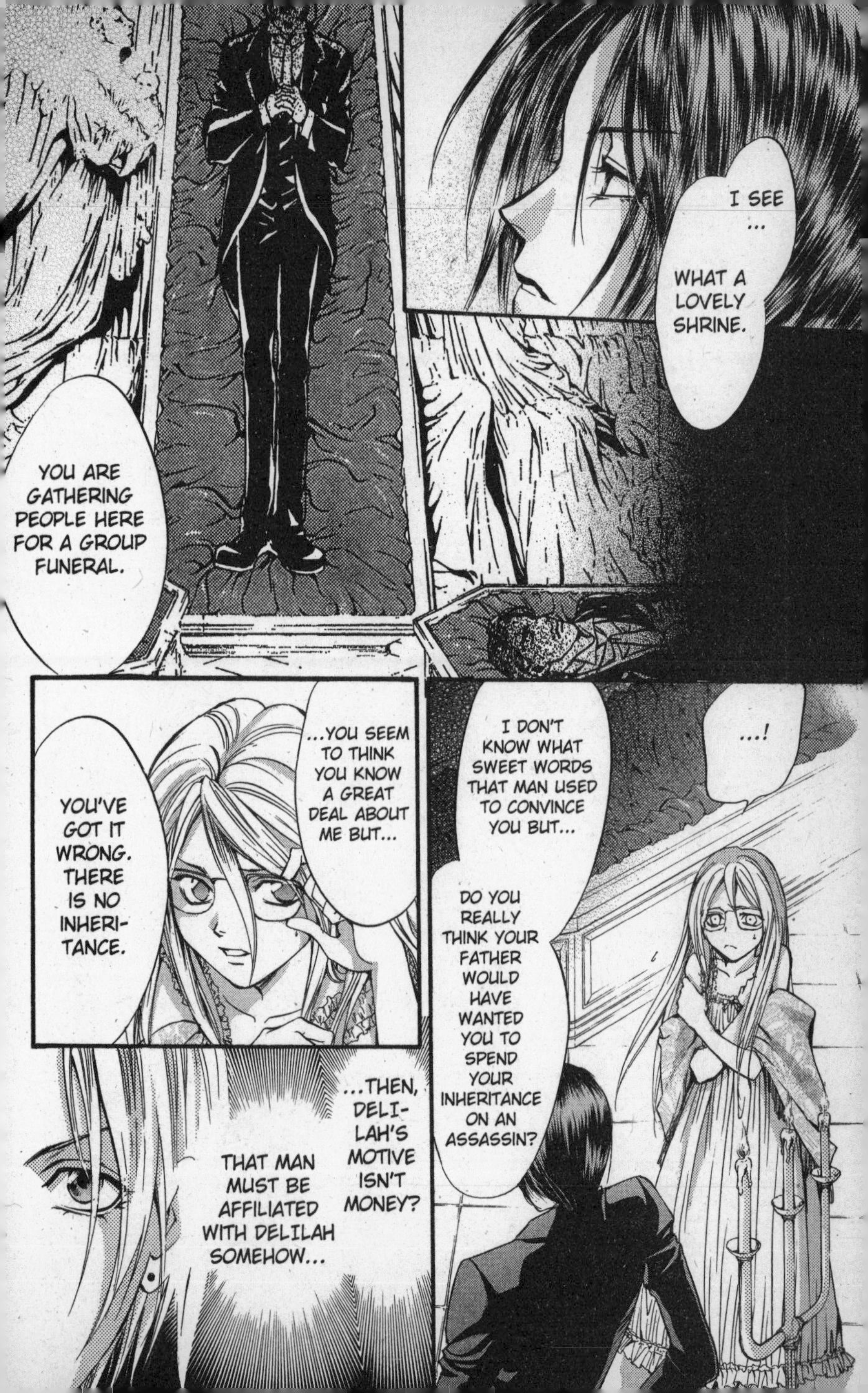
I SEE ...
WHAT A LOVELY SHRINE.
YOU ARE GATHERING PEOPLE HERE FOR A GROUP FUNERAL.
...!
I DON'T KNOW WHAT SWEET WORDS THAT MAN USED TO CONVINCE YOU BUT...
DO YOU REALLY THINK YOUR FATHER WOULD HAVE WANTED YOU TO SPEND YOUR INHERITANCE ON AN ASSASSIN?
...YOU SEEM TO THINK YOU KNOW A GREAT DEAL ABOUT ME BUT...
YOU'VE GOT IT WRONG. THERE IS NO INHERI-TANCE.
...THEN, DELI-LAH'S MOTIVE ISN'T MONEY?
THAT MAN MUST BE AFFILIATED WITH DELILAH SOMEHOW...

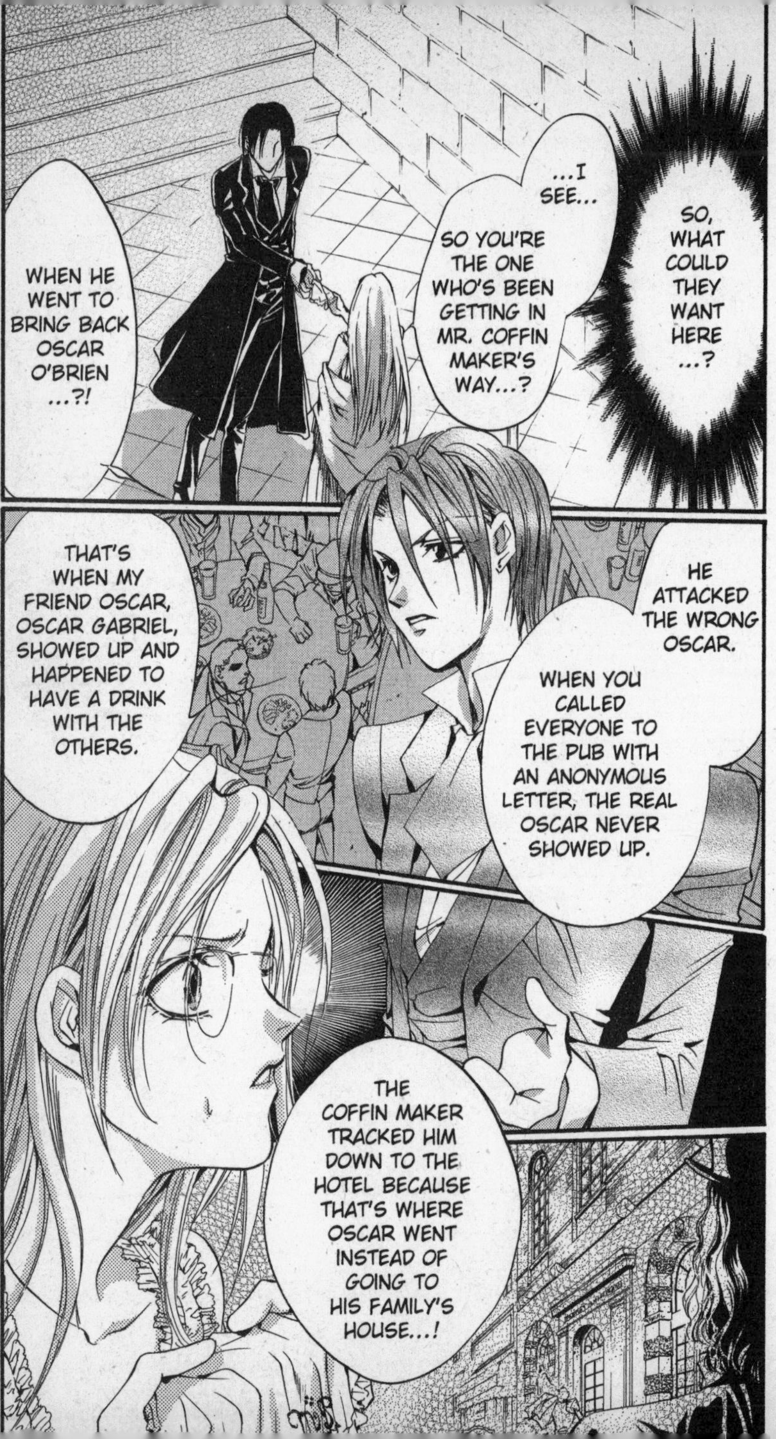
SO, WHAT COULD THEY WANT HERE ...?
...I SEE...
SO YOU'RE THE ONE WHO'S BEEN GETTING IN MR. COFFIN MAKER'S WAY...?
WHEN HE WENT TO BRING BACK OSCAR O'BRIEN ...?!
HE ATTACKED THE WRONG OSCAR.
WHEN YOU CALLED EVERYONE TO THE PUB WITH AN ANONYMOUS LETTER, THE REAL OSCAR NEVER SHOWED UP.
THAT'S WHEN MY FRIEND OSCAR, OSCAR GABRIEL, SHOWED UP AND HAPPENED TO HAVE A DRINK WITH THE OTHERS.
THE COFFIN MAKER TRACKED HIM DOWN TO THE HOTEL BECAUSE THAT'S WHERE OSCAR WENT INSTEAD OF GOING TO HIS FAMILY'S HOUSE...!

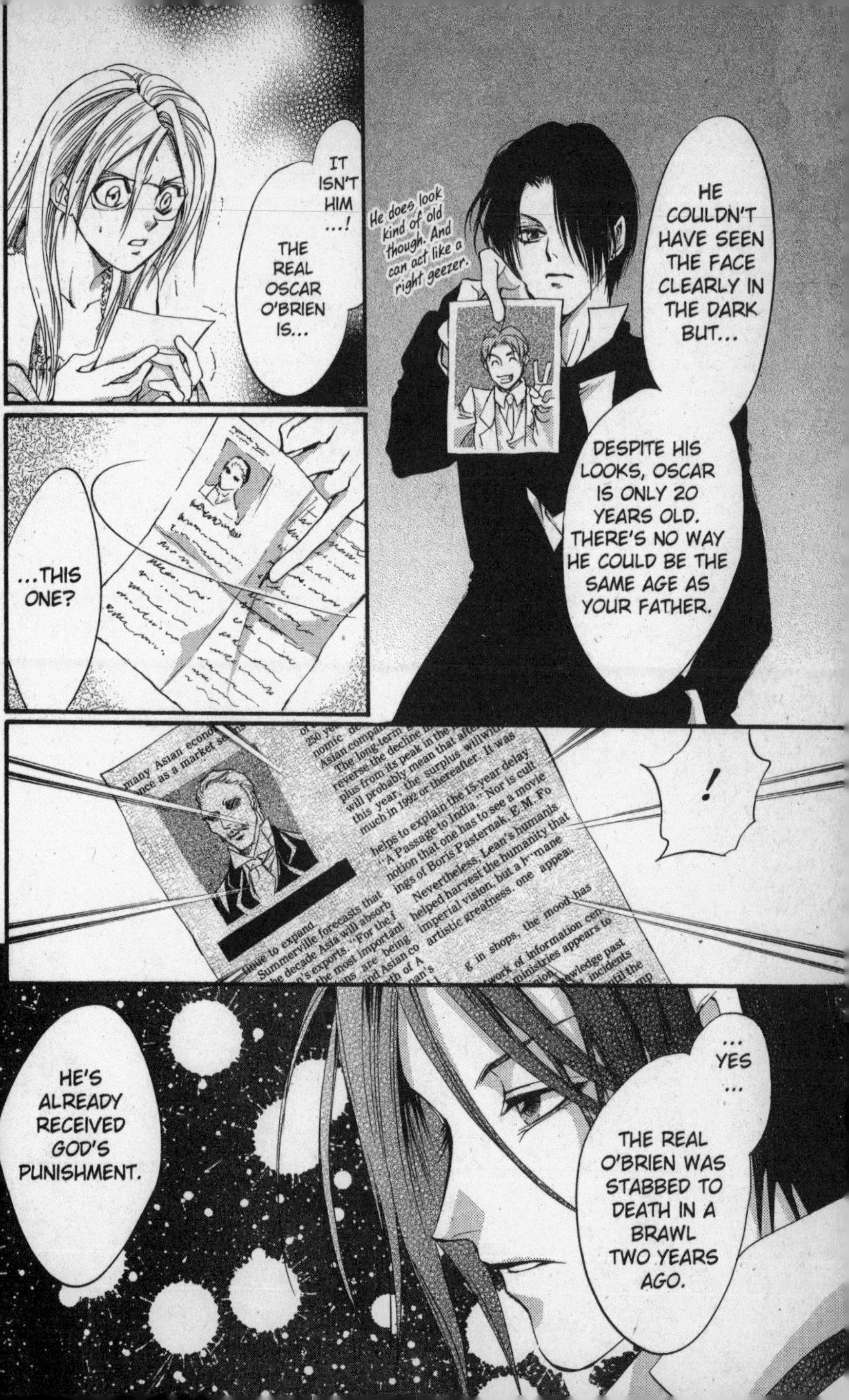
HE COULDN'T HAVE SEEN THE FACE CLEARLY IN THE DARK BUT...
DESPITE HIS LOOKS, OSCAR IS ONLY 20 YEARS OLD. THERE'S NO WAY HE COULD BE THE SAME AGE AS YOUR FATHER.
He does look kind of old though. And can act like a right geezer.
IT ISN'T HIM ...!
THE REAL OSCAR O'BRIEN IS...
...THIS ONE?
!
... YES ...
THE REAL O'BRIEN WAS STABBED TO DEATH IN A BRAWL TWO YEARS AGO.
HE'S ALREADY RECEIVED GOD'S PUNISHMENT.

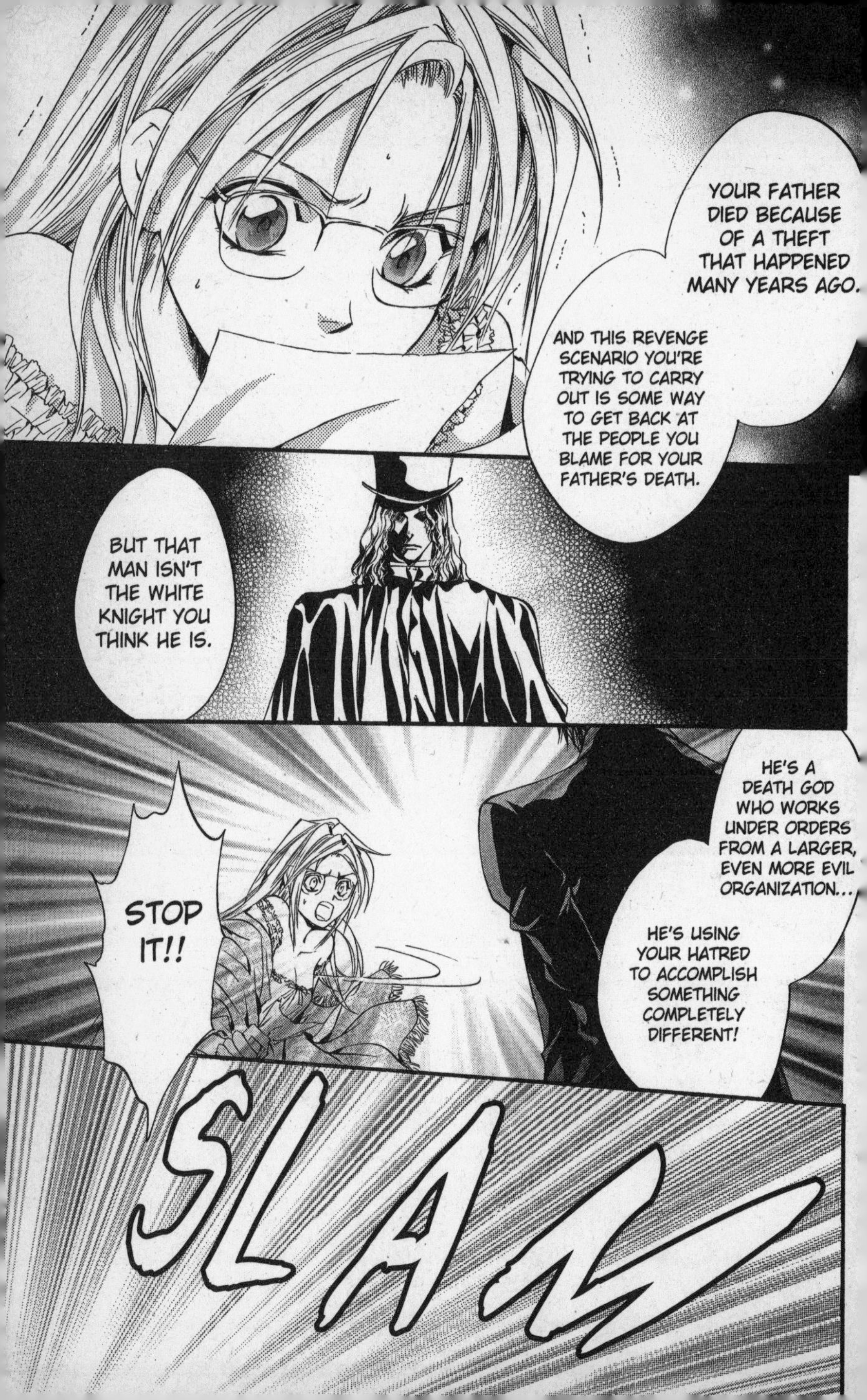
YOUR FATHER DIED BECAUSE OF A THEFT THAT HAPPENED MANY YEARS AGO.
AND THIS REVENGE SCENARIO YOU'RE TRYING TO CARRY OUT IS SOME WAY TO GET BACK AT THE PEOPLE YOU BLAME FOR YOUR FATHER'S DEATH.
BUT THAT MAN ISN'T THE WHITE KNIGHT YOU THINK HE IS.
HE'S A DEATH GOD WHO WORKS UNDER ORDERS FROM A LARGER, EVEN MORE EVIL ORGANIZATION...
HE'S USING YOUR HATRED TO ACCOMPLISH SOMETHING COMPLETELY DIFFERENT!
STOP IT!!
SLAM

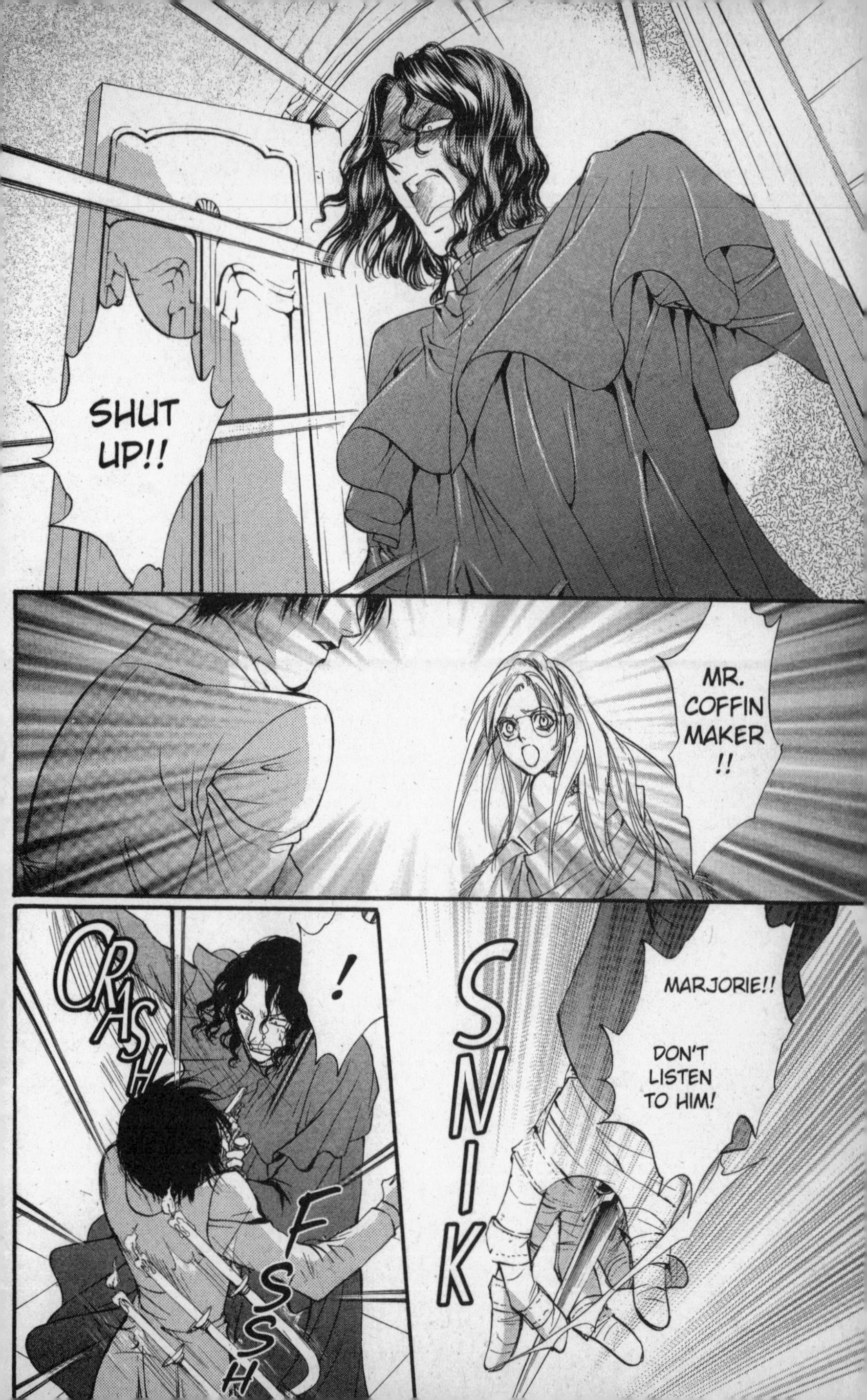
SHUT UP!!
MR. COFFIN MAKER !!
MARJORIE!!
DON'T LISTEN TO HIM!
SNIK
!
CRASH
FSSH

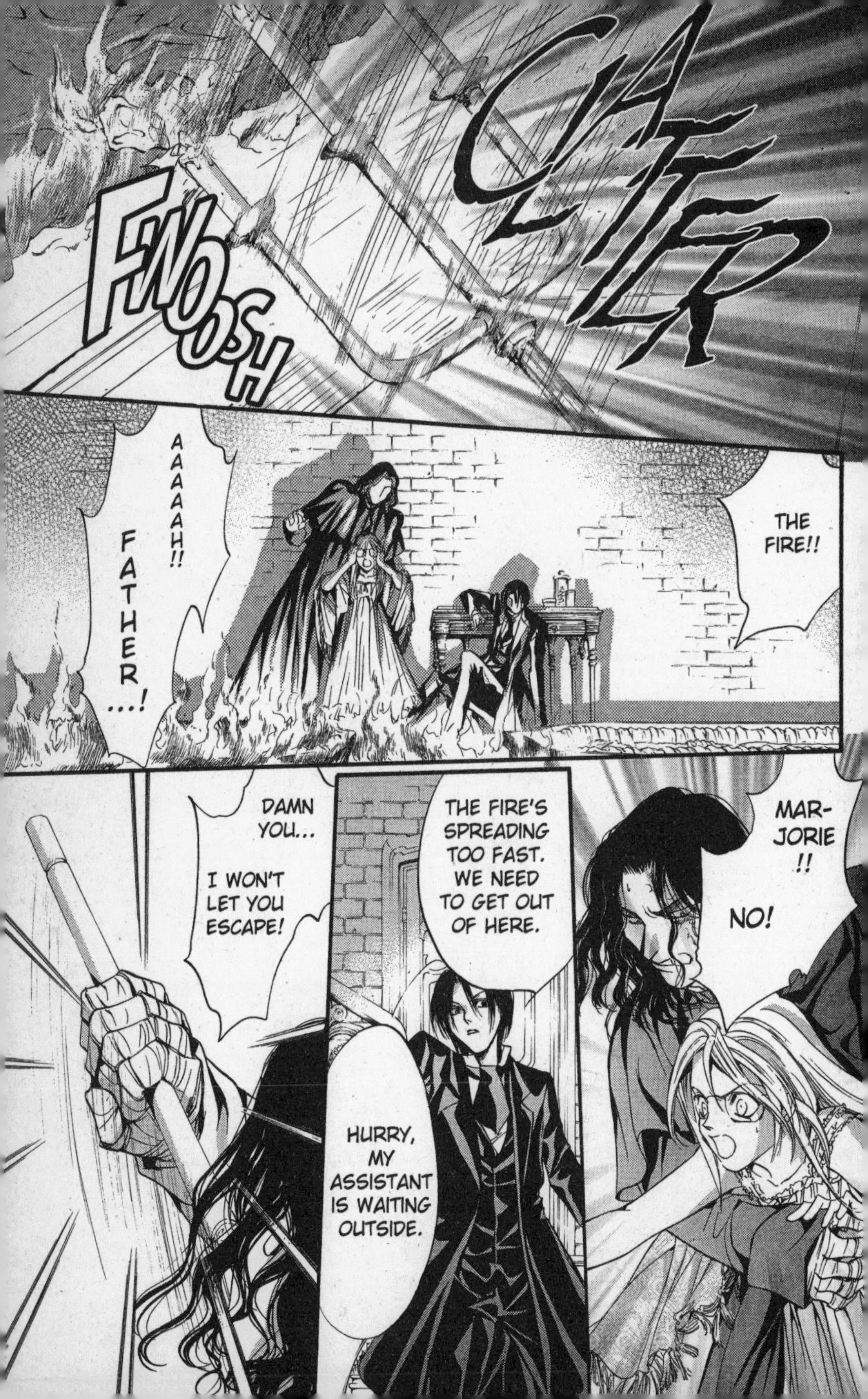
CLATTER
FWOOSH
THE FIRE!!
AAAAAH!!
FATHER...!
MAR-JORIE!!
NO!
THE FIRE'S SPREADING TOO FAST. WE NEED TO GET OUT OF HERE.
HURRY, MY ASSISTANT IS WAITING OUTSIDE.
DAMN YOU...
I WON'T LET YOU ESCAPE!

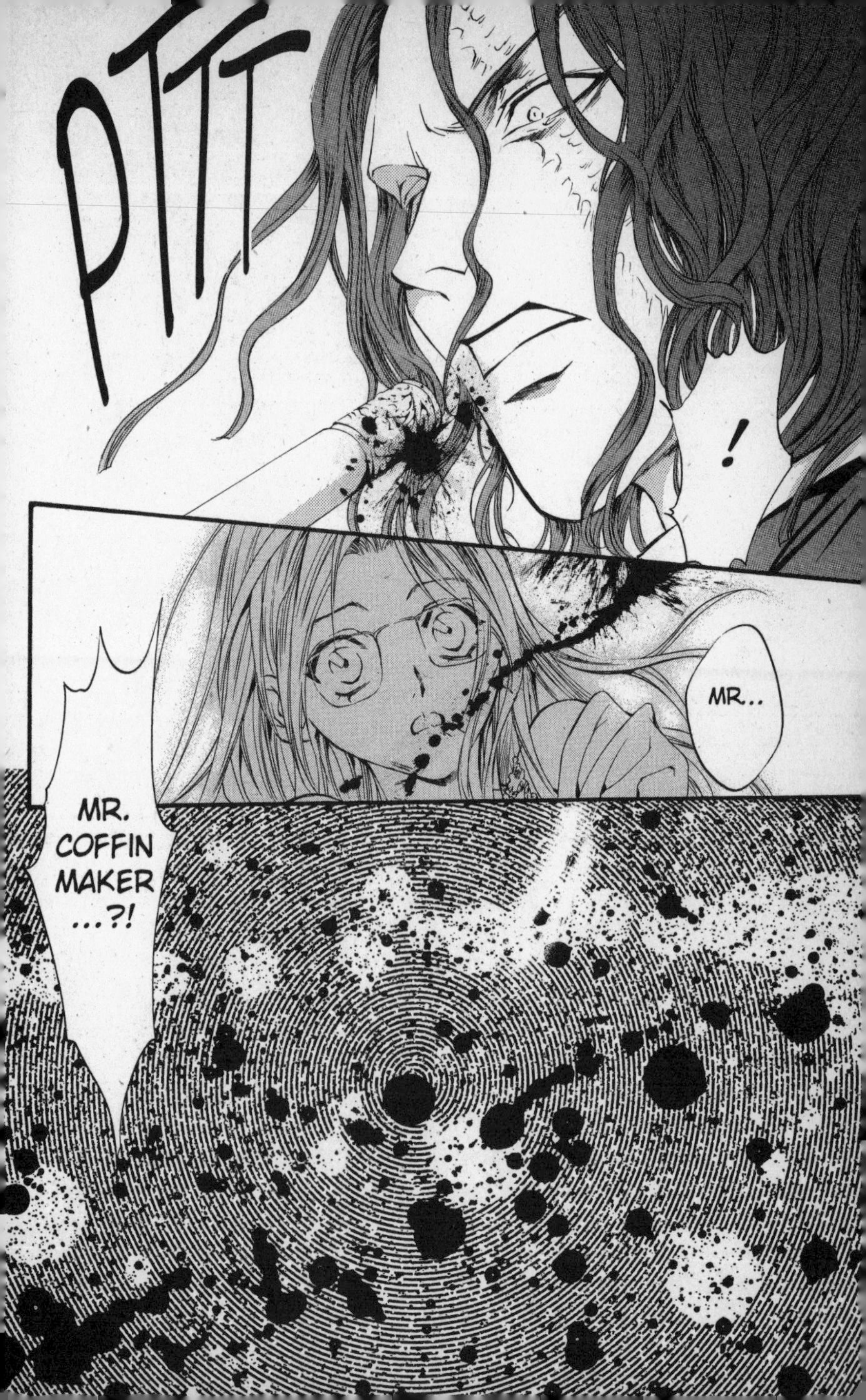
PTTT
!
MR..
MR. COFFIN MAKER ...?!

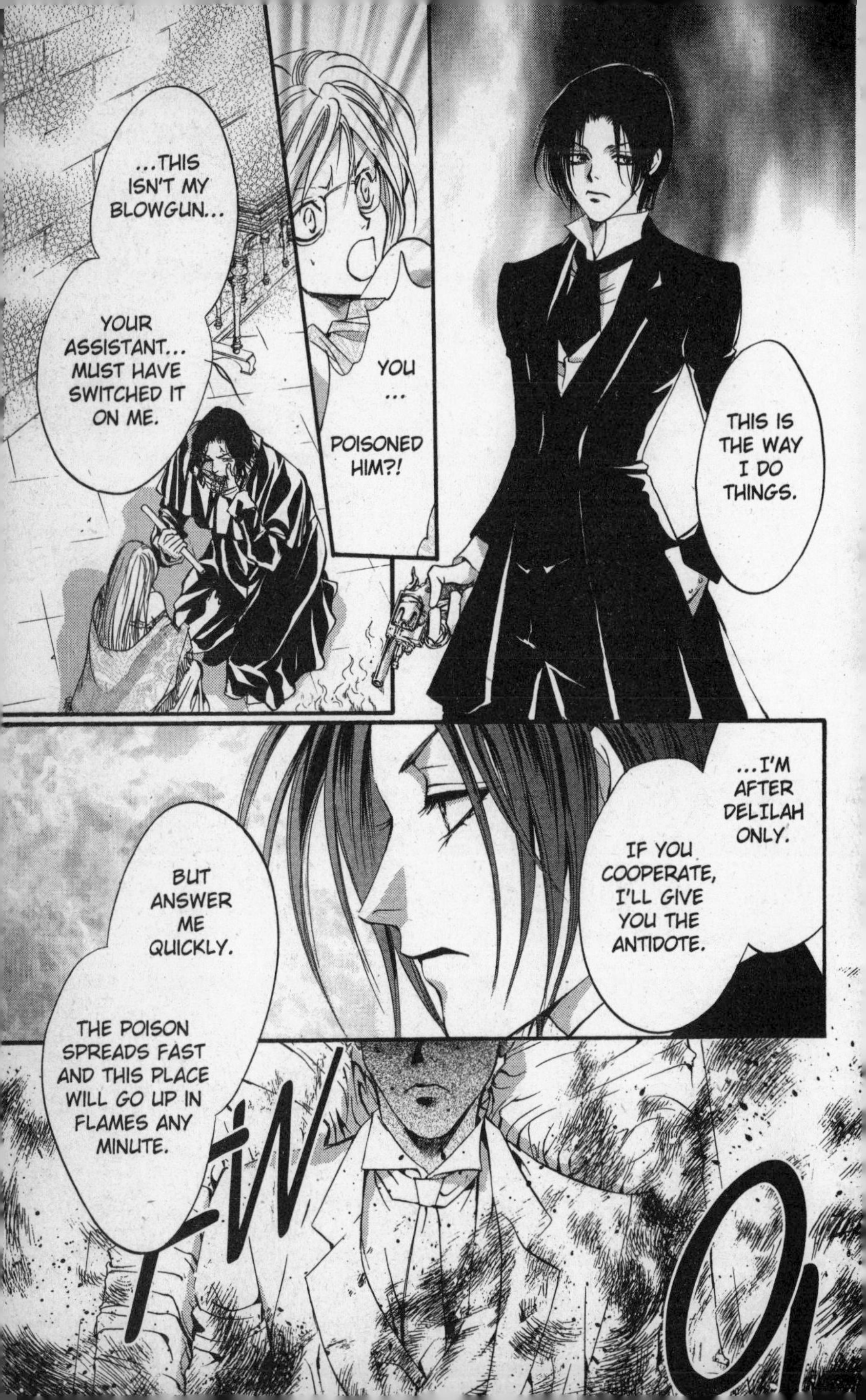
THIS IS THE WAY I DO THINGS.
YOU ... POISONED HIM?!
...THIS ISN'T MY BLOWGUN...
YOUR ASSISTANT... MUST HAVE SWITCHED IT ON ME.
...I'M AFTER DELILAH ONLY.
IF YOU COOPERATE, I'LL GIVE YOU THE ANTIDOTE.
BUT ANSWER ME QUICKLY.
THE POISON SPREADS FAST AND THIS PLACE WILL GO UP IN FLAMES ANY MINUTE.

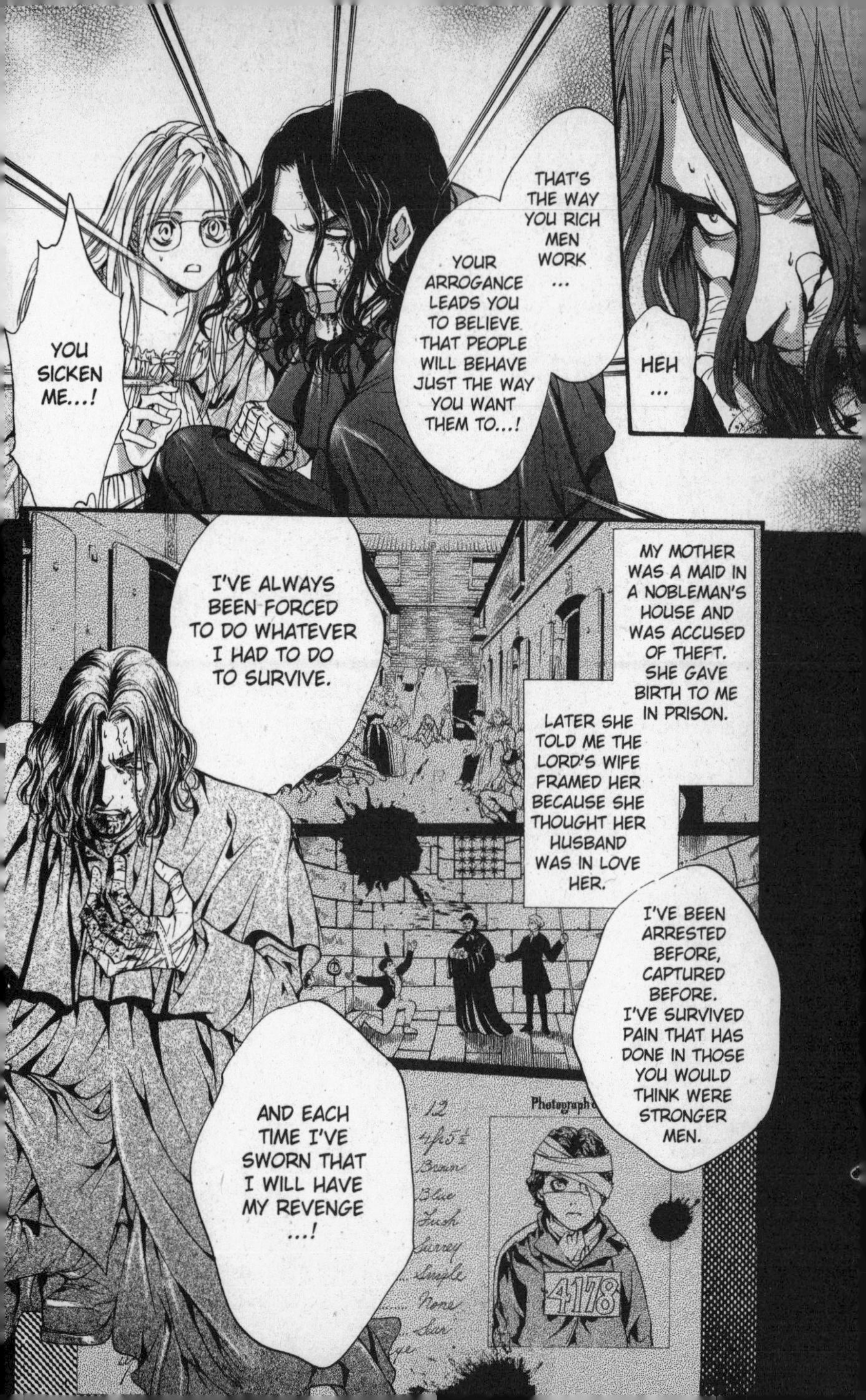
HEH ...
THAT'S THE WAY YOU RICH MEN WORK ...
YOUR ARROGANCE LEADS YOU TO BELIEVE THAT PEOPLE WILL BEHAVE JUST THE WAY YOU WANT THEM TO...!
YOU SICKEN ME...!
MY MOTHER WAS A MAID IN A NOBLEMAN'S HOUSE AND WAS ACCUSED OF THEFT. SHE GAVE BIRTH TO ME IN PRISON.
LATER SHE TOLD ME THE LORD'S WIFE FRAMED HER BECAUSE SHE THOUGHT HER HUSBAND WAS IN LOVE HER.
I'VE ALWAYS BEEN FORCED TO DO WHATEVER I HAD TO DO TO SURVIVE.
I'VE BEEN ARRESTED BEFORE, CAPTURED BEFORE. I'VE SURVIVED PAIN THAT HAS DONE IN THOSE YOU WOULD THINK WERE STRONGER MEN.
AND EACH TIME I'VE SWORN THAT I WILL HAVE MY REVENGE ...!
4178

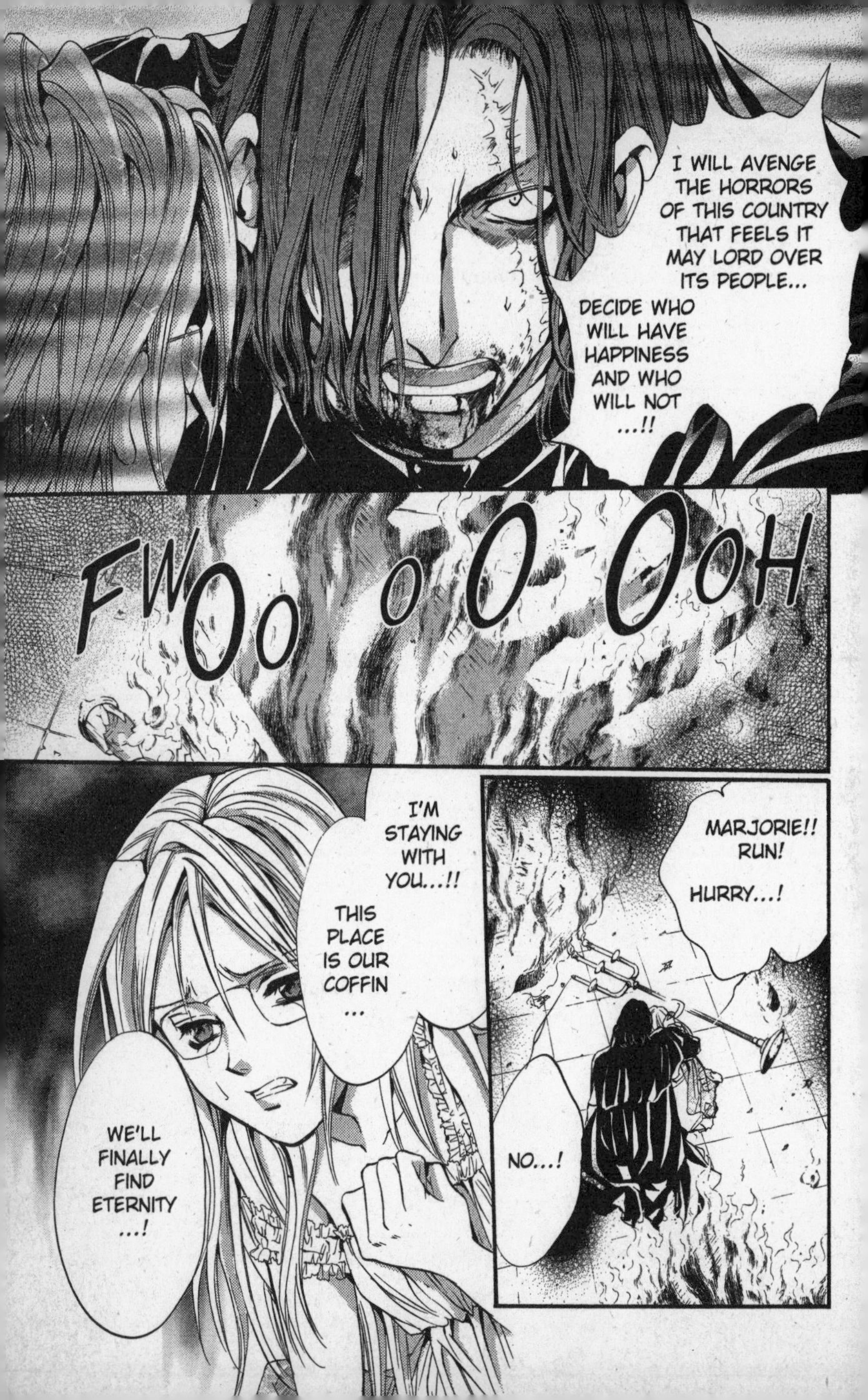
I WILL AVENGE THE HORRORS OF THIS COUNTRY THAT FEELS IT MAY LORD OVER ITS PEOPLE...
DECIDE WHO WILL HAVE HAPPINESS AND WHO WILL NOT ...!!
FWOOOOOOH
MARJORIE!! RUN!
HURRY...!
NO...!
I'M STAYING WITH YOU...!!
THIS PLACE IS OUR COFFIN ...
WE'LL FINALLY FIND ETERNITY ...!

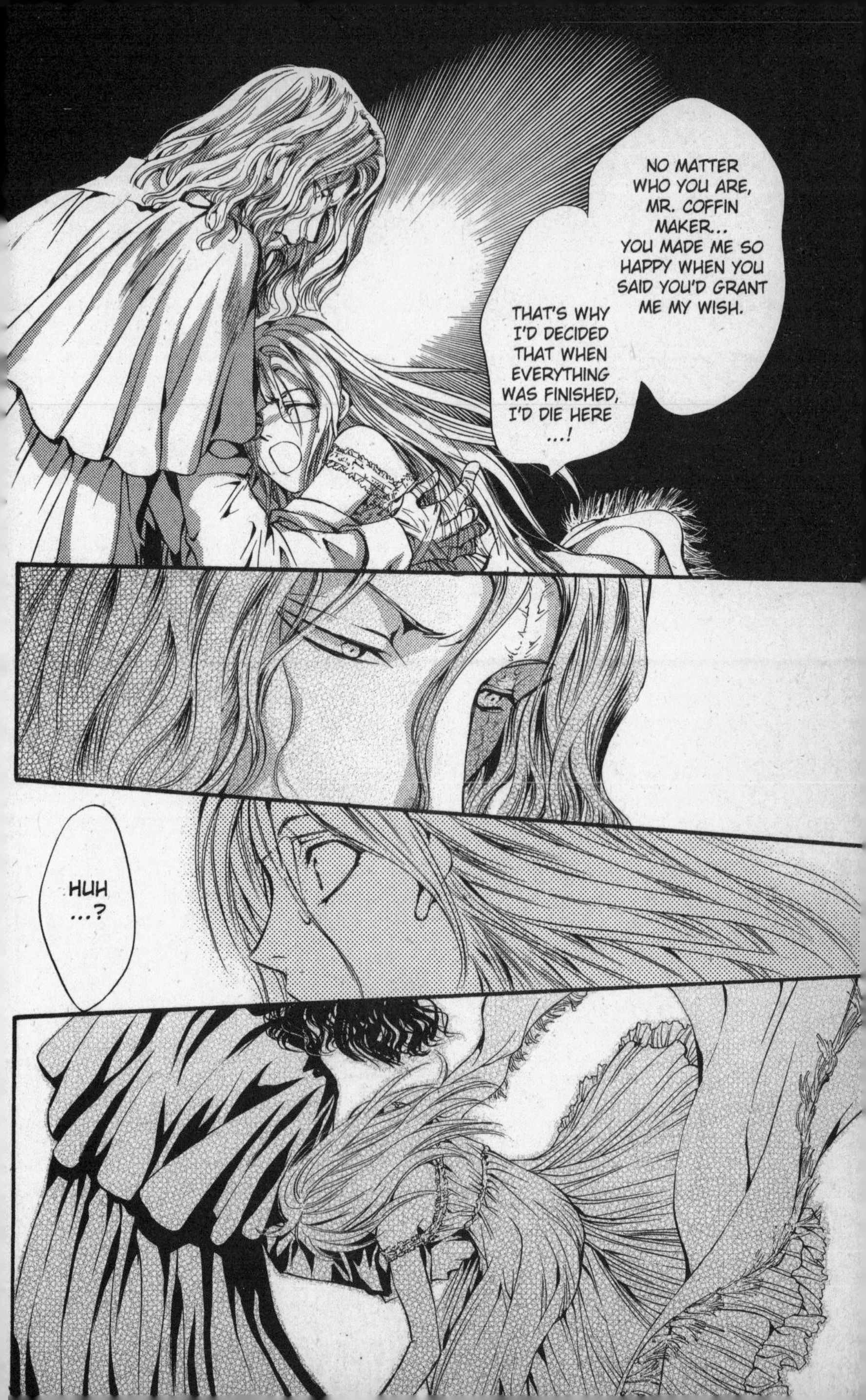
NO MATTER WHO YOU ARE, MR. COFFIN MAKER... YOU MADE ME SO HAPPY WHEN YOU SAID YOU'D GRANT ME MY WISH.
THAT'S WHY I'D DECIDED THAT WHEN EVERYTHING WAS FINISHED, I'D DIE HERE ...!
HUH ...?

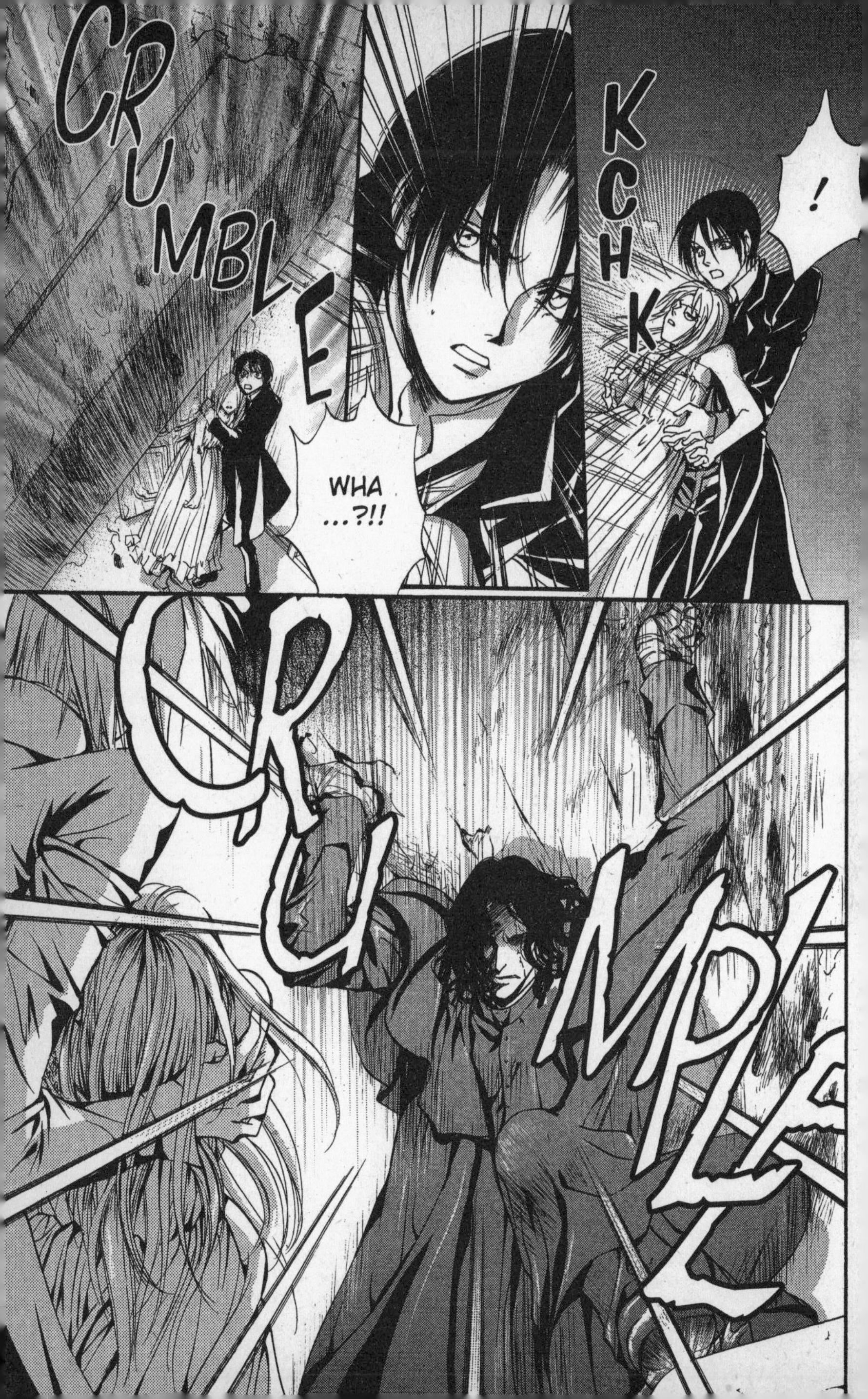
KCHK
!
WHA ...?!!
CRUMBLE
CRUMPL

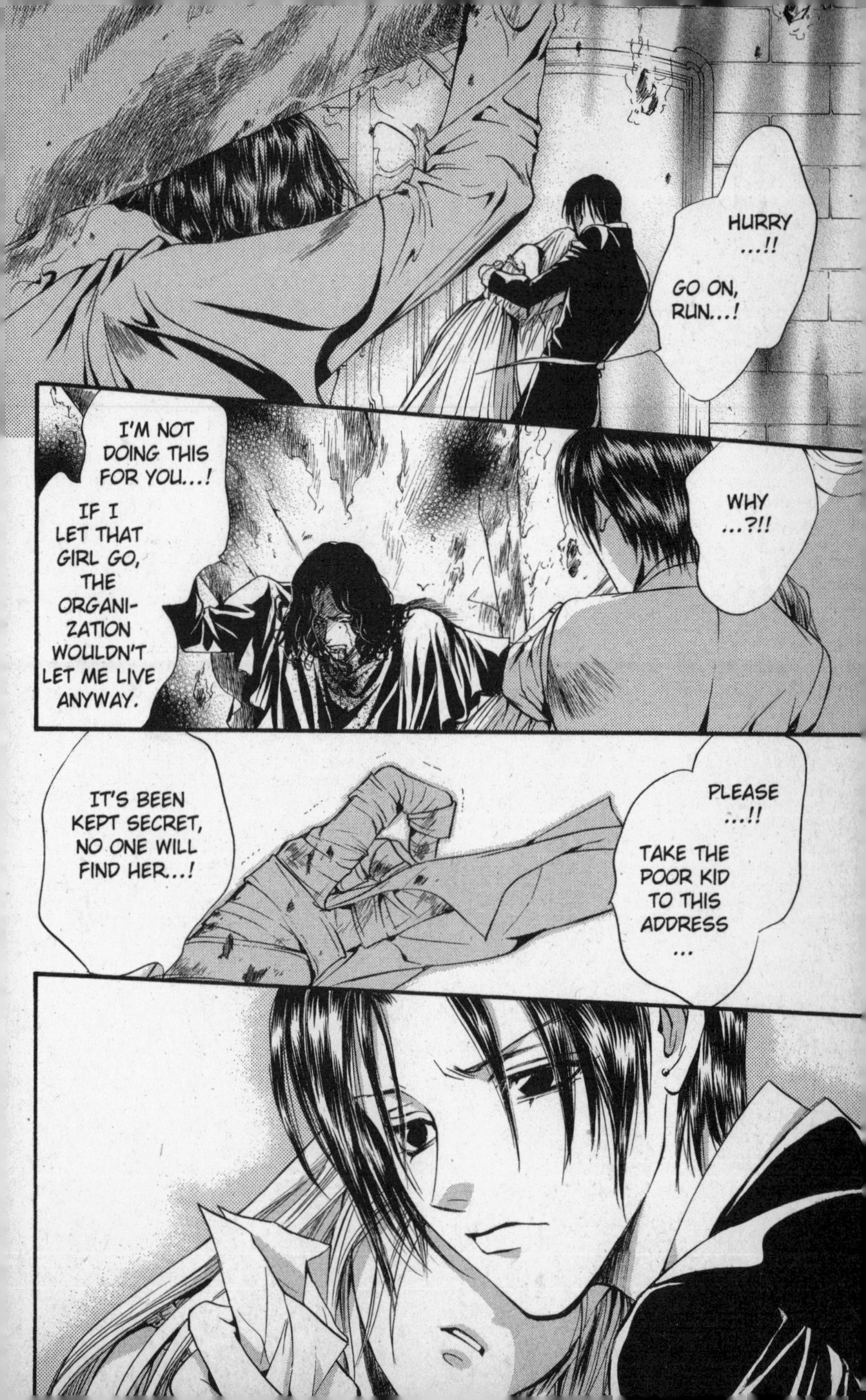

HURRY ...!! GO ON, RUN...!
WHY ...?!!
I'M NOT DOING THIS FOR YOU...! IF I LET THAT GIRL GO, THE ORGANIZATION WOULDN'T LET ME LIVE ANYWAY.
PLEASE ...!! TAKE THE POOR KID TO THIS ADDRESS ...
IT'S BEEN KEPT SECRET, NO ONE WILL FIND HER...!

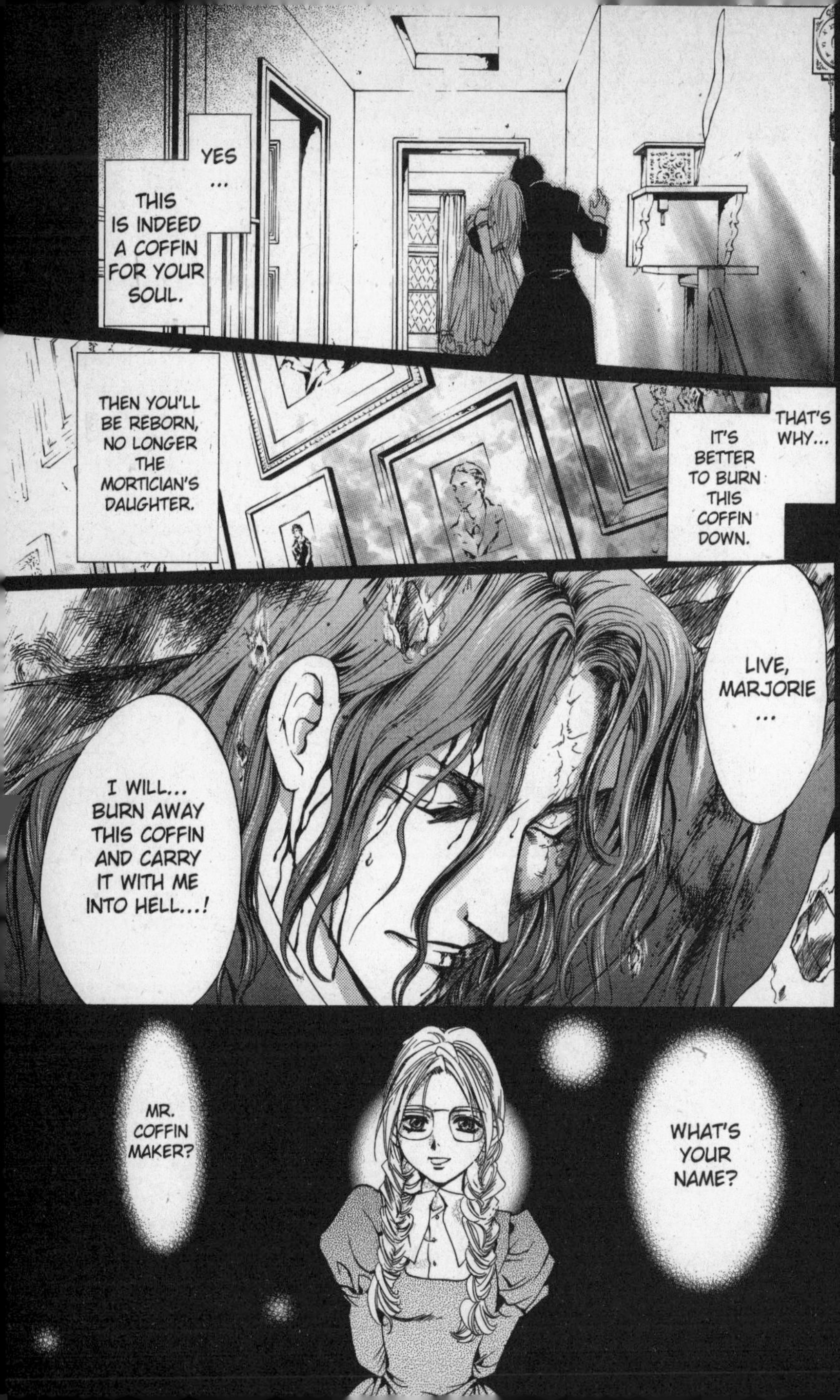
YES ...
THIS IS INDEED A COFFIN FOR YOUR SOUL.
THAT'S WHY...
IT'S BETTER TO BURN THIS COFFIN DOWN.
THEN YOU'LL BE REBORN, NO LONGER THE MORTICIAN'S DAUGHTER.
LIVE, MARJORIE ...
I WILL... BURN AWAY THIS COFFIN AND CARRY IT WITH ME INTO HELL...!
WHAT'S YOUR NAME?
MR. COFFIN MAKER?

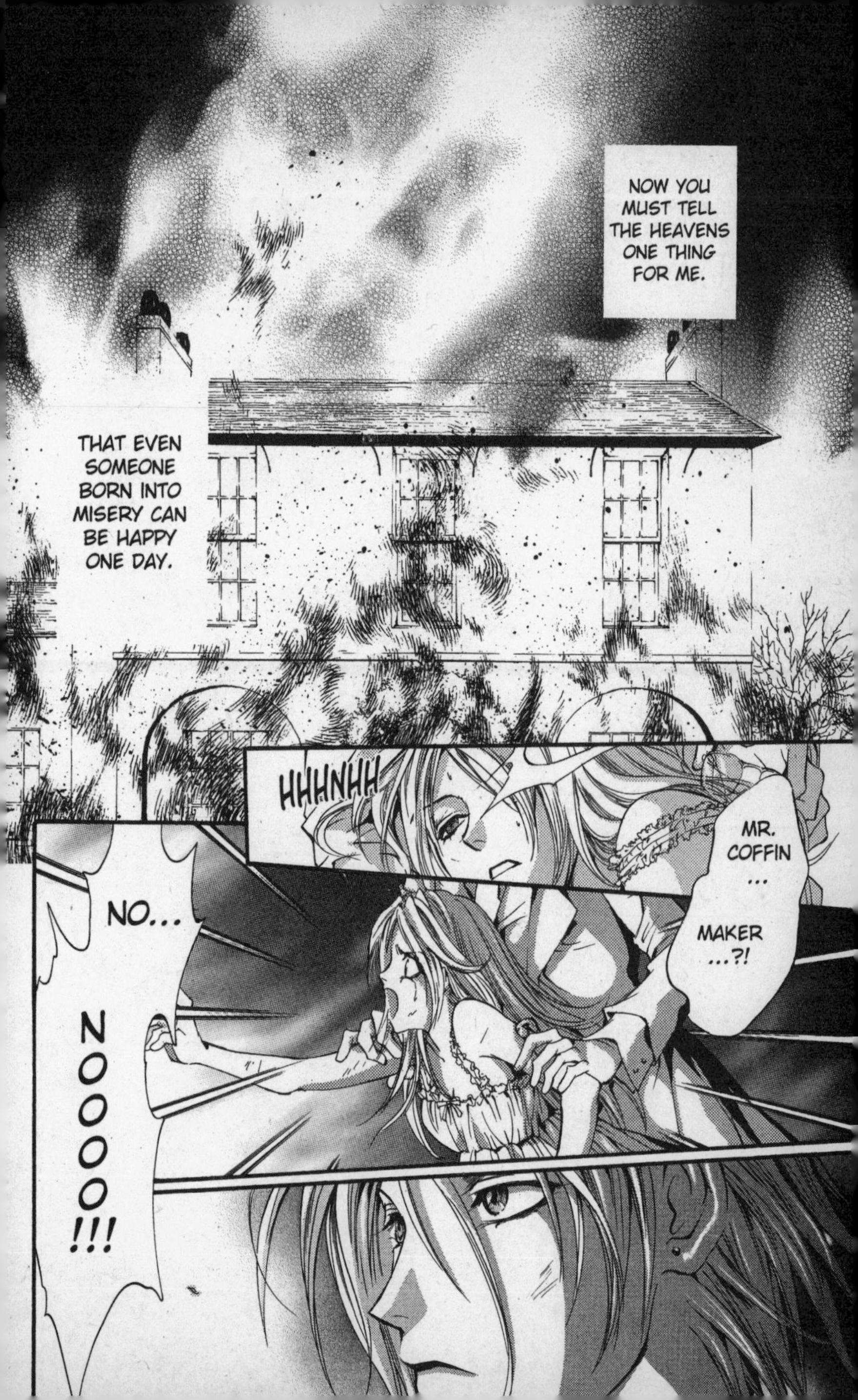
NOW YOU MUST TELL THE HEAVENS ONE THING FOR ME.
THAT EVEN SOMEONE BORN INTO MISERY CAN BE HAPPY ONE DAY.
HHHNHH
MR. COFFIN ...
MAKER ...?!
NO...
NOOOOO!!!

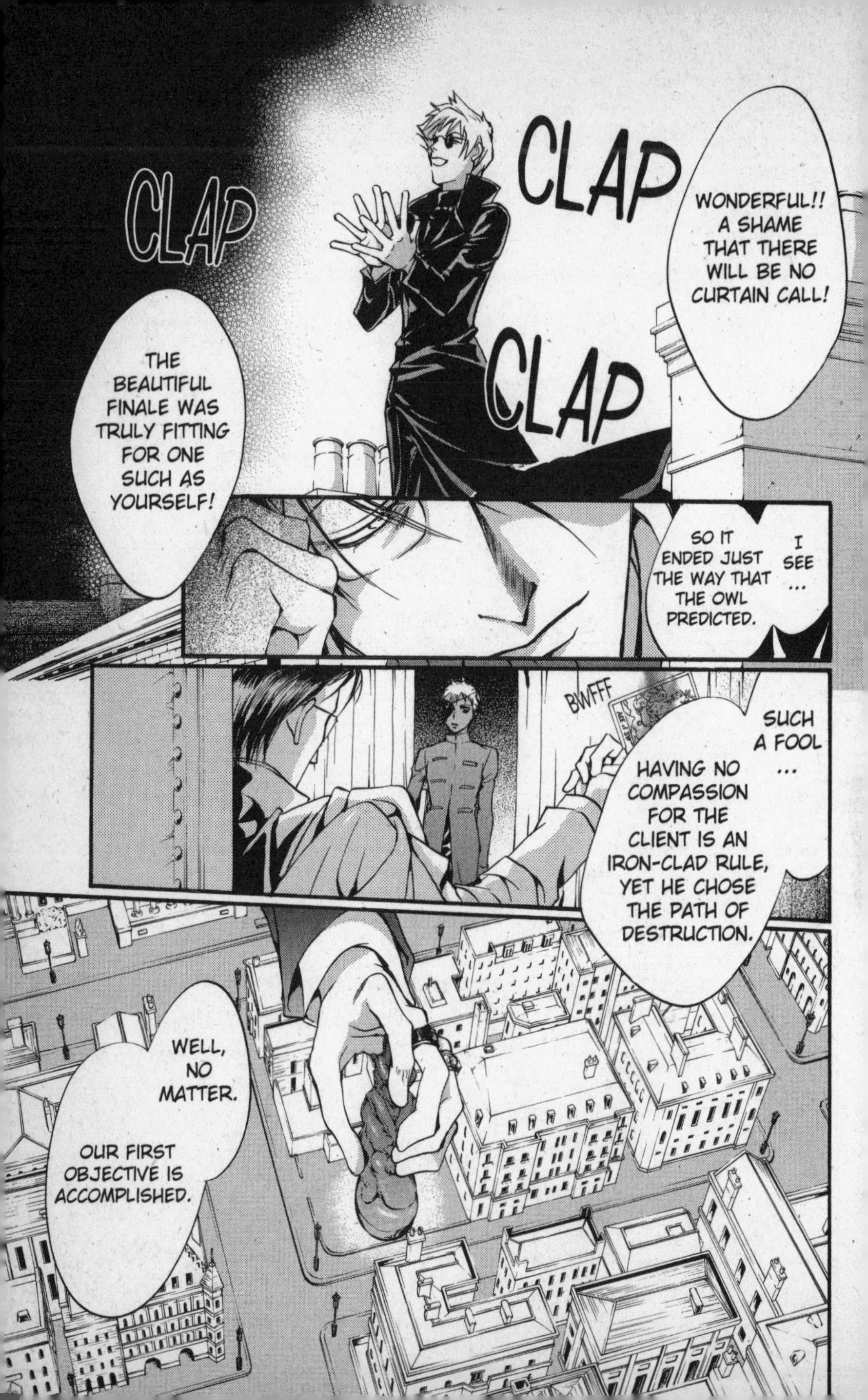
WONDERFUL!! A SHAME THAT THERE WILL BE NO CURTAIN CALL!
CLAP
CLAP
CLAP
THE BEAUTIFUL FINALE WAS TRULY FITTING FOR ONE SUCH AS YOURSELF!
I SEE ...
SO IT ENDED JUST THE WAY THAT THE OWL PREDICTED.
BWFFF
SUCH A FOOL ...
HAVING NO COMPASSION FOR THE CLIENT IS AN IRON-CLAD RULE, YET HE CHOSE THE PATH OF DESTRUCTION.
WELL, NO MATTER.
OUR FIRST OBJECTIVE IS ACCOMPLISHED.

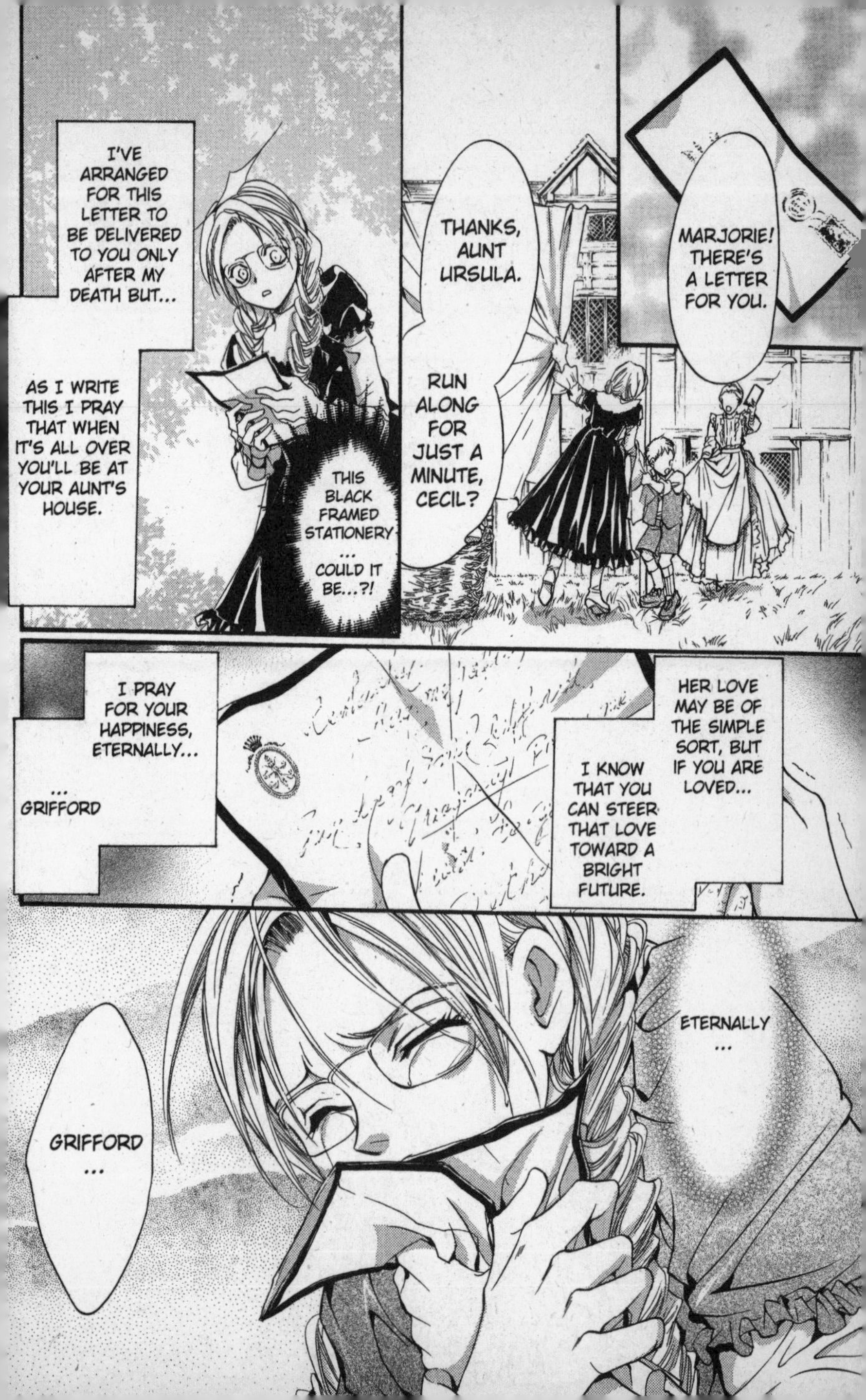
MARJORIE! THERE'S A LETTER FOR YOU.
THANKS, AUNT URSULA.
RUN ALONG FOR JUST A MINUTE, CECIL?
THIS BLACK FRAMED STATIONERY ... COULD IT BE...?!
I'VE ARRANGED FOR THIS LETTER TO BE DELIVERED TO YOU ONLY AFTER MY DEATH BUT...
AS I WRITE THIS I PRAY THAT WHEN IT'S ALL OVER YOU'LL BE AT YOUR AUNT'S HOUSE.
HER LOVE MAY BE OF THE SIMPLE SORT, BUT IF YOU ARE LOVED...
I KNOW THAT YOU CAN STEER THAT LOVE TOWARD A BRIGHT FUTURE.
I PRAY FOR YOUR HAPPINESS, ETERNALLY...
... GRIFFORD
ETERNALLY ...
GRIFFORD ...

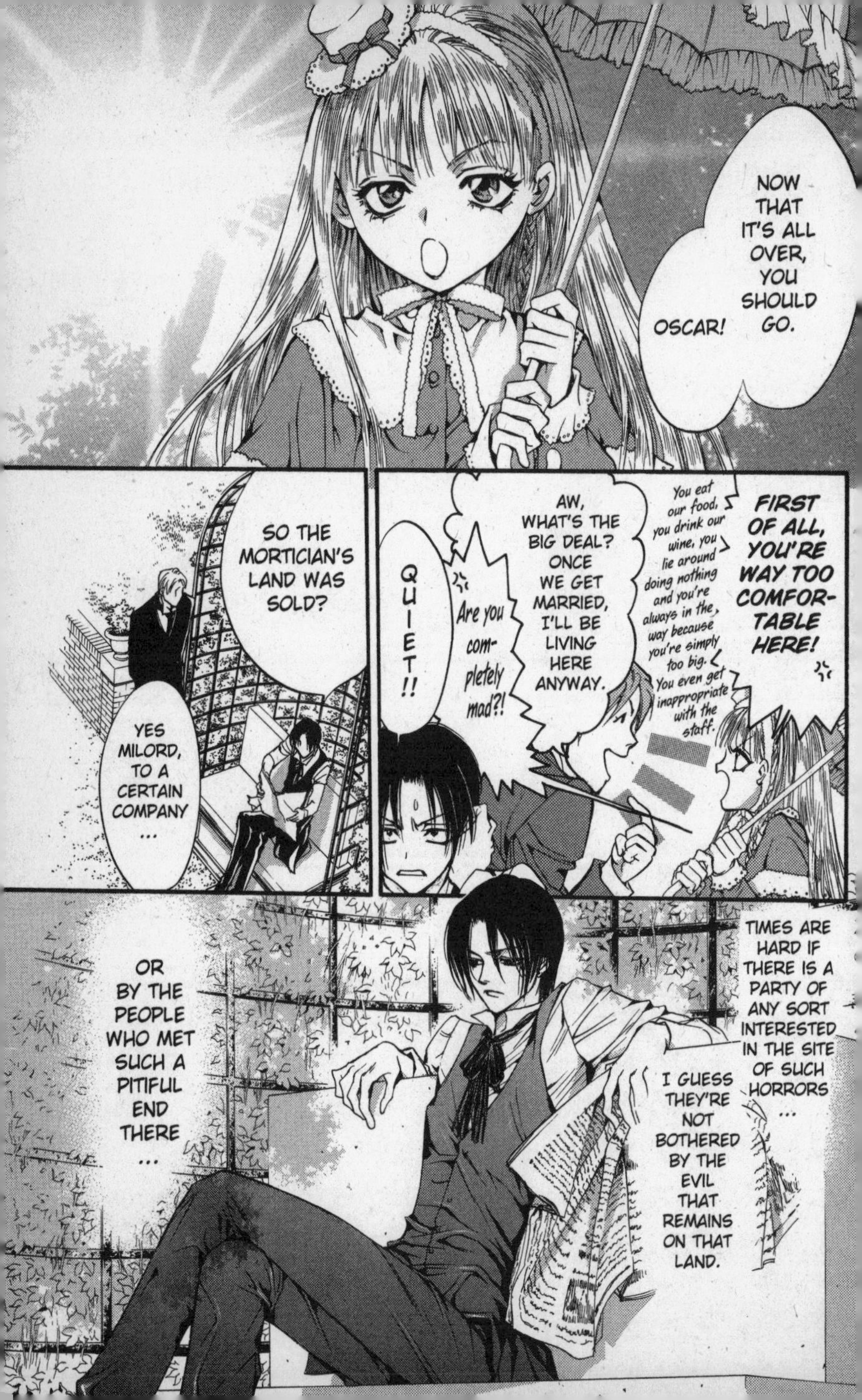
NOW THAT IT'S ALL OVER, YOU SHOULD GO.
OSCAR!
FIRST OF ALL, YOU'RE WAY TOO COMFORTABLE HERE!
You eat our food, you drink our wine, you lie around doing nothing and you're always in the way because you're simply too big. You even get inappropriate with the staff.
AW, WHAT'S THE BIG DEAL? ONCE WE GET MARRIED, I'LL BE LIVING HERE ANYWAY.
Are you completely mad?!
QUIET!!
SO THE MORTICIAN'S LAND WAS SOLD?
YES MILORD, TO A CERTAIN COMPANY ...
TIMES ARE HARD IF THERE IS A PARTY OF ANY SORT INTERESTED IN THE SITE OF SUCH HORRORS ...
I GUESS THEY'RE NOT BOTHERED BY THE EVIL THAT REMAINS ON THAT LAND.
OR BY THE PEOPLE WHO MET SUCH A PITIFUL END THERE ...

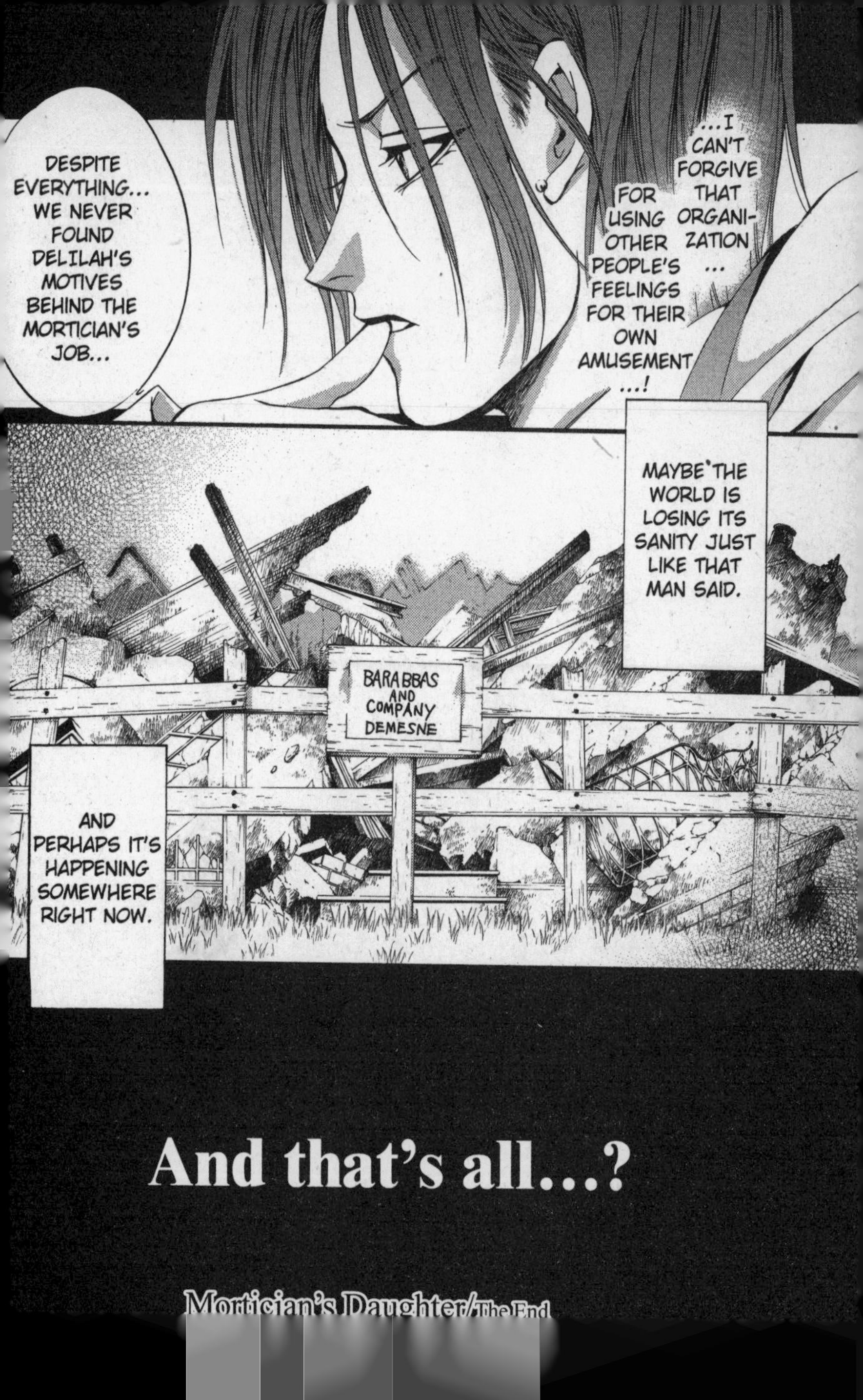
...I CAN'T FORGIVE THAT ORGANIZATION... FOR USING OTHER PEOPLE'S FEELINGS FOR THEIR OWN AMUSEMENT...!
DESPITE EVERYTHING... WE NEVER FOUND DELILAH'S MOTIVES BEHIND THE MORTICIAN'S JOB...
MAYBE THE WORLD IS LOSING ITS SANITY JUST LIKE THAT MAN SAID.
BARABBAS AND COMPANY DEMESNE
AND PERHAPS IT'S HAPPENING SOMEWHERE RIGHT NOW.

And that's all...?

Mortician's Daughter/The End

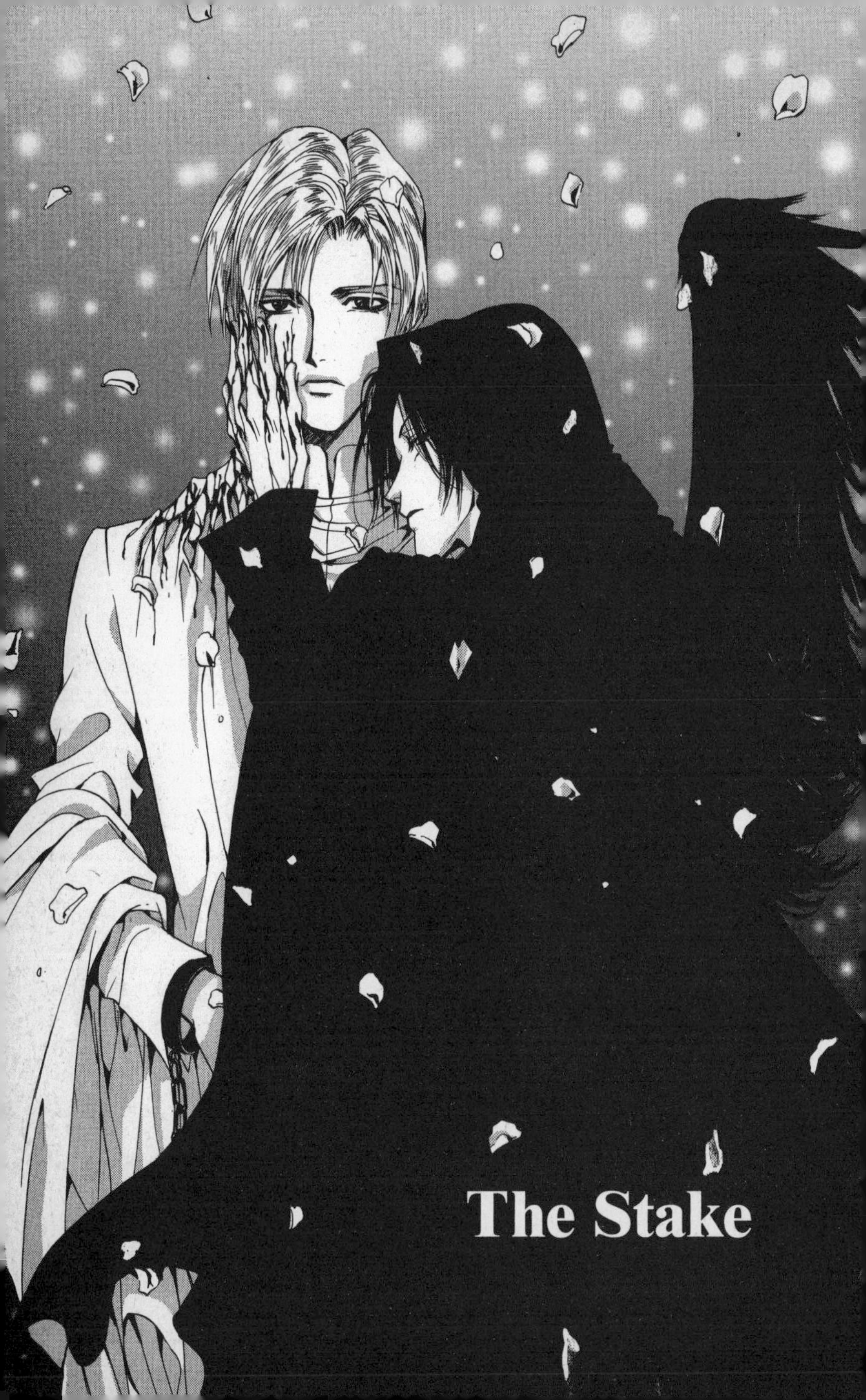

The Stake

The Stake

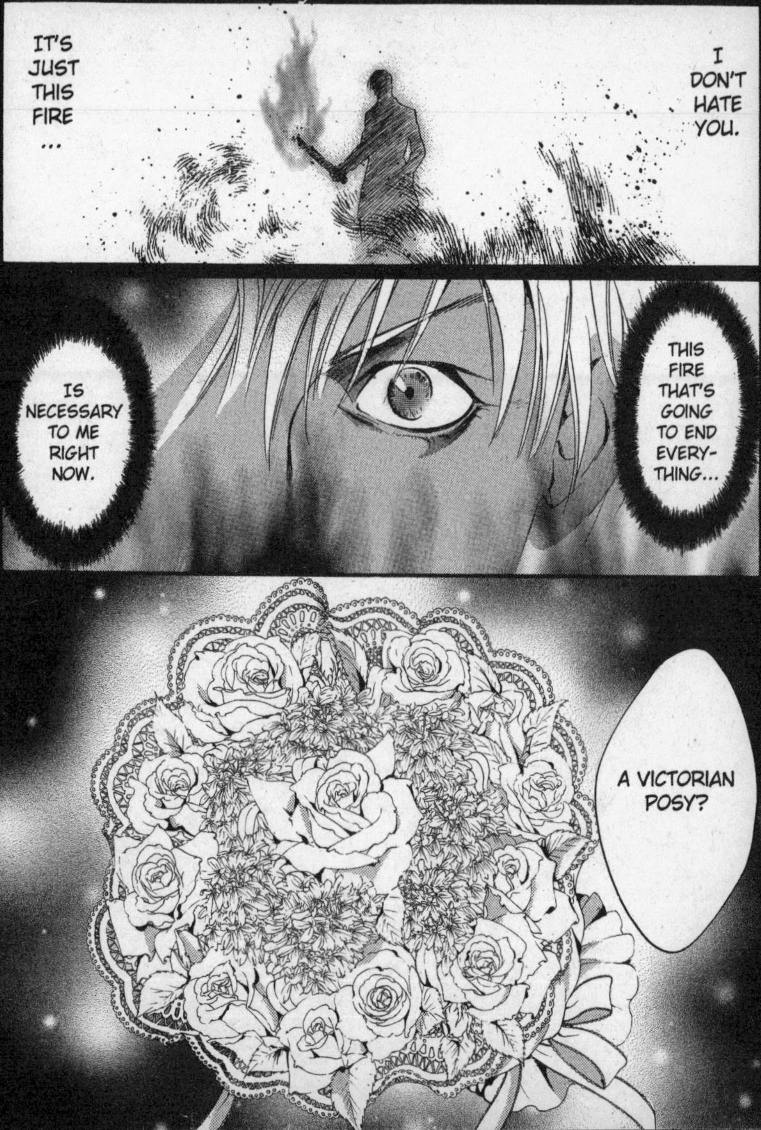
I DON'T HATE YOU.
IT'S JUST THIS FIRE ...
THIS FIRE THAT'S GOING TO END EVERY-THING...
IS NECESSARY TO ME RIGHT NOW.
A VICTORIAN POSY?

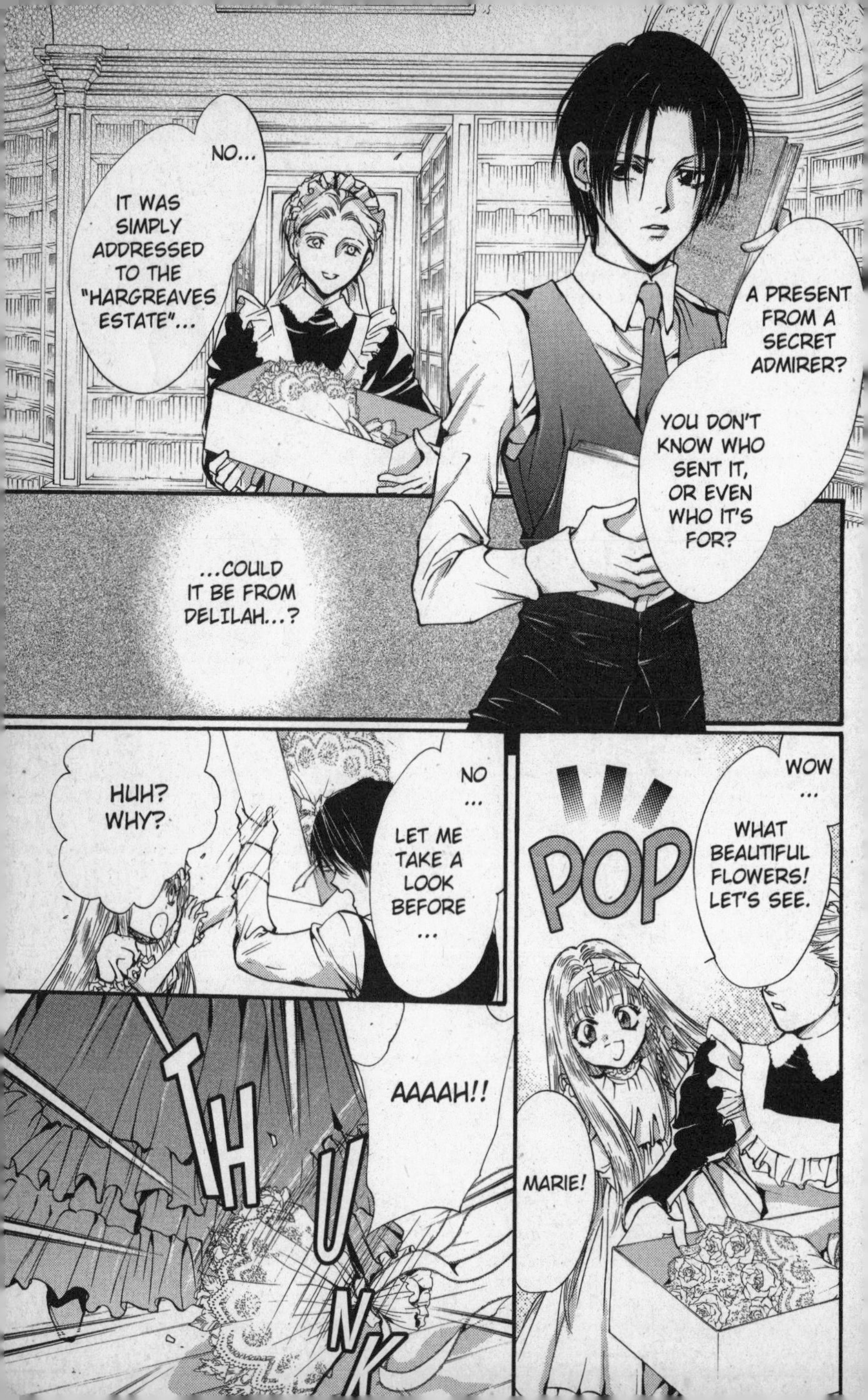

NO... IT WAS SIMPLY ADDRESSED TO THE "HARGREAVES ESTATE"...
A PRESENT FROM A SECRET ADMIRER?
YOU DON'T KNOW WHO SENT IT, OR EVEN WHO IT'S FOR?
...COULD IT BE FROM DELILAH...?
WOW ... WHAT BEAUTIFUL FLOWERS! LET'S SEE.
POP
MARIE!
NO ... LET ME TAKE A LOOK BEFORE ...
HUH? WHY?
AAAAH!!
THUNK

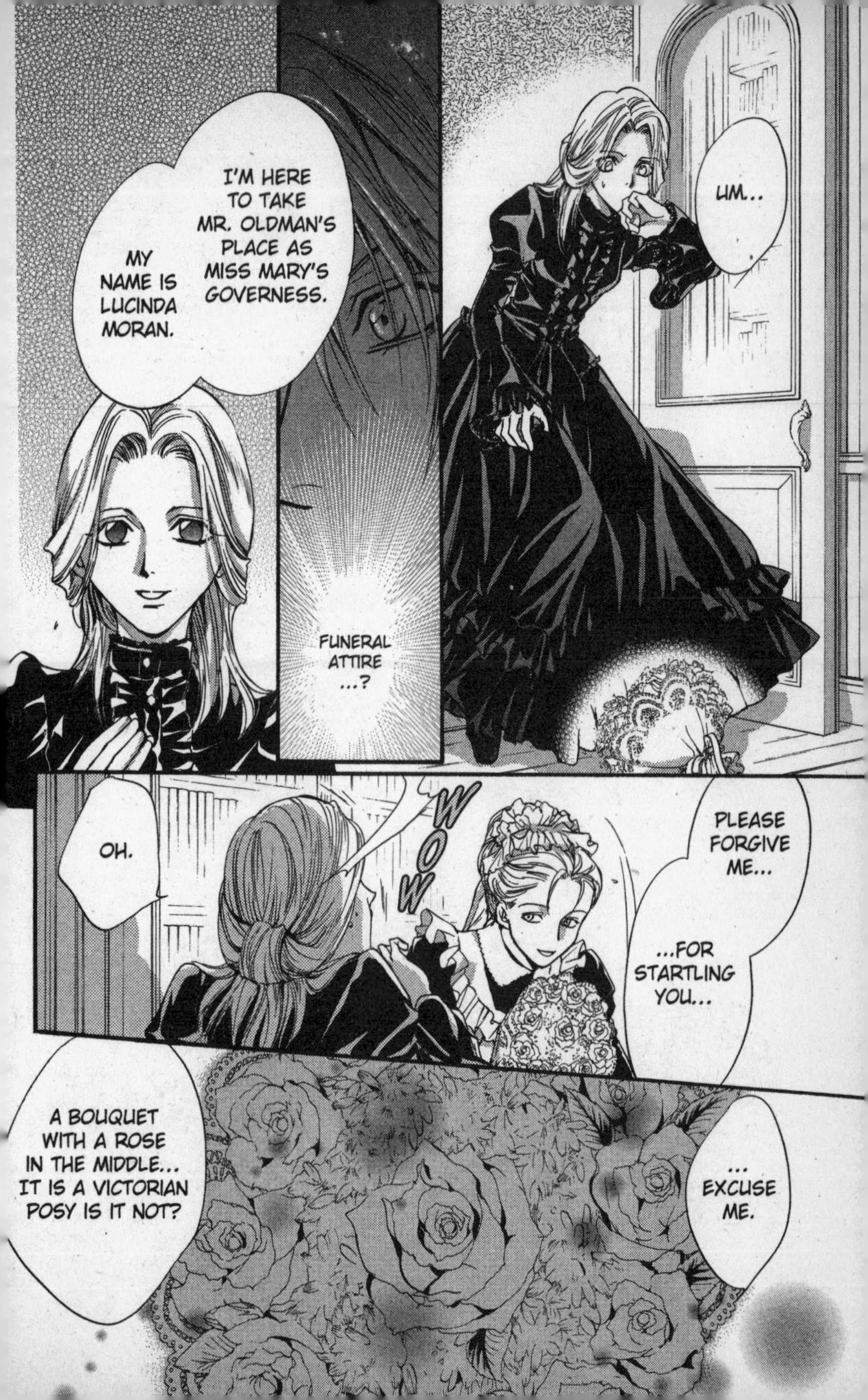
UM...
FUNERAL ATTIRE ...?
MY NAME IS LUCINDA MORAN. I'M HERE TO TAKE MR. OLDMAN'S PLACE AS MISS MARY'S GOVERNESS.
PLEASE FORGIVE ME...
...FOR STARTLING YOU...
WOW
OH.
... EXCUSE ME.
A BOUQUET WITH A ROSE IN THE MIDDLE... IT IS A VICTORIAN POSY IS IT NOT?

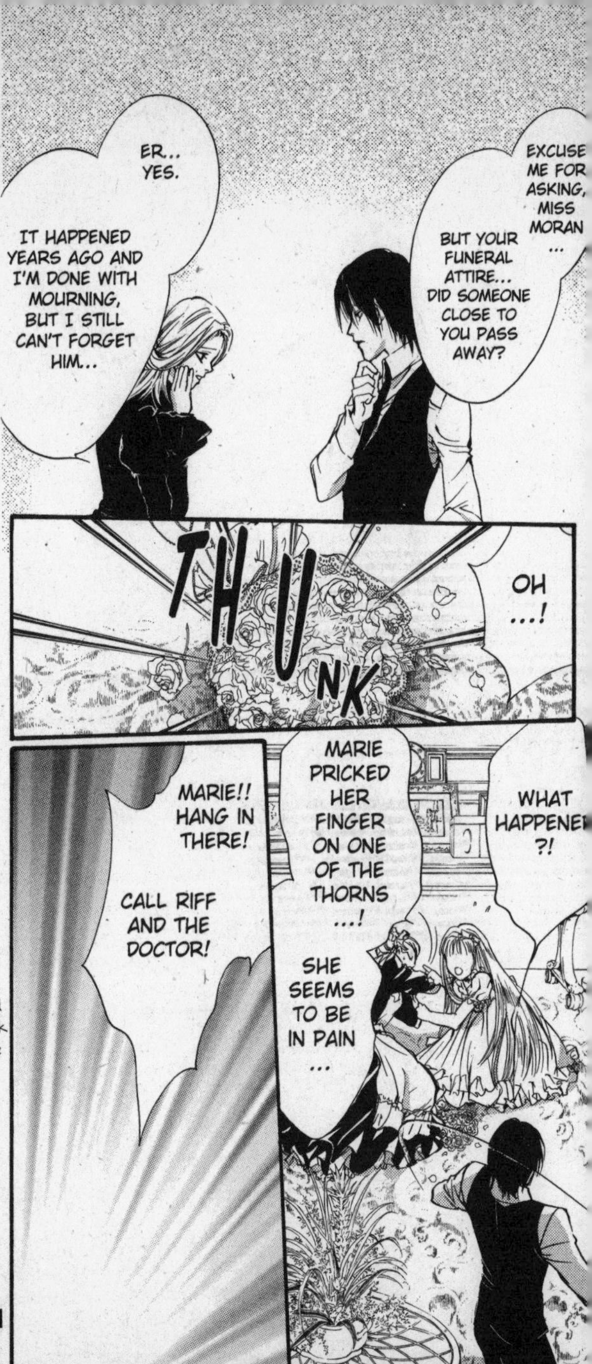
EXCUSE ME FOR ASKING, MISS MORAN ...
BUT YOUR FUNERAL ATTIRE... DID SOMEONE CLOSE TO YOU PASS AWAY?
ER... YES.
IT HAPPENED YEARS AGO AND I'M DONE WITH MOURNING, BUT I STILL CAN'T FORGET HIM...
OH ...!
THUNK
WHAT HAPPENE ?!
MARIE PRICKED HER FINGER ON ONE OF THE THORNS ...!
SHE SEEMS TO BE IN PAIN ...
MARIE!! HANG IN THERE!
CALL RIFF AND THE DOCTOR!

This Lucinda story is another one that I was finally able to write... At the time I thought it was a low-key story but now that I look at it, it's pretty intense. I don't want to keep saying the same thing but I wrote this episode much later than the previous one so the same explanations are included for the first-time readers as well as for readers who might have forgotten some things that occurred in previous episodes. (Not to mention some of the same dialogue.) So to all the readers who've kept up with the story, please pay no attention to it and read on. Even my drawing style is changing... Could I be growing as an artist? My old drawings aren't that easy to look at right now.

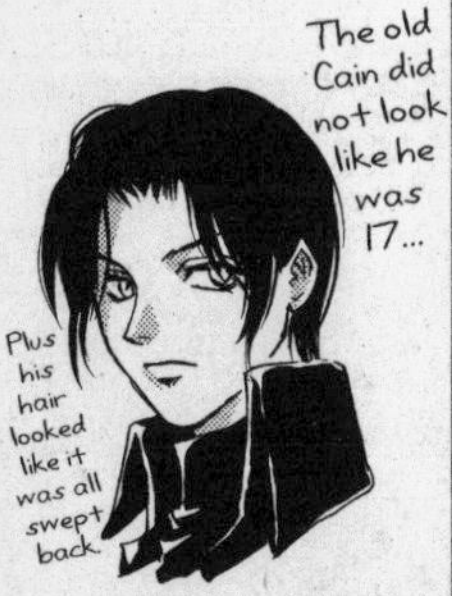
The old Cain did not look like he was 17...
Plus his hair looked like it was all swept back.

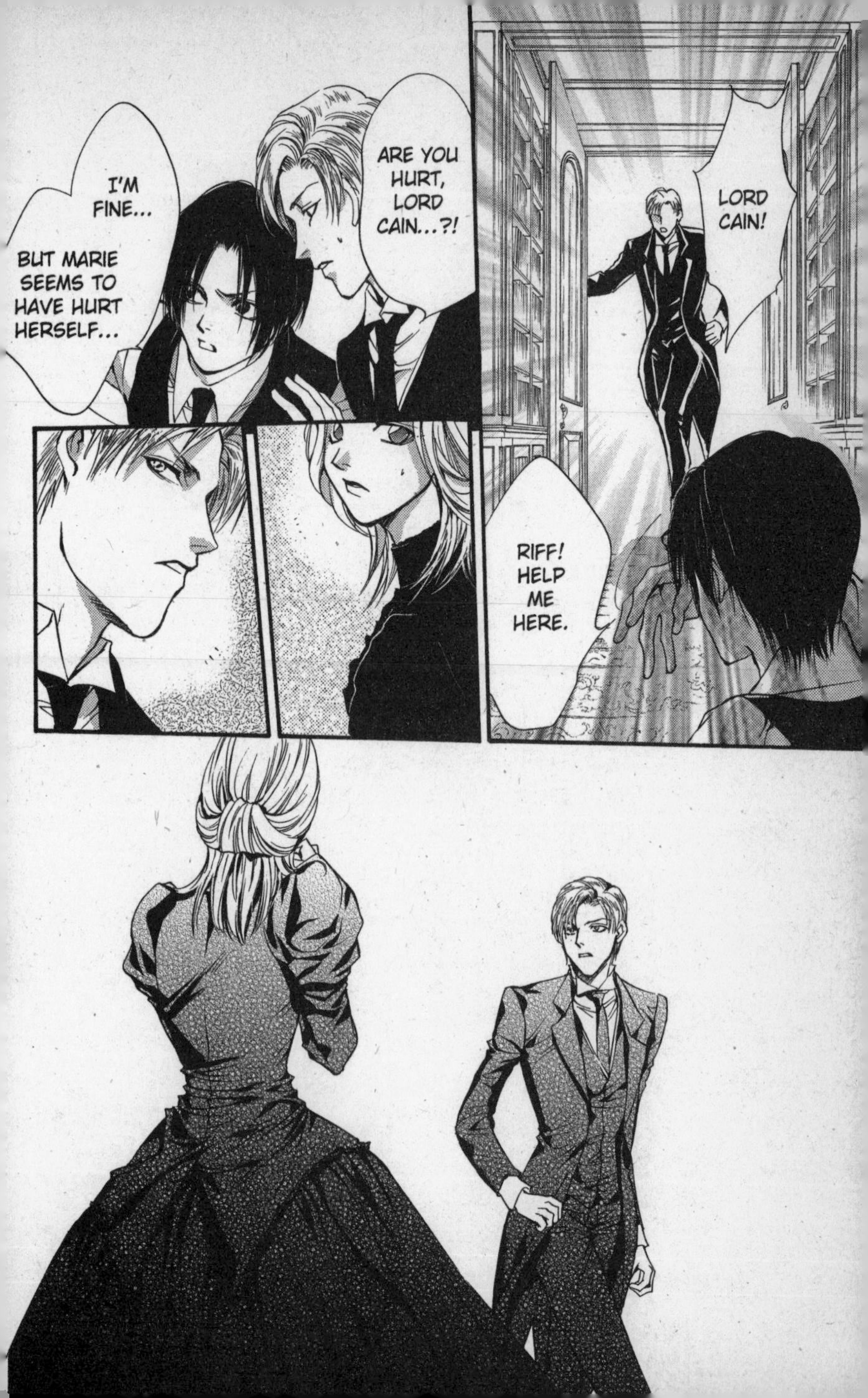
LORD CAIN!
RIFF! HELP ME HERE.
ARE YOU HURT, LORD CAIN...?!
I'M FINE...
BUT MARIE SEEMS TO HAVE HURT HERSELF...

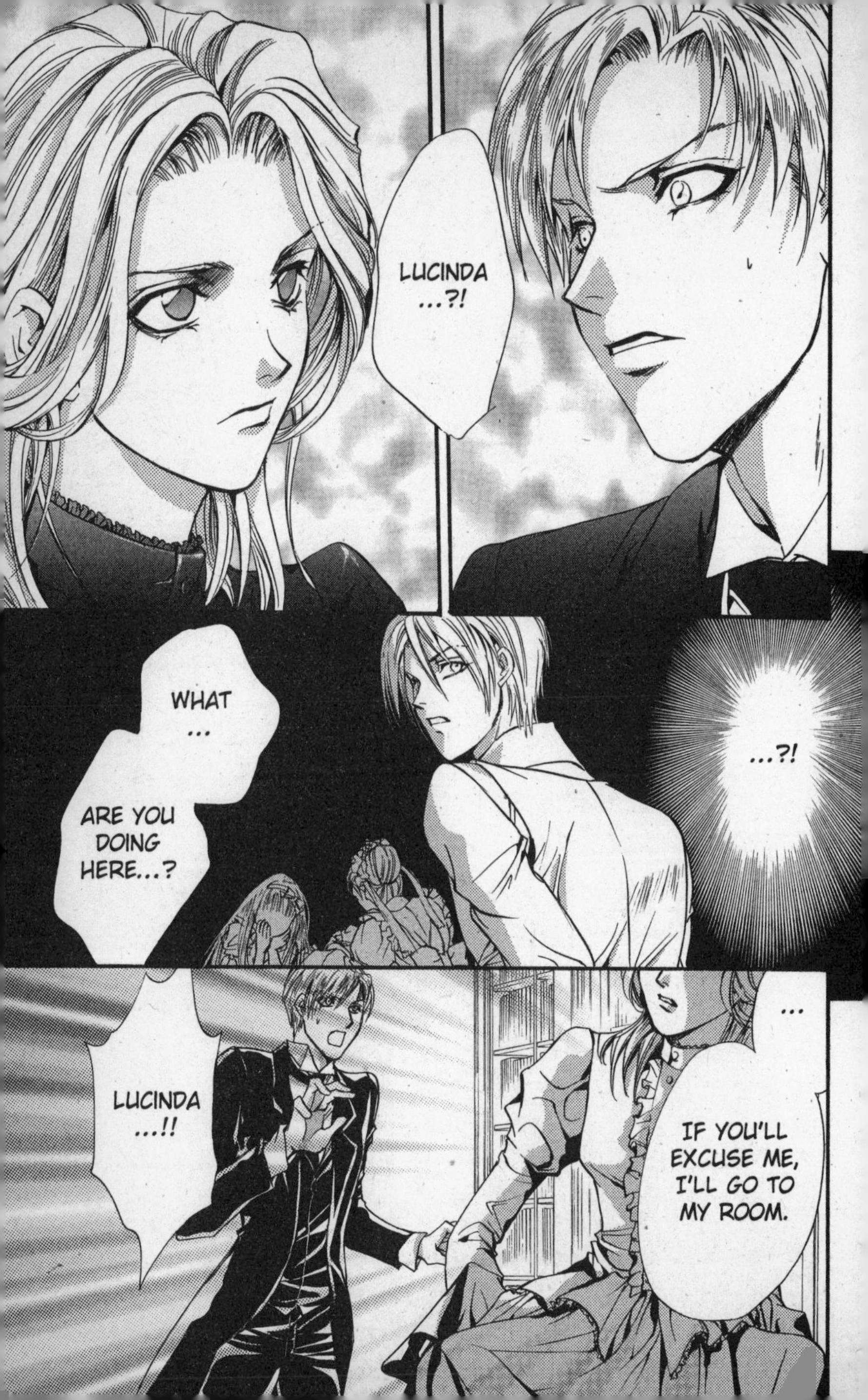
LUCINDA ...?!
...?!
WHAT ...
ARE YOU DOING HERE...?
...
IF YOU'LL EXCUSE ME, I'LL GO TO MY ROOM.
LUCINDA ...!!

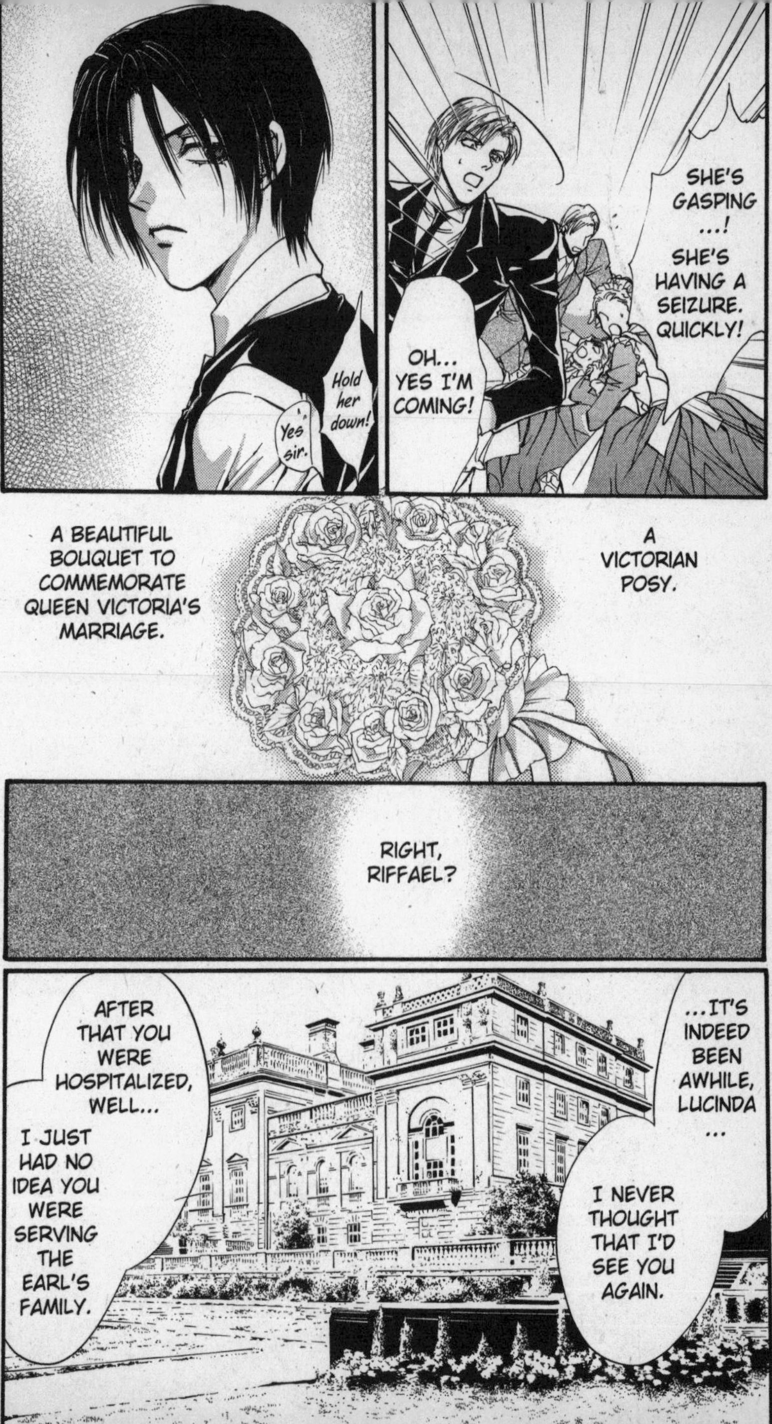
SHE'S GASPING ...!
SHE'S HAVING A SEIZURE. QUICKLY!
OH... YES I'M COMING!
Hold her down!
Yes sir.
A VICTORIAN POSY.
A BEAUTIFUL BOUQUET TO COMMEMORATE QUEEN VICTORIA'S MARRIAGE.
RIGHT, RIFFAEL?
...IT'S INDEED BEEN AWHILE, LUCINDA ...
I NEVER THOUGHT THAT I'D SEE YOU AGAIN.
AFTER THAT YOU WERE HOSPITALIZED, WELL...
I JUST HAD NO IDEA YOU WERE SERVING THE EARL'S FAMILY.

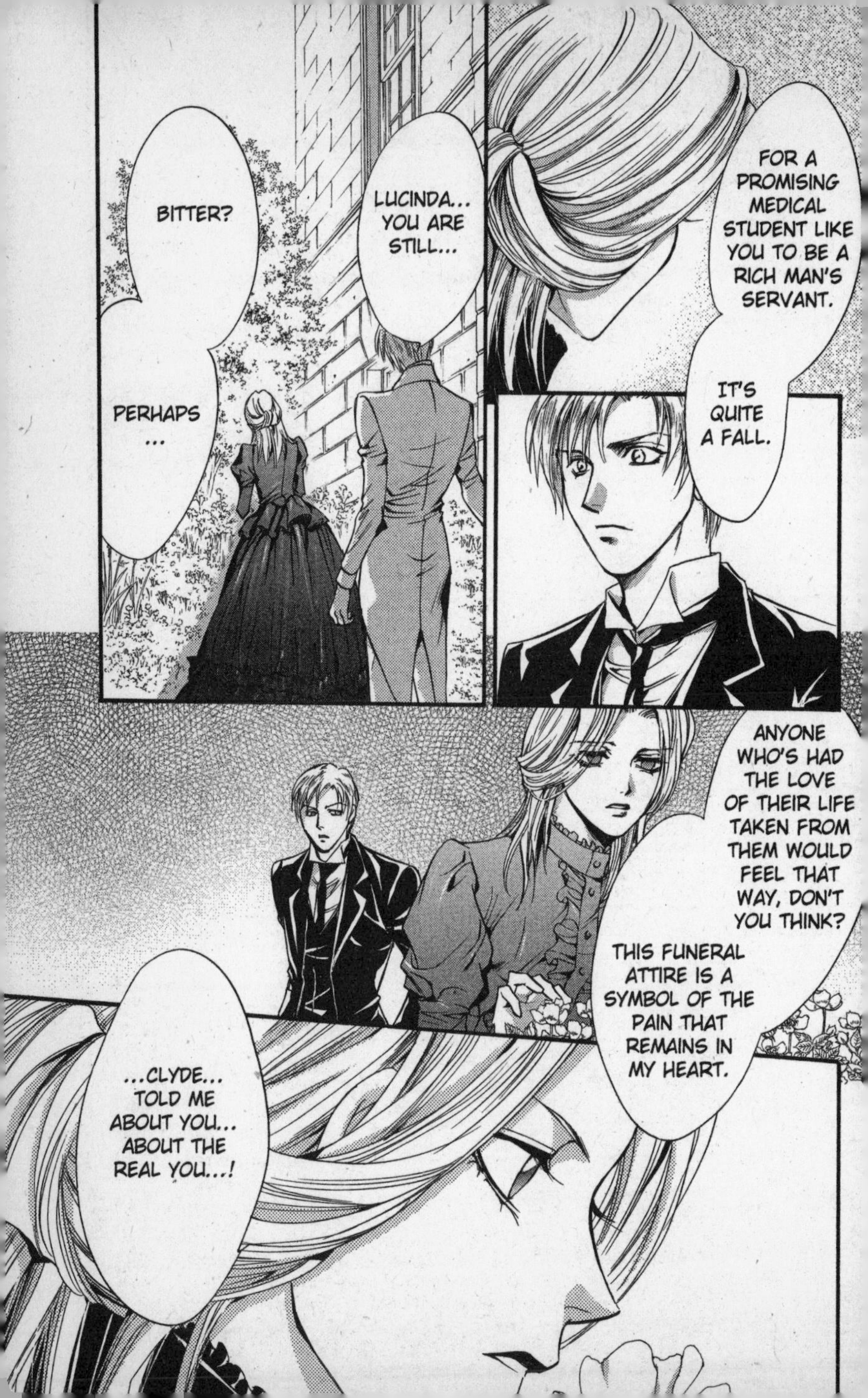
FOR A PROMISING MEDICAL STUDENT LIKE YOU TO BE A RICH MAN'S SERVANT.
IT'S QUITE A FALL.
LUCINDA... YOU ARE STILL...
BITTER?
PERHAPS ...
ANYONE WHO'S HAD THE LOVE OF THEIR LIFE TAKEN FROM THEM WOULD FEEL THAT WAY, DON'T YOU THINK?
THIS FUNERAL ATTIRE IS A SYMBOL OF THE PAIN THAT REMAINS IN MY HEART.
...CLYDE... TOLD ME ABOUT YOU... ABOUT THE REAL YOU...!

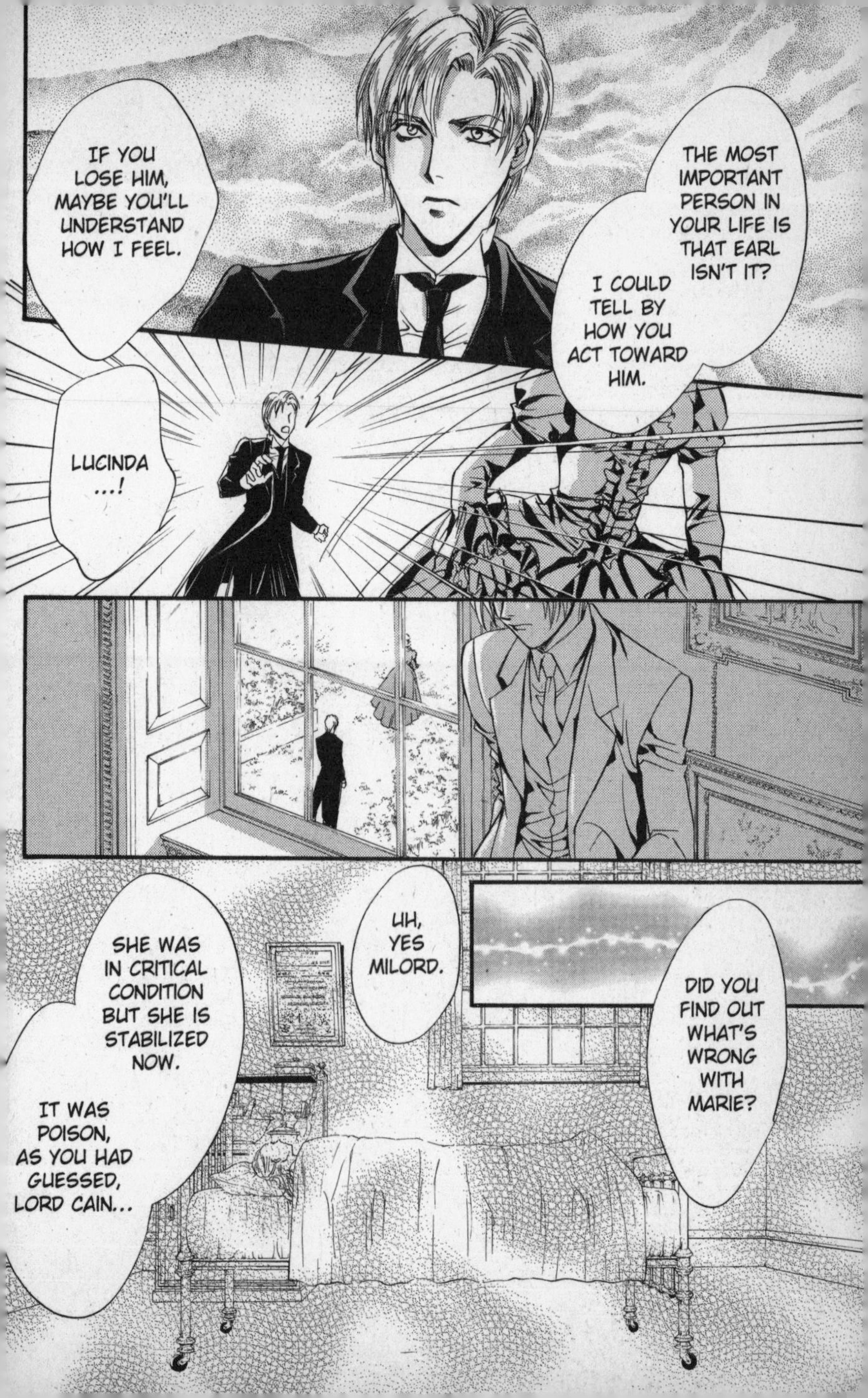
THE MOST IMPORTANT PERSON IN YOUR LIFE IS THAT EARL ISN'T IT?
I COULD TELL BY HOW YOU ACT TOWARD HIM.
IF YOU LOSE HIM, MAYBE YOU'LL UNDERSTAND HOW I FEEL.
LUCINDA ...!
DID YOU FIND OUT WHAT'S WRONG WITH MARIE?
UH, YES MILORD.
SHE WAS IN CRITICAL CONDITION BUT SHE IS STABILIZED NOW.
IT WAS POISON, AS YOU HAD GUESSED, LORD CAIN...

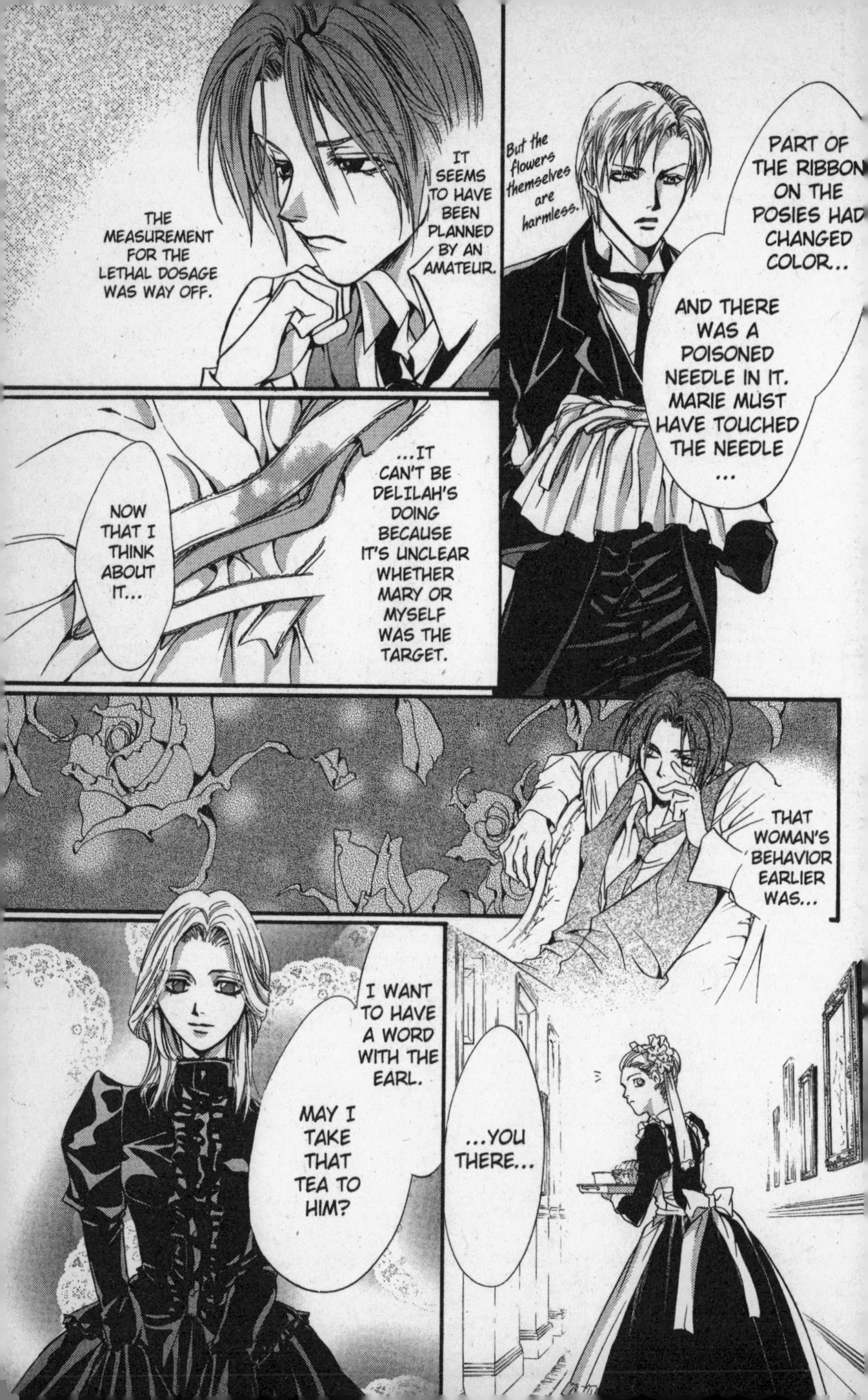
PART OF THE RIBBON ON THE POSIES HAD CHANGED COLOR...
AND THERE WAS A POISONED NEEDLE IN IT. MARIE MUST HAVE TOUCHED THE NEEDLE ...
But the flowers themselves are harmless.
IT SEEMS TO HAVE BEEN PLANNED BY AN AMATEUR.
THE MEASUREMENT FOR THE LETHAL DOSAGE WAS WAY OFF.
...IT CAN'T BE DELILAH'S DOING BECAUSE IT'S UNCLEAR WHETHER MARY OR MYSELF WAS THE TARGET.
NOW THAT I THINK ABOUT IT...
THAT WOMAN'S BEHAVIOR EARLIER WAS...
...YOU THERE...
I WANT TO HAVE A WORD WITH THE EARL.
MAY I TAKE THAT TEA TO HIM?

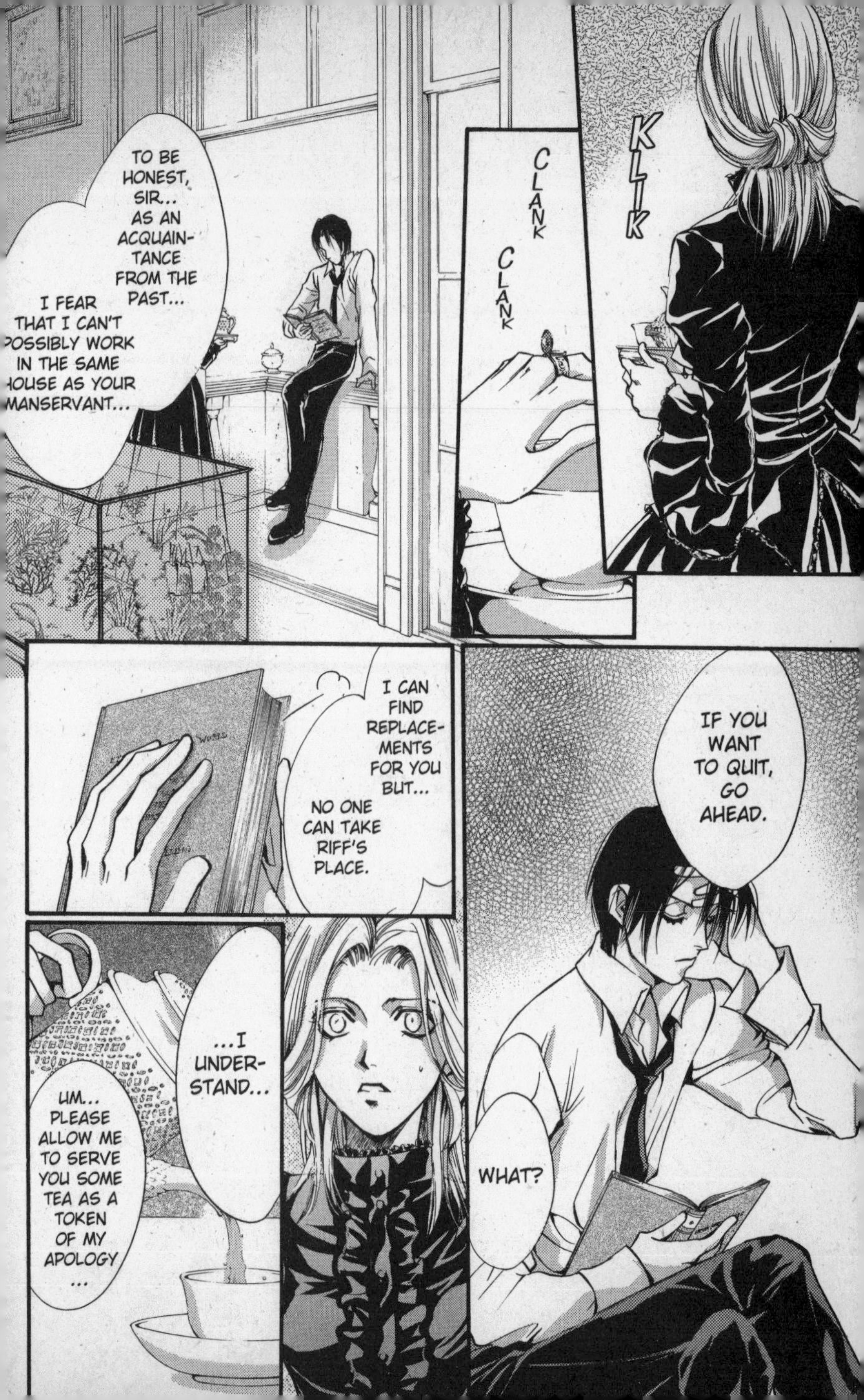
KLIK
CLANK CLANK
TO BE HONEST, SIR... AS AN ACQUAINTANCE FROM THE PAST...
I FEAR THAT I CAN'T POSSIBLY WORK IN THE SAME HOUSE AS YOUR MANSERVANT...
IF YOU WANT TO QUIT, GO AHEAD.
WHAT?
I CAN FIND REPLACEMENTS FOR YOU BUT...
NO ONE CAN TAKE RIFF'S PLACE.
...I UNDERSTAND...
UM... PLEASE ALLOW ME TO SERVE YOU SOME TEA AS A TOKEN OF MY APOLOGY...

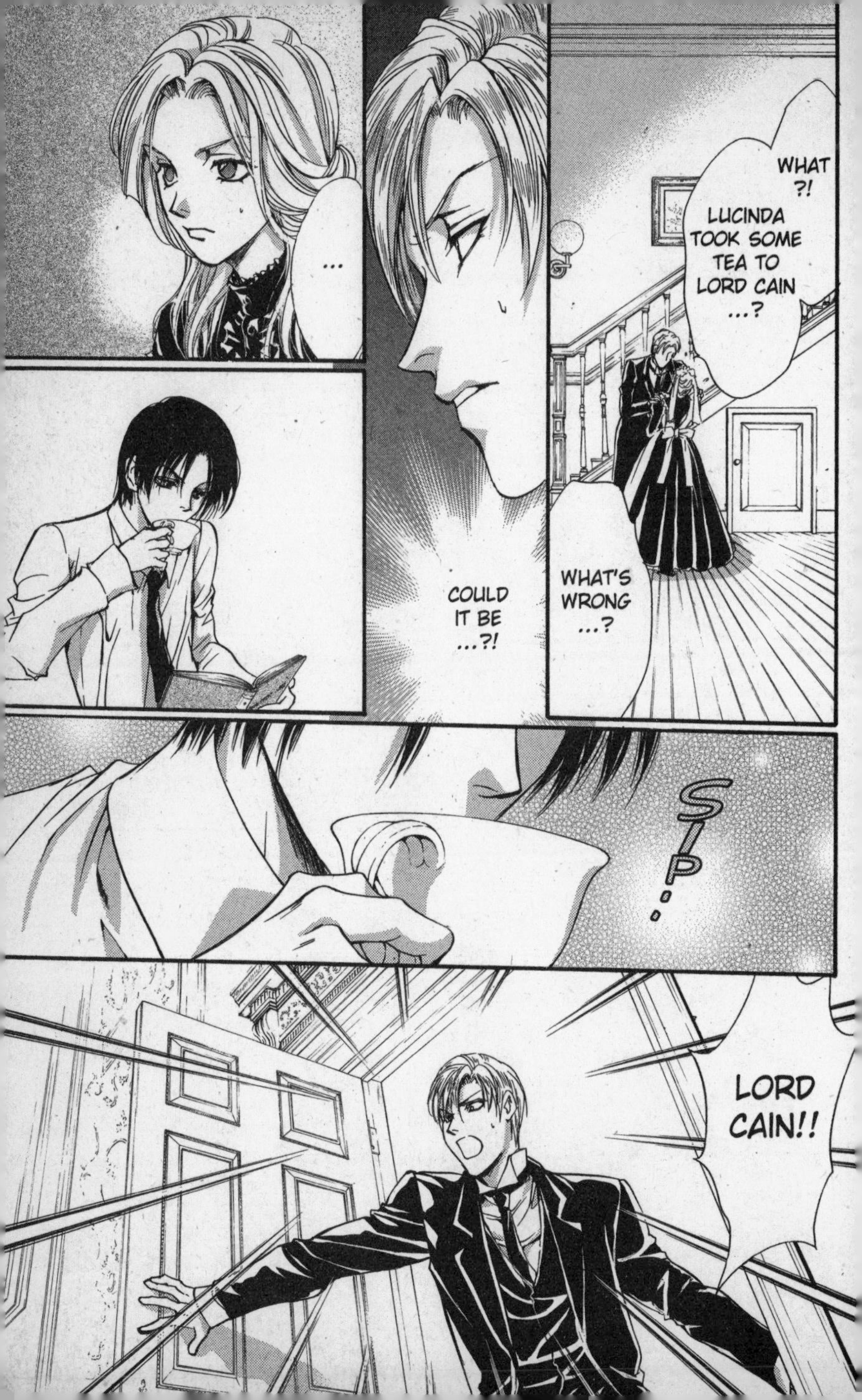
WHAT ?!
LUCINDA TOOK SOME TEA TO LORD CAIN ...?
WHAT'S WRONG ...?
COULD IT BE ...?!
...
SIP!!
LORD CAIN!!

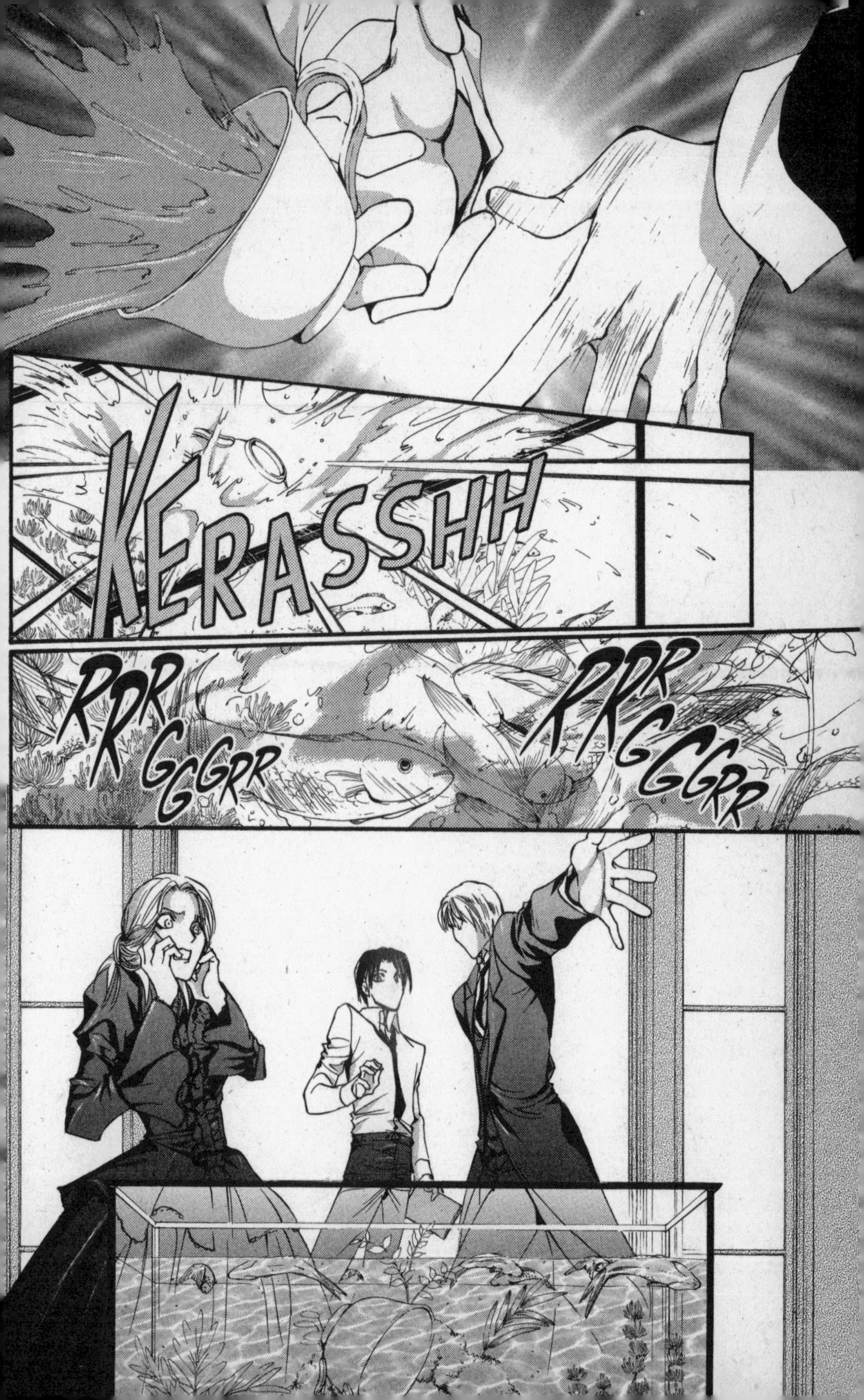
KERASSHH
RPRRGGGRR
RPRRGGGRR

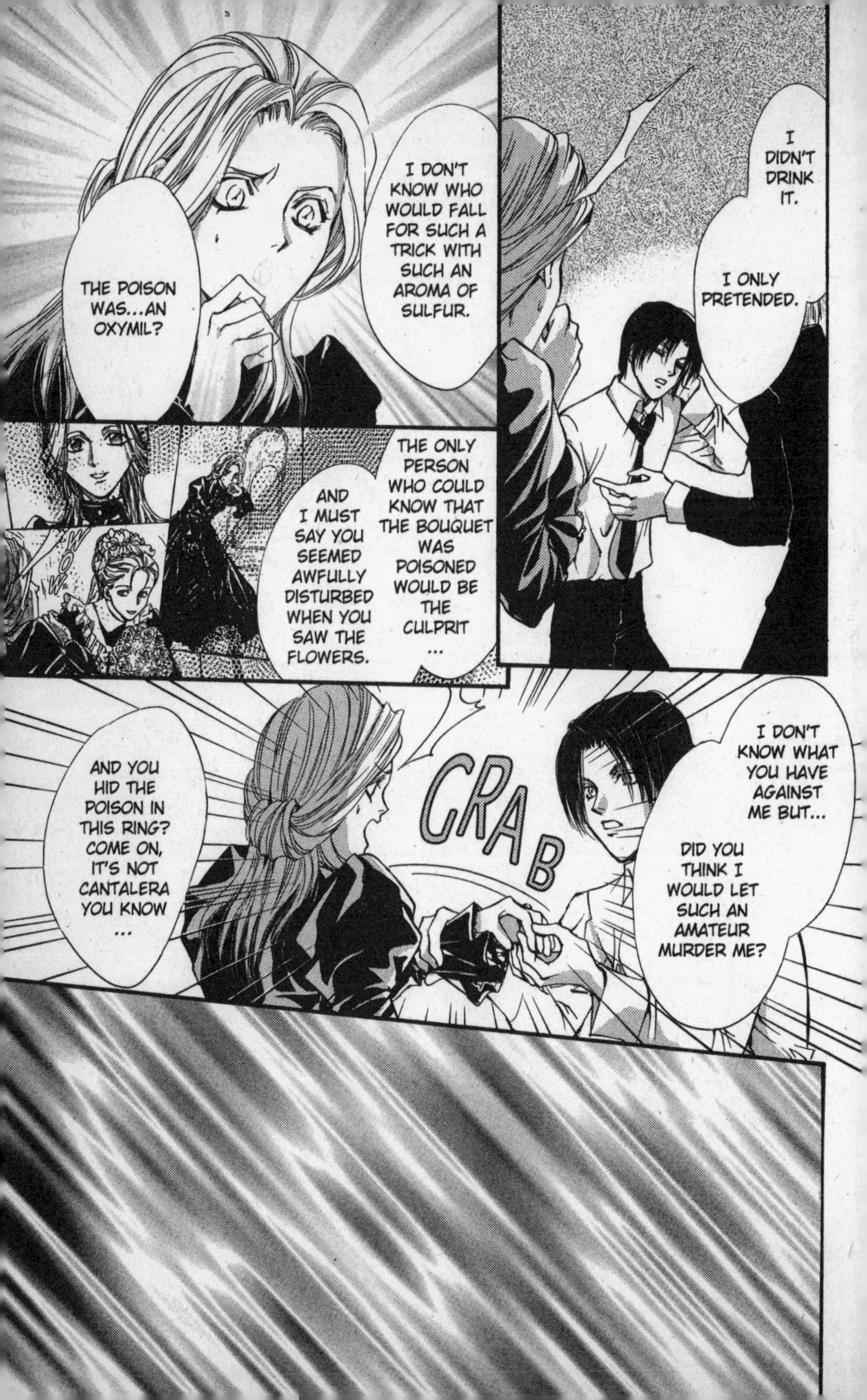
I DIDN'T DRINK IT.
I ONLY PRETENDED.
I DON'T KNOW WHO WOULD FALL FOR SUCH A TRICK WITH SUCH AN AROMA OF SULFUR.
THE POISON WAS...AN OXYMIL?
THE ONLY PERSON WHO COULD KNOW THAT THE BOUQUET WAS POISONED WOULD BE THE CULPRIT ...
AND I MUST SAY YOU SEEMED AWFULLY DISTURBED WHEN YOU SAW THE FLOWERS.
WOW
I DON'T KNOW WHAT YOU HAVE AGAINST ME BUT...
DID YOU THINK I WOULD LET SUCH AN AMATEUR MURDER ME?
CRAB
AND YOU HID THE POISON IN THIS RING? COME ON, IT'S NOT CANTALERA YOU KNOW ...

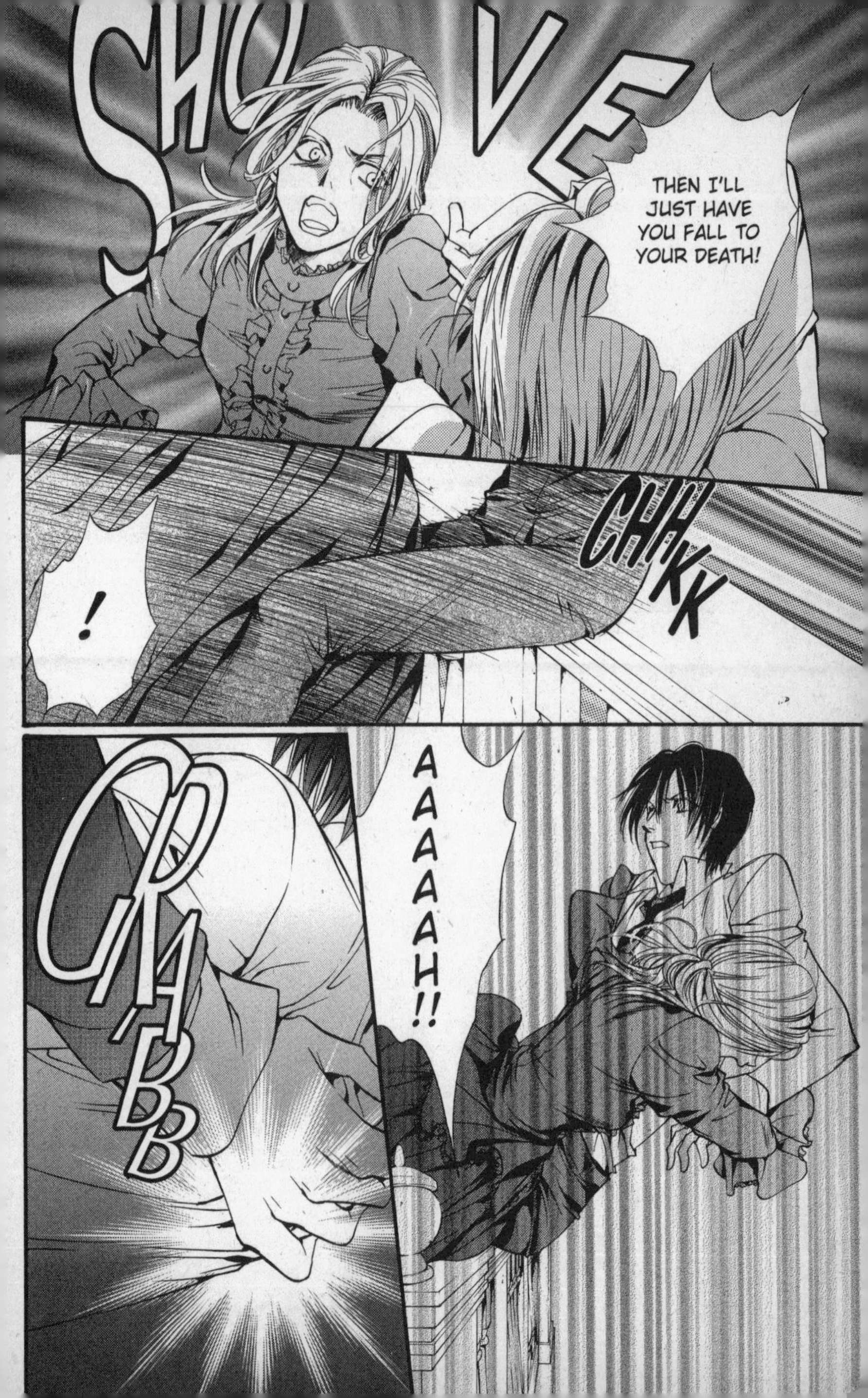
SHOVE
THEN I'LL JUST HAVE YOU FALL TO YOUR DEATH!
CHHKK
!
AAAAAAH!!
CRABB

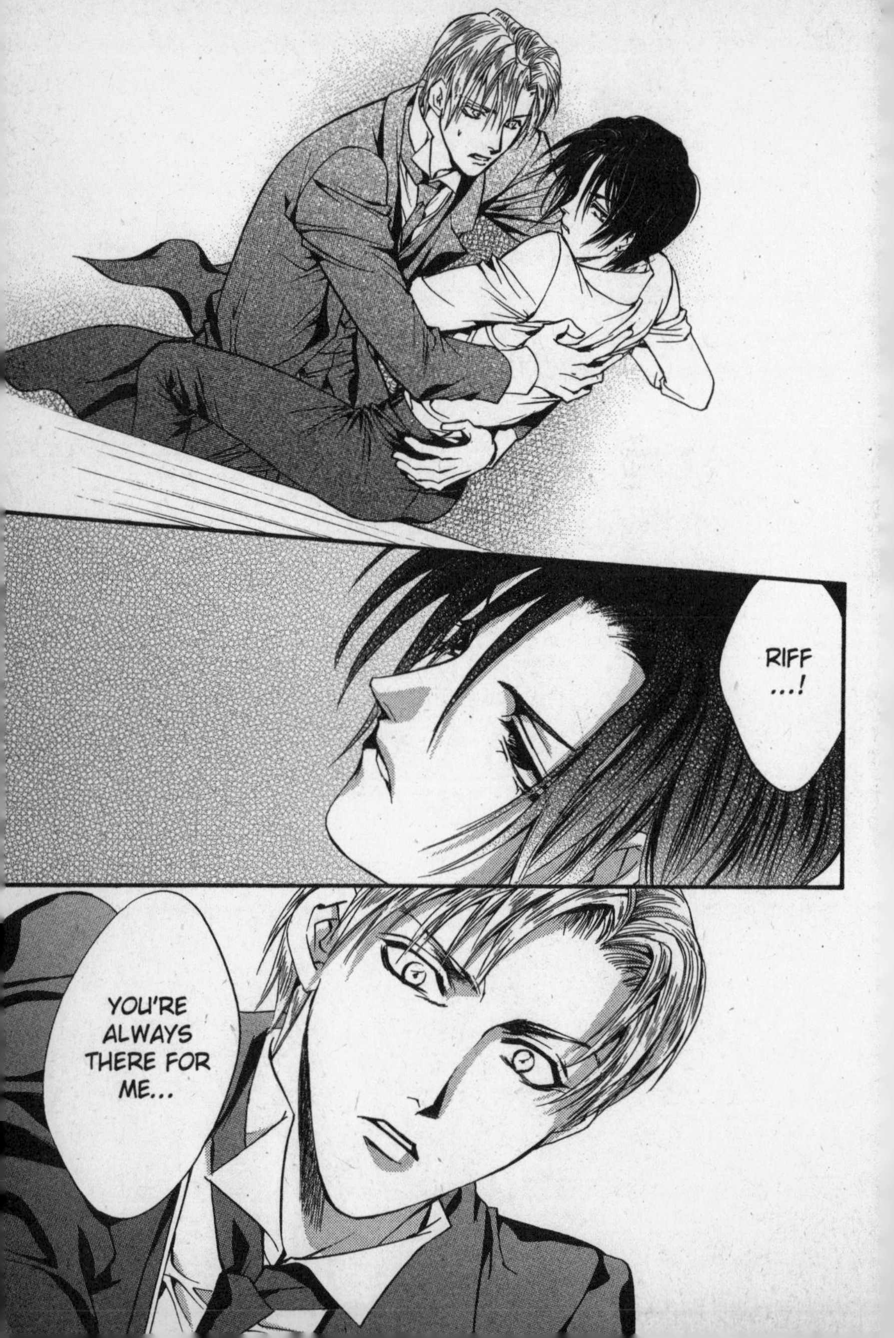
RIFF ...!
YOU'RE ALWAYS THERE FOR ME...

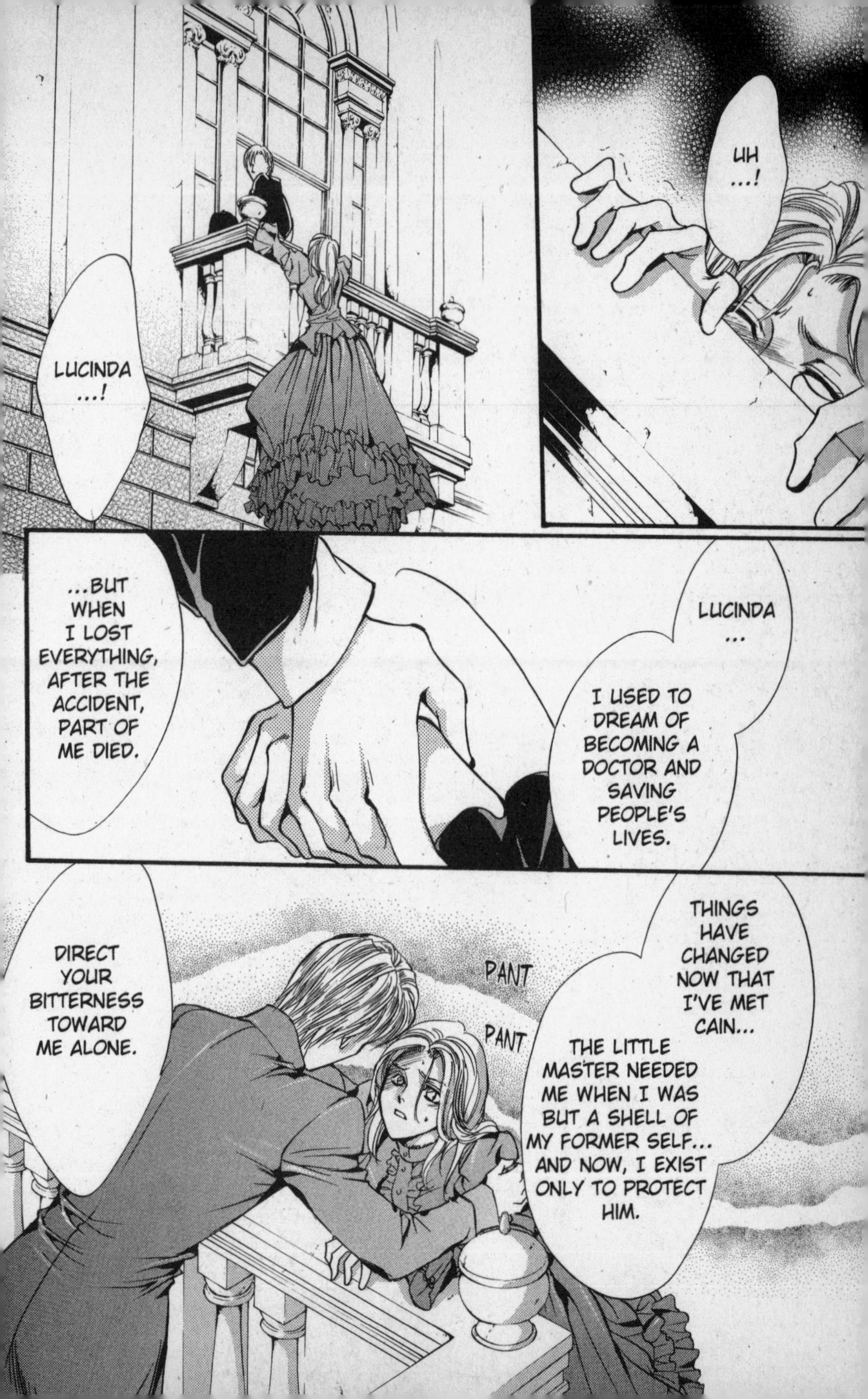
UH ...!
LUCINDA ...!
LUCINDA ...
I USED TO DREAM OF BECOMING A DOCTOR AND SAVING PEOPLE'S LIVES.
...BUT WHEN I LOST EVERYTHING, AFTER THE ACCIDENT, PART OF ME DIED.
THINGS HAVE CHANGED NOW THAT I'VE MET CAIN...
THE LITTLE MASTER NEEDED ME WHEN I WAS BUT A SHELL OF MY FORMER SELF... AND NOW, I EXIST ONLY TO PROTECT HIM.
PANT
PANT
DIRECT YOUR BITTERNESS TOWARD ME ALONE.

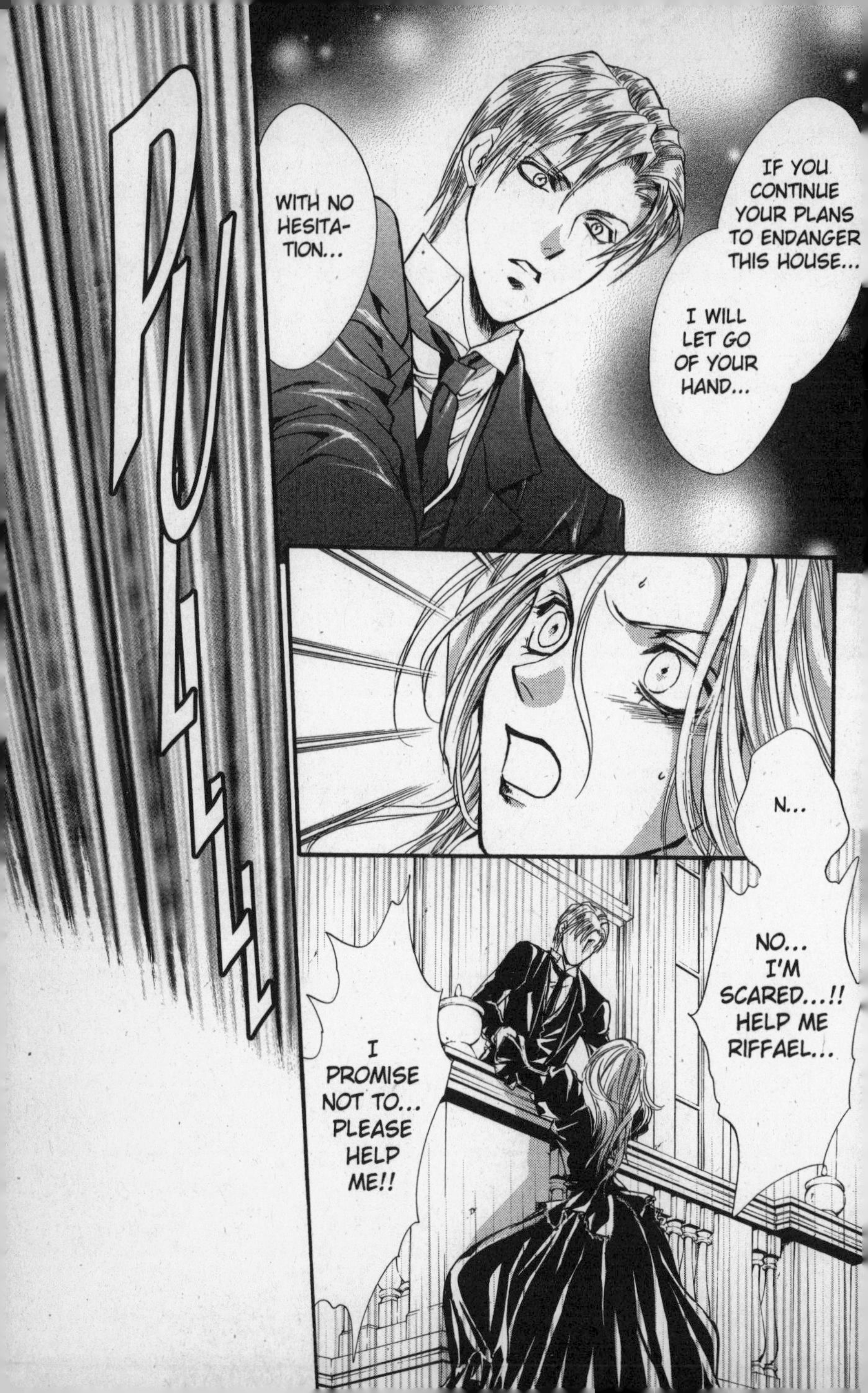
IF YOU CONTINUE YOUR PLANS TO ENDANGER THIS HOUSE...
I WILL LET GO OF YOUR HAND...
WITH NO HESITA-TION...
N...
NO... I'M SCARED...!! HELP ME RIFFAEL...
I PROMISE NOT TO... PLEASE HELP ME!!
PULLLL

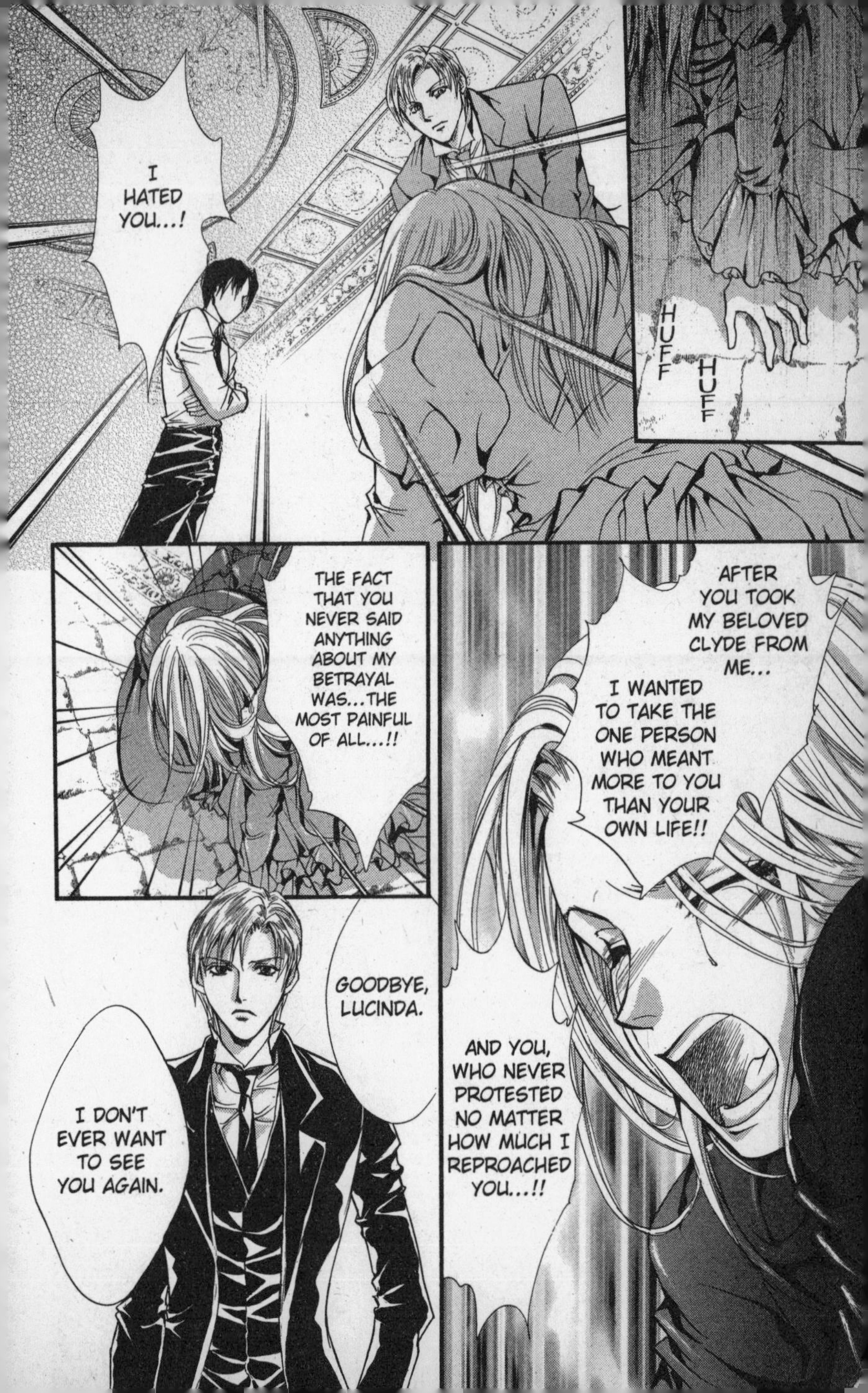
HUFF HUFF
I HATED YOU...!
AFTER YOU TOOK MY BELOVED CLYDE FROM ME...
I WANTED TO TAKE THE ONE PERSON WHO MEANT MORE TO YOU THAN YOUR OWN LIFE!!
AND YOU, WHO NEVER PROTESTED NO MATTER HOW MUCH I REPROACHED YOU...!!
THE FACT THAT YOU NEVER SAID ANYTHING ABOUT MY BETRAYAL WAS...THE MOST PAINFUL OF ALL...!!
GOODBYE, LUCINDA.
I DON'T EVER WANT TO SEE YOU AGAIN.

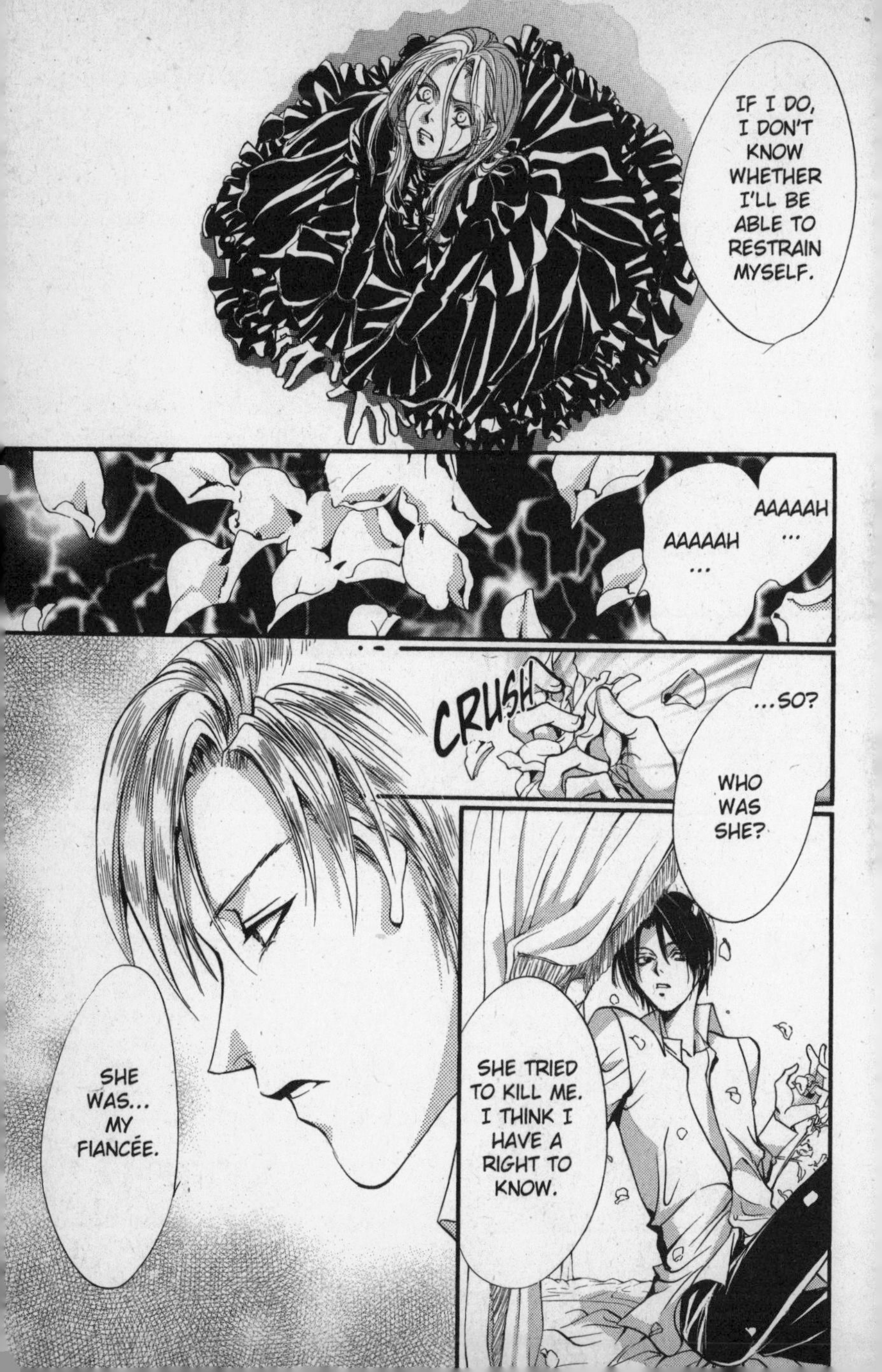
IF I DO, I DON'T KNOW WHETHER I'LL BE ABLE TO RESTRAIN MYSELF.
AAAAAH ...
AAAAAH ...
CRUSH
...SO?
WHO WAS SHE?
SHE TRIED TO KILL ME. I THINK I HAVE A RIGHT TO KNOW.
SHE WAS... MY FIANCÉE.

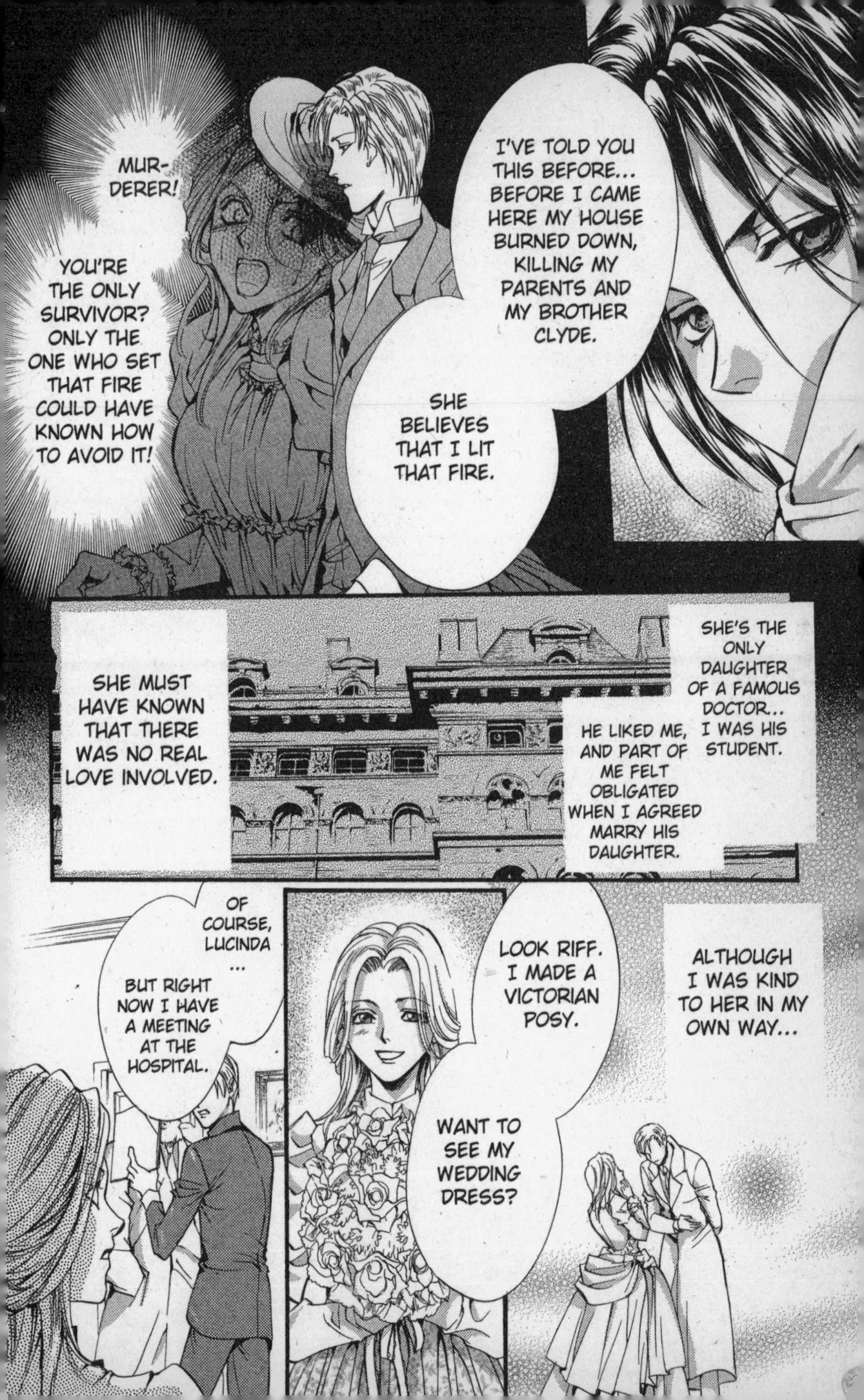
I'VE TOLD YOU THIS BEFORE... BEFORE I CAME HERE MY HOUSE BURNED DOWN, KILLING MY PARENTS AND MY BROTHER CLYDE.
MUR-DERER!
YOU'RE THE ONLY SURVIVOR? ONLY THE ONE WHO SET THAT FIRE COULD HAVE KNOWN HOW TO AVOID IT!
SHE BELIEVES THAT I LIT THAT FIRE.
SHE'S THE ONLY DAUGHTER OF A FAMOUS DOCTOR... I WAS HIS STUDENT.
HE LIKED ME, AND PART OF ME FELT OBLIGATED WHEN I AGREED MARRY HIS DAUGHTER.
SHE MUST HAVE KNOWN THAT THERE WAS NO REAL LOVE INVOLVED.
ALTHOUGH I WAS KIND TO HER IN MY OWN WAY...
LOOK RIFF. I MADE A VICTORIAN POSY.
WANT TO SEE MY WEDDING DRESS?
OF COURSE, LUCINDA ...
BUT RIGHT NOW I HAVE A MEETING AT THE HOSPITAL.

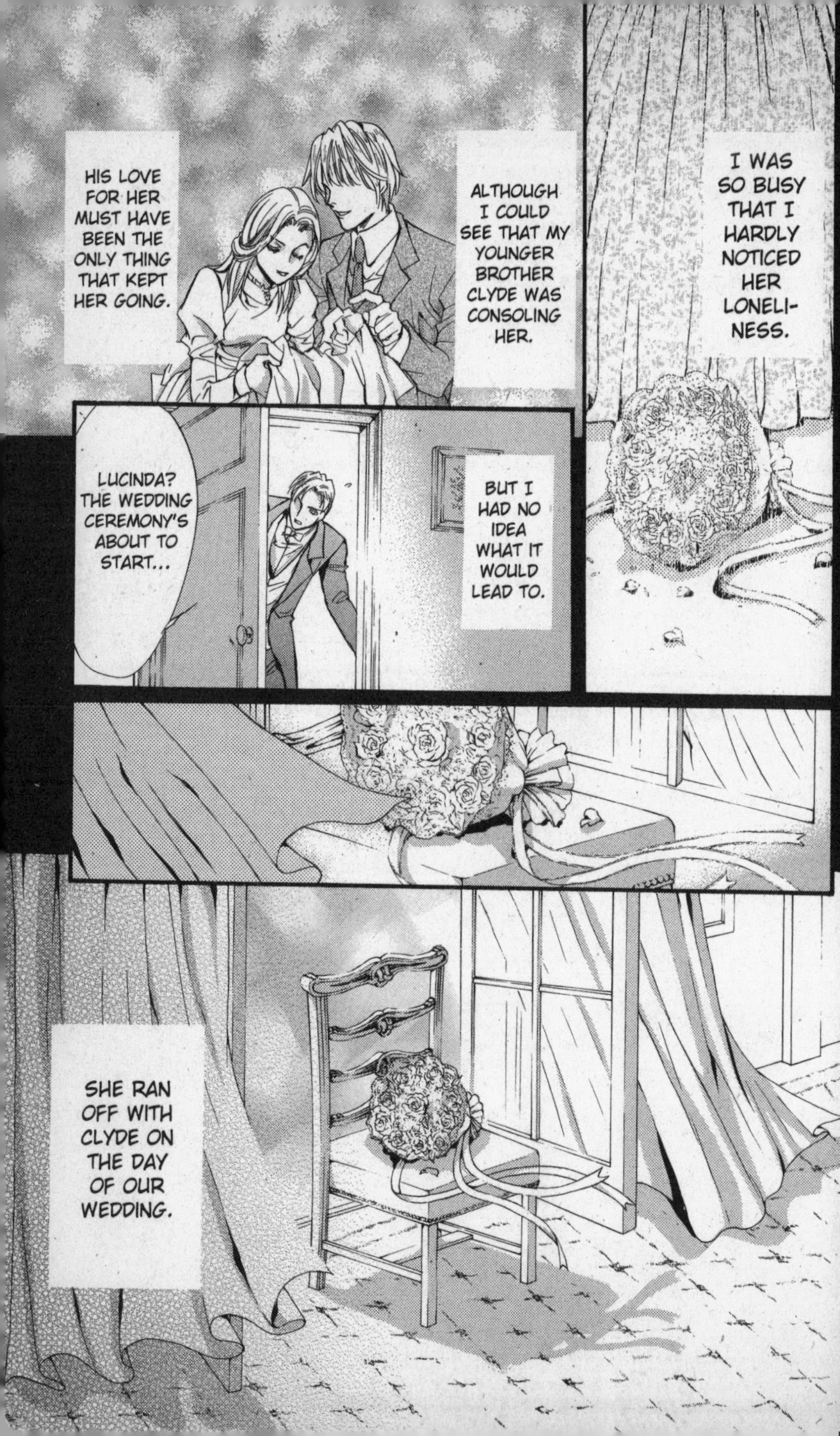
I WAS SO BUSY THAT I HARDLY NOTICED HER LONELI-NESS.
ALTHOUGH I COULD SEE THAT MY YOUNGER BROTHER CLYDE WAS CONSOLING HER.
HIS LOVE FOR HER MUST HAVE BEEN THE ONLY THING THAT KEPT HER GOING.
BUT I HAD NO IDEA WHAT IT WOULD LEAD TO.
LUCINDA? THE WEDDING CEREMONY'S ABOUT TO START...
SHE RAN OFF WITH CLYDE ON THE DAY OF OUR WEDDING.

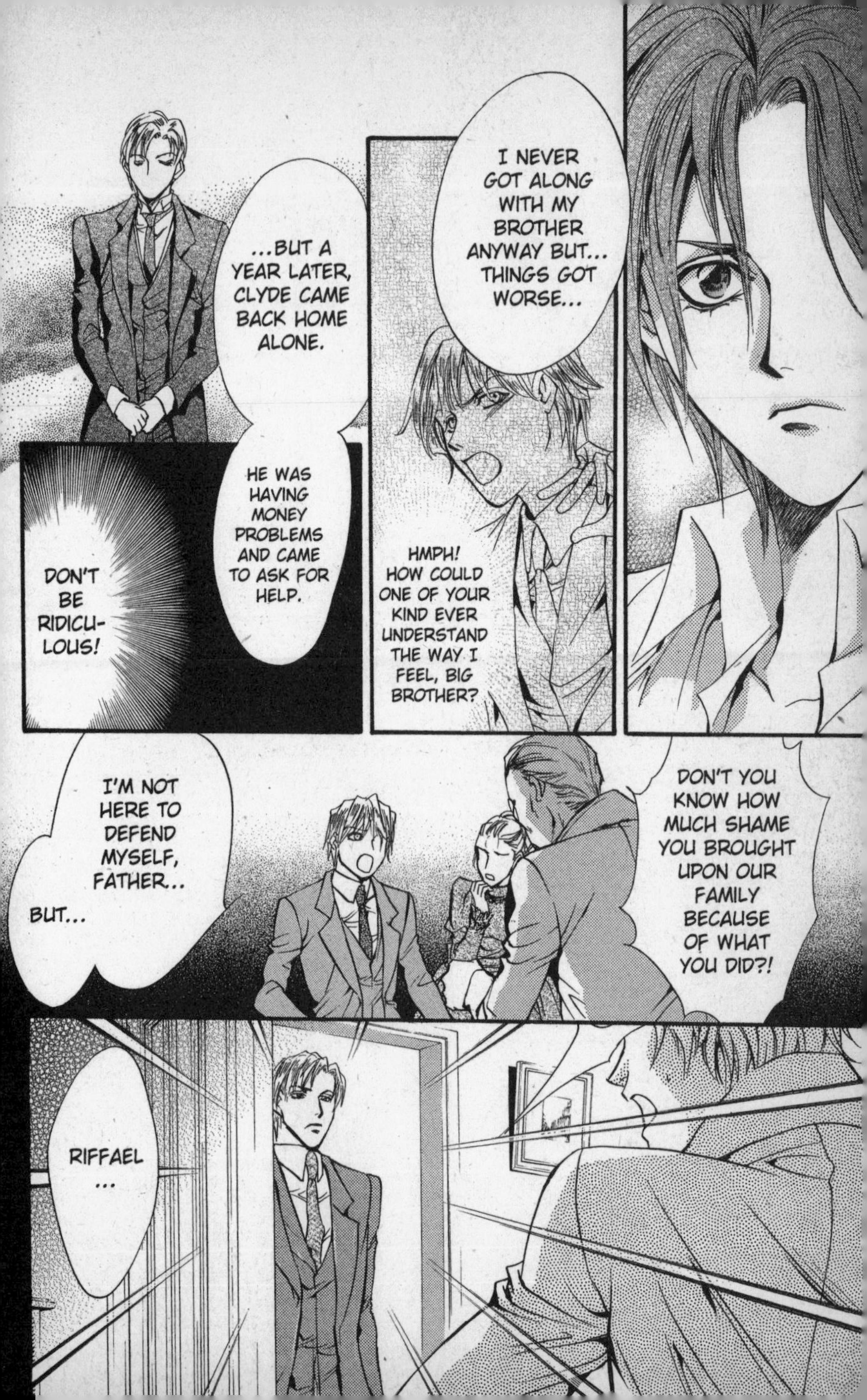
I NEVER GOT ALONG WITH MY BROTHER ANYWAY BUT... THINGS GOT WORSE...
HMPH! HOW COULD ONE OF YOUR KIND EVER UNDERSTAND THE WAY I FEEL, BIG BROTHER?
...BUT A YEAR LATER, CLYDE CAME BACK HOME ALONE.
HE WAS HAVING MONEY PROBLEMS AND CAME TO ASK FOR HELP.
DON'T BE RIDICU-LOUS!
DON'T YOU KNOW HOW MUCH SHAME YOU BROUGHT UPON OUR FAMILY BECAUSE OF WHAT YOU DID?!
I'M NOT HERE TO DEFEND MYSELF, FATHER...
BUT...
RIFFAEL...

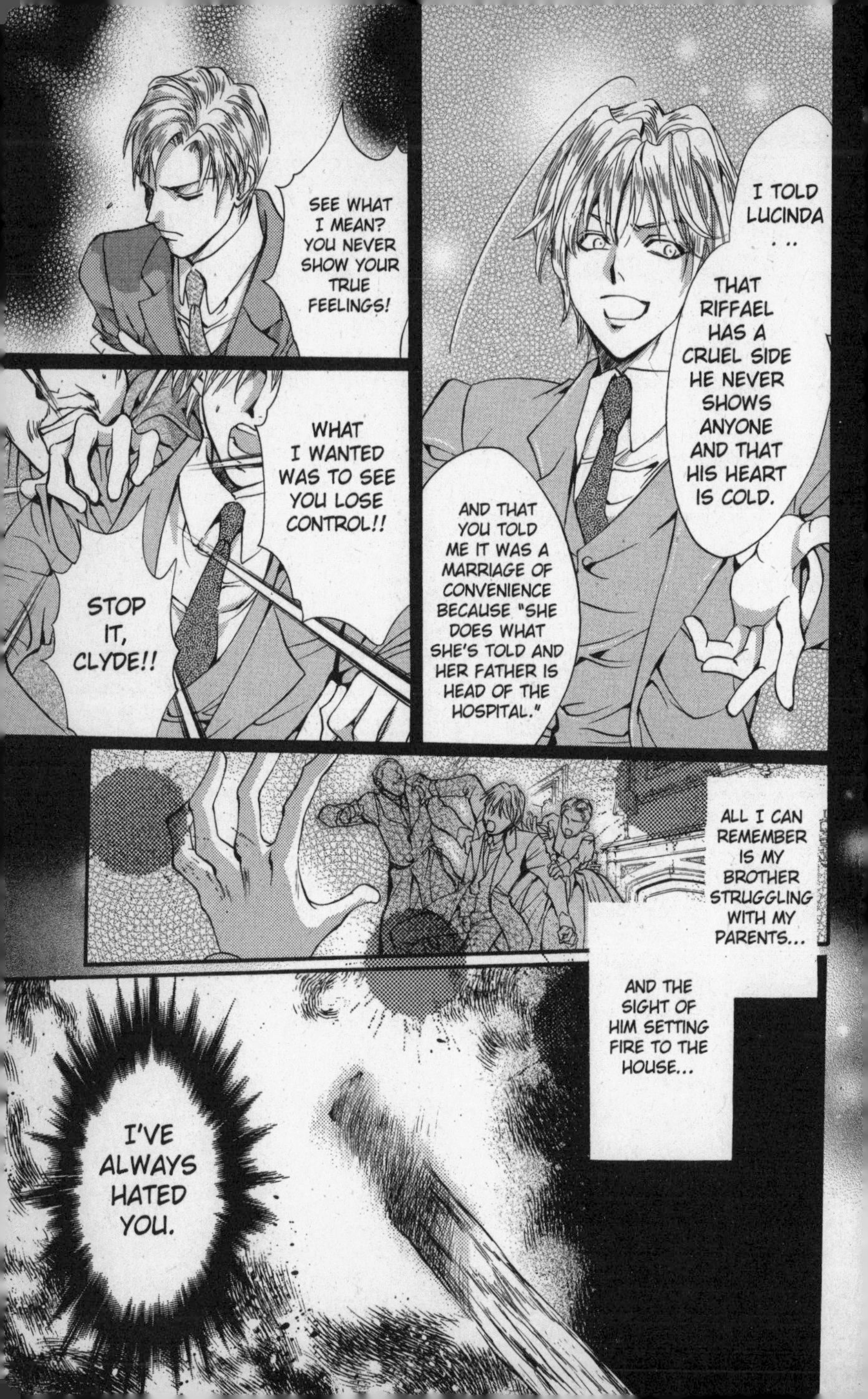
I TOLD LUCINDA . . .
THAT RIFFAEL HAS A CRUEL SIDE HE NEVER SHOWS ANYONE AND THAT HIS HEART IS COLD.
AND THAT YOU TOLD ME IT WAS A MARRIAGE OF CONVENIENCE BECAUSE "SHE DOES WHAT SHE'S TOLD AND HER FATHER IS HEAD OF THE HOSPITAL."
SEE WHAT I MEAN? YOU NEVER SHOW YOUR TRUE FEELINGS!
WHAT I WANTED WAS TO SEE YOU LOSE CONTROL!!
STOP IT, CLYDE!!
ALL I CAN REMEMBER IS MY BROTHER STRUGGLING WITH MY PARENTS...
AND THE SIGHT OF HIM SETTING FIRE TO THE HOUSE...
I'VE ALWAYS HATED YOU.

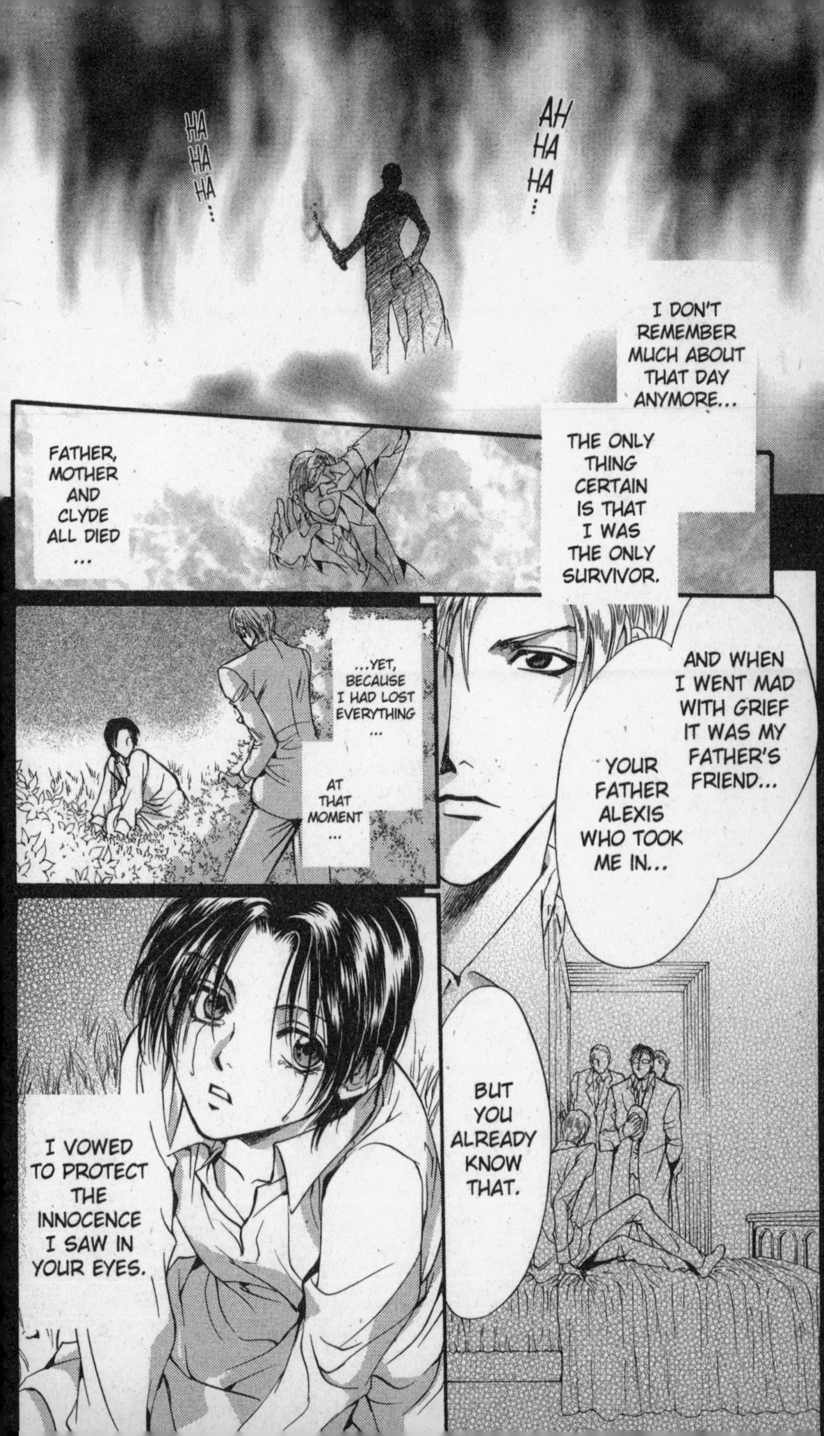
AH HA HA...
HA HA HA...
I DON'T REMEMBER MUCH ABOUT THAT DAY ANYMORE...
THE ONLY THING CERTAIN IS THAT I WAS THE ONLY SURVIVOR.
FATHER, MOTHER AND CLYDE ALL DIED ...
AND WHEN I WENT MAD WITH GRIEF IT WAS MY FATHER'S FRIEND...
YOUR FATHER ALEXIS WHO TOOK ME IN...
BUT YOU ALREADY KNOW THAT.
...YET, BECAUSE I HAD LOST EVERYTHING ...
AT THAT MOMENT ...
I VOWED TO PROTECT THE INNOCENCE I SAW IN YOUR EYES.

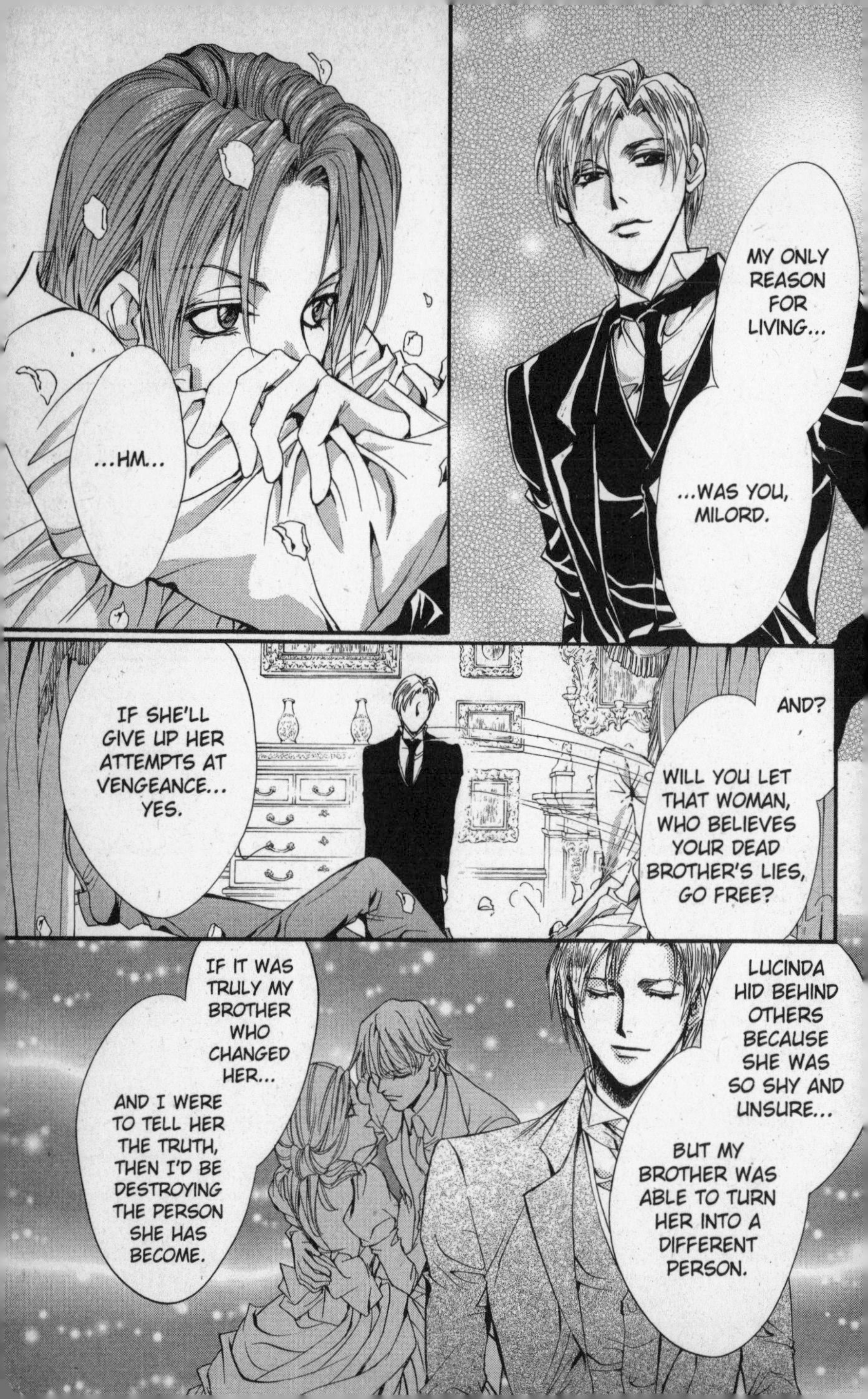
MY ONLY REASON FOR LIVING...
...WAS YOU, MILORD.
...HM...
AND?
WILL YOU LET THAT WOMAN, WHO BELIEVES YOUR DEAD BROTHER'S LIES, GO FREE?
IF SHE'LL GIVE UP HER ATTEMPTS AT VENGEANCE... YES.
LUCINDA HID BEHIND OTHERS BECAUSE SHE WAS SO SHY AND UNSURE...
BUT MY BROTHER WAS ABLE TO TURN HER INTO A DIFFERENT PERSON.
IF IT WAS TRULY MY BROTHER WHO CHANGED HER...
AND I WERE TO TELL HER THE TRUTH, THEN I'D BE DESTROYING THE PERSON SHE HAS BECOME.

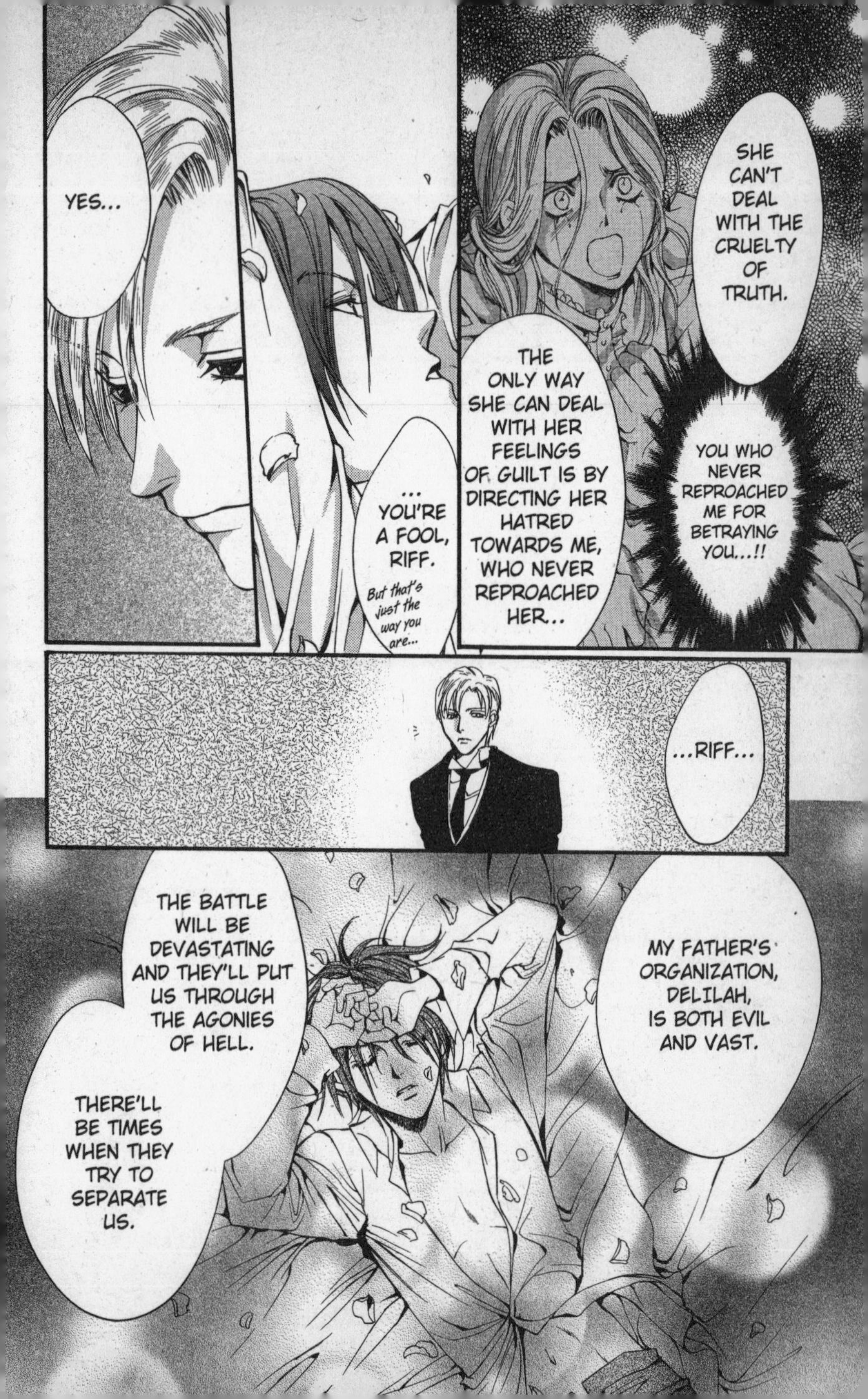
SHE CAN'T DEAL WITH THE CRUELTY OF TRUTH.
THE ONLY WAY SHE CAN DEAL WITH HER FEELINGS OF GUILT IS BY DIRECTING HER HATRED TOWARDS ME, WHO NEVER REPROACHED HER...
YOU WHO NEVER REPROACHED ME FOR BETRAYING YOU...!!
YES...
... YOU'RE A FOOL, RIFF.
But that's just the way you are...
...RIFF...
MY FATHER'S ORGANIZATION, DELILAH, IS BOTH EVIL AND VAST.
THE BATTLE WILL BE DEVASTATING AND THEY'LL PUT US THROUGH THE AGONIES OF HELL.
THERE'LL BE TIMES WHEN THEY TRY TO SEPARATE US.

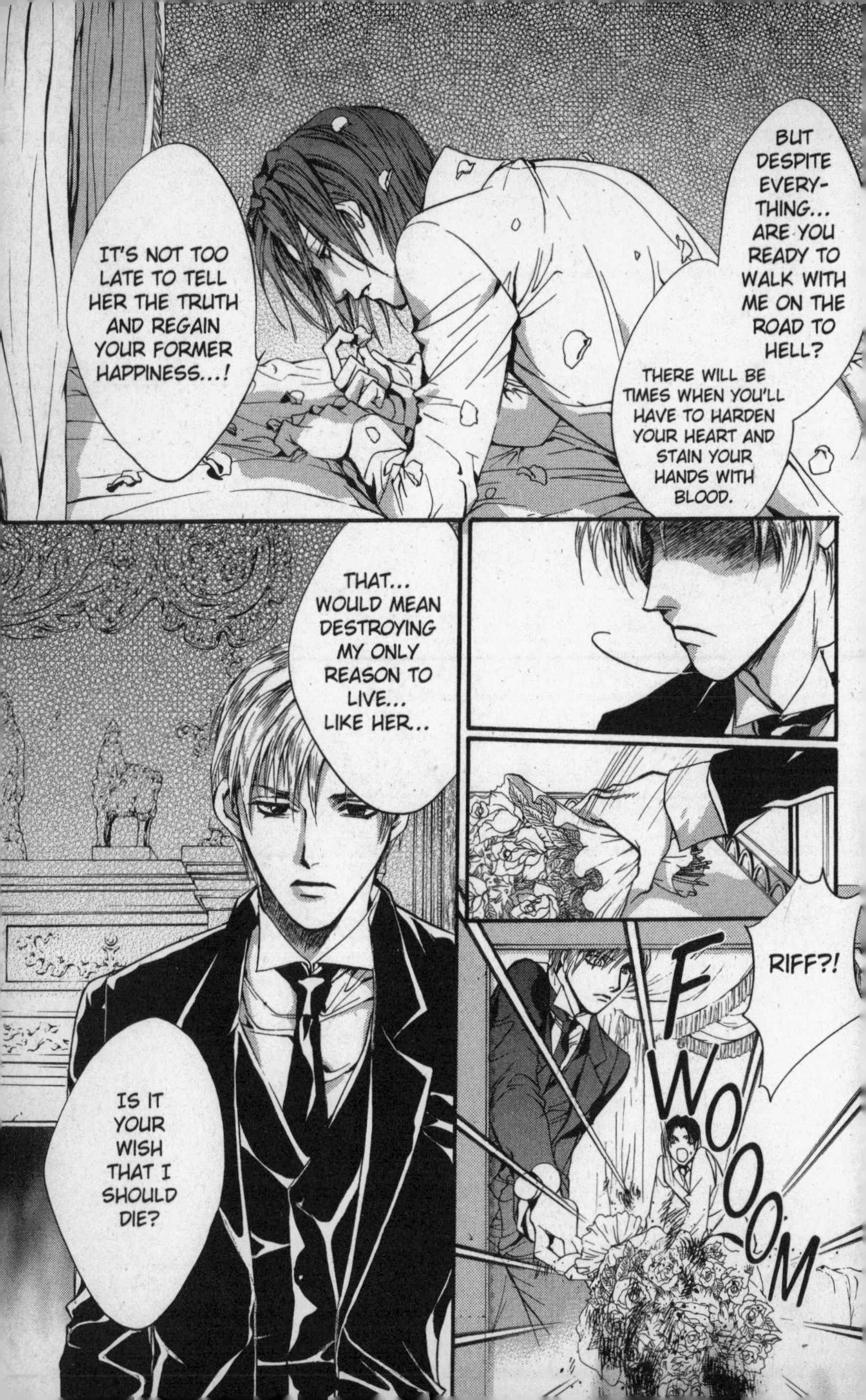
BUT DESPITE EVERY-THING... ARE YOU READY TO WALK WITH ME ON THE ROAD TO HELL?
THERE WILL BE TIMES WHEN YOU'LL HAVE TO HARDEN YOUR HEART AND STAIN YOUR HANDS WITH BLOOD.
IT'S NOT TOO LATE TO TELL HER THE TRUTH AND REGAIN YOUR FORMER HAPPINESS...!
RIFF?!
FWOOOM
THAT... WOULD MEAN DESTROYING MY ONLY REASON TO LIVE... LIKE HER...
IS IT YOUR WISH THAT I SHOULD DIE?

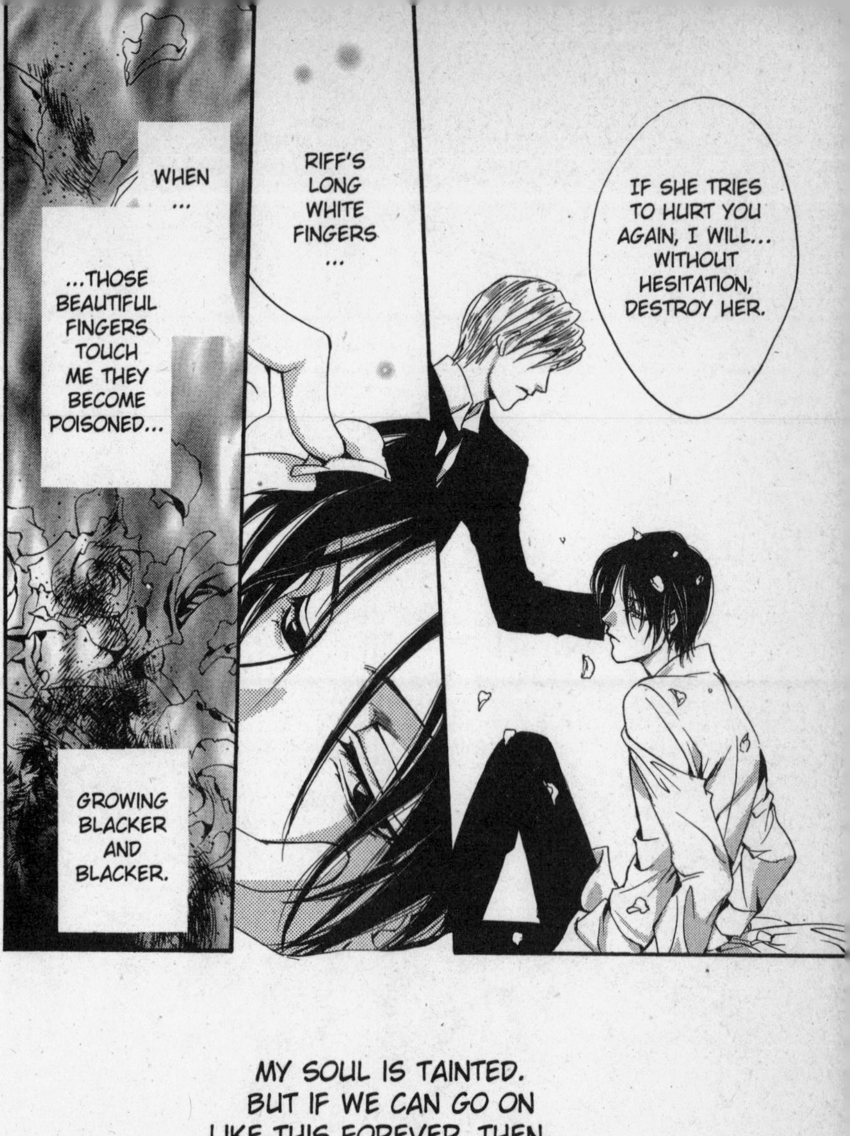
IF SHE TRIES TO HURT YOU AGAIN, I WILL... WITHOUT HESITATION, DESTROY HER.
RIFF'S LONG WHITE FINGERS ...
WHEN ...
...THOSE BEAUTIFUL FINGERS TOUCH ME THEY BECOME POISONED...
GROWING BLACKER AND BLACKER.

MY SOUL IS TAINTED.
BUT IF WE CAN GO ON
LIKE THIS FOREVER, THEN...

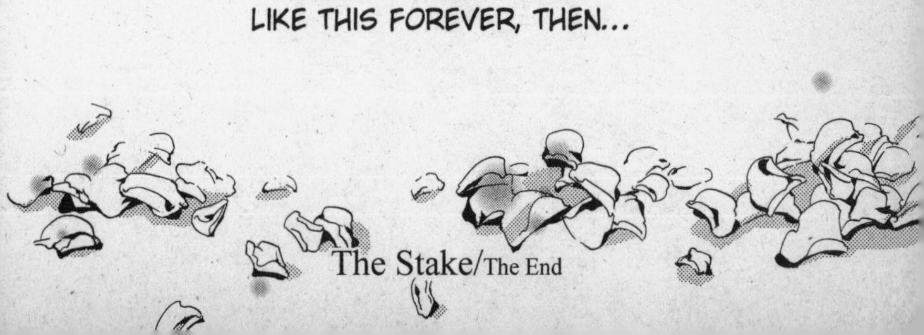
The Stake/The End

GOD ◾◾◾ 👤 ◾◾◾ CHILD

I was really into a game called "Space Channel 5 Part 2." The music is awesome and the characters are fascinating... it was fun! I haven't played many games lately but I loved this one! I even told my friend Ashi about it and we played it together. To be honest, I'm not much of a gamer, and I tend to stay away from lots of games but this one was so cool. The climax of the last scene and the things that you can do after you clear the game are great too. ♪ I even bought the soundtrack CD and have been listening to it with the sounds "chu chu" going through my head... I even bought a copy of Part I on sale, but I haven't been able to find a Dreamcast anywhere... That's why I don't think I'll be able to play "Part I" for awhile...

Let's just have fun.
B.Y. PAGY

Shut up, swine.
Mr. Hughes.

Hm... it looks like time to say goodbye again. Well, I'll see you all next time in Volume 4. I eagerly await your letters. I even made a preview page. Turn the page and take a look!
← ♡ 20020523

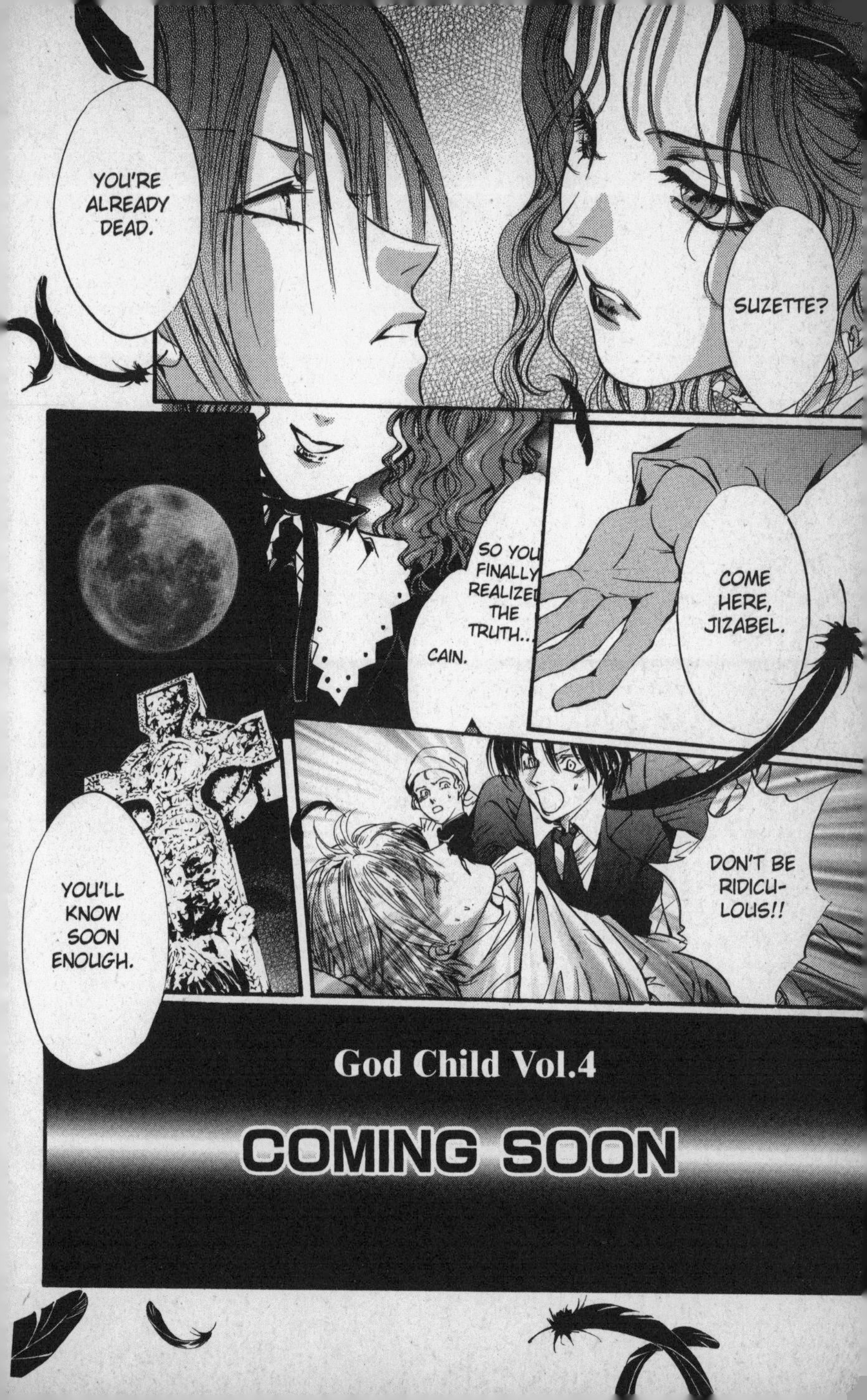
SUZETTE?
YOU'RE ALREADY DEAD.
COME HERE, JIZABEL.
SO YOU FINALLY REALIZED THE TRUTH... CAIN.
DON'T BE RIDICU-LOUS!!
YOU'LL KNOW SOON ENOUGH.
God Child Vol.4
COMING SOON

Creator: Kaori Yuki

Date of Birth: December 18

Blood Type: B

Major Works: *Angel Sanctuary* and *The Cain Saga*

Kaori Yuki was born in Tokyo and started drawing at a very early age. Following her debut work *Natsufuku no Erie* (Erie in Summer Uniform) in the Japanese magazine *Bessatsu Hana to Yume* (1987), she wrote a compelling series of short stories: *Zankoku na Douwatachi* (Cruel Fairy Tales), *Neji* (Screw), and *Sareki Ôkoku* (Gravel Kingdom).

As proven by her best-selling series *Angel Sanctuary* and *The Cain Saga*, her celebrated body of work has etched an indelible mark on the gothic comics genre. She likes mysteries and British films, and is a fan of the movie *Dead Poets Society* and the show *Twin Peaks*.

GODCHILD, vol. 3
The Shojo Beat Manga Edition

STORY & ART BY KAORI YUKI

Translation/Akira Watanabe
English Adaptation/Trina Robbins
Touch-up Art & Lettering/James Gaubatz
Design/Courtney Utt
Editor/Joel Enos

Managing Editor/Megan Bates
Editorial Director/Elizabeth Kawasaki
VP & Editor in Chief/Yumi Hoashi
Sr. Director of Acquisitions/Rika Inouye
Sr. VP of Marketing/Liza Coppola
Exec. VP of Sales & Marketing/John Easum
Publisher/Hyoe Narita

Printed in Canada

Published by VIZ Media, LLC
P.O. Box 77010
San Francisco, CA 94107

Shojo Beat Manga Edition
10 9 8 7 6 5 4 3 2 1
First printing, November 2006

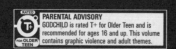

PARENTAL ADVISORY
GODCHILD is rated T+ for Older Teen and is
recommended for ages 16 and up. This volume
contains graphic violence and adult themes.

store.viz.com

Read Kaori Yuki's entire Earl Cain Series

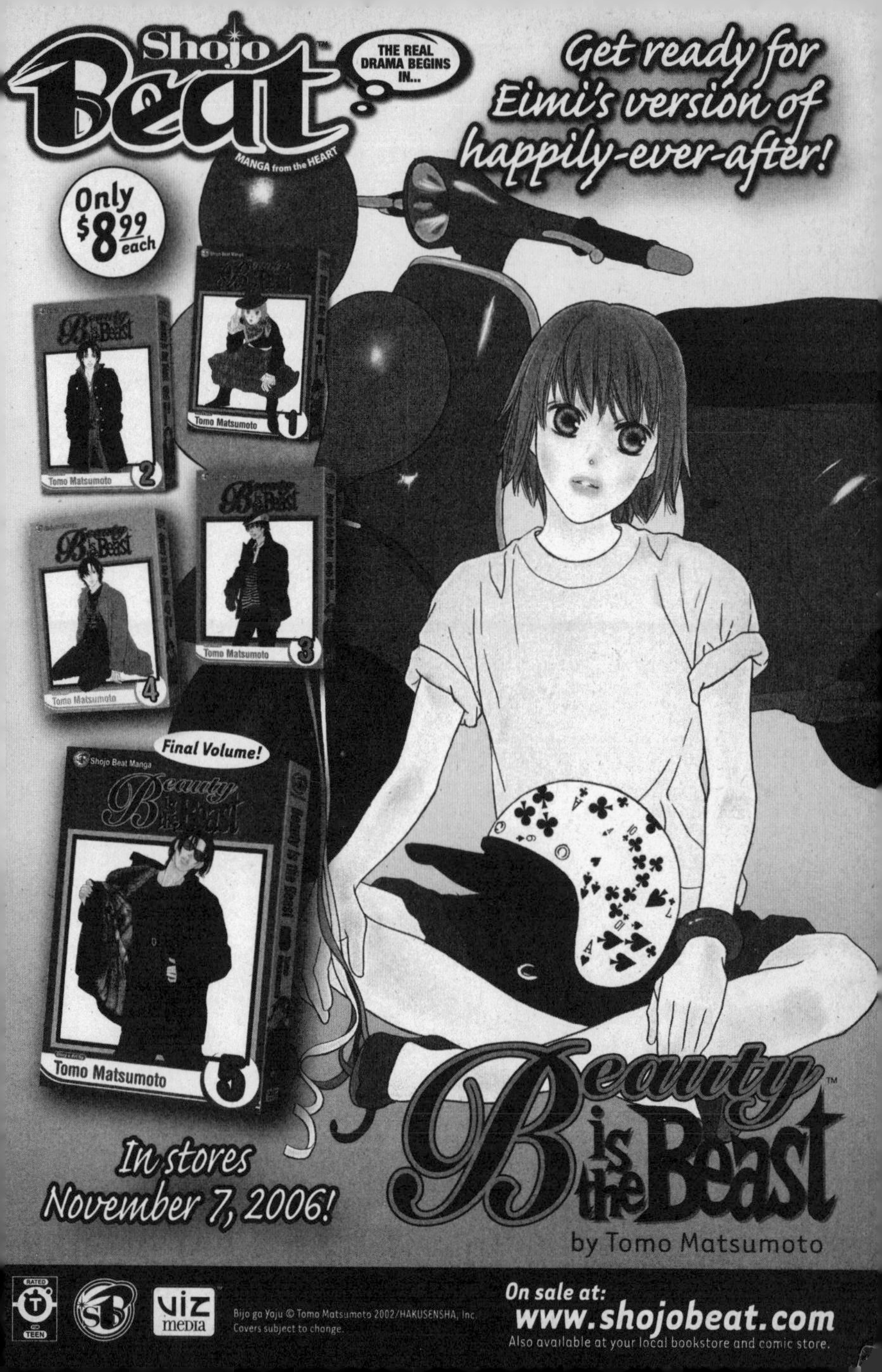
Shojo Beat
MANGA from the HEART
THE REAL DRAMA BEGINS IN...
Get ready for Eimi's version of happily-ever-after!
Only $8.99 each
Tomo Matsumoto
Final Volume!
Shojo Beat Manga
Beauty is the Beast
In stores November 7, 2006!
Beauty is the Beast
by Tomo Matsumoto
RATED T TEEN
viz media
Bijo ga Yoju © Tomo Matsumoto 2002/HAKUSENSHA, Inc.
Covers subject to change.
On sale at:
www.shojobeat.com
Also available at your local bookstore and comic store.

Skip·Beat!™

by Yoshiki Nakamura

Will Kyoko's grudge cost her a chance at fame?

Only $8.99 each

In stores November 7, 2006!

Shojo Beat™

MANGA from the HEART

THE REAL DRAMA BEGIN IN...

On sale at:
www.shojobeat.com
Also available at your local bookstore and comic store

   viz media

Save OVER 50% OF[F]

MANGA from the HEART

Six of the most addictive Shojo Manga from Japan:
Nana, Baby & Me, Absolute Boyfriend (by superstar creator Yuu Watase!!), and more! Plus the latest on what's happening in Japanese fashion, music, and culture!

Save 51% OFF the cover price PLUS enjoy all the benefits of the Sub Club with your paid subscription—your issues delivered first, exclusive access to ShojoBeat.com, and gifts mailed with some issues.

only **$34⁹⁹** for 12 HUGE issues!

☑ **YES!** Please enter my 1-year subscription (12 GIANT issues) to *Shojo Beat* at the special subscription rate of only $34.99 and sign me up for the Sub Club.

NAME _____

ADDRESS _____

CITY _____ STATE _____ ZIP _____

E-MAIL ADDRESS _____ P6BGNC

☐ **MY CHECK, PAYABLE TO SHOJO BEAT, IS ENCLOSED**

CREDIT CARD: ☐ **VISA** ☐ **MASTERCARD**

RATED **T+** FOR OLDER TEEN

ACCOUNT # _____ EXP. DATE _____

SIGNATURE _____

☐ **BILL ME LATER PLEASE**

CLIP AND MAIL TO ➤ SHOJO BEAT
Subscriptions Service Dept.
P.O. Box 438
Mount Morris, IL 61054-0438

1 JUL 2008

Canada add $12 US. No foreign orders. Allow 6-8 weeks for delivery.

11-07 *TML*